COMICS AND MODERNISM

HISTORY, FORM, AND CULTURE

EDITED BY JONATHAN NAJARIAN

UNIVERSITY PRESS OF MISSISSIPPI / JACKSON

Publication of this book has been generously supported by a subvention from Colgate University.

The University Press of Mississippi is the scholarly publishing agency of the Mississippi Institutions of Higher Learning: Alcorn State University, Delta State University, Jackson State University, Mississippi State University, Mississippi University for Women, Mississippi Valley State University, University of Mississippi, and University of Southern Mississippi.

www.upress.state.ms.us

The University Press of Mississippi is a member of the Association of University Presses.

Copyright © 2024 by University Press of Mississippi
All rights reserved

∞

The essay "Four Repulsive Women: Marjorie Organ, Nell Brinkley, Kate Carew, Djuna Barnes" by Jean Lee Cole is forthcoming in *Modernism/modernity Print Plus*. Copyright © Johns Hopkins University Press. Reprinted by permission.

Library of Congress Cataloging-in-Publication Data

Names: Najarian, Jonathan, editor.
Title: Comics and modernism : history, form, and culture / Jonathan Najarian.
Other titles: Tom Inge series on comics artists.
Description: Jackson : University Press of Mississippi, 2024. | Series: Tom Inge series on comics artists | Includes bibliographical references and index.
Identifiers: LCCN 2023039956 (print) | LCCN 2023039957 (ebook) | ISBN 9781496849571 (hardback) | ISBN 9781496849588 (trade paperback) | ISBN 9781496849595 (epub) | ISBN 9781496849601 (epub) | ISBN 9781496849618 (pdf) | ISBN 9781496849625 (pdf)
Subjects: LCSH: Comic books, strips, etc.—Philosophy. | Comic books, strips, etc.—History and criticism. | Graphic novels—Philosophy. | Graphic novels—History and criticism. | Philosophy in comics. | Modernism (Art)
Classification: LCC PN6714 .C649 2024 (print) | LCC PN6714 (ebook) | DDC 741.5/9—dc23/eng/20231010
LC record available at https://lccn.loc.gov/2023039956
LC ebook record available at https://lccn.loc.gov/2023039957

British Library Cataloging-in-Publication Data available

CONTENTS

Acknowledgments VII
Comics and Modernism: An Introduction 3
   JONATHAN NAJARIAN

Section I: Modernism and Comics

Entanglements of Style: The Uniqueness of Modernism in Comics 15
   GLENN WILLMOTT

Modernism for the Masses: The Armory Show in Comics 33
   KATHERINE ROEDER

The Dreamer's Modern Body: Winsor McCay and the Everyday
Sensorium. 49
   NOA SAUNDERS

A Thoroughly Modern Kat 70
   DAVID M. BALL

Section II: Print, Ephemera, Circulation

Four Repulsive Women: Marjorie Organ, Nell Brinkley, Kate Carew,
Djuna Barnes. 87
   JEAN LEE COLE

Jackie Ormes's *Torchy Brown in "Dixie to Harlem"*: Modernism in the
African American Funny Pages. 113
   CLÉMENCE SFADJ

In Dialogue and Debate: Comics, Little Magazines, World Literature . . 129
LOUISE KANE

Section III: Pop/Art: Comics Low and High

Telling Details: Feminine Flourish in Midcentury Illustration and
Comics 157
SCOTT BUKATMAN

Speed Lines: Futurism and Superheroes. 184
DANIEL WORDEN

"Our First Literature": The Poetics Underground of Joe Brainard's
New York School Comics 206
NICK STURM

Section IV: Comics as Modernism

Profane Transfigurations: On a Detail of a Painting in a Panel in an
Installment of *Little Annie Fanny*, 1963, or How Harvey Kurtzman and
Arthur Danto (Mostly) Agree, and Deep Down Really Disagree Too . . 229
ANDREI MOLOTIU

Art Spiegelman and the Ghost of Picasso 257
JONATHAN NAJARIAN

Little Tommy Lost and the Anachronistic Comic 284
MATTHEW LEVAY

Afterword: Graphic Modernisms. 301
HILLARY CHUTE

Selected Bibliography 310
About the Contributors 317
Index 320

ACKNOWLEDGMENTS

Writing an acknowledgments page for an edited collection is like taking credit for a group project where everyone has actually done what they were supposed to do: this book would quite literally not exist without the dedicated work of all the contributors. I've learned so much reading these essays—about comics and modernism, about museums and film, about newspapers and journalism and little magazines, about midcentury illustration and midcentury superhero comics and midcentury poetry, about art history and about contemporary comics—and I'm so grateful to have worked with a brilliant, patient, and friendly group of scholars. So first and foremost, a heartfelt thank you to everyone who contributed. Your work has made this process so enjoyable and the results so much fun.

A special thank you goes to Andrei Molotiu and David M. Ball, who were the first to mention to me the possibility of a book-length project about comics and modernism; without them, this collection, in its current form, might never have gotten underway. I emailed Andrei asking whether he'd like to contribute to a special issue of a journal, and he agreed, but he thought a book might be a better forum. Thank you, Andrei, for your vision. Dave Ball, whom I first met at the Modernist Studies Association in Columbus, Ohio, in 2018, had the same idea, and he encouraged me to write to him if I wanted to turn my special issue project into a book. Dave first recommended me to the University Press of Mississippi and was unconditionally supportive of the project. Thank you, Dave, for your encouragement.

The editorial team at the University Press of Mississippi has offered tremendous support and guidance. Thank you to Katie Keene, who believed in this project from the very beginning. Lisa McMurtray offered speedy and careful guidance in the later stages of the submission process. Joey Brown and the folks in the marketing department have been gracious and kind in their help shaping the final project. Kerri Jordan's meticulous, perceptive proofreading has made this project significantly better. And a very special thank you to Michael Martella, who had to deal closely with me at the worst stages of publication, when I was scrambling for more time, refusing to answer his emails promptly, and making promises I couldn't keep about deadlines I wouldn't meet. Michael: I'm sorry, and thank you for your patience and gentleness.

A long list of mentors and friends have sustained me, personally and professionally, throughout work on this project. Rob Chodat was a model advisor and has become a dedicated mentor and friend, in Boston, in London, and now remotely. Hillary Chute has been an unyielding proponent of my work; her scholarship on comics has shaped so much of my own thinking about the medium, and I'm very grateful to be publishing her contribution here. At Colgate, I've enjoyed that rare academic privilege: a genuinely supportive, collegial, and closely connected department. Thank you to Jennifer LeMesurier, Suzanne B. Spring, Jenn Lutman, Jeff Spires, Rob Mills, and Ritika Popli, who have made the past year the best of my academic career. And thank you to Meg Worley, for letting me teach Rhetoric of Comics, and for your leadership and guidance. Your knowledge of comics—and, actually, of basically everything—is immense.

All of the late nights and solitary hours of working on a project like this one would be almost impossible to manage without the loving support of my partner Katie and my young bubu Crosby. Katie was perhaps the first person I ever met with whom I felt I could be fully and totally myself, and who can see me more clearly than I do. I cherish what we have, and I fully believe that I wouldn't be who I am—emotionally, personally, intellectually—without your companionship. And my Crosby is younger than this project: I first submitted the proposal for *Comics and Modernism* in summer 2020, and he was born in May 2021. He's a source of unending inspiration; recently, when we've asked him if he's ready to head upstairs and get ready for his bath, he will nod and whisper a quick "yeah" before pausing on the staircase to give a goodnight kiss through the banister. I've never met someone I love more.

Finally, I want to mention John Paul Riquelme, who passed away too soon in March 2022, and to whom this book is dedicated. John Paul was an exemplary scholar and mentor: rigorous without being unfair, demanding without being harsh, and dedicated to seeing his students and mentees produce their best work. He thought of himself as an editor first, which I believe was related to the unyielding generosity of his spirit; he was so committed to the work of others that he left this world without having finished all those monographs he had underway. I wish I could read what he had to say about Oscar Wilde's gothic modernism, and I wish he could read this book, which brings together many of his ongoing interests about comics art, about the legacies and afterlives of modernism, and about looking backward from the vantage point of the present. If he does ever have the chance to read this book, I'll look forward to our conversation, where I imagine he'll gently but definitively point out all of my grammatical missteps and challenge me to find a more precise conceptual formation for my ideas. Where there are errors, John Paul, I claim them as my own.

COMICS AND MODERNISM

Figure 1. Frank King, *Gasoline Alley*, first published November 2, 1930.

COMICS AND MODERNISM

An Introduction

JONATHAN NAJARIAN

There will be no high and low cultural levels; one single and mighty art will prevail, understood equally by all, for they will all encounter themselves in it.
—IVÁN HEVESY, "MASS CULTURE, MASS ART," 1919

On Sunday, November 2, 1930, Frank King published one of his masterful full-page, peripatetic *Gasoline Alley* comics (figure 1). These ambulatory "nature walk" strips, which King tended to write in the late fall months, were not the norm—they diverged sharply from the ambitiously quotidian daily strips, which reveled in the quiet beauty of middle-class America. Yet many offered sophisticated reflections on art: aesthetics, production, reception. In one strip, Walt and his adopted son Skeezix, who refers to his father as "Uncle Walt," study the rich (and stylized) brilliance of nature, while Skeezix notes all the opportunities nature affords to paint; in another, the pair marvel at their landscape rendered in "the style of the old woodcut pictures." The November 2 iteration begins not in nature but inside, in the space of the museum, with Walt and Skeezix bent over a modernist painting vaguely reminiscent of a Braque seascape. "Modernism is a bit beyond me," confesses Walt, hunched toward the painting, as if getting closer will reveal the mysteries he feels have eluded him. Skeezix, intellectually nimble, is hungry: "Yes but I'd like to go there. Let's, Uncle Walt."

Father and son traverse a mix of rural and urban backdrops: in some panels, trees buckle under the weight of their own existence, and in others, telephone poles snake upward, rigid and uncertain. Visually, Walt and Skeezix stand apart from their surroundings; the line used for their bodies remains cleaner, thinner, and more precise than the "modernist line" used for the surroundings. In this strip, it's modernism, not comics, that appears stylized, distorted, even cartoonish. Walt and Skeezix are by no means depicted realistically, but their stylization is masked, tempered by the overt, extreme stylization of the rest of the page. The cartoon characters—lines of ink contorted across the page—become the only stable foothold on reality. This stability begins to give in the middle of the strip, when Skeezix, queasy, comments: "I'm beginning to feel crooked myself, Uncle Walt."

Skeezix might be feeling more than just crooked. In the last panel, he and Uncle Walt dissolve into a spatter of ink, flooding the landscape with a fluid mosaic of reds, blues, and yellows. What was in the title panel simply an image on the wall of a museum, separated safely by an elaborate frame, has become Walt and Skeezix's reality. Modernism, then, is initially configured not merely as a style, nor even as a movement, but as a *place*, somewhere Walt and Skeezix can go. The strip reveals a subtle ontological truth: Walt and Skeezix can "go there," to modernism, because they too are merely images, a consequence of style, projections in readers' imaginations. "Nature was wonderful," Walt laments, "but how she has changed." Walt exists within this world fully; he doesn't mourn how depictions or renditions of nature have changed, but how *nature itself* has contorted to the pressures of a modernist visual style. Does King feel more like Walt, like modernism is a bit beyond him, or more like Skeezix, who wants to go there?

The final panel complicates any easy either/or reading of the strip. The central paradox of King's strip is that by walking into modernism, Walt and Skeezix in fact bring modernism into comics and reveal that the divide was never so sharp as one might expect. This strip, like all of King's other *Gasoline Alley* strips, was published in the newspapers; the next day, November 3, we're back to car gags, this one a wry quip about keeping a brand-new automobile under thirty-five miles per hour for the first five hundred miles. So Walt and Skeezix aren't literally trapped within modernism, condemned to exist merely as swirling puddles of multicolored ink.

This wasn't the first time, of course, that a modernist visual style had appeared in newspapers. As Katherine Roeder summarizes in her essay in this volume, comics artists mimicked and modeled the styles on display in the famous 1913 Armory Show. Some of these responses invoke the confusion that many museumgoers felt, turning the obscure, inscrutable visual styles in the exhibition into a punchline or gag; other responses, though, seem almost admiring, exhibiting a sly acknowledgement of the stylistic proximity between modernism and comics, however subtle. One of the most radical paintings on display, Marcel Duchamp's *Nude Descending a Staircase (No. 2)* (see figure 9.4), displays a marked similarity to how newspaper cartoonists were already experimenting with visual depictions of motion. What seemed so radical in Duchamp's painting, with its hectic constellation of overlapping lines that coalesce into a sequential blur, was already old hat for a cartoonist attuned to the complexity of drawing for the sports pages, trying to capture that perfect intersection of stillness and motion. "In many ways," writes Michael Tisserand, in his biography of George Herriman, "Duchamp was just catching up."[1] Just as the *Gasoline Alley* strip from 1930 represents two divergent responses to modernist art—both "it's a bit beyond me" and "I want to go there"—so early comics responses to the art on exhibit at the Armory Show display a complicated sense of affinity toward artists like Picasso and Duchamp. Modernist art was challenging, provocative, and experimental; but then, comics was too.

And for their part, the modernist avant-garde loved comics. Gertrude Stein saved the American newspapers so Picasso could read the funnies; T. S. Eliot and e. e. cummings adored Herriman's *Krazy Kat* (and the latter famously introduced the first selected edition of *Krazy* comics, published just two years after Herriman's death); the poet Dorothy Parker wrote astutely about the cultural value of comics in her columns for the *New Yorker*; even that titan of the modernist novel James Joyce, on entering a local bookshop, would often skip the literary reviews and head straight for the comics. These connections are more than just anecdotal and allusive; comics art is woven into the fabric of modernist aesthetic praxis. As Jared Gardner has written, "It is hard not to see intimate connections between the formal experiments with the novel by Joyce or Faulkner and the fragmentary, looping narratives" that characterize so much comics art.[2] Indeed, popular comics and avant-garde modernism had a lot to teach each other. Scholars such as Daniel Stein have tracked a "specific type of visual modernism [that] includes intertextual and intermedial references to modernist visual art" in Herriman's *Krazy Kat*, and cartoonists from Winsor McCay to Art Spiegelman have remained keenly aware of the developments and experiments, successes and failures associated with modernist art and literature.[3] As David M. Ball has pointed out, Picasso's famous portrait of Gertrude Stein exhibits more than a passing similarity to Rudolph Dirks's Ma Katzenjammer, a visual echo that suggests that newspaper comics, like African art, could have informed Picasso's stylistic evolution.

As the anecdotal connections between modernism and comics relayed above suggest, the divisions between high and low forms of art were never as strong as conventional accounts of modernism made them seem. In *The Popular Culture of Modern Art*, Jeffrey Weiss offers an account of modernism that abandons the rigid high/low hierarchies, advocating instead for a renewed understanding of the "tangled mess" of "modern esthetic experience":[4]

> The role of popular culture does not turn here on a point of subversive intent, of mass culture being elevated by artists into the realm of "high art," or of painting and sculpture being indecorously dressed down. As

a tidy contrast, this arrangement is clearly inadequate to the record of period discourse, as well as the art itself. At stake, instead, is the growing malleability of these categories of cultural experience during the period, the manner in which elements of new art and popular culture might, at times, be appreciated as part of a single train of thought. The esthetic life of the epoch can be addressed broadly in this way, as a realm of activity and paradoxical discourse in which the devices of innovation that are drawn from popular stock (long familiar in that context to the audience for new art) resemble the terms of popular incomprehension.[5]

Even a figure like T. S. Eliot, "the personification of aesthetic modernism's resistance to modern commodification,"[6] is, on close inspection, fully embroiled in this "paradoxical discourse," the "tangled mess" of a culture that produced him. As Michael North has observed, in 1921 the critic Clive Bell wrote "an elaborate denunciation of jazz in which both Eliot and Joyce are accused of being ragtime artists."[7] "When Eliot alludes to the Shakespearean rag in the second section of *The Waste Land*," North continues, "he is alluding to an actual popular song and to the common modern process of mining the past for current fashions as well as using a designation that had recently been applied to his own work."[8] Eliot meets Bell's charge with playful riposte (albeit one buried in a thicket of dense, allusive modernist poetry). Eliot, inveterate lover of crosswords and *Krazy Kat*, seems mostly undisturbed by Bell's denunciation, happy to deploy his own punning gag at Bell's expense and accept his place among the highest of the low artists. North writes that the modernists and their "popular" contemporaries "all lived in the same world of film, music, advertising, and promotion that is still around us" and observes that "they had various and not entirely negative reactions to it."[9] Eliot and Herriman and Joyce and McCay and Woolf and King and Duchamp and Fisher and Pound and Barnes: all immersed in the same changing city streets, all responding to the same aesthetic impulses, all trying to make sense of a world that defied reason and logic.

From a disciplinary perspective, a volume like this one is the product of two concurrent scholarly developments. The first is the rise of the New Modernist Studies, which ushered in a drastic revaluation of the modernist canon and directed scholars to new avenues of exploration, both vertical (between so-called "high" and "low" artforms) and horizontal or spatial (across geographic regions). Of particular interest for the essays collected here was the New Modernist Studies emphasis of periodicals, ephemera, and the mélange of print cultures that constitute the modernist moment. Over the last several decades, we've come to see the significance of magazines and journals such as the *Little Review*, *Blast*, and *Camera Work* in both disseminating and shaping modernist aesthetic values. This scholarship has provided a specific material context for the ongoing scholarly project of challenging rigid binaries between high and low art. As Lise Jaillant writes of the publishing house Tauchnitz, which offered both modernist and mass-market novels, "Readers were encouraged to read as many Tauchnitz titles as possible, from high modernism to popular fiction."[10] Beyond observing, anecdotally, how much Picasso, Joyce, Eliot, cummings, or Parker loved comics, we can now specify a particular set of historical conditions that facilitated the relationship between high and low art, and between modernism and comics.

The other scholarly development, which was largely distinct from but historically continuous with the emergence of the New Modernist Studies, was the widespread explosion of comics studies. Before roughly the year 2000, comics studies was mostly relegated to a few niche scholars, some of whom, like Bill Blackbeard, had no academic affiliation and had to argue tirelessly for the academic study of comics.[11] In the late 1990s and early 2000s—after Art Spiegelman won a Pulitzer Prize for *Maus*, and after he and Françoise Mouly had migrated from independent publishing over to the *New Yorker*—academic scholarly attention finally started to turn in earnest to the comics. In 2006, the journal *Twentieth-Century Literature* published their first essay devoted to comics, Hillary Chute's "'The Shadow of a Past Time': History and Graphic Representation in *Maus*." As Sebastian Domsch, Dirk Vanderbeke, and Dan Hassler-Forest have written, "From the mid-2000s onwards, comics studies has become one of the most prolific fields of inquiry across a variety of disciplines. Literary studies, cultural studies, media studies, art history and aesthetics have all contributed to research into a cultural phenomenon that had previously been neglected if not vilified in the Anglophone world."[12]

For the last two decades, the New Modernist Studies and comics studies have been in continual orbit and with increasing frequency are coming into contact. Yet to date, no single, book-length volume has explored the overlapping material and aesthetic conditions of early twentieth-century art and literature and the form of comics. *Comics and Modernism: History, Form, and Culture* seeks to fill the gaps in current scholarship—and, in turn, to outline new gaps and point the way toward future scholarship—by bringing together recent interdisciplinary research from both established scholars and emerging voices in the field.

The essays in this book offer no single definition or theory of modernism. One of the great strengths of a collection like this one is that, in bringing together scholars with diverse backgrounds, methodological training, and disciplinary specialties, we are able to explore a complicated period from a rich, productive array of scholarly perspectives. Taken as a whole, the essays here offer something of a survey of modernist studies, or at least what modernism can mean in a particular discourse. In the chapters by Noa Saunders, Jean Lee

Cole, and Clémence Sfadj, for example, *modernism* most closely corresponds to particular conditions and lived experiences: respectively, the shock and trauma of everyday life, the grotesque distortions of gendered hierarchies, the unattainable promise of urban life. In the essays by Louise Kane and Daniel Worden, we're reminded of the conceptually irreconcilable elements of modernist politics, which flex both revolutionary leftist (as in Russian constructivism) and regressively nationalist (as in certain strains of futurism). Kane examines the emerging global culture, where styles and artworks and influence and inspiration were being freely traded; and Worden reminds us of the converse (and consequent) impulse, the eruption of fascist ideals out of a dormant nativism.

Of course, this would not be a book about modernism without some extended treatment of formalism and style. Whether we accept the much-contested Greenbergian stance that defines modernism primarily in relation to its own formal autonomy, we can't deny that form figures prominently in theories of art and literature from the period (theories produced both in and since modernism). For Glenn Willmott, Katherine Roeder, and Scott Bukatman, formal detail, and visual style in particular, is central to how we orient comics alongside modernism. All three of their essays move beyond easy proclamations about experimentation—the idea that Joyce, Picasso, McCay, and Herriman pushed the boundaries of their respective media. Audience and ownership, the museum and the public sphere, realism and style and detail all come under renewed scrutiny when we understand comics and modernism as equal participants in the aesthetic culture of the period.

And in the essays by David M. Ball, Matt Levay, and myself, we return to modernism's rigorously historical impulse, what T. S. Eliot would call "tradition," that simultaneous "sense of the timeless as well as of the temporal."[13] Make it new, Pound declared, which so many modernists did, like Stephen Dedalus, rere regardant, looking backward to the past with a hopeful sense that there they might find the future. Their project of mining the old to generate the new would prove impossible (though not fruitless), and as Ball writes, we don't need Paul de Man to figure out why the modernists struggled, finally, to sever their connection with history; it was right there in Herriman's *Krazy Kat* all along. Yet many comics artists, like their modernist forebears, have remained obsessively, compulsively consumed with the past. Modernism in contemporary comics—the ghost of Picasso in Art Spiegelman's work, the anachronistic visual style in Cole Closser—might not be a nightmare from which cartoonists are trying to awake, but it is certainly a powerful, generative presence.

Just as these essays advance no single understanding of modernism, neither do we insist on any single definition of comics. Comics, in this volume, refers to single-panel cartoons and newspaper strips; to magazine illustrations and superhero comics; to *Mad* magazine and experimental underground comix and contemporary graphic narratives. Most often, comics refers to a particular style or mood—but even then, the style is by turns satiric and grotesque, the mood playful and serious. While you need not read the book cover to cover to appreciate the nuances of each argument contained here, doing so offers a rich, sophisticated history of the medium of comics spanning the twentieth century. The narrative is not complete—we're missing an extended treatment of Lyonel Feininger, of King's modernist masterpiece *Crazy Quilt*, of Flannery O'Connor's cartoons, of the surrealist innovations of Sally Cruikshank's animation, of the pervasive influence of modernist titans on Alison Bechdel, of comics produced outside of the American tradition—but it nonetheless offers an important template for how we can approach comics' relation to other art forms. We learn, in this present volume, how modernism was disseminated in the newspapers, accepted into the world of magazine illustration, and finally memorialized in the space of the comics page.

...

The book is divided into four sections that move roughly chronologically through the twentieth century, spanning from early-century newspaper comics through midcentury magazine illustration and silver age superhero comics and ending with the work of contemporary cartoonists such as Art Spiegelman and Cole Closser. The first section, "Modernism and Comics," offers an account of modernist art and culture that intersects with the history of comics. The section begins with Glenn Willmott's theoretically rich chapter, "Entanglements of Style: The Uniqueness of Modernism in Comics." Recognizing that, from an institutional standpoint, comics was not modernism, Willmott proposes that the "kindred strategies of aesthetic and semiotic disruption" that we find in both forms can be understood most powerfully through *style*: "the aesthetic means by which the defamiliarizing or subversive effects that are experienced as modernist difficulty in the arts of the avant-garde are, in comics, uniquely conveyed." Building on this argument, Katherine Roeder's chapter, "Modernism for the Masses: The Armory Show in Comics," shows how newspaper cartoonists co-opted, parodied, and, ultimately, admired the aesthetically challenging visuals on display in the International Exhibition of Modern Art in 1913. Comics, Roeder argues, effectively brought modernism from the galleries into people's homes through the medium of the newspaper.

The next two essays, Noa Saunders's "The Dreamer's Modern Body: Winsor McCay and the Everyday Sensorium" and David M. Ball's "A Thoroughly Modern Kat," both attend to the shifting, unpredictable conditions of the modern world, seeking to locate comics in a sociocultural milieu that was subject to intense theorization, uncertain speculation, and aesthetic provocation. For

Saunders, this registers most powerfully in "the everyday sensorium," that compendium of seemingly tedious, quotidian experiences that, taken together, constitute the shock of modern life; Winsor McCay's comics register this experience through what Saunders terms "the iterative image." Ball's essay is similarly attentive to repetition and iteration, and conveys how the serialized quality of Herriman's *Krazy Kat* complicates modernism's desire for a complete break with the past.

Section II of the book, "Print, Ephemera, Circulation," directs our attention to the dispersive quality of comics art, tracing its circulation across media platforms (newspapers, magazines, books) and geographic boundaries. In "Four Repulsive Women: Marjorie Organ, Nell Brinkley, Kate Carew, Djuna Barnes," Jean Lee Cole uncovers an important circle of women journalists in the male-dominated world of newspaper comics and reporting. Cole is especially attentive to the "grotesque transformations of bodies, especially female ones" in response to patriarchal modernity. In "Jackie Ormes's *Torchy Brown in "Dixie to Harlem"*: Modernism in the African American Funny Pages," Clémence Sfadj directs our attention to another artist using the medium of comics to resist hegemonic and patriarchal norms: Jackie Ormes, whose strip *Torchy Brown in "Dixie to Harlem"* made her the first syndicated African American woman cartoonist. Many of Ormes's strips invoke canonically modernist literary techniques: blurring the boundaries between Torchy's inner consciousness and her exterior surroundings and allowing a fantastical dreamscape to overwhelm her panels; bombarding Torchy with the overwhelming sensory experience of the modern city; indulging a fragmented, almost desultory mode of narrative progression. For Louise Kane, modernism's arena is not the local but the global: the divergent collection of forms that coalesced on the world stage. Her chapter "In Dialogue and Debate: Comics, Little Magazines, World Literature" uncovers the parallel histories of little magazines and comics, both of which were developed in the middle to late nineteenth century; flourished in the early decades of the twentieth; participated in multiple genres and invoked various media traditions; and prefigured the rise of what we know today as "world literature."

Section III, "Pop/Art: Comics High and Low," offers a survey of vastly divergent comics forms: lifestyle illustration, superhero comics, and experimental "comic bokes." Scott Bukatman's essay "Telling Details: Feminine Flourish in Midcentury Illustration and Comics" reveals the rich complexity of seemingly superfluous "ornamental" details, which he connects to contemporary practices in Hollywood melodrama. In "Speed Lines: Futurism and Superheroes," Daniel Worden reads the superhero as a quintessentially modernist trope, arguing that superheroes participate in both modernism's visual, formal experimentation and in its problematic fascination with fascist politics. In "'Our First Literature':

The Poetics Underground of Joe Brainard's New York School Comics," Nick Sturm surveys the challenging, subversive work of Joe Brainard, putting the artist in conversation with various underground cartoonists (many of whom Brainard prefigures by at least ten years). As Sturm writes, "We should see Brainard's work as establishing a legitimate and sophisticated role for comics as a critical and imaginative form that engages both visual art and literature."

The final section of the book inverts the first: "Modernism and Comics" has become "Comics as Modernism," the *and/as* a cheeky nod to the suggestive, complex interplay between the forms. In "Profane Transfigurations," Andrei Molotiu puts Harvey Kurtzman, the legend behind *Mad* magazine, in conversation with a surprising interlocutor: the art critic and philosopher Arthur Danto. Reading these two figures alongside one another "allows us to establish more complex parallels and avenues of communication between art and comics without falling into the trap of high and low, of upward aspiration or downward appropriation, of celebration or resentment," while also looking ahead toward the rise of the comix underground in the sixties and seventies. My own essay, "Art Spiegelman and the Ghost of Picasso," picks up exactly where Molotiu leaves off, examining Art Spiegelman's early comic "Ace Hole, Midget Detective." Deploying techniques he learned reading *Mad* magazine, Spiegelman reveals comics to be the natural inheritor of a modernist aesthetic tradition. And in "*Little Tommy Lost* and the Anachronistic Comic," Matthew Levay examines the tendency of contemporary cartoonists to adopt distinctly anachronistic visual styles, ones that mimic the aesthetic of early newspaper comics. Understanding these unique, revealing formal innovations allows us to see clearly Cole Closser's political project: "to critique the conservative social and political ideologies" that permeated the work of Harold Gray, the cartoonist behind *Little Orphan Annie*.

The book ends with Hillary Chute's suggestive afterword, "Graphic Modernisms." Chute offers an important glimpse at some central figures not discussed at length in the book—Robert Crumb, Alison Bechdel, Joe Sacco—while also reflecting on the etymology of *the graphic*. Tracing the graphic to its etymological roots in Homer's *Iliad*, when a spear punctures a shoulder, Chute demonstrates the relentless materiality of the comics form, in both its hand-drawn images and its insistence on the visual display of bodies. As a concept, the graphic helps to explain what is so powerful about comics: "The wounding power of comics' graphic form—its power to inscribe bodies on the page—is part of its great possibility." In both modernism and comics, we're left, ultimately, with the historical conditions that facilitate the production of art.

Notes

1. Michael Tisserand, *Krazy: George Herriman, A Life in Black and White* (New York: HarperCollins, 2016), 241.

2. Jared Gardner, *Projections: Comics and the History of Twenty-First-Century Storytelling* (Stanford, CA: Stanford University Press, 2012), xi.

3. Daniel Stein, "The Comic Modernism of George Herriman," in *Crossing Boundaries in Graphic Narrative: Essays on Forms, Series and Genres*, ed. Jake Jakaitis and James F. Wurtz (New York: McFarland, 2012), 56.

4. Jeffrey Weiss, *The Popular Culture of Modernism: Picasso, Duchamp, and Avant-Gardism* (New Haven, CT: Yale University Press, 1994), xvi.

5. Weiss, xvii.

6. Michael North, *Reading 1922: A Return to the Scene of the Modern* (Oxford: Oxford University Press, 2002), 26.

7. North, 26.

8. North, 27. For more on Eliot's affiliation with popular culture, see David Chinitz, *T. S. Eliot and the Cultural Divide* (Chicago: Chicago University Press, 2003).

9. North, 29.

10. Lise Jaillant, *Cheap Modernism: Expanding Markets, Publishers' Series and the Avant-Garde* (Edinburgh: Edinburgh University Press, 2017), 9.

11. There are a handful of notable exceptions, one of which is the University Press of Mississippi, publisher of the present volume, which issued Joseph Witek's *Comic Books as History* in 1989 and M. Thomas Inge's *Comics as Culture* in 1990.

12. Sebastian Domsch, Dirk Vanderbeke, and Dan Hassler-Forest, "Comics Studies: Survey of the Field," in *Handbook of Comics and Graphic Narratives*, ed. Sebastian Domsch, Dan Hassler-Forest, and Dirk Vanderbeke (Berlin: De Gruyter, 2021), 1.

13. T. S. Eliot, "Tradition and the Individual Talent," *Egoist* 6, no. 4 (1919): 55.

Section I

MODERNISM AND COMICS

ENTANGLEMENTS OF STYLE

The Uniqueness of Modernism in Comics

GLENN WILLMOTT

MODERNISM

What follows is a theory of modernism in comics. It begins by grappling with a seeming paradox: in an important historical sense, comics were never modernist, because they were not art. In *Comics versus Art*, Bart Beaty influentially explored this exclusion: modernism names the institution of an art world that came to power in the middle of the twentieth century, which distinguished itself definitively against and above the ignoble, creative welter of commercial media culture. And to that other world, comics inextricably belonged.[1]

Even defiantly so. When George Herriman's comic strip, *Krazy Kat*, was performed as an avant-garde jazz ballet in 1922, it received extravagant praise from New York's high-brow magazine, the *New Republic*. Herriman quickly penned two pages of tongue-in-cheek complaints to its author, the academic-turned-theater-critic, Stark Young. He described how this newly conferred cultural status had rendered Krazy and the rest of the denizens of the strip, erstwhile "nobodies," suddenly strutting, vain, and pretentious. "I can't blame them," Herriman concludes: "publicity of that kind is strong medicine—the air is rarer up there—and we can't stand too much of it—we who live close to the sidewalks."[2] While his tone with Stark is affectionate, one can't miss Herriman's edgy reluctance to be identified with oxygen-deficient high art and its elite class status. We, he emphasizes—meaning both he and his cartoon animals—belong on the street, not in the art world.

This is exactly what Clement Greenberg would say about comics nearly two decades later, but looking in the reverse direction, downward. Comics, he said, were kitsch, beneath notice—or rather, only noticed as a contrasting background, cultural murk, to set off the rare, refulgent aura of modern art.[3] I'll return to Greenberg's idea of kitsch momentarily. Such deprecations of comics as low entertainment, at best a raw resource to be slyly repurposed by an Andy Warhol or a Roy Lichtenstein, were commonplace and have become a cliché to comics readers. But why should Herriman, of all people, affirm this degradation? He is flattered by the high-brow attention, yes, but also scornful of it, defensive of where he feels he belongs, where the creatures of his art belong.

What Herriman means by living "close to the sidewalks" points to his identification with a popular commons, but more importantly, it points to that commons as an audience whom he means to address and thus to whom he feels ethically committed, the people in whose imaginations the funny animals, Krazy Kat, Ignatz Mouse, Offisa Pupp, Joe Stork, Kolin Kelly, and Walter Austridge are brought alive. These readers were coming to Herriman's daily newspaper strip in 1922 with different expectations, for example, than did contemporary readers of *Ulysses*, whose pricy, limited first editions on handmade paper, typically obtained through special subscription, were marketed as collector art objects. Herriman's readers did not expect art as such. But I suggest that they expected something of which art was made—even if this something was disposable—and which was recognized among modernists as distinctly, aesthetically modern. I do not think there is a word yet for this aesthetic substance, this genetic feature buried across modern art and popular culture. We need a word that will capture the pursuit of creative ideas and experimental practices, playing transgressive games with social and psychological norms, in both *Mrs. Dalloway* and *Polly and Her Pals*. This word must preserve a certain detachment, not assimilable to art.

This I will call, borrowing from the lexicon of modernism itself, *style*. On the one hand, avant-garde modernists exemplify style as form made meaningful, as a signature fusion of individual vision and aesthetic practice. On the other hand, the modern culture industry, with its frenzied, mass consumption of goods and entertainment, exemplifies style as fashion, as sensation, as mere style. The differences between these two worlds of style, on the street and in the gallery, have little to do with aesthetics or content and more to do with what we expect them to do for us.

Style names a chameleonic doubling of the art world in the open commerce of the street, in another modernism, bound to modern art genetically yet distinct from it sociologically; style sees comics and art living uncanny parallel lives, like twins separated at birth.[4] What made this separation? Purely formal or aesthetic understandings of comics are no help in answering this question. Indeed, Scott McCloud's brilliant and seminal anatomy of comics form associates comics with canonical art traditions and observes, in particular, a convergence with modernism in the breakdown of distinctions between word and image.[5] To track the implications for style in the separation of comics and art, we may return to Beaty, who shows that comics cannot adequately be defined by formal or media criteria: as a creative tradition, it is more convincingly recognized by institutional criteria, where an institution is any network of social relations and values organized around a purpose or activity—for example, making and reading comics. Just as is the case with the modernist "art world," says Beaty, "comics" is most accurately defined as a set of aesthetic conventions and practices that is understood by historical communities to constitute comics.[6]

Comics and the art world both grew up within the wild abundance of creative practices that we now include in expanded notions of modernism. They evolved from the same fire and slime of twentieth-century history, and they adopted kindred strategies of aesthetic and semiotic disruption and experiment to express and to make sense of it. Yet they took shape in different institutions: the art world comprised unique art objects validated for consumers by expert tastemakers and specialized spaces for exhibition and appreciation, motivated by ideas of ownership (status, self-image), readership (insight, alienation), and authorship (vision, autonomy). The comics world depended on different ideas of ownership, readership, and authorship. It comprised mass produced, disposable objects validated for consumers by faceless corporations, like newspaper syndicates and later small publishers, and it was motivated by an ideology of consumption (thrills, adventure, play, sensation). Comics and art worlds overlapped in many ways, but as institutions, they habituated readers to approach them differently.

Modern art solicited a desire for trouble, and especially a desire to trouble pleasure with cognitive, moral, or emotional difficulty. Modern comics, I suggest, solicited instead a desire for abandon, a loose, extravagant feeling in which cognitive, moral, or emotional expectations for sensitive taste and meaningful insight—whose confounding would raise difficulties—are left aside, leaving only an expectation for kinds and degrees of (not necessarily unintelligent) pleasure. It is not that a troublesome taste or insight must be absent. Far from it. But comics habituated the reader to a surface reading in which modernist vision and formal experiment have no hidden layer that is difficult to apprehend. If the idea of an accessible difficulty sounds paradoxical, then one must only think of humor, which works to express dissonant or troubling content in a ludic, pleasing way. Comics of course takes its name from a historical association with humor, but even completely unfunny comics work this way, to express the dissonant or troubling, the difficult, in ways our expectations are habituated to find accessible.

Because an institutional definition of comics involves a particular contract with its readers, a particular set of expectations and engagements with aesthetic and semiotic strategies, this seemingly sociological definition must eventually circle back to the stuff of genre, to matters of form or content. Readers of a particular genre are engaged in it both by a normative interlocking of institutional conditions (conventional reader expectations) and by aesthetic designs (techniques and concerns in the work of art). Neither of these can work without the cooperation of the other. One can anachronistically undo this interlock in modernism; one might legitimately be expected, in a twenty-first-century context, to look at a bigfoot-style comics panel as a work of authorial vision and gallery art; or conversely, at an abstractionist painting as kitsch, as an ornamental, anonymous background for a doctor's waiting room or kitchen utensil advertisement.[7] In either case, what the panel or painting means is going to be driven by the particular deployment of its bigfoot or its abstractionist style; yet what we are meant to do about that meaning will differ with institutional expectations. How we look at comics in modernism depends on "generic contracts" for the reader or viewer, then, that are both imposed externally, by historical convention, and also conditioned internally, by what is afforded by, even urged by, the power of aesthetic design.[8]

There is a danger of losing sight of this doubleness in simply adopting an expanded, currently progressive idea of art, in asserting that comics simply is art, or more specifically to our purpose, that comics is a modernist art. Art and comics undertook different kinds of affective and ethical work in the early twentieth century, from very different positions in modern social experience. Yet they are bound by modernism as style and by some of the aims of that style. I will now return to what that means for comics.

DIFFICULTY VERSUS ABANDON

In modernist art, style is difficult. This is a generic expectation, linked to where we find it, what we do with it and why, and it is also a matter of form and content in the work itself. It may be difficult conceptually, morally, or emotionally; notoriously difficult, for example, to make sense of (as in in Stein's syntax), to accept as art (Duchamp's readymades), to countenance (Lawrence's obscenities), or simply to undergo (Stravinsky's dissonance). And any of these may be mixed and matched (the 1913 Armory Show; see Katherine Roeder's essay in this volume).

In Greenberg's account of modernism, difficulty is a necessary experience of "genuine art," which demands interaction from the viewer and demands reflection, while mere kitsch is passively consumed.[9] Certainly, early comics are rarely difficult in this art-world sense—disturbing us into deliberate, reflective work on the aesthetic experience they offer us. But do they belong to thoughtless kitsch? For Greenberg, kitsch names an undifferentiated juggernaut of "popular, commercial art and literature with their chromeotypes, magazine covers, illustrations, ads, slick and pulp fiction, comics, Tin Pan Alley music, tap dancing, Hollywood movies, etc., etc." Alas, comics gets further singled out at the juggernaut's leading edge: kitsch "surrounds and presses in" on the struggling man of culture "from the moment he is old enough to look at the funny papers."[10] In this institutional modernist point of view, comics represents both a mass-mechanized institution of thoughtless reading as well as the individual text designed to require no thought.

Curiously, the only example Greenberg gives of a kitsch style does not derive from comics or other modern entertainment media; rather, he invents an historical battle scene rendered by an eminent realist painter, Ilya Repin, with which he asks a hypothetical "Russian peasant" to compare a similarly invented portrait painted by the vanguard cubist, Pablo Picasso. The uncultivated peasant swoons enthusiastically before the transparent, naturalistic magic of Repin, which seems a window on another world, hardly art at all. In contrast, all the peasant gleans from the "austere" Picasso painting is a "play of lines, colors and spaces that represent a woman," whose meaning is not evident.[11] I recount Greenberg's imagined scene in part to underline the power of institutionally confining audience expectations. The simplified, caricatured, nonrealist style of early comics—which I have elsewhere placed in a longer evolution of the grotesque[12]—surely contrasts in every way with the almost photorealist effects Greenberg attributes here to kitsch—while conversely, many early comics exemplify the abstractionist style to which he assimilates cubist modernism. Greenberg is blind to this irony.

But I recount this imagined scene from an exhibition for another purpose, too. There is a deeper meaning here, which is the antithesis Greenberg ends up dramatizing between two forms of empathy. There is a bad, easy empathy, in which artistry erases itself and turns any unfamiliar content, which might have been a challenge for his peasant, into something immediately recognizable, familiar, and sympathetic—in a word, relatable. Or there is a good, difficult empathy, in which obtrusive, unconventional artistry demands that his peasant bridge a profound gap between sign and content, between aesthetic experience and recognition. The unfamiliar forces its otherness on the viewer. Only this kind of empathy reveals something unexpected. The difficulty of style, then, turns out to be the difficulty of empathy. If this is so, and comics are closer to Picasso than to Repin, then why do comics feel so easy? Why is comics' plastic play with the world not similarly difficult? Why should it be so easy imaginatively to enter the highly stylized and abstract worlds, and barely humanoid lives, of comics storyworlds—of Slumberland, of the Kewpies, of Silly Symphony, or of planet Mongo?[13]

For a poignant answer to this question, we may turn to a writer at the other temporal bookend of the high modernist period, Wilhelm Worringer, and his 1908 treatise, *Abstraction and Empathy: A Contribution to the Psychology of Style*. This work is highly suggestive for comics studies because it places figural abstraction, the very basis of comics art, at the heart of its modernist aesthetics. Unlike Greenberg, who thought about abstraction as a sign of art considering its own materials, Worringer takes abstraction in its more literal sense of a drawing forth, as a distortion or extrapolation of existing, complex, heterogeneous real-world forms in the direction of ideal or imaginary order, coherence, and simplicity. In this sense, abstraction is at the heart of all style, because style gives form and unity to representation. And any particular style offers a particular, psychological engagement or grip on the world:

> No psychology of the need for art—in the terms of our modern standpoint: of the need for style—has yet been written. It would be a history of the feeling about the world and, as such, would stand alongside the history of religion as its equal. By the feeling about the world I mean the psychic state in which, at any given time, mankind found itself in relation to the cosmos, in relation to the phenomena of the external world.[14]

Thus different styles emerge "at any given time" in a historical trajectory and geographic diversity, as forms of cultural expression in response to feelings about existence itself as it seems to impose itself upon the artist there and then. But that's not all. Within style itself, the "need" it expresses is ever tugged in two opposing directions: toward empathy or toward abstraction. Worringer means something a little unconventional by empathy: he is trying to name a psychological drive that he posits, an attraction toward all life, everything vital in the world, that expresses itself in the desire to reproduce that life-world mimetically. Style that expresses the need for empathy aims naturalistically to reproduce the full, "organically beautiful vitality" of the world in which we live.[15] Style that pursues a need for abstraction, on the other hand, is much less comfortable in that vital immersion, indeed is distressed by it. Abstraction predominates, says Worringer, when we feel that the world around us is overly complex, shifting, chaotic, and incoherent—in which we may struggle and suffer with our consciousness of "the unfathomable entanglement of all the phenomena of life" or "the relativity of all that is."[16] To the quandary of difficulty posed by Greenberg's example of comics, then, the answer suggested by Worringer is that empathy may be difficult when naturalistic and abstract urges are paradoxically fused—when phenomena are revealed in all their chiaroscuro depths of "obscurity and entanglement," yet also made plainly accessible, captured by the simple line, unified by geometrical regularity, and surfaced into two-dimensional space.[17]

For Worringer, the drives to empathy and abstraction in style are hardly limited to the art world. Because they are cultural expressions, they range across all forms of art and craft, even to mere decoration. While most interested in where styles fit into a developmental trajectory between empathy and abstraction, he briefly considers ornamental styles that simultaneously express both. For example, he finds decorative line drawings of wave motifs to be "pure ornament on an organic fundament," that is, a fusion of a naturalistic experience of the primal, fluidly ungraspable element, water, with an accessible abstraction. The same fusion is found in ornamental animal motifs across cultures, which are highly stylized and often fantastical. In these examples, a feeling for organic instability and entanglement (the fact that beings in real life are not unified or isolated from their environments, but ever exceeding our grasp, overflowing our perception) pulls abstraction away from the austerity of geometry or pure ornament, and toward the real world.[18]

This fusion of a mimesis of existential excess with abstract unity and order may sound contradictory or impossible, but it well describes the magical style of comics, in which the abstraction of outline drawing, simplified figures, and two-dimensionality works to express a kind of material unity without homogeneity, a kind of open visibility without ready decodability, and thus a kind of immersive empathy that demands something more profoundly indulgent or eccentric from the reader than mere thoughtless recognition. This is an extravagant demand, perhaps, but one that comics was born with. The accessible difficulty of its style is matched by an institutional culture of comics in which one is habituated to meet its disturbingly quasi-human or flagrantly distorted worldbuilding not with an expectation of trouble (decoding work, conceptual hardship, emotional distress, or ethical confrontation), but with a leisurely expectation of abandon. Early comics culture does not expect its readers to rise to a challenge, but it does need them, sometimes in markedly unconventional ways, simply to let go.

THREE DIMENSIONS OF COMICS STYLE

Graphic style is the aesthetic means by which the defamiliarizing or subversive effects that are experienced as modernist difficulty in the arts of the avant-garde are, in comics, uniquely conveyed. This concept of style is narrower than the one introduced above as a name for the aesthetic ground of modern art and popular culture industries. It is the particular practice of comics on that ground, with emphasis on its nonsemiotic (in the sense of merely stylistic) yet powerful qualities. Specifically, I understand graphic style to refer to the usage in comics of nonmimetic properties of line, shape, expressivity, tone, spatial composition, and color to characterize a represented storyworld, along with mimetic elements we cognitively apprehend rather than conventionally read. The latter may include universal conceptual metaphors like higher versus lower, or universal facial expressions like surprise or sadness.[19] Thus the qualities and effects of style reach beyond words and icons, and may be described independently from language functions. In comics, style is special in three interrelated ways:

(1) Entanglement. As a totalizing element in the portrayal of characters and storyworlds, style in comics is an aesthetic unifier—and material entangler, to borrow Worringer's word—of represented selves and environments, however distinct or diverse in themselves.[20] Whether as an unthinking daydream, as a curious experiment, or as flickering sensation in-between, style in comics provides to readers a means to imagine the often transgressive affects and unaccountable agency of beings explicitly drawn into a single storyworld. In theory, following Worringer, such immersive entanglement might be the stuff of nightmares. After all, if one of Rose O'Neill's Kewpies were to burst into our room, or we took a wrong turn into the vertiginous, volatile wastes of Coconino County, the claustrophobic, starkly inked locales of Dick Tracy, or the sweeping, chromatic currents of planet Mongo, we would be terrified. We aren't terrified of such apparitions, though, because we do not come to them, when we do, expecting to decode them for ourselves, to recognize them. Instead, our expectation is to abandon ourselves to them as something satisfyingly recognized only as artifactual, as intrinsically stylized. The anxious drama of subjective recognition of others that courses through all fiction is here short-circuited, grounded like lightning, in an artifactual recognition of style. We simply go along with it. We are entangled first by style, then by style's worlds and creatures.

(2) Rehumanization. As an effect of entanglement, style in comics offers unique modes of empathy, of immersion and identification for its reader, according to which humanness is reshaped—whether very subtly, or quite outrageously—without ceasing to be experienced as human. Rehumanization is not a return to but a remaking of the human figure, both cognitive and semiotic.

(3) Diaphany. Style is the means by which a specifically heteroglossic field of signs and images is fantastically, playfully, or anxiously unified; sutur-

ing into imaginary coherence its persons, places, and objects.[21] Style is thus not only dialogic (signifying across), in that it provides the graphic substratum to articulate different discourses together, but also and definitively "diaphanic" (showing across), in that style articulates different mimetic and affective communications together. Indeed, diaphany arguably assimilates discursive dialogism as a subordinate element into the iconic continuum of comics form.[22] Diaphany, in this view, reveals itself to be a key to understanding the social and political implications of an accessible modernist style in comics, in comparison to the more trouble-making work of the avant-garde art world. Diaphany is the mode in which a work either hews to a monologic purpose that trivializes the effects of immersive entanglement and rehumanizing identification, or more adventurously and subversively, it explores radically alternative ways of understanding the self, its agency, and its natural and social conditions.

These three propositions can be illustrated in diverse strips of the early and mid-twentieth century. I'll briefly discuss a strip that was appreciated as singularly modern and innovative in its time, the aforementioned *Krazy Kat*, as well as two less outwardly experimental works: the family humor strip *Cap Stubbs and Tippie*, by Edwina Dumm, and the fantasy adventure strip *Flash Gordon*, by Alex Raymond.

MODERNIST DIAPHANIES

The story for the *Krazy Kat* ballet was drawn from a strip Herriman published the previous year, in which Krazy sees a public poster advertising a Grand Ball and is inspired, with the help of a tutu borrowed from a clothesline, to break into a joyful, free-style dance (figure 1.1). In the opening panel we see in the foreground an anthropomorphic cat, Krazy, sleeping with head propped against a potted, palm-like tree, set near a tall wall. Offissa Pupp strolls by in the near middle ground, eyeing Krazy. Flat ground stretches in every direction, relieved only by a few pebbles, all the way to a flat horizon, above which a few clouds drift in a sky that shades from daytime bright on the left to nighttime dark on the right. Plant, pot, cat, dog, wall, desert, sky—these are unashamedly heterogeneous elements that do not come together into a scene that we recognize, that we can identify, except within the world of Krazy Kat itself. None have an obvious relationship to each other. They are inexplicable in their environment, even as they appear utterly at home in it, pulled together by brute pictorial fact and the fancies of the plot.

Figure 1.1. George Herriman, *Krazy Kat*, first published July 31, 1921.

This is what Worringer calls entanglement, the unpoliceable conspiracy of things to belong with other things with vitality and motivation, but without recognizable coherence or symmetry. Thrown into this world, *Krazy Kat*'s reader might feel puzzled, disoriented, even vaguely disturbed by such heterogeneity, such multiplied otherness, if it were not all unified by a unique, expressive style. Literally, each unlike thing is visibly made of the material and gestures of every other unlike thing, visibly belonging to a single aesthetic fabric. Heterogeneity and entanglement are surfaced and simplified—as an experience—in style. Aesthetic justification allows actions and effects that in our world we would judge difficult to accept or to interpret, such as the appearance of a tutu strung between tree stumps in the middle of the desert, or a palm-like tree that seems to move in response to the story, like a Greek chorus. What is life? What is our environment? These questions have profoundly difficult answers in Krazy's world, yet we do not find them difficult, because we abandon ourselves to visible, sensual answers before the questions are asked. Offissa Pupp sums it up: "All's well."

The most powerful motif of entanglement, the one we are invited to identify with, to empathize with, is Krazy Kat, the anthropomorphic protagonist. Krazy is made out of elements of cat, elements of human, and elements neither human nor cat but stylistic, and is notoriously gender fluid. In Herriman's highly theatricalized storyworld, this entanglement of genders and species is performed rather than revealed, a matter of style rather than essence. In drawing the reader into this style, the storyworld draws us into empathy with unconventional, unsettled images of humanity. We don't have to be "human" in a fully recognizable way. What counts as a person and as a human are reimagined, rehumanized. Herriman will often play with signs of identity in language—Krazy speaks an idiosyncratic ethnic-class mélange rife with puns—and in visual icons, such as the feminine ballet tutu that when worn alone, suddenly implies nakedness; the imagery of black versus white skin; or the mix of human and cat features in Krazy. Yet these iconic elements are not only dialogic: they are embedded in and interact with pictorial effects of style that are diaphanic. For example, the bill sticker mixes legible dog and human elements with a nonsignifying geometric ornament resembling a Jasper Johns painting on its back. When we take in this bill sticker as readers, we do not so much decode as we directly apprehend the creature's fusion of the organic (animal) and the artifactual (craft, ornament), making them something quietly but strangely cyborgian. Something closer to pure diaphany is expressed in the relationship of the potted-tree figure to the other figures in the first three panels. In the first, the tree stands upright, with a mere crook in its trunk echoing the elbow of the passing Offissa Pupp. In the second, the tree leans toward the wall and poster, its foliage extended, echoing the posture and attention of Krazy and the bill sticker. In the third, the tree's trunk and foliage are jagged and dynamic, again echoing Krazy in their dance, perhaps in sympathy, perhaps in recoil. There is a kind of mimetic contagion or reciprocity, in other words, between the potted tree and the other characters that—again, quietly, obscurely—allows us to register the tree as not merely an object, nor quite a character. Entangled visually with the characters, we abandon ourselves to the presence of a being that exists somewhere between object and subject, only partly readable, only partly knowable, that is just doing its thing. Herriman's diaphanies are challenging. Even if not troubling, they subvert normalized and naturalized ideas of the human, of gender, and of social purposes and values.[23]

Similar challenges may be found in comics less overtly experimental than *Krazy Kat*. Edwina Dumm, one of the most successful women in early comics, was a close contemporary of Herriman, and was known both for her editorial cartoons and her comic strips. Her long-running strip, *Cap Stubbs and Tippie*, triangulates the mindsets of animals, children, and adults in everyday domestic dramas involving a rambunctious boy, Cap, his rambunctious pet bulldog, Tippie, and a long-suffering parental figure, usually his Grandma. In a five-panel strip from 1920 (figure 1.2), the confusion of an animal-human distinction that we saw in Krazy Kat is played out in the figural style—compare Cap's face in panel four to Tippie's face in panel five—but reassuringly naturalized, even thematized, as a childish perception. Yet even here there is a pleasing, subversive edge to the nature of the animal, as well as of the human. In the first panel, Tippie is represented as fearful of the scolding Grandma. In the second panel, he is resentful, a more complex emotion that is implicitly explained by Cap's speech (a curious example of what McCloud calls the "additive" use

Figure 1.2. Edwina Dumm, *Cap Stubbs and Tippie*, first published September 4, 1920.

of word and image to reinforce the same message) as belonging to a more human, or at least not dog, mind.[24] The third panel has Tippie turning to Cap as if in response to this speech, with the same resentful expression. Across the two panels, Cap has lowered himself into a crouch that mimics Tippie's own posture and height, establishing a shared identity; this mirroring will return in the final panel, as their freedom from adult (and normatively human) mentality is rendered affectively, for the reader, as a freedom from gravity. In the climactic fourth panel, the dog now leaps upward, staring down Grandma face to face, just as he did Cap, but the sense of equivalence is here ludic and bizarre. To underscore this diaphanic play of bodies and gazes, Cap gazes at Tippie "kissing" Grandma, while a portrait in the background (grandfather?) placidly stares directly at the reader, an ineffectual patriarch and super-ego, helpless before this libidinal chaos.

Dumm's own version of a realist style holds everything together: nothing like a naturalistic mimesis, it is a style that draws on conventional periodical cartooning and illustration practices of découpage to sketch figures against fragmentary, empty spaces. One might call it a spontaneous realism, where despite some closely observed anatomy and clothing details, the force of abstraction is felt in the freedom of figures to emerge and interact in a storyworld space ungrounded in anything much more than the picture plane itself. It is remarkable, for example, how few lines ground the presence of the sofa, or how the baseboard melts into two-dimensional emptiness, isolating the figures of the remaining characters and objects in their own, private fury of linework. In a narrative context, such découpage takes on new meaning: things are free to bind each to each according to a conventional order, or not. When the figures are brought into unfamiliar or unrecognizable relationships, as especially in panel four, there is a sense of freedom in their doing so that arises from their normalized isolation as magically autonomous agents. Thus Dumm's style effects a fantastically egocentric storyworld, but one without a ruling, normative ego. The reader sees this without having to interpret it.

Figure 1.3. Alex Raymond, *Flash Gordon*, first published November 22, 1936.

The diaphany of a comic strip's style need not be humorous to solicit our abandon and convey subversive apprehensions. Alex Raymond's *Flash Gordon* is the most somber of the early adventure strips, a stylistic effect of the storyworld well displayed in this episode from 1936 (figure 1.3). The physical stances are heavy, statuesque, almost melancholic. The faces are downturned, brooding, or grimly intent. Conventional découpage is at work here too, but without a sense of agential isolation: the figures—and holistically, the panels—are woven together by moody currents of swooping, flowing lines, as if some kind of pantheistic force were immanent in characters, objects, substances, and even in spatial shadings that approach nonfigural abstraction and belong only to an affective sense of its world. Hence, despite the powerful inertia of the figural style—even in the midst of action, time oozes, loses direction—the strip throbs with sensual motion. The visually dominant image, an inexplicably huge, writhing, muscular tree, seems to yearn toward and entangle the other figures like so many limbs and leaves; each panel echoes or extends gestures and motifs of its whorl, roots, and trunk. This nonsignifying diaphany of figures and nonfigural ornament establishes a weird, vital unity in which is embedded, like signifying shards, a dialogic play of conflicting icons of life (male, female; earthling, alien; creature, artifact; oriental, occidental; modern, primitive). We are expected to read and affirm the ideological hierarchies, the casual racism and familiar patriarchy, of those conventional signs; but we are also invited to observe and indulge their indiscriminate entanglement and deconstruction in style. In giving ourselves up shamelessly to the undefinable pleasure of exotic, bald aliens in breastplates and loincloths, along with looming arms and fingers of entwining vegetation, along with pendulous, gleaming technologies, along with languid mantles and waters, we sink into the erotic current of a polymorphous, posthuman voyeurism.

IMMERSION

In 1827, Thomas De Quincey added murder to the fine arts. Today, a leisurely online browse of books in print will reveal "the art of" many more things, such as war, cocktails, mindfulness, business strategy, breastfeeding, motorcycle maintenance, not giving a f*ck, and cartooning. To be sure, comics is an art—and for most readers of this chapter, it is art in the fine art and literature sense. But in order to talk about modernism in comics, I here bracketed the term art, reserving it to refer historically to the Protean, counter-cultural art communities of the early twentieth-century avant-garde, against which, but also in conversation with, comics emerged as another flowering of modernist style. I want to refurbish the term style to refer to something that transcends the troubling borders of modernist art and wanders in the innumerable other worlds of creative practices and institutions, including in popular and commercial economies, yet which may be equally modernist. I have taken this approach, which counts art as a field of institutions within a larger field of creative practices traversed by styles, in order thereby to cast a direct light on the unique modernism of comics, here seen in sharp relief as a generic alternative to the normatively troublesome modernism of the avant-garde.

In so doing, I have been reading style in comics as an expressive form, as an aesthetic practice that mediates a normally unrecognized condition of life and agency—in particular, of the permeability and plasticity of notions of the human, which include ideologically ordered signs of species, race, and gender—with cartoonish accessibility. This vocation for style, as the formal expression of difficult or unacknowledged content, is itself a modernist one,[25] and it may be recognized as yet another genetic link between the early twentieth-century worlds of comics and the avant-garde. In the art world, style in this sense tends to be read intentionally, as an expression of the individual artist's vision. But to read style as vision in comics means departing from the generic expectation of a normatively difficult modernism and instead reading comics as either evasive or symptomatic. A symptomatic reading will see comics expressing a larger cultural condition unconsciously mediated by the artist—taking, for example, Ignatz's comically irrational but codependent hatred of Krazy as a displacement of anxieties about American racism, or taking Tippie's animalized agency overwhelming Grandma's sedentary boundaries as a displaced refusal of modern norms of human personhood. If the vision in comics is read not as unconscious, however, but as intentional, then it must be evasive, a safely ambiguous expression of the artist's sensibility—for example, interpreting the queerly fluid sensuality of planet Mongo as a deliberate invitation to sensationalism and eroticism that Raymond offers with plausible deniability.

But modernist subversion is not the only effect of style. The styles of Jimmy Swinnerton's funny animal comic *The Journal Tigers*, Hal Foster's fantasy adventure *Prince Valiant*, and Harold Gray's social drama *Little Orphan Annie* all flatten diaphany—through minimal animalization, minimal découpage, and sentimental mise-en-scéne respectively—and so suppress the experiences of personal or environmental entanglement. Arguably, even each of the artists I've discussed tethers their stylized subversions to reassuring strategies of ideological containment that invite the reader not to take seriously, that is, to forget or discount anything actually profound they may feel in their briefly moving abandon to modernist defamiliarizations or transgressions. This tether, for Herriman, is a tradition of animalized nonsense; for Dumm, it is a discourse of childish naivete; and for Raymond, it is the icon of a white savior. But if so tethered, it is by a long leash.

In sum, the uniqueness of modernism in comics arises from its paradoxical yet seamless fusion of overtly abstract and mimetic effects in cartoon style, which when brought to narrative form and worldbuilding produces an aesthetics of stylized diaphany—a volatile, shifting, showing across and showing through—of the barely acknowledged, existential entanglements that make us what we are and embed us in our environment. "In the destructive element, immerse," said Conrad, of the fluid ungroundedness of life in *Lord Jim*; the same might also be said of modernist comics. This divergent modernism conjures a special experience of empathy whose signal disposition, normalized by generic contract, is psychological abandon. All that is solid melts into air, Marshall Berman famously claimed of modernity; and so too, for the comics reader, all that is difficult melts into style. We let go of what we think of ourselves. We let ourselves be drawn in. We identify shamelessly, for a moment, as cartoons, as wondrous, abstract artifacts. And where modernism subversively flourishes, we identify as artifacts shamelessly, wonderfully entangled with others unexpectedly just like us.

Notes

1. I summarize here more than one strand in Bart Beaty, *Comics versus Art* (Toronto, ON: University of Toronto Press, 2012), see esp. 3–7, 20, 74, 99.

2. George Herriman to Stark Young, n.d., Stark Young Collection, MS-4629, Harry Ransom Center, University of Texas at Austin. See also Stark Young, "Krazy Kat," *New Republic*, October 11, 1922, 175–76.

3. Clement Greenberg, "Avant-Garde and Kitsch," in *Art and Culture: Critical Essays* (Boston: Beacon, 1961), 3–21.

4. The life of the sidewalk irresistibly calls to mind Walter Benjamin's vision of Baudelaire's urban *flâneur*, the archetypal modernist figure of the streets who registers capitalist culture's psychic and bodily experience in all its shocks, its mechanized heterogeneity and ephemerality, in "On Some Motifs of Baudelaire," in *Illuminations: Essays and Reflections*, ed. Hannah Arendt, trans. Harry Zohn (New York: Schocken, 1969). The *flâneur*'s aestheticized registration of "shock" may indeed inform the staccato pictorial regimentation or the sensationally entangled styles of modernist period comics: Benjamin tells us that the shock effects of the pictorial advertising pages of the newspaper, to the reader's eye and sensibilities, are analogous—in leisurely violence, seduction, and enchantment—to those of the walker among the busy traffic of the street (163, 169, 175). The modernist dreams of a kind of writing that belongs to the street and predicts the new style of pictorial writing that Herriman and other comics creators would come to draw:

> Who among us has not dreamt, in his ambitious days, of the miracle of a poetic prose? It would have to be musical without rhythm and rhyme, supple and resistant enough to adapt itself to the lyrical stirrings of the soul, the wave motions of dreaming, the shocks of consciousness. This ideal . . . will grip especially those who are at home in the giant cities and the web of their numberless interconnecting relationships. (Baudelaire quoted by Benjamin, 165)

5. Scott McCloud, *Understanding Comics: The Invisible Art* (1993; repr., New York: Harper Perennial, 1994), 147–48.

6. Beaty, *Comics versus Art*, 36–44.

7. "Bigfoot style" refers to the simplified, stylized, caricatural drawing style of humor comics in the Golden Age (and revived later by comix artists). Figures often had exaggeratedly large feet; for example, Olive Oyl and Mickey Mouse.

8. Fredric Jameson describes "genres" as

> essentially contracts between a writer and his readers; or rather, to use the term which Claudio Guillen has so usefully revived, they are literary *institutions*, which like the other institutions of social life are based on tacit agreements or contracts. The thinking behind such a view of genres is based on the presupposition that all speech needs to be marked with certain indications and signals as to how it is properly to be used. (Fredric Jameson, "Magical Narratives: Romance as Genre," *New Literary History* 7, no. 1 [1975]: 135)

9. Greenberg, "Avant-Garde and Kitsch," 15.

10. Greenberg, 9, 11.

11. Greenberg, 14.

12. Glenn Willmott, "The Animalized Character and Style," in *Animal Comics: Multispecies Storyworlds in Graphic Narratives*, ed. David Herman (London: Bloomsbury Academic, 2017), 53–77.

13. Greenberg fends off this kind of question by asserting that kitsch in a style comparable to modernist art, that is, modernist kitsch, is a simulacrum that may look like modernism without acting on the viewer as modernism ("Avant-Garde and Kitsch," 10–11, 15–16). Since the criteria for distinguishing the two detaches itself entirely from formal style, and is only projected by the audience, and indeed by a critic's psychological speculations thereof, this explanation is a tautology of the form: kitsch is recognizable because I see it as kitsch. The argument does, however, obliquely express the institutional *seeing* that underpins his theory of modernism.

14. Wilhelm Worringer, *Abstraction and Empathy: A Contribution to the Psychology of Style*, trans. Michael Bullock (Chicago: Ivan R. Dee, 1997), 13.

15. Worringer, 14.

16. Worringer, 16. Note that for Worringer, abstraction tends to nonliving forms, especially geometrical, that are not identifiably organic or human. Thus his idea of abstraction is quite different from, but not incompatible with, Scott McCloud's view of abstraction as pure sensory form and quality (*Understanding Comics*, 50–51). McCloud's speculation (42–43) that an abstract face is more likely to encourage empathy may, in this context, seem paradoxical. Yet one might explain it as an abstract simplification and suppression of self that allows for empathetic release into the wider, stranger storyworld of the comic.

17. Worringer, 20, 40.

18. Worringer, 72, 61–62.

19. On conceptual metaphors as a human experience transcending cultural differences, see George Lakoff and Mark Johnson, *Philosophy in the Flesh: The Embodied Mind and Its Challenge to Western Thought* (New York: Basic Books, 1999). On universal versus culturally specific facial expressions of emotion, see the review of research in D. Matsumoto, "Culture and Emotion," in *The Handbook of Culture and Psychology*, ed. D. Matsumoto (Oxford: Oxford University Press, 2001), 171–94.

20. Notes on entanglement and homogeneity: (1) Worringer's characterization of existential reality as entangled resonates with Karen Barad's description of her ontology of agential realism in *Meeting the Universe Halfway: Quantum Physics and the Entanglement of Matter and Meaning* (Duke University Press, 2007). Both of these writers defy hasty summary, but I find it intriguing that Worringer's vision of the cosmos (including the self) as restless, entangled activity upon which we impose abstract orders offers a step in the direction of Barad's posthumanist view, with the important difference that such orders, for Barad, have a relational validity that is denied by the simpler existentialist dualism and its implication of a transcending consciousness. (2) While in modernist and later comics, a homogenous style is by far the most common, there have always been storyworld styles that combine stylistic modes. For example, in Cliff Sterrett's *Polly and Her Pals*, Polly is always drawn in a more realistic, proportional way, with fewer distorting caricatural conventions, than the other characters, who are more grotesquely comedic. Another more striking example is Jeff Smith's *Bone*, in which a highly abstract, simplified figural style for Bone and his friends is combined with more realistic human figures. This kind of orchestrated styling may be evident not only between character types but also between characters and noncharacter objects and backgrounds. In such cases, I speculate that stylistic unity remains shared enough, for example in line style and inking, so as not to disrupt the sense

of a coherent storyworld. Some artists have experimented with very different stylistic modes within strips: Art Spiegelman's surrealist work prior to *Maus* is often very difficult to scan or "enter" into as a reader because it combines radically contrasting styles.

21. On heteroglossia see Mikhail Bakhtin, *The Dialogic Imagination: Four Essays* (Austin: University of Texas Press, 1981), 291.

22. Scott McCloud argues that pictorial and nonpictorial icons are the basis of comics in *Understanding Comics*, 26–28. I find this argument illuminating for the analysis of words and figures in comics, and I am here—at the invitation of modernism—attempting better to understand the role of abstraction.

23. For a reading of Kat's subversion of social and economic norms, see Glenn Willmott, *Modern Animalism: Habitats of Scarcity and Wealth in Comics and Literature* (Toronto, ON: University of Toronto Press, 2012), 65–68.

24. McCloud, *Understanding Comics*, 154.

25. Ben Hutchinson, *Modernism and Style* (New York: Palgrave, 2011), 3, 27.

MODERNISM FOR THE MASSES

The Armory Show in Comics

KATHERINE ROEDER

The 1913 Armory Show, which famously introduced audiences in the United States to European avant-garde art, has long been acknowledged as a transformative moment in American art history. Officially labelled the *International Exhibition of Modern Art*, the exhibition was on view for less than a month at New York City's 69th Regiment Armory on Lexington Avenue, but it had a pervasive impact on the public dialogue surrounding avant-garde art.[1] Even audiences who did not attend the show in person were able to experience the shock of some of the works on display, as newspaper comics magnified the reach of the exhibition. As a reporter describing attendees in Chicago noted, "The Cubist room attracts the largest crowds, no doubt largely on account of attention drawn to it by comic writers and cartoonists."[2] The wide range of responses to the 1913 Armory Show, from up-and-coming cartoonists to recognized names, was startling. Winsor McCay drew a comic in response to the show, titled "The Modern Art Show: Familiar Scenes as the Newest Artists Would See Them," and published it in the *New York Herald* in 1913. In six panels he shows New York street scenes, including a crowded Brooklyn Bridge and a trolley car on Chambers Street, as drawn by a modernist. His distortions here are intended to amuse his audience and possibly belittle current trends.

And yet the abstractions he employs are not far removed from his existing style, rendering his derision inert. European modernists deployed visual strategies that cartoonists had engaged with for years, and the subsequent attention the modernists drew at the Armory Show may have bemused or even frustrated commercial artists whose work engaged with similar ideas. McCay and many of his colleagues had embraced fractured forms and self-referentiality, developing a new, medium-specific visual shorthand to describe conditions of modern life. By combining innovative pictorial approaches with satire, the comics parodies of the art show enabled the viewing audience to encounter modernist art techniques in a direct, personal way and in the process acclimated the masses to the visual language of abstraction and undermined the false dichotomy between high and low art.

The large exhibition, which displayed over twelve hundred works by European and American artists, opened on February 17, 1913, and closed on March 15, 1913. It then travelled to the Art Institute of Chicago and Boston's Copley Society, where the tour concluded on May 19, 1913.[3] Approximately 87,000 people visited the show in New York, a figure more than doubled by the Chicago audience, which numbered 188,650. An additional 14,400 visitors attended the Boston exhibition.[4] Although credited with acquainting Americans with the art of such artists as Picasso, Picabia, and Duchamp, it is worth noting that works by these artists filled only a single gallery in the back corner of the large hall. The vast majority of the exhibition featured more conventionally representational paintings and sculpture. Even so, the show is largely remembered for the extensive debates around modern art that it inspired in the mass media. It can be difficult to disambiguate the hyperbolic discourse that surrounded the exhibition from the content of the show itself. The mythmaking around the Armory Show was firmly in place as early as 1922, when Carl Van Vechten wrote in his novel *Peter Whiffle: His Life and Works* that "it was possibly the last exhibition of paintings held in New York which everybody attended. Everybody talked about it. Street-car conductors asked for your opinion of the *Nude Descending the Staircase*, as they asked you for your nickel.... It was cartooned, it was caricatured, it was Dr. Frank Craned."[5]

Comics artists and cartoonists were quick to respond to and satirize the art on display, especially the cubist paintings and sculptures. Dozens of comics and caricatures were made in direct response to the exhibition in 1913, and these comics are often used to this day as a means of illustrating how shocked Americans were by the contents of the show. Rarely are the comics panels themselves examined as aesthetic works in their own right: sophisticated in terms of their visual strategies, engaged with a rapidly changing world, and worthy of attention and analysis. Indeed, comics were often as experimental and formally radical as the high art they were theoretically lampooning.

Before turning our attention to the comics art, it should be acknowledged that the high-low divide between the modernist art on display and the comics they inspired has always been an inherently false dichotomy. A cartoonist was, in crucial respects, instrumental to the creation of the exhibition itself. Walt Kuhn, along with painter Arthur B. Davies, organized the exhibition and selected the objects on display. Kuhn was also largely responsible for the show's publicity. The delineation between cartoonists and fine artists was quite permeable at this historical moment, and Kuhn drew comics and commercial illustrations in addition to painting. His cartoons appeared regularly in the pages of *Life*, *Judge*, and *Puck*. In 1912 he had a weekly comic panel that ran in the *Brooklyn Daily Eagle* called *Funny Birds*, which was taken over by another cartoonist once Kuhn became too busy planning the exhibition.[6] Kuhn's familiarity with the newspaper industry was undoubtedly put to use when he corresponded with national newspapers to promote the exhibition. Kuhn's knowledge of mass media and promotional tactics were critical to the exhibition's popularity. He was also secretary of the Association of American Painters and Sculptors (AAPS), the arts organization that put on the exhibition. AAPS was formed as a progressive alternative to the National Academy of Design, which was known for their narrow and conservative aesthetic approach.

Kuhn included his own work in the show, alongside artworks by friends of his who were also cartoonists, including Rudolph Dirks and Gus Mager. Mager was best known for his strip *Sherlocko the Monk*, and he also worked with Dirks on *Captain and the Kids*. Though many of the American contributions to the Armory Show were conservative compared to their European counterparts, Mager's paintings in the years following the exhibition showed a continental influence, and his work was acquired by the Whitney Museum and the Newark Museum of Art.[7] Rudolph Dirks submitted two landscapes demonstrating a postimpressionist influence. Yet in their exploration of movement and advancement of visual metaphors, Dirks's groundbreaking comics pushed boundaries further than his paintings ever did, even though his comics were not included in the exhibition.[8]

Dirks's canvasses did not distinguish him among the crowded field of painters, but his groundbreaking comics art forged new means of expression. As the cartoonist and comics historian Brian Walker has written, "Dirks pioneered the use of many comic devices that eventually became part of the art form's visual language. Parallel lines and dust clouds to indicate speed, dotted lines to represent eye contact, and sweat beads to suggest fear or nervousness appeared regularly."[9] While Dirks's landscapes were largely derivative, his innovative comic-strip work attracted the attention of admirers near and far. Gertrude Stein was known to save the Sunday comic supplements of American newspapers for Picasso to peruse and recounted handing Picasso a bundle of comics that included Dirks's *Katzenjammer Kids* in her 1933 book, *The Autobiography of Alice B. Toklas*.[10]

Beyond Kuhn and his friends, other exhibition participants were connected to the newspaper comics world as well, including several from the circle of Robert Henri. Henri was an influential art instructor and leader of the group of artists known as The Eight, who coalesced around their rejection of the academic traditionalism of the National Academy of Design. Associated with a form of urban realism that came to be known as the Ashcan School, several of

Henri's followers also worked as newspaper illustrators or cartoonists, including George Luks, William Glackens and John Sloan. Among the Armory Show exhibitors was Marjorie Organ, who was Henri's wife. Organ was the only female cartoonist on staff at William Randolph Hearst's *New York Journal*; her most famous strip, *Little Reggie and the Heavenly Twins*, was published from 1902 to 1905. Organ knew Rudolph Dirks from working at the *Journal*, and it was Dirks who introduced her to Henri, her future husband. Six of her drawings were displayed at the Armory Show. Denys Wortman was a student of Henri's who also participated in the show. His best-known comic, *Metropolitan Movies*, featured naturalistic city scenes with a strong Ashcan influence. Other cartoonists including George Luks, Herbert Crowley and T. E. Powers all contributed artworks to the show as well. Powers submitted two landscape paintings and also satirized the show in a cartoon that appeared two days after the exhibition opened.[11]

Alek Sass was among the very first cartoonists to respond to the Armory Show, publishing his comic in the *New York World* on the day the show officially opened to the public. Sardonically titled *Nobody Who Has Been Drinking Is Let in to See This Show* (figure 2.1), the comic depicts allusions to specific artworks on display in gallery I and the comically outraged responses of a visiting critic, who is ultimately taken away in an ambulance. Gallery I was where the cubist works were located, the so-called "chamber of horrors." With over twelve hundred works on display overall, the cubist gallery accounted for only a small percentage of the works on view even though the sensational press coverage focused on them nearly exclusively. Sass depicts a stylized drawing of Georges Braque's *Violin: "Mozart Kubelick,"* from 1912, an analytic cubist painting that fractures form and movement while making reference to a live performance by the Czech violinist Jan Kubelik. The version by Sass is captioned "this post-impression portrait of Kubelik playing Mozartian rag-time impressed us most." The sculpture in Sass's comic refers to Alexander Archipenko's sculpture *La Vie Familiale*. Francis Picabia's *The Procession, Seville* (now in the National Gallery of Art's collection) is also presented, with an outraged figure representing the artist standing in front of it. His contorted posture, the corkscrew motion line on the floor indicating his sudden movement, his hat levitating above his head, and his wild hair extending in all directions are further abstractions signifying his surprise. The caption reveals the source of his alarm: his masterpiece has been hung upside down. A sequence of six successive panels shows an art critic becoming increasingly agitated by the exhibition, until he is finally carted off to Bellevue by ambulance in the final panel.

Satires of modern art were not new. Nineteenth-century French avant-garde exhibitions similarly inspired comic responses, as in when Jules Renard, using the pseudonym Draner, drew caricatures for *Le Charivari* in which a pregnant

Figure 2.1. Alek Sass, *Nobody Who Has Been Drinking Is Let in to See This Show*, New York World, February 17, 1913.

woman is advised to avoid encountering impressionist art.[12] The trope of providing a warning to viewers is similar to the cautionary notice in the Sass title, which bans those who have been drinking from visiting the show. This type of hyperbole was later embraced by the Brooklyn Art Museum in 1999, when they advertised the notorious *Sensation* exhibition with a mockup of a surgeon general warning that "the contents of this exhibition may cause shock, vomiting, confusion, panic, euphoria and anxiety."

As Michele Bogart has observed, the division between commercial art and fine art was porous during the early twentieth century, when newspapers relied heavily upon illustration and art departments were staffed with struggling artists.[13] This double identity is embodied in Ashcan artist John Sloan, who displayed works in the show but still found time to mock cubism in a comic he sketched for socialist magazine *The Masses* (figure 2.2). Accompanied by rhyming couplets, his drawing featured a man composed entirely out of cubes, living in a cubic house, with cubic cat and mouse. Sloan's short-hand formulation of cubism—art composed of literal cubes—made for a visual gag that was easily grasped by the public but bore little relationship to the analytic cubist

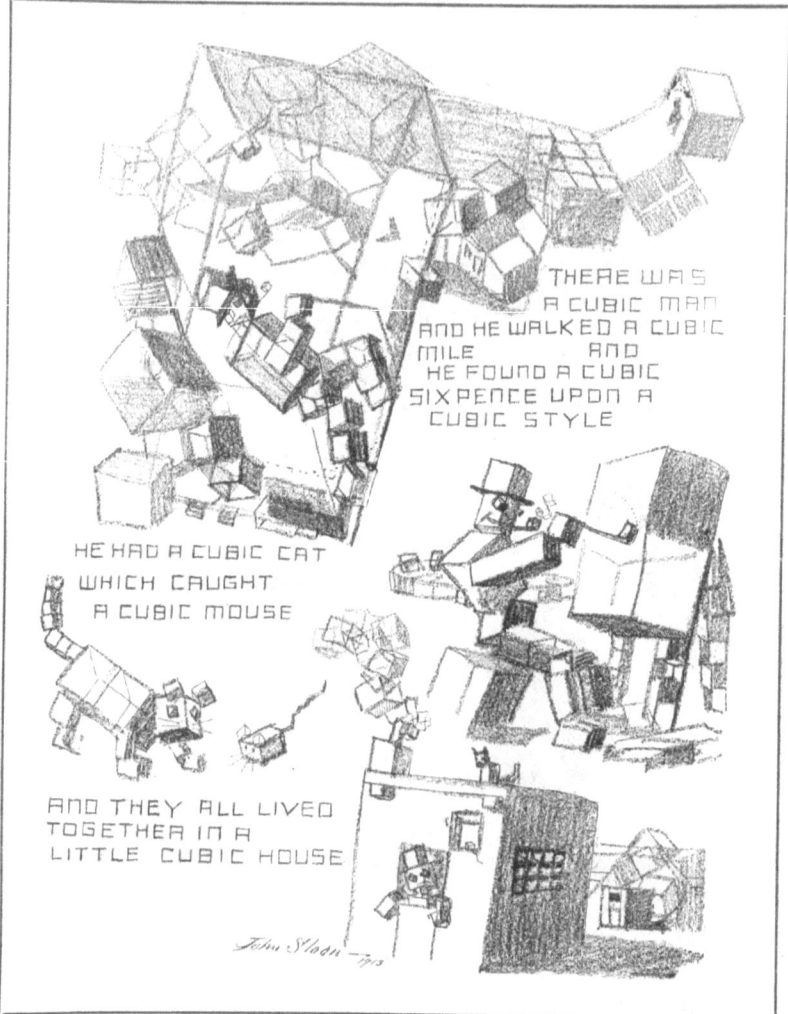

Figure 2.2. John Sloan, *A Slight Attack of Third Dimentia Brought On by Excessive Study of the Much-talked of Cubist Pictures in the International Exhibition at New York*, The Masses, April 1913.

paintings by Braque and Picasso that were on display. Even so, Sloan manages to economically communicate the idea of cubism as a reduction and fracturing of form. Sloan's cartoon, which begins with a singular square at the upper right corner of the page, depicts cubes in dynamic motion spreading down the page and multiplying as they transform into figures and structures, challenging the viewer to look at the geometry of the surrounding objects.

By all accounts, Walt Kuhn drove the initial press coverage of the exhibition. As one of his contemporaries recalled,

Walt wanted to make sure that this thing was an intensely popular sort of show and his instructions to us when we were distributing posters was to put them in every gin mill on Second, Third, and Ninth Avenues and to cover not only the part of the town that would normally be interested but to get into the parts of town that would not ordinarily think in terms of art exhibitions.[14]

Kuhn was interested in appealing to a broader audience, and this campaign extended beyond New York. He sent posters to museums, libraries, and colleges and wrote directly to newspaper and magazine editors around the country. In a letter to Edwin Goewey, an editor at the *Kansas City Post* and himself a former cartoonist, Kuhn pitched his exhibition as a feature: "I could furnish you a fine selection of photos, and in fact a story if you require it, which would make a very attractive Sunday page. We are doing this according to American methods and have already spent a good deal of money on advertising."[15] The "American methods" of promotion that Kuhn references considered any publicity to be beneficial. Whether Kuhn expected the negative press or not, he quickly adapted to using it to his advantage. This was evidenced by his clever move, while working in cooperation with Frederick James Gregg, the Chicago exhibition's public relations director, to publish a pamphlet titled *For and Against: Views on the International Exhibition Held in New York and Chicago*, which compiled positive and negative reviews from various newspapers and magazines.[16] Five thousand copies of the pamphlet were printed and sold at the door in Chicago.

Louis Glackens's parody of the exhibition, which appeared just prior to the Chicago opening on *Puck* magazine's cover published March 19, 1913 (figure 2.3), exemplified how interrelated the worlds of art and cartooning were at that moment. Louis Glackens was the older brother of William Glackens, an artist steeped in both worlds: he was a newspaper illustrator and member of The Eight, alongside Robert Henri; in 1912 he went to Paris and purchased works by Picasso, Van Gogh, and Cézanne on behalf of the collector (and William's high-school friend) Albert Barnes and became an important advisor to the collection which would become the Barnes Foundation; he was a founding member of AAPS; he was involved in selecting works for the Armory Show; and, finally, he was himself a participant. Louis Glackens would therefore be well acquainted with developments in contemporary art from his brother and their shared social circles. The *Puck* cover image shows a chicken with newly laid, multifaceted colored eggs in the foreground, as other farm animals look on in confusion. Below the image a caption reads, "The Latest in Easter Eggs: The Cubist Influence Reaches the Barnyard." The idea that sophisticated European art movements had become so widespread that they were turning up on

THE LATEST IN EASTER EGGS.
The Cubist Influence Reaches the Barnyard.

Figure 2.3. Louis Glackens, cover for *Puck*, March 19, 1913.

rural farms was a reference to both the exhibition traveling to the heartland and becoming the topic of national debate. The issue was published during Easter week, which also happened to be the week in which the contents of the Armory exhibition arrived in Chicago for their Midwest debut. The fact that this parody made the cover of *Puck*, a national magazine typically focused on current events and politics, was indicative of how widespread the conversation about modern art had become.[17]

Cubism was not merely fodder for cartoonists; it inspired everything from children's books to fashion lines. In Philadelphia, Wanamaker's department store launched a campaign, promoting "for the first time in America, Color Combinations of the Futurists" and the "Cubist Influence in Fashions in the new Paris models for spring."[18] The advertisement, which appeared in the March 13 edition of the *New York Evening Sun*, even bore the exhibition's pine tree logo. This instance of the commodification of cubism as fashion is further parodied in a cartoon from April 8, 1913, credited to F. Fox that appeared in that same newspaper, as if responding directly to the consequences of the marketing push. F. Fox, the penname of Fontaine Talbot Fox Jr., drew the popular, long-running comic *Toonerville Folks*. His "Cubisto Picture Composed by Dad, Under the Inspiration of the Incoming Bills for the Ladies' Spring Purchases" shows a father as artist, having painted a cubist portrait of his daughter composed entirely of overlapping rectangles formed by payment envelopes and bills for clothing and hats. When Picasso began making cubist collages in 1912 (none of which appeared in the Armory Show), he mined the detritus of modern life to produce works incorporating newspaper clippings, sheet music, and scraps of labels. In works like *Still-Life with Chair Caning* (1912, Musée Picasso Paris), such components added a typographic element as well as an additional layer of social commentary. So too does Fox's usage, where he marries geometric abstraction with pointed references to commodity culture and the appropriation of cubism by the fashion industry.

Comics that mocked cubism and modern art were nevertheless introducing the ideas to mass audiences in a palatable way. They also demonstrated the ways in which avant-garde art tactics were uniquely suited to critiquing modern life. In the intervening years, scholars have tended to use cartoonist responses to the Armory Show to illustrate the small-minded response of the wider American public to European art. In Milton Brown's landmark history of the Armory Show, he indicated that the comics satires of the exhibition were an example of "lampooning things we simply do not understand."[19] This conventional wisdom has been problematized by recent scholarship. Michael Leja has suggested that the relationship between the public and modern art was more complicated than it might appear, and Sarah Burns, in looking at the visual culture surrounding the exhibition, determined that the comics were "instrumental in the creation of an oppositional culture of homegrown connoisseurship that circumvented critical authority and endorsed autonomous judgement." In this regard they "invited audiences to enjoy avant-garde art on their own terms."[20]

The cartoon parodies invited readers to participate in a larger conversation about modern art, while also drawing attention to commonalities between the avant-garde strategies and the techniques pioneered by comic-strip artists. Depictions of speed and bodies in motion were a preoccupation of futurist artists and figured prominently in Marcel Duchamp's *Nude Descending a Staircase (No. 2)* (see figure 9.4), which depicts a blurred figure, simplified and reduced to geometric planes, walking down a staircase. However, David Kunzle dates the use of motion lines in comics to the nineteenth century, noting examples from Rodolphe Töpffer and Wilhelm Busch.[21] Arthur Burdett Frost drew upon the stop motion photography of Eadweard Muybridge decades before Duchamp channeled Étienne-Jules Marey's chronophotography in *Nude Descending a Staircase*. Winsor McCay used motion lines as well, in *Dream of the Rarebit Fiend* comics exploring the disorienting features of modern life (see Noa Saunders's chapter in this volume). The comics spoofs gave cartoonists entry to the conversation about modern art as well as a platform to display how their own work anticipated the formal innovations that were being solely attributed to the European artists.

Indeed, Duchamp's *Nude Descending a Staircase* was the most frequent target of criticism. The *American Art News* invited the public to locate the nude in the painting, with a $10 reward as a prize for the winning entry.[22] The *New York Evening Sun* offered readers, whom they referred to as "our Cubist Editors," a chance to send in their own versions of the controversial work. Critics and cartoonists flooded the newspapers with parodies such as *Huntsman Descending a Staircase with his Dog*, and *Aviator Descending from an Airplane*.[23] While such efforts may have been intended to foment derision, they nevertheless directed the wider viewing public to grapple with modern art head-on, in a focused and engaged way. Among the published Duchamp-inspired cartoons, J. F. Griswold's *Rude Descending a Staircase (Rush Hour at the Subway)* (figure 2.4) was among the most widely cited. Griswold's cartoon was part of a series called "Seeing New York With a Cubist," which was published by the *New York Evening Sun*.[24] Little is known about Griswold outside of this series of cartoons; graphic designer Alex Jay has used census records and passport applications to propose that J. F. Griswold was likely a commercial artist living in New York at the time named Julia Frances Griswold.[25]

While Duchamp refracted the form of a single figure as it moved down a staircase, Griswold's cartoon engages with the direct experience of the cantankerous crowds one encounters in a crowded subway. With brilliant economy, Griswold conveys the stance of long-suffering commuters lurching down the stairs, intermingled with agitated figures with raised fists and elbows, and angry, yelling faces. The repetition of dark hatched lines replicates the suggestion of motion produced by Duchamp's painting. At least one figure, at lower right, appears to have fallen to the ground and is being trampled. A foot can be seen upon his forehead. The comic's success in translating the scandalous artwork into a canny critique of modern commuting further inspired imitators. In October 1913, caricaturist Oscar Cesare depicted the impeachment of New

Figure 2.4. J. F. Griswold, *The Rude Descending a Staircase (Rush Hour at the Subway)*, *New York Evening Sun*, March 20, 1913.

York Governor William Sulzer by members of the Tammany Hall political machine with an abstracted composition he titled *The Rude Descending on Sulzer*.[26] Compositionally, Cesare departs from both the Duchamp original and the Griswold parody, both of which are oriented around the diagonal of the staircase. While similarly reducing his figures to geometric forms, Cesare uses a circular design as the focal point to capture the spiraling chaos of the state assembly floor. He also incorporates text into the design. But his title seems to purposely reference both Duchamp's painting and Griswold's "rude" comic.

Professional cartoonists relished deriding cubist artists in particular.[27] Chicago-based cartoonist Clare Briggs, for example, drew a granny stitching a crazy quilt of jagged, contrasting geometric forms and titled it "The Original Cubist."[28] With her extended arm holding the thread taut, and a proud smile on her wizened face, she declares, "I tuk the fust prize at the fair last fall." The single panel cartoon makes the shrewd suggestion that a homegrown, vernacular form of cubism could be traced to the crazy quilt technique popularized by American women at the end of the nineteenth century. Crazy quilts featured patchworks of irregularly shaped fabric pieced together with embellished seams and stitching that serve to highlight its means of construction. In linking cubism to quilting, Briggs's cartoon also unintentionally reveals both the regional and gender bias that subordinated the aesthetic production of rural women.[29]

Burns understands this panel as a form of domesticating and taming modernism by folding it into existing traditional artforms,[30] but it also points to the ways in which popular art forms were pioneering the use of radical aesthetic strategies before they were codified by fine artists as high modernism.

Briggs left for New York in 1914, but his former colleagues at the *Chicago Tribune* carried the analogy further in the short-lived but radically experimental jam comic *Crazy Quilt*. Running from April to June 1914, the comic was a weekly collaborative effort led by Frank King, with contributions from Charles Lederer, Quin Hall, Everett Lowry, Dean Cornwell and Lester J. Ambrose. Just like many actual "crazy quilts" being stitched by rural women across the country, the *Tribune*'s jam comic featured contributions from different cartoonists assembled on a page in a riot of different styles and angles, colliding with one another in what Chris Ware refers to as "comic-strip-as-collage."[31] While the term collage makes sense in this context, the word was coined by Braque and Picasso from the French word "to glue." It seems significant that the *Tribune* artists looked to a popular American art form rather than the European modern tradition to name their experimental comics. Like comics, quilting was considered a low art tradition that only belatedly received critical attention from the academy.[32]

While the comics responding to the Armory Show often express a surface disdain for modernism, their form actually reveals a close affinity with modern art. The disjunction between language and pictorial expression compels the viewer to wrestle with the competing visual and verbal rhetoric on the page. To some extent, the comics artists must have recognized an affinity between abstraction and their own approach to form. Parodying modern art was a way to place comics and modernism in conversation, allowing audiences to see these similarities for themselves. In the process such comics acclimate their readers, with a blend of humor and fractured form, to modernist experimentation in a less alienating venue than the rarefied atmosphere of the art gallery or museum. Comics are distinct from other art forms in the manner in which they build their audiences over time; they instruct their audience in how to read and understand their distinctive visual language. Reading comics is a bodily experience; one is directly engaged with the newspaper page, holding it in one's hands, moving it closer or farther away.[33] The haptic, personal nature of print comics fostered a more direct relationship with the viewer, which in turn propagated the spread of modernist ideas and abstraction into American homes in the early decades of the twentieth century.

To be clear, criticism of the event was not limited to cartoonists.[34] Established art critics like Royal Cortissoz, art editor of the *New-York Tribune*, accused the participating artists of being "foolish terrorists" and claimed that they wanted to "turn the world upside down."[35] The existential threat posed by the modern artists was also decried in a *New York Times* editorial that referred to modern art as a "general movement, discernible all over the world, to disrupt and degrade if not to destroy, not only art, but literature and society, too."[36] Notably, such accusations were being levelled at cartoonists of this period as well. A 1909 editorial published in *The Outlook* (and republished in national newspapers everywhere from Texas and Oklahoma to the *Brooklyn Daily Eagle*) made similar claims of the comic supplement, asserting: "We are teaching them lawlessness: we are cultivating the lack of reverence in them; we are doing everything we can, by cheapening life, to destroy the American homes of the future."[37] Dozens of articles appeared between 1907 and 1915 making similar claims about the detrimental impact of comics on society. Both comics and modern art stood accused of degrading and disrupting American culture.

One cannot help but wonder if poking fun at modern art became broadly popular because it gave cartoonists a license to experiment. In 1913, Mary Mills Lyall published *The Cubies' ABC*, an alphabet book written in rhyming verse and illustrated in comics style by her architect husband, Earl Harvey Lyall. Three green-haired pyramidal figures are our guides to the topsy-turvy world of modernist art. They are the titular "Cubies," as the text explains: "A" begins, "A is for Art in the Cubies' domain / (Not the Art of the Ancients, brand-new are the Cubies) / Archipenko's their guide, Anatomics their bane; / They're the joy of the mad, the despair of the sane." It remains unclear who the intended audience was—alphabet books are typically read to young children, yet the vocabulary and references would surely be lost on newly emerging readers. Francis Naumann, a dealer and scholar of the American Dada movement, declared that he saw the book as "an attack on Modern Art."[38] While the book is clearly a satire, it is "Dedicated by the Cubies to the Association of American Painters and Sculptors, to which they owe their incubation." *The Cubies*'s illustration for the letter *K*, "K's for Kandinsky's Kute 'improvisations,'" shows the three imps attempting to re-assemble the puzzle pieces of a painted composition, nodding toward the ways in which abstraction breaks down and reconstitutes formal elements. Cubist comics and satires allowed commercial artists to play with form and push boundaries under the guise of mockery. These mockeries brought modernist ideas and sensibilities directly into people's homes, whether through fashion, food, or art, thereby casually introducing them to abstraction with a wink and a nod.

Frank King, with a four-panel comic called "After the Cubist Food Exhibit," added himself to the chorus of cartoonists mocking cubism. The comic was referencing a cubist food display organized by a Catholic women's club for a domestic science fair.[39] Here King is mocking the broad appropriation of cubism by the larger culture, in a sequence of panels depicting a man becoming overcome with "cubic indigestion" after consuming a meal of cubed food.

The man consults a square-headed doctor in a checked suit, who prescribes him a "cubic treatment." King produced this comic early in his career, while working at the *Chicago Tribune*, where he worked alongside Clare Briggs and other prominent, established cartoonists. Jeet Heer suggests that it was King's exposure to the Armory Show that served as catalyst for his mature style, inspiring him to become the "master of domestic modernism."[40]

Frank King would go on to engage periodically with modern art within the Sunday color spreads of his epic narrative *Gasoline Alley*. On one occasion, he used the conceit of Skeezix trying out a new compass to create interlocking, overlapping, and concentric circles that resembled the colorful modern art abstractions of Robert Delaunay and Stanton McDonald-Wright.[41] In a Sunday comic published in 1930, Uncle Walt and Skeezix visit the Art Institute of Chicago, the very museum that the Armory Show travelled to and that introduced midwesterners to European art (see figure 1 in this volume). The title panel shows them in a gallery, examining a painting. Uncle Walt declares, "Modernism is a bit beyond me. I'd hate to live in the place that picture was painted," before he and Skeezix physically walk through a series of abstract landscapes inspired by Kandinsky, Kirchner, and Picasso. Once again, the antimodernist rhetoric on the page is belied by King's faithfulness depicting a variety of artistic styles, from German expressionism and fauvism to cubism. The final panel is a return to normalcy, a common comic framing device, with Skeezix declaring, "That was an awful dream Uncle Walt! Or was it a dream?" as the pair walks toward a traditional landscape while trailing paint behind them. Each of the nine individual panels is its own abstract composition, yet they work together as a full-page spread through the repetition of diagonal and curving lines and a unified color palette. Seventeen years after the Armory Show, abstraction still has the power to shock. Yet in spite of Uncle Walt and Skeezix's protests to the contrary, the comic page itself makes a direct appeal for modern art to the viewer. This is evidence of a push-pull operational aesthetic taking place within comics, an aesthetic that verbally articulates the reader's apprehensions about modern art while visually acclimating them to its formal language of abstraction.

Reconsidering the relationship between comics and the Armory Show allows us to re-frame the dynamic between commercial and modernist artists at the beginning of the twentieth century. The divide between high and low art was elastic, with cartoonists involved in both producing and commenting upon the Armory Show. To understand comics as offering merely an oppositional, populist response to the avant-garde is reductive. Instead, we should understand comics as a form of engagement and mediation that extended the aesthetic discussion beyond the walls of the gallery and directly into the hands of the larger public, while also drawing attention to the groundbreaking and experimental work of the cartoonists themselves.

Notes

1. Marilyn Satin Kushner, Kimberly Orcutt, and Casey Nelson Blake, eds., *The Armory Show at 100: Modernism and Revolution* (London: Giles, 2013), 13.

2. "Art in Chicago," *Outlook*, April 12, 1913, 790.

3. Kushner, Orcutt, and Blake, 15.

4. Kushner, Orcutt, and Blake, 16.

5. Carl Van Vechten, *Peter Whiffle: His Life and Works* (New York: Alfred A. Knopf, 1922), 123. Dr. Frank Crane was a minister and widely read national columnist known for his "four-minute essays."

6. Ralph D. Suiter III, "'Vulgarizing American Children': Navigating Respectability and Commercial Appeal in Early Newspaper Comics" (PhD diss., George Mason University, 2016), 166.

7. Suiter, 168.

8. Despite Kuhn's background, no thought was given to displaying comics art or illustration at the Armory. It would not be until the thirties that museums and galleries began exhibiting original comics art. For more, see Kim Munson, *Comic Art in Museums* (Jackson: University Press of Mississippi, 2020), 66–67.

9. Brian Walker, *The Comics Before 1945* (New York: Harry N. Abrams, 2004), 36.

10. Gertrude Stein, *The Autobiography of Alice B. Toklas* (New York: Vintage Books, 1990), 23. In 2020, the Musée Picasso Paris delved into this topic further with its exhibition *Picasso and the Comics* (July 21, 2020–January 3, 2021).

11. Thomas E. Powers, "Art at the Armory by Powers, Futurist," *New York American*, February 22, 1913.

12. Sarah Burns, "Cubist Comedy and Futurist Follies: The Visual Culture of the Armory Show," in Kushner, Orcutt, and Blake, *The Armory Show at 100*, 348.

13. Michele Bogart, *Artists, Advertising and the Borders of Art* (Chicago: University of Chicago Press, 1995), 16.

14. "Reminiscences of Wood Gaylor," Wood Gaylor and Adelaide Lawson papers, Archives of American Art, Smithsonian Institution.

15. Walt Kuhn to Edwin Goewey, January 31, 1913, Walt Kuhn family Papers and Armory Show records, 1859–1978, Archives of American Art, Smithsonian Institution.

16. Kenyon Cox, ed., *Documents of the 1913 Armory Show: The Electrifying Moment of Modern Art's American Debut* (Tucson: Hol Art Books, 2009), 167.

17. Heather Campbell Coyle, "The Latest in Easter Eggs," *Essays on Illustration* (blog), Rockwell Center for American Visual Studies, March 21, 2013, https://rockwellcenter.org/essays-illustration/the-latest-in-easter-eggs/.

18. Advertisement, *New York Evening Sun*, March 13, 1913, repr. in Kushner, Orcutt, and Blake, *The Armory Show at 100*, fig. 60.

19. Milton Brown, *The Story of the Armory Show*, 2nd ed. (New York: Abbeville, 1988), 17, 140.

20. Burns, "Cubist Comedy," 349, 346.

21. David Kunzle, *The History of the Comic Strip*, vol. 2, *The Nineteenth Century* (Berkeley: University of California Press, 1990), 348.

22. Francis Naumann, *New York Dada, 1915–23* (New York: Harry N. Abrams, 1994), 17.

23. Burns, "Cubist Comedy," 350.

24. J. F. Griswold, *The Rude Descending a Staircase (Rush Hour at the Subway)*, New York *Evening Sun*, March 20, 1913.

25. Alex Jay, "Creator: J. F. Griswold 'The Rude...' Artist," *Tenth Letter of the Alphabet* (blog), February 20, 2017, http://alphabettenthletter.blogspot.com/2017/02/creator-j-f-griswold-rude-artist.html.

26. Oscar Cesare, *The Rude Descending on Sulzer*, 1913, Library of Congress, Prints and Photographs Division, https://www.loc.gov/item/2016685391/.

27. They also particularly enjoyed deriding futurist artists, although the exhibition did not in fact include any work by Italian futurists.

28. Clare Briggs, "The Original Cubist," *New York Evening Sun*, April 1, 1913.

29. The ongoing institutional recognition of the groundbreaking artistry of the Gee's Bend quiltmakers, beginning with a series of museum exhibitions in 2002, represents a much belated attempt to rectify this omission.

30. Burns, "Cubist Comedy," 355.

31. Chris Ware, "A Young Man's Game," in *"Crazy Quilt": Scraps and Panels on the Way to "Gasoline Alley*," ed. Peter Maresca (Palo Alto, CA: Sunday Press, 2017), 5.

32. Jonathan Najarian describes the way *Crazy Quilt* orients its readers to navigating an increasingly complex print culture, where advertisements filled a growing percentage of the visual field, thereby helping them accommodate to shifting demands on their attention. See his essay "*Crazy Quilt*, Advertising, and the *Chicago Tribune*," *American Periodicals* 32, no. 2 (Fall 2022): 109–15.

33. For more on the haptics of reading comics, see especially Scott McCloud, *Understanding Comics: The Invisible Art* (1993; repr., New York: Harper Perennial, 1994), 206.

34. As Leonard Diepeveen discusses in *Mock Modernism: An Anthology of Parodies, Travesties, Frauds, 1910–1935* (Toronto, ON: University of Toronto Press, 2014), even other modernists were mocking the modernists; James Joyce apparently wrote a satiric poem in the style of Eliot's "Waste Land."

35. Cortissoz, quoted in Brown, *Story of the Armory Show*, 131.

36. *New York Times*, March 16, 1913, sec. 4, p.6.

37. "The 'Comic' Nuisance," *Outlook*, March 6, 1909, 527.

38. See Alec Wilkinson, "Cubies," *New Yorker*, February 24, 2013.

39. "Club Women to Display 'Cubist' Food this Week," *Chicago Daily Tribune*, April 22, 1913, cited by Burns, "Cubist Comedy," 357.

40. Jeet Heer, "Crazy Quilts, Krazy Kats and King's Cartoons," in Maresca, *"Crazy Quilt*," 6.

41. Frank King, *Gasoline Alley*, *Boston Herald*, May 10, 1931. Delaunay and McDonald-Wright pioneered synchromism, an early abstract, color-based mode of painting, which was the first American avant-garde art movement to receive international attention.

THE DREAMER'S MODERN BODY

Winsor McCay and the Everyday Sensorium

NOA SAUNDERS

In one of Winsor McCay's famous *Dream of the Rarebit Fiend* strips—the one that inspired Thomas Edison and Edwin Porter's 1906 film—the dreamer, tumbling through the night sky, gets caught by a weathervane that jars her awake, and her discombobulated body appears twice in the same position. To guide the eye from the nightmare's pandemonium to the comforts of the average American home, McCay retains the image of the dreamer by drawing her in the same pose: upside down, caught by the seat of her nightgown, arms outstretched below her. As this dreamer falls, she embodies anxiety in a form that, as Sianne Ngai would suggest, is spatial as much as it is temporal. Extending Heidegger's thrownness into Being to illustrate the projective and "expectant" qualities of feeling anxious, Ngai identifies other spatial metaphors for the loss of agency as well as for the episteme of expectation in the forms of "fleeing," "turning," or "seeking."[1] McCay might also offer us "launching," as our dreamer is cast into the darkness across the comic page, the graphic spread elaborating the unease until, finally, McCay turns on the lights, and she is shocked to discover she's still at home. The spatial and temporal instabilities of anxiety are well-suited in the comics' panels, where time, as Hillary Chute puts it, is "dispersed rather than propulsive," and motion is only represented by stopping it.[2] Because the comic page complicates linear progression, it seems paradoxical to say anything happens "suddenly," but when McCay duplicates the dreamer's body as a transition through profound change, he captures an affective experience of immediacy, a mixture of surprise and epiphany. With this technique of iterating images, McCay displays a sense of modern contingency to sudden change in the everyday life of the American public. With every comic, our dreamer wakes to conclude that a rarebit, perhaps a late-night grilled cheese, caused the nightmare, and the return to normalcy buries any anxieties the nightmare may have exposed.

This technique of doubling bodies across comic panels demonstrates what I call the iterative image, a visual trope that occurs throughout the modern media ecology. Most clearly visible in mechanically reproduced media like photography and film, the trope produces and reproduces nearly exact images across consecutive frames. The apparatus of the camera's shutter makes this duplication inevitable; without stilling the frames and observing the celluloid reel as an object, we would not see the prevalence of these repetitions that fly through the projector. When we watch a movie, the persistence of vision seals these nearly exact images together in a fluid cohesive action. As an innovator of animation, McCay pays close attention to the motion pictures and borrows techniques that are otherwise mechanically reproduced. As much as the work of iteration is the work of the camera, it is also the work of the cartoonist, whose labor is delicately repetitive on a daily basis.

Rather than implying that McCay is merely bringing the machine back to the hand, I suggest that his use of this ostensibly filmic technique illustrates how the iterative image resists a narrative of medial progression and instead represents a set of nonlinear aesthetic and cultural exchanges. Prominent scholars like Katherine Roeder, Scott Bukatman, and Tom Gunning have each emphasized that comics has the capacity for multiple media forms to make meaningful a phenomenological and epistemological investment in the temporalized body that pervades both science and art.[3] Like these scholars, I consider the exploration of motion in time as an ongoing cultural legacy that manifests in conscious and unconscious ways. The iterative image as a particular visual trope both reveals the material conditions of aesthetic production and, moreover, uncovers the increasingly complex intersection between media exposure and everyday life in the early twentieth century.

Rarebit Fiend is situated by everyday occasions, like sleeping in bed, riding a commuter bus, or walking through busy streets, and McCay uses the comic as a receptacle for commonplace anxieties. Because iterative images can expose strident graphic contrast, they become useful for approximating simultaneous experience, sudden change, and surprise in a form that severely regiments temporal and spatial progression. When expressed visually, this temporal paradox betrays the potential for commonplace anxieties like income, professional life, marriage, health, and commodity to deepen into more profound cultural trepidations that manifest in or manipulate the composure of daily life. Time in comics distributes singular moments across the page, and McCay's waking dreamer is stuck between them so that the iterative image in fact performs anxiety itself.

McCay presents everyday life through the everyday sensorium: the day-to-day emotions and sensations that are exhibited and exploited in popular news sources, vaudeville performances, entertainments, movies, toys, and advertisements. These sensations—anxiety, boredom, and melancholy as well as pleasure, delight, and surprise—rarely ask to be interrogated because of their ubiquity. Without questioning these sensations per se, McCay uses the iterative image to curate them, which, I suggest, heralds significant material ruptures in systems of class and power that structure the American way of life. What's at stake for the sensational success of the *Rarebit Fiend* is not so different from what's at stake for the Bolshevik revolution, the stock market crash, and the rise of fascism.

To iterate images necessitates a set of expressive and visual strategies that are cross-pollinating in the complex media ecology engendered by the everyday sensorium. Out of about 800 *Rarebit Fiend* strips, McCay uses the technique of iterating images only for about twenty.[4] But the technique is quite common in early cinematic analogues of dreamers suddenly waking—so common that it's peculiar that Edison and Porter do not use it in their adaptation. Charlie Chaplin (as well as other comedians and trick cinema directors) use it namely through the match cut. Because the iterative image can simulate the experience of sudden change, it exposes a latent anxiety under capitalism, but where Chaplin finds a radicalizing politics that connects one iterative body to another, McCay is prone to dismissing the unrest his dreamers face. Lost among the popular media transfusions are the politics of the middle class that figures like William Randolph Hearst—who employed McCay in 1911 and severely undercut his formal ambitions[5]—would be supervising.

As products of the newspaper, American comics inhere epistemological stakes in the medium's ability to mold public attitude. By examining lowbrow modernism in comics and film together, we gain insight into the dynamic negotiation of hegemonic complacency in twentieth-century politics, a struggle with what Miriam Hansen calls "reflexivity" over the traumas from modern structures of power, progress, and ideology.[6] Though *Rarebit Fiend* ornately illustrates the anxieties of modern life, the resolution of normalcy pacifies those anxieties with too much certainty for the strip to productively reflect on the anxieties it witnesses. With the strip's conventional return to normalcy that hinges on the iterated body, McCay produces a cultural-political ambivalence towards addressing uncertainties under capitalism.

STILLNESS, SIMULTANEITY, AND THE ITERATIVE IMAGE

McCay's characters, creatures, and fantasies showcase a clear curiosity about the gestures of the body as it moves through space, and Eadweard Muybridge's chronophotography provided a spectacular way of rendering the incremental movements of the body. McCay's comics borrow Muybridge's attention to the body as a form. The iterative image—images that repeat over consecutive panels—inherits a formalism caught between photography and comics, where a duplicated image not only estimates the change around it but becomes a conduit for affective responses to that change. Iteration illustrates its environmental changes, its affective evolutions, and more importantly the resilience of the body through myriad transmissions. Serializing the body's movements, in Muybridge, McCay, and other media, offers more than a visualization of progress over time; it also elucidates what Walter Benjamin calls "the optical unconscious," where the space between each movement of the body is loaded with cultural and political possibility that, before the invention of the camera, could not be recognized and made mobile.[7] The iterated image offers us the ability to name the political potential as our bodies are stilled, equated, reflexed, and simultaneously bombarded, isolated, and moved. For McCay, to borrow from Muybridge is not only for a comics artist to absorb the technology of another medium and use it to propel his own developing medium forward but to define a precise moment of epiphany in the context of modern uncertainties by seizing upon what images share.

While Louise Hornby observes in Muybridge the drive towards technological prowess, comics have an ontological freedom to revel in suspension, which permits McCay to explore the affective range in images precluded from photography.[8] By having a horse run through a set of multiple cameras that each go off as the horse trips wires in its path, Muybridge measures the changes the horse's body undergoes at each stage of its trajectory. Muybridge's work, which fractures individual moments into many, suspends each frame from its collection, so much so that a man walking appears to cover several yards in the series rather than just to take a single step. So too is McCay's dreamer suspended in their mediation, their modern body being wholly dreaming and wholly not. Serial photographs provide us a visual vocabulary for the body's continuity in space as regimented by modern technology, but this visual vocabulary derives from dramatizing a process too quick for the human eye. The iterative image becomes expressive through the visual series' rendering of the body, not as it progresses, but as it renegotiates space over and over again. When we consider the stillness of the series, we better observe its negativity, the space between each step, the gap between limbs, like the gutter between panels: what the body is rather than how the body changes.

The spatial juxtaposition of comics also discloses an affective stillness, what Hillary Chute has described as simultaneity. Chute describes a readerly experience of comics where a graphic series collapses into a synchronous instant; while the comic's images, presented beside one another, create a narrative that propels us from left to right, from up to down, the eye of the reader takes in the composite page all at once. Comics hang on this paradox of stillness and

Figure 3.1. Winsor McCay, *Dream of the Rarebit Fiend*, first published August 4, 1907. Reprinted in Ulrich Merkl, ed., *The Complete Dream of the Rarebit Fiend (1904–1913)*.

motion, garnering them not quite the illusion of movement but an imaginative leap outward from the image. In photography, as Hornby writes, a still photograph "points away from itself, drawing attention to what is about to happen and to the apparatus as a machine of and about motion by way of its finite suspension."[9] This dynamic is compounded in comics, where one panel gestures outward to the next and simultaneously looks backward to the preceding panel. The paradox of stillness and motion therefore begets an additional paradox, one of inward and outward affinities.

Like Muybridge's presentation of photographs side by side, where we rely on the graphic stability of the horse's body that appears paradoxically still as its limbs shift, one of McCay's strips from 1907 presents a series of incremental moments, what Chute terms "a material register of seriality" (figure 3.1).[10] But the iterative image in this comic also expresses a *literal* simultaneity of sleep and dreaming, allowing the reader to observe the dreamer's two realities happening at once. Snoring under the covers, our dreamer is lying motionless in bed as a mysterious shuffling of insects and creatures swarms his face, body, and pillow. Repeating the dreamer's form offers us a notable graphic stability, where the twenty panels each hold the same frame on the dreamer's face to sustain a wallpaper-like pattern across the page. McCay iterates the face to show the increasing number of invading pests, making the dreamer himself a stable fixture. In fact, part of the nightmare is that he *cannot* move, and the iteration of his face evokes a stillness that reflects that paralysis. The dreamer's duplicated body presents the affective responses of the changes around him, thereby undercutting the graphic stability its form implies.

The narrative linearity of the comic is also compromised as the dreamer's repetitive speech bubbles underscore the graphic sense of a singular experience rather than a progressive one. Because the sleeper cannot open his eyes to the dream world, he learns nothing new throughout the dream. While our experience of the dreamer is regimented by McCay's panels, the dreamer's own experience is stunted; the nineteen separate sleepers on the page are identical but also redundant. Though each panel stills the dreamer even as peculiar sensations creep all over him, he is simultaneously launched into the masses of fellow dreamers in the neighboring panels. If, for Hornby, the "apparatus as a machine" refers to the camera, we might ask, To what apparatus does McCay's hand-drawn serial direct us? I argue that these juxtaposed iterations direct us toward their coequal images because they have no semiotic referent but themselves. The singularity of this experience puts pressure on particular images as sources of affect and sensation.

The dreamer's bodily form becomes an index for subjective receptions of the world, even if they're ignorant and vulnerable. Though McCay uses photographic means to delineate the experience graphically, the nightmare-world of the *Rarebit Fiend* exhibits its chaos without the dreamer understanding it. Suggestively, the dreamer doesn't mention the creatures at all. Instead, his perspective is ironically removed from what we witness on the page, as he thinks to himself, "*What* is that pain on my head?" or "I *seem* to be smothered" (emphasis added). The dreamer knows he cannot breathe, but he does not know it is a worm that crawled up his nose. These expressions reveal the dreamer to be uninformed of what causes his suffering, and his distress results not from disgust (as it may for readers) but from uncertainty. While McCay spares his dreamer from trauma, an unknown phantom haunts his dreamer, yielding a horror that is sensed but not tangible. The dreamer's puzzlement over what ails him relays the terror of unknowing that anthropologist Kathleen Stewart uses as a common motif in *Ordinary Affects*: "Something is happening to me." Stewart's affects engage comparably peculiar feelings that come and go throughout everyday life and find no firmer realization: an indescribable "something"; an obscurity that unravels into ideology; a coincidence that leads often to serendipity, or, just as often, to accidents; "public feelings that begin and end in broad circulation, but [are] also the stuff that seemingly intimate lives are made of."[11] The dilation of affects across public and private spheres makes Stewart's picture of ordinary life defamiliarizing as much as it is familiar.

Figure 3.2. Winsor McCay, *Dream of the Rarebit Fiend*, first published 1909. Reprinted in Ulrich Merkl, ed., *The Complete Dream of the Rarebit Fiend (1904–1913)*.

McCay also draws out of his dreamers' lives recognizable anxieties—arachnophobia, claustrophobia—and at the same time reveals the way everyday life is often fraught with unpredictability. The medium of McCay's manual repetitions assumes a modern transmedial constitution; through it, our dreamer's uncertainty invokes a public sensorium that operates just as ephemerally as the anxieties that burden it. The strangeness of McCay's historic circumstance, particularly in proximity to Hearst's "yellow journalism"[12] and the oncoming cultural shifts for gender and class, indicates that, epistemologically, everyday life is not as stable as it seems. McCay expresses exactly "public feelings that begin and end in broad circulation"—his intuition about the American public's fears and fantasies being what brought him into the hands of Hearst. The familiar fear of bugs imparts some of the strip's ordinariness, but so too does manifesting that fear as losses of agency, orientation, and acknowledgment. McCay's "What," just like Stewart's "Something," foments an insecurity about the possibilities of the world, stirring, as a reader takes the bus home or rests in their chair after an exhausting day of work, an uneasiness about their subjugation to modernity—if only briefly. Comics' relationship to cinema (as well as other "vernacular" media) may affect how we anticipate personal, social, and cultural changes because comics indicate that we cannot actually anticipate such changes.

In a 1909 *Rarebit Fiend* strip featuring a commuter's accidental nap on public transit, McCay illustrates a common anxiety of social perceptions while formally juxtaposing public connectivity and alienation (figure 3.2). Throughout the comic, the woman's agoraphobia is gendered, as she frets over the impossibility of finding a dress that pleases everyone; when she wakes, she continues to indulge these anxieties, "wonder[ing] if anyone noticed" her napping.[13] While she seems embarrassed, thinking other commuters might have caught her midday snooze, she simultaneously hopes no one noticed her getting worked up over fashion expectations as she fails to resolve a gendered insecurity about her dress. She hangs her own opinion on the rest of the public: "No one seems to rave over it." There's a revealing tension between her reliance on public opinion and her reluctance to be perceived. When she wakes, she forgets the entourage of other checker-dressed ladies. The checkers enumerate a theory of self that her duplication agitates: as her number increases, we see each check more clearly, as if individualism becomes the dream's climactic horror. She, in fact, *doesn't* want to stand out, preferring to be part of the unremarkable crowd. Epiphany for our dreamer, her "immediate and instantaneous consciousness," appears as a feeling of self-ridicule or denial that McCay veils as reassurance in normalcy.[14] The comic therefore enacts the persuasion of the public, where the dreamer yields to an undisruptive milieu.

It is important that we read the iterative image in McCay's comic simultaneously and not progressively because of the material multiplication its process entails. For McCay, to observe our dreamers in the first panels and then in the following panels is not to ask what happens between them or how one frame precedes the other, but to ask what they mean to each other in the same moment. Due to the repetition of the dreamer, the dream displays separate but identical dreamers having the exact same nightmare. Through the repetition, McCay facilitates a simultaneity of multiplied dreamers on the page that the reader consumes at once. The spatial juxtaposition of the comics form offers us an opportunity to reconceive the component parts of narrative progression as materially bound; the materiality of the graphic page follows a linear progression only by convention. Interrogating that convention affords insights as to how visual media render their affective worlds.

Chute suggests that simultaneity is a form of modernist epistemology because of its "proliferation of perspectives and temporalities," and in the *Rarebit Fiend*, multitudinous perspectives make impositions on each other; the sleeper reluctantly yields to the power of the dream, but in the end the dream disappears just as swiftly.[15] For McCay, this simultaneity is not harmonious but rather full of tension because it betrays how certain discursive modes overwhelm or detract from others. Through simultaneity, McCay manifests the increasingly critical hermeneutic of suspicion that calls attention to the difference between what a text appears to do and what it does in actuality. McCay has a deeper simultaneity at work here that he fails to recuperate: the simultaneous experience of having modern anxieties and living in a world that consistently attempts to dissuade you of them. Where, in the last panel, the dreamer exclaims, "Confound! That rarebit I ate last night!" McCay displaces the sudden epiphany, locating it in an imaginative space that precedes the diegetic world of the strip. Like the one-gag's punchline, each dreamer wakes in exasperation, thinking a cheese sandwich was the cause of their wild dream. The realization alleviates the anxieties conjured by the dream and condemns the dream as ultimately insignificant. Blaming the rarebit drives the dreamer further into their alienation, further away from others experiencing the same anxieties, despite the mechanism of connectivity in the newspaper's mass circulation. In its investment in modern anxieties, McCay's comic abandons the affective and cultural implications that the nightmares engender. The dreamers return to normalcy, resituated by ambivalence, and the strips resort to mere parody of suspicion.

Hornby insists that the modern visual epistemology is one of stillness rather than motion, and what she calls "the duality of stillness"—that it simultaneously resists motion and suspends it—demands of the viewer a critical contemplation and embodied reception of the image that asks to be viewed and then reviewed. Perhaps the iterative image is posed to be similarly reflexive, but rather than demonstrating a scientific principle of vision, it demonstrates the affects of reflection itself: anxiety, even suspicion, followed by epiphany. Just as the iterative image in photography shows precisely the ways change unfolds across space and time, so it becomes in McCay the means of expressing immediate change for the disturbed dreamer by contracting temporality into a singular presence. This visual operation connotes immediacy, potentially turning Gunning's "art of succession" into an art of interruption. The iterative image, then, might offer the possibility of jolting the public out of complacency, except that, as I will demonstrate, McCay's politics restrict this reflexive power.

EPIPHANY, SLAPSTICK, AND THE POLITICS OF ITERATION

The anxieties plaguing McCay's *Rarebit Fiend* dreamers come from quotidian life in the metropolis, usually involving tight urban quarters, identity loss in the chaos of the crowd, the speed of mass transportation, and the spectacular bombardment of images and advertisements.[16] The dreamer's sense of uncertainty is followed always by epiphany: a return to normalcy. There is a sudden rush of understanding that turns the nightmare into nothing more than a midnight snack. Always, the problem for the dreamer is the cheese sandwich giving them indigestion and *not* the dangers modernity actually poses to them. McCay's middle-class politics might be observed more strikingly in the insistence of this normalcy. The anxieties I consider here are worth interrogating because they indicate various ways capitalist modernity begets sudden, uncontrollable change in everyday life—of income, of commodity culture, of technology—that are never acknowledged as anxieties that need rectification. When the dreamer awakens, the sudden relief puts into question the dream's reality as well as the anxiety it represents. McCay does not confront ambivalence; he's directly complicit with it. Despite McCay's interest in the psychological representation of sudden change, his iteration of the dreamer's body becomes a modern mode of dismissing anxieties, not of apprehending them.

Popular modernisms like comics and slapstick expose these mundane anxieties. Participating in rich cultural exchanges with mass audiences, slapstick and comics derive a modernity that intimately nurtures the everyday sensorium. The senses I'm concerned with here, which don't normally receive extended meditation, are occasioned by an empty afternoon's trip to the cinema, or the noisy bus that takes you home at the end of the day. These occasions are ephemeral, with seemingly low stakes, and yet I see something recoverable in these experiences—I read them as an important vehicle for cultural reflection, not despite but because of their nearly invisible incorporation into ordinary life. For Miriam Hansen, lowbrow modernism provided an occasion to examine how "the traumatic effects of modernity were reflected, rejected or disavowed, transmuted or negotiated."[17] Being "crucially anchored in sensory experience and sensational affect," Hansen's "reflexivity" leads us to ask questions about what it feels and looks like to be surprised or anxious and whether or not that representation says something about what caused it—whether or not the medium allows its viewers "to confront the constitutive ambivalence of modernity."[18] Moviegoers, Hansen estimates, learn about themselves by allowing the cinema to situate them in a political, ideological, and affective matrix, and throughout this essay I've suggested a similar matrix is at work in the funny papers.[19]

To fully understand the political potential that McCay denies the iterative image, it is instructive to compare his use of the technique with its appearance as the match cut in the work of Charlie Chaplin. As comics and films experiment with their own techniques for orienting the reader or viewer, transitioning between images, and navigating affective registers, they each arrive at iteration as a way of expressing sudden change and its psychological reality. By using the match cut to illustrate change, Chaplin primarily showcases adaptions and alternatives to modernity's subjections. Being put square in the center of each frame, Chaplin's body is a fixed point around which all else changes. The match cut, which is both performed and technical, requires surveyor tools at each of the filming locations to ensure Chaplin's position is a perfect match across each frame. The iterative image therefore articulates a politics of shared gestures, desires, and vulnerability because, in the hands of Chaplin, image iteration reveals itself to be simultaneously alienating and rejoining. Comparing comics to film regarding their use of iterative images gives us insight to the ways developing aesthetic forms influence the evolving dynamics of twentieth-century politics.

The match cut is a cinematic technique that uses the same or similar figures across multiple frames, usually to smooth a transition that is otherwise mere juxtaposition. Scott McCloud shows in his guide to comics that sequencing panels orients space and time much the same way cinematic editing effects transitions.[20] While the match cut became a common way of making a scene change fluid in narrative cinema, trick films and slapstick comedy complicate this emerging convention; where the match cut would make a scene legible, it comes to express surprise rather than accommodation. Chaplin's match cut in his 1915 film *The Bank* reflects a politics of the body's vulnerability and desires: Chaplin suddenly finds his dream meaningless not because of its outrageous terror (like McCay's dreamer) but because of its clichéd and manufactured ideals (figures 3.3 and 3.4).

Because of the difficulty of coordinating physical bodies of performers for the match cut, the disruptive mediation of the iterative image becomes more apparent on film, wherein "the eye is able to slow, to handle, and finally to use its perceptions, as if actually seeing them for the first time."[21] Like any celluloid cut, the frames are divided materially and recombined according to a narrative or affective arbitration. Using the body as the conduit of transition strains the subject with affective tensions; the graphic stability of the recurring body that seems unmoving and unchanging is actually destabilized by its affective insecurities—the lack of movement is the feeling of being stunned, of being out of time and out of sync. As an affective repository, the iterative body is not moving but rather is somehow moved. While the body finds a new arrangement, it is also a mediator that marks the change.

Chaplin's iterative image in *The Bank* begets the power that Chaplin then flouts. In *The Bank*, Charlie works as a janitor at a bank and, with his unfazed

Figures 3.3. Still images, *The Bank*, dir. Charlie Chaplin, 1915.

dignity, keeps his coat, cane, and mop in the safe instead of money. After falling in love with the president's daughter (Edna Purviance) and after a debacle with a fellow suitor with the same name, Charlie falls asleep among his brooms and rejected flowers. He dreams that the bank is robbed, and when the other suitor, a trusted bank teller, reveals himself to be a coward, Charlie sees himself save Edna and the bank. Our match cut in question shows Charlie embracing Edna, who in the next moment is revealed to be Charlie's dirty mop. When he wakes up, his heroic fantasy disappears, and his rejection remains. He dreams of desire, not anxiety: a longing for Edna, yes, but also for a class utopia where Edna is attracted to courage rather than stature. Charlie's dream is euphoric, and its disappearance yields a forlorn realization—his mop being significantly less relieving than the comfortable beds of McCay's dreamers. The epiphany of the iterative image inverts that of McCay's dreamers, where, rather than relief of the dream's insignificance, we see Charlie's disappointment.

Charlie's epiphany prominently displays iteration's temporal lag. When he wakes to find Edna is really his broom, he is still adapting to the previous setting, manifesting "firstness," or what Gilles Deleuze calls "a category of the possible"—where what Chaplin perceives "is not a sensation, a feeling, an idea, but the quality of a possible sensation, feeling or idea."[22] In this sensational moment where the lovely becomes the disgusting, Chaplin becomes suddenly unimpressed with the ideals his dream enunciates. Chaplin's dream shows an

Figure 3.4. Still images, *The Bank*, dir. Charlie Chaplin, 1915.

idealized self, and the attitudes of the people around him fall into appropriate order. Furthermore, Chaplin exhibits an ambition that upholds a capitalist hierarchy, inserting himself as a contender to both Edna and her father because of his loyalty to his workplace, even entertaining the impulse to protect the wealthy literally. Returning to his situation among the mops becomes an occasion for reexamining what he wanted in the first place: his humble flowers remain crumbled to his chest; Edna still clings dotingly to the wrong Charlie. Our final shot is Charlie walking away proudly after determining his own right to reject the situation he has been given.

While Chaplin uses the iterative image to reject capitalist alienation, McCay's dreamer denies that alienation exists in the first place. The success of the epiphany is the erasure of the nightmare's threat, but for McCay, waking from the dream also puts the dreamers themselves into doubt. McCay's dreamer is a practically different person after they wake; they must be in order to deny their dreaming's modernity. Chaplin's iterations, by contrast, rejoice in the ways they retain themselves. When Chaplin's character wakes, he does not forget himself; he retains himself across the match cut. A scenario wherein Charlie is both barred from upward socioeconomic mobility as well as isolated in his interpersonal relationships underscores the alienation between individuals. Iterating the body on film is literally alienating because it detaches the subject from its surroundings, rendering the old surroundings false and the new surroundings unknown. But the iterative image also insists on the endurance of images, especially when they're put together. Through Chaplin's destruction of a false ideal, we associate the epiphany with multiplicity, possibility, and power; his affective register takes on a public manifestation as if the body becomes a public itself.

As quotidian forms of media, comics and film each elucidate the way the affective curation of modern life involves their collectiveness. Walter Benjamin, for instance, shows how Chaplin occupies the popular occasion for cinema:

> The majority of city dwellers, throughout the workday in offices and factories, have to relinquish their humanity in the face of an apparatus. In the evenings these same masses fill the cinemas, to witness the film actor taking revenge on their behalf not only by asserting *his* humanity (or what appears to them as such) against the apparatus, but by placing that apparatus in the service of his triumph.[23]

By apparatus, Benjamin means the cultural infrastructure of capitalism, that which is responsible for the divisions of public and private, work and leisure—the very structure that augments everyday life. As an after-hours activity, the cinema then facilitates and organizes the affects that have been dissociated by capitalist industry. Similarly, McCay's regular *Rarebit Fiend*, which was consumed primarily by commuters in the same after-hours context as Benjamin envisions for moviegoers, presents, and is presently incorporated in, an affective dimension of everyday life that is contingent upon capitalist divisions of time. Chaplin, for Benjamin, straddles this apparatus in order to expose it as oppressive; in Chaplin, alienation is corrected or confronted, dishonored, disarmed. McCay's alienation, on the other hand, is denied or dismissed. The mechanical reproduction of both modern newspapers and film gives full expressive range to those individually subjective experiences; but, precisely because they are mechanically reproduced, these media simultaneously contextualize seemingly private, seemingly subjective experiences with the rest of the public. The iterative image is loaded with potential and can serve different politics. Where Chaplin accesses its radicalizing potential on the basis of graphic sameness, equity, and reflection, McCay fails to marshal the anxieties that his readers internalize every evening after work.

Both comics and slapstick have the potential to engage "the contradictions of modernity at the level of the senses, the level at which the impact of modern technology on human experience was most palpable and irreversible."[24] In this *Rarebit Fiend* comic (figure 3.5), McCay displays a recognizable fear of industrial machinery. Our dreamer's body is thrown, bent, hit, twirled, and slammed. Finally, the dreamer wakes in a sudden change, visual contrast, and

Figure 3.5. Winsor McCay, *Dream of the Rarebit Fiend*, first published July 10, 1907. Reprinted in Ulrich Merkl, ed., *The Complete Dream of the Rarebit Fiend (1904–1913)*.

iterated body position. The stillness of the iterative image gives the ephemeral body weight, a form that makes time and space into objects that come and go rather than the other way around. The modern body is: an affective repository that receives an environment; one of many, its own public that is interconnected with others; constantly subjected to capitalist, political, epistemological, and technological interventions *suddenly*. When McCay doubles the image of an old man he makes his image redundant, as an attempt to neutralize the dream. When he wakes, there's no real problem in the world. McCay's impulse to still the exact moment upon waking by doubling the dreamer's body fulfills a desire to recapture control over one's subjectivity.

Ultimately, however, McCay relinquishes that impulse as he arrives at the conclusion that the dream has no significance, the conclusion that normalcy has not been and should not be breached. When we see the doubled body, we recognize the two as one. We remember what the dreamer forgets. The epiphany (a false one, as he returns to reality) resounds within the span of iteration. But McCay fails to utilize that visual memory, choosing not to confront it, yielding a psychologized prioritization of the arrived present. When Chaplin duplicates his image, he recalls himself, respecting the Chaplin that came before. By blaming the rarebit, McCay in fact attempts to reverse the impact of modern technology on the dreamer. McCay himself as a cartoonist is susceptible to this same impact: feeling it in his daily repetitions—a practice driven by capitalist enterprise, a circulation and distribution maintained by the modern press—as well as translating this impact to his dreamer's bodies, who endure not only awful dreams and confused awakenings but also the graphic dualism of their iteration.

AMBIVALENCE AND THE BODY'S LABOR

The iterative image of the *Rarebit Fiend* dramatizes vision itself, as if on one side of the dream, we have an image, and on the other, we have its afterimage. Our topic, in this way, has been the modern body in the twin happenings of perception and subjection, wherein comics mediation presents to us what it feels like to have change occur in the time it takes for an image to seep into the flesh of the retina before that image disappears. The dreamer's body endures its own imprinting to show us not only the temporality of perception but the paradox of affixing certainty's visage at all.

In comics, the iterative image evokes the experience of a modern reprocessing of temporality. McCay subjects his dreamers to the powerful structures of capitalism, especially its efforts to compartmentalize everyday life through Ford-Taylorist production practices.[25] Mary Ann Doane makes a similar claim about film. Tracing a historical trajectory beginning with the intensive regulation of time during the industrial revolution, Doane argues that the cinema provides its own epistemology through its fixation of fleeting moments that document the experience of presence. Meanwhile, these Ford-Taylorist standardizations render the public contingent such that its cultural wellbeing is unessential to capitalist expansion. This contingency to capitalism becomes the site of minor affective experiences: anxieties about being late to work turn into anxieties of being hit by a bus; anxieties about health turn into anxieties about commodified health solutions; anxieties of one displacement evolve into anxieties of others. The technology supporting modern capitalism shares much with the technologies of newspapers and film, and they each provide new language for the experience of our subjection to them.

As an element of technological modernity, iteration itself became a newspaper comics convention in the ways serials would consistently present recurring familiar characters, who "day after day," in Thierry Smolderen's words, "ceaselessly perform their own specialty like automatons."[26] Unlike McCay's boy dreamer Nemo, who follows such a recurring story line in *Little Nemo in Slumberland*, the *Rarebit Fiend* features a different individual for every strip, a figure who represents any average American and in whom the public can see "their world, values, mores, and prejudices . . . exactly reflected."[27] McCay's dreamers endure significant unease regarding money (being late for work, asking for raises) and bodily safety (car and train accidents; bodies being chased, caught, or squashed; mysteriously growing or shrinking). The site of dreaming ushers the strange into our nightly routines, but the dreamer's mediation illustrates the shock of waking itself as a modern experience. In the ways the comic fractures the perceptions of self, environment, and change, what seems extraordinary in the *Rarebit Fiend* in fact represents the ordinariness of life under capitalism. McCay continues to be a compelling figure as we witness the conflict between his expressive capacities towards the public and the developing generic conventions of the newspaper comic that were simultaneously cementing a cultural politics.

McCay's repetitive labor as a cartoonist and animator, his regular sitting down to work and drawing, speaks to the material conditions around which these cultural politics are based. In superficial ways, McCay imitates, by hand, the mechanical reproduction of images. Duplicating images is a technique that becomes particularly useful in McCay's developments of the "split system" in early animation. Before common use of clear celluloid sheets called "cels" that relieve much of an animator's work in copying, McCay and his assistant produced an estimated 3,000 original drawings for his vaudeville act *Gertie the Dinosaur*.[28] To save them from redundancy, some of these drawings were "cycled," or photographed multiple times, to represent repeated motions of the characters in his story, like Gertie's breathing or lifting her feet.[29] Using the same material, the sequence of drawings therefore mimes Gertie's repeated gestures. But for McCay to outline the body of the *Rarebit Fiend* dreamer again and again involves a method of duplication that requires the creation of two indexical forms rather than one. This process of creating one figure and another identical to the first issues important implications not only about image production but also what the generation of like images means. If McCay's crafting of two bodies by hand means he is imitating mechanical reproduction, he is simultaneously imitating the creation of democratic access and the pattern of equity. However, the iterative image at the moment of a dreamer's epiphany has a formal structure of both visual and political recognition only if it is encouraged.

For all his comics' investment in the everyday, McCay's own everyday experiences—including the assembly-line regiment of producing a daily comic strip—are curiously missing from his archive. Most of what McCay left behind are his instructions for making animated motion pictures, published in course books or artist studies. Among the only documents of his daily experience is his 1908 diary and calendar, where he indexed his regular routine with different symbols: whether he worked in the city or stayed home; whether he felt good or bad; which comic he worked on; whether he paid or received money.[30] I read McCay's archival absence as a testament to his active work life. When he did record his experiences, he confirms this dogged devotion. On his visit to San Simeon at William Randolph Hearst's request in 1920, he felt he "was simply an employee on the job." While Hearst's other guests "enjoyed every kind of sport," McCay kept close to Hearst: "I went no where, I saw nothing. . . . I sat up in the telegraph hut on the hill for hours each day near 'The Chief,' pen poised, ink and drawing board ready." Though Hearst told him to enjoy the "vacation," it is clear McCay never did.[31] McCay on several occasions referred to his work life as its own rarebit nightmare, which indicates how he anticipated contingencies about his job that behooved him to make prudent choices regarding his own labor and expressions.

Indeed, McCay was eventually forced to halt his aesthetic pursuits because Hearst regarded McCay's wildly popular comics and vaudeville performances as trivial compared to the political values of nationalism, American isolationism, anti-immigration, anticommunism, and the threats of big government that his newspapers aimed to forward. Many McCay scholars are quick to bemoan McCay's involvement with Hearst's political agenda as one that is circumstantial, concluding that, because McCay was unhappy with the editorial work, whose craftsmanship was shoddy and uninspired (with the strong exception of *Lusitania*), McCay's political sensibilities were never aligned with Hearst in any substantial way. This essay speculates that McCay's role in Hearst's journalism has been critically overlooked because we presume his politics to be active rather than complacent. McCay's aesthetic salience with multiple media exposes a buried trapdoor through which fantasy and fear stumble into political revelation. Within McCay's conservatism was a sensitivity to his own ordinary discomforts, and that sensitivity harbors a potential for contextualizing everyday anxieties when they are given a platform of mass circulation. The *Rarebit Fiend* therefore imports a latent confrontation over anxieties of capitalist industry—those of job security, urban sprawl, consumerism, xenophobia, and more. It is ironic then that Hearst failed to recognize the strip's ultimate ambivalence towards those anxieties, an ambivalence that would maintain a status quo and lend him more influence over the contrivance of middle-class political life.

McCay's situation incurs an ordinary expectation for this medial shimmering indulged by the iterative image to shake out an unconscious politics that nevertheless behaves dynamically. As part of this ordinary expectation of media's comportment that we are developing here, the material environment contextualizes McCay in the rhetoric of capitalism literally: his vaudeville performances, for instance, were often publicized in the same pages as advertisements. In the *Detroit Times* in 1912, a review of McCay's performance at Temple Theatre is featured right next to products with nightmarish headlines and magical cures.[32] An ad for a special soap openly emphasizes skin-crawling ailments: "Baby's Face All Scales"; "Pimples Began to Itch and Burn." What follows turns a reader's alarm into commercial rhetoric for the miraculous work of commodities. Like *Rarebit Fiend*'s convention of putting the reader in the horror directly, these large-set headlines induce an immediate anxiety that their commercial product soothes, anticipating the use of comics art as advertisements that in the 1930s were placed in the funny paper sections.[33]

While McCay elucidates a skepticism of commodity culture, he neutralizes it immediately in the *Rarebit Fiend* comic where a wife and husband accidentally take each other's pills. After purchasing one "Get-Fat-Quick" bottle for her husband and one "Anti-Fattino" bottle for herself, a middle-class woman mixes the bottles up, and when she grows enormously bulbous, her husband shrinks to a thin line.[34] As a magic pill, the commodified medicine promises to cure emaciation, but the nightmare reveals the commodity's risks and confusions. Upon waking, the dreamer forgets the problems of commodity culture, of vanity, of gender regulations that had characterized the experience of the dream. Instead, the dreamer is called back to a reality where the pills work correctly without being misunderstood and without overturning cultural expectations for women. They return to a place where taking the pills still seems reasonable.

McCay's techniques for image-making cannot express the same historical or material contingency as film, but they can express a *regard* for that contingency. Highlighting the proximity between the public's ordinary routines and newspapers, vaudeville, and the cinema helps to clarify the cultural and political ingress that popular modernisms share. By placing *Rarebit Fiend* in relation to other "mass-produced and mass-consumed phenomena," we can better recognize the heterogeneous quality of modernity's markings.[35] McCay shows us that the ecological transfusions between modern media should be considered an expectation of ordinary life. Sitting at the nexus of standardized time and the aesthetic wrangling of its affective havoc, the *Rarebit Fiend* serves as a public reservoir in which the visual epistemes of anxiety continue to incite questions of political contingency, perceptual change, and the sensorium we inhabit every day.

Notes

1. Sianne Ngai, *Ugly Feelings* (Cambridge, MA: Harvard University Press, 2005), 215. See also Ernst Bloch's *The Principle of Hope*, vol. 1 (Cambridge, MA: MIT Press, 1995).

2. Hillary Chute, *Disaster Drawn: Visual Witness, Comics, and Documentary Form* (Cambridge, MA: Harvard University Press, 2016), 84. Louise Hornby has written that photography, too, represents motion by stopping it. See Hornby's *Still Modernism: Photography, Literature, Film* (Oxford: Oxford University Press, 2017).

3. Katherine Roeder's *Wide Awake in Slumberland: Fantasy, Mass Culture, and the Art of Winsor McCay* (Jackson: University Press of Mississippi, 2014) provides new channels of inquiry regarding the expressions of everyday life in McCay's comics, by placing him in a trajectory of historical developments of art in advertising. Scott Bukatman's *The Poetics of Slumberland: Animated Spirits and the Animating Spirit* (Berkeley: University of California Press, 2012) adopts Noel Busch's term "motionless voyage" to describe comics' paradoxical sense of movement derived from still images, such that the flatness of comics makes the experience of them somewhere between *tableau vivant* and film. Tom Gunning's essay "The Art of Succession," in *Critical Inquiry: Comics & Media* (Chicago: University of Chicago Press, 2014), provides a formalist purview of the visual inheritance the comic strip finds in such disparate genres as chronophotography, cinematography, the moving panorama, optical toys, and hieroglyphs.

4. The *Rarebit Fiend* ran initially in the *New York Evening Telegram*, published by James Gordon Bennett Jr. as a part of the *New York Herald*, from 1904–1911, then dispersed as variant offshoots until 1925.

5. John Canemaker, *Winsor McCay: His Life and Art* (Boca Raton, FL: CRC, 2018), 22.

6. Miriam Hansen, "The Mass Production of the Senses: Classical Cinema as Vernacular Modernism," *Modernism/modernity* 6, no. 2 (April 1999): 69–70.

7. Walter Benjamin, "The Work of Art in the Age of Its Technological Reproducibility," in *The Work of Art in the Age of Its Technological Reproducibility and Other Writings on Media*, ed. Michael W. Jennings, Brigid Doherty, and Thomas Y. Levin, trans. Edmund Jephcott et al. (Cambridge, MA: Belknap Press of Harvard University Press, 2008), 37.

8. Hornby, *Still Modernism*, 108–12.

9. Hornby, *Still Modernism*, 19.

10. Hillary Chute, "Comics as Literature? Reading Graphic Narrative," *PMLA* 123, no. 2 (2008): 454.

11. Kathleen Stewart, *Ordinary Affects* (Durham, NC: Duke University Press, 2007), 2.

12. Ben Procter even calls it "journalistic entertainment." See his *William Randolph Hearst: The Early Years, 1863–1910* (Oxford: Oxford University Press, 1998), 86.

13. Ulrich Merkl, ed., *The Complete Dream of the Rarebit Fiend (1904–1913)*, by Winsor McCay (self-pub., Ulrich Merkl, 2007), 493.

14. Gilles Deleuze, *Cinema I: The Movement Image* (Minneapolis: University of Minnesota Press, 1986), 98.

15. Chute, *Disaster Drawn*, 86.

16. Roeder, *Wide Awake in Slumberland*, 153–81.

17. Hansen, "The Mass Production of the Senses," 69.

18. Hansen, 70, 71.

19. Reflectivity requires a passive yielding to the cinema's enervations, recalling Gunning's observation that the cinema, and the moving panorama before it, delivers images to a stationary spectator. See Gunning's "The Art of Succession."

20. See Scott McCloud, *Understanding Comics: The Invisible Art* (1993; repr., New York: Harper Perennial, 1994), 68–73. For McCloud, comic transitions can happen moment-to-moment, action-to-action, subject-to-subject, and scene-to-scene. To demonstrate the moment-to-moment, McCloud has two panels with the same woman, one with her eyes open, the next with her eyes closed. The panel slows time and calms the scene by iterating the woman at the same angle. On the other extreme, McCloud shows that scene shifts often display radical changes in time and space.

21. Michael North, *Machine-Age Comedy* (Oxford: Oxford University Press, 2008), 45.

22. Deleuze, *Cinema I*, 98.

23. Benjamin, "The Work of Art," 31.

24. Hansen, "Mass Production," 70.

25. See Mary Ann Doane, *The Emergence of Cinematic Time: Modernity, Contingency, the Archive* (Cambridge, MA: Harvard University Press, 2002).

26. Thierry Smolderen, *The Origins of Comics: From William Hogarth to Winsor McCay* (Jackson: University Press of Mississippi, 2014), 150.

27. Canemaker, *Winsor McCay*, 81.

28. See Donald Crafton and David Nathan, "The Making and Re-making of Winsor McCay's *Gertie* (1914)," *Animation: An Interdisciplinary Journal* 8, no. 1 (2013): 23–46.

29. Canemaker, *Winsor McCay*, 179.

30. McCay's agenda book, John Canemaker Collection, SPEC.CGA.JC, box JC1, folder 5, Billy Ireland Cartoon Library and Museum, Ohio State University. McCay wrote few notes to his family, though when he did, they often included doodles of himself and his wife Marion, or, once, a Black caregiver (whose Blackness he signals with the same minstrel lips as his Imp character). When his grandson was born, McCay sent him a letter that consisted entirely of baby-talk sounds.

31. McCay writes on his visit to San Simeon, John Canemaker Collection, SPEC.CGA.JC, box JC1, folder 5.

32. Newspaper review of McCay performance. John Canemaker Collection, SPEC.CGA.JC, drawer AC H3 190, Billy Ireland Cartoon Library and Museum, Ohio State University.

33. Ian Gordon, *Comic Strips and Consumer Culture, 1890–1945* (Washington, DC: Smithsonian Books, 1998), 81.

34. Winsor McCay, *Dreams of the Rarebit Fiend* (1905; repr. New York: Dover, 1973), 37.

35. Hansen, "Mass Production," 60.

A THOROUGHLY MODERN KAT

DAVID M. BALL

Late nineteenth- and early twentieth-century readers of American newspaper comics lived in an echo chamber. There they could have read any of a number of Winsor McCay's masterful repetition compulsions: *Little Sammy Sneeze*, whose eponymous ejaculations erupted like clockwork in the fifth panel of his rigid grid; *Dream of the Rarebit Fiend*'s food-induced nightmare visions, the repeated injunction against nighttime indulgence perpetually forgotten; and *Little Nemo in Slumberland*'s own reprise of this theme, its fanciful departures invariably concluded amidst the rumpled sheets of a childhood bed.¹ Even the anarchic, youthful violence endemic to so many of these early strips—the cacophonies of immigrants and tenement dwellers surrounding the Yellow Kid, the endless pranks perpetrated by the Katzenjammer Kids and their imitators, the proliferating indignities heaped upon Happy Hooligan—occurred with a metronomic regularity. Due to the fierce competition for cartooning talent during the period, multiple, simultaneous, and contending versions of the escapades first of the Yellow Kid and then the Katzenjammer Kids could be read in the pages of rival newspaper syndicates.² Mass-market reproduction can thus be taken not only as the context from which early American comics emerged but also as one of its most recognizable narrative strategies. Seriality constitutes both early newspaper comics' form and its content.

Despite this proliferating dynamic throughout the early age of American newspaper comics, perhaps no graphic narrative represents the omnipresence of repetition better than George Herriman's groundbreaking creation *Krazy Kat*. First published in William Randolph Hearst's *New York Evening Journal* in 1913 and running up until Herriman's death in 1944, *Krazy Kat* offered apparently endless invention out of a remarkably simple-seeming premise. Krazy Kat is a feline naïf of indeterminate gender whose unrequited love for Ignatz Mouse is rewarded more often than not with a brick to the head—a brick nonetheless taken as a token of affection—an ambivalent violence that is policed with intermittent success by Offissa Pupp. This repeated structure is a "scrambled system," Kevin Cooley writes, "that acts out a narrative cycle as regular as it is chaotic."[3] It is infused throughout with a kaleidoscopic verbal and visual imagination: Herriman's characters traverse a formally inventive and shifting desert landscape while speaking a pun-laden pidgin that spans multiple languages to create its own. Most often read as an anthropomorphic Oedipal triangle or a kind of visual-verbal analogue to jazz, *Krazy Kat* is also a study in iteration and alterity, endlessly riffing and innovating out of the seemingly limited parameters of this generative device. Indeed, *Krazy Kat* arguably remains the most influential strip for comics artists into the twenty-first century.

The cumulative effect of reading the more than fifteen hundred pages of the collected Sunday strips *alone* is one of a strangely enclosed verbal and visual assault, a chaotic world endlessly revolving in a tightly contained space. Such fascinations with repetition in the funny papers are best understood neither simply as the gratifications derived from formula fiction nor as the propagative visions spawned from creative constraint, although they are also both of these things. One generative way to think about comics' iterative qualities throughout this period is in counterpoise to the more conventionally celebrated aesthetic innovations and text-image experiments of its artistic contemporary: modernism. Placing the history of graphic narrative in conversation with critical understandings of art and literature in the late nineteenth and early twentieth centuries makes visible the significant role that comics have had on modernist works in both literature and the fine arts.

Perhaps no comics artist has been more widely recognized for "bringing modernist formal techniques and concerns into the newspaper comic strip," in the words of Paul Peppis, than Herriman, who was feted by many arbiters of literary modernism in his day such as Gilbert Seldes and e. e. cummings.[4] Herriman also worked within one of American modernism's most recognizable visual registers: the iconography of the American Southwest that drew modernist writers and artists such as Willa Cather and Georgia O'Keeffe.[5] Newspaper comics as a whole achieved a period of formal inventiveness in the work of Herriman, McCay, Lyonel Feininger, and Rudolph Dirks, among many others, contemporaneous with the development of artistic *and* literary high modernism. Dirks's *The Katzenjammer Kids* was imported from America to Paris and passed lovingly between Gertrude Stein and Pablo Picasso during their foundational modernist collaborations, and Dirks's work itself was exhibited at the influential 1913 Armory Show, the artistic epicenter for American modernism in the fine arts.[6] The exhibition at the Whitney Museum of American Art of Lyonel Feininger's comics alongside his innovations in expressionism and cubism, as well as the reprinting of Lynd Ward's "pictorial narratives" of the 1920s and '30s by the Library of America, speaks to the rich possibilities that are opening up for the correlation of the history of graphic narratives with that of modernism.[7] Yet despite such rich overlap between comics and modernism—a dawning acknowledgment represented most forcefully in the publication of this very volume—comics have never made, to my knowledge, an appearance in conventional anthologies or histories of modernist literature and have until very recently yielded only occasional mentions in modernist scholarship.[8] Herriman thus represents a valuable touchstone for considering the intersections between comics and modernism more broadly.

I argue in this essay that a crucial contribution *Krazy Kat* makes to modernist discourse was the means by which it participated in, and complicated, modernism's desire for both a radical break from history and a perceived distance from popular culture.[9] Comics' constitutive repetition, as both the structural necessity of serial images and a thematic lynchpin of popular cultural texts, becomes the emotional and narrative center of Herriman's masterwork. Ignatz Mouse and Krazy Kat's continual chase after one another is thus a theater of seriality that enacts the central drama of modernist creation; the characters' lively antics also portray the animal consciousness that allowed for the belief in an absolute break from history. Much of the delight of reading Herriman's work, and a key to understanding his formal invention, occurs precisely within this repetition and alteration of narrative and aesthetic formulas as generative devices toward artistic creation. Yet despite the layered repetitions of *Krazy Kat*'s varying compositions, their insistence upon recurrence as the fountainhead of artistic generation, perhaps no comics artist has been regarded as so sui generis, such the auteur, as George Herriman.

Rightly seeing Herriman as a modernist of a piece with the literary, artistic, and comics innovations happening around him, and the role of comics more generally in the long history of modernism, asks us to revisit our notions of just how radical a break modernism represents from historical and formal precedents. Comics scholars, once secure in their sense that Herriman's generation represented the inaugural moment of comics history, have had to revise their histories of the medium. So too might scholars' recognition that modernists' professions of radical singularity and authentic newness represent generative but inexecutable aspirations serve to forge a needed bridge between comics and modernist artistic innovation.[10] In so doing, we allow for a more complex and multimodal genealogy of modernism, one that could begin to incorporate the achievements of American graphic narratives within it. Doing so would allow for a range of American comics artists to be considered alongside more conventionally regarded modernist authors and artists, and would simultaneously ask us to rethink comics history in terms of the more widely regarded histories of literary and artistic modernism.

. . .

A Thoroughly Modern Kat

THE FAMILY UPSTAIRS

Figure 4.1. George Herriman, *The Family Upstairs*, first published July 26 and 27, 1910. The images depict the first instances of the characters of *Krazy Kat*.

At first glance Herriman's repetitions seem at odds with the visual and verbal rhetoric of radical innovation and deracination so customarily associated with artistic and literary modernism. Take as one example the "birth" of Krazy Kat, as it were, in the margins of one of Herriman's earliest strips, *The Family Upstairs*.[11] Another representative study in repetition, this strip narrated the travails of the Dingbat family as they daily sought, and were thwarted in their attempts to confront, their disruptive upstairs neighbors. (Herriman went to extravagant extremes to maintain this conceit—objects dropped on the vacationing Dingbats from their unseen neighbors' rented aircraft, and the strip concluded with the entire floor removed above the Dingbats in the process of their building's demolition—remaining true to this constraint up until the final panel.)[12] While for its entire run the goings-on of the upstairs neighbors of E. Pluribus Dingbat would be withheld from readers and characters alike, the actions of their menagerie of animals increasingly occupied Herriman's compositions, in some episodes occasionally subordinating the human actors to the subpanels and eventually supplanting them entirely with the launch of *Krazy Kat* as its own strip. The strips published on July 26 and 27, 1910 (figure 4.1), play exactly on the thematics of repetition that yielded the larger structure of the Dingbats' narrative. The first panels to serially lay out the characters that would become Ignatz and Krazy in later iterations, these strips make clear the ways in which Krazy's mortifications serve as mirror images of E. Pluribus Dingbat's. Positioned relative to Dingbat in successive panels, Krazy takes his punishment both visually aligned to and simultaneous with Dingbat's, a double repetition within the constraints of the strip's own generic expectations. Indeed, E. Pluribus's very name cuts short the "Unum" from the familiar motto, prizing plurality yet sacrificing singularity, evading the expectations of discrete subjectivity.

If Krazy's travails are originally presented as mere echoes of Dingbat's, how then explain the ways in which Herriman's animals soon supplant his human characters in his and his readers' interest and attention? One possible explanation might be the animal's—even the anthropomorphized animal's—differing relationship to consciousness, or our projections of what that differing consciousness might entail. While Dingbat expresses rage or elicits sympathy, no matter in what slapstick version these qualities arrive to us, Krazy's state serves more as a blank screen upon which our responses might be more fully projected. In the July 26 strip, Krazy's emanata and direct, blank stare in the final panel connote vacuity as opposed to the fuller palette of Dingbat's consolations, while in the concluding panel of the July 27 strip, where Dingbat is roused to express fury, Krazy is disallowed such a human response to his dunking, disappearing from the composition entirely. The pose Krazy would soon assume while being "beaned" by Ignatz's bricks—cantilevered forward, eyes agog, expressing pleasure—figures exactly this remove from the more human drama taking place among the urban cliff dwellers of *The Family Upstairs*. If, as Umberto Eco famously argued, the "oneiric climate" of the superhero's perpetual present protects him from the passage of time, the perpetual pleasure Herriman will craft for Krazy in his debasement similarly shields him from the human consequences of time.[13] Once Krazy learns to desire his beaning, his delight will be the most unyielding element of *Krazy Kat*'s formulaic expectations in the Sunday strips. Such an ability to forget may well be the source of much of the pleasure Herriman and his readers take in his mature work.

One route to better understand the pleasures and motivation of reading Herriman's funny animals, representations of which, José Alaniz reminds us, "facilitated aesthetic breakthroughs for the artform [of graphic narrative] as a whole,"[14] is Friedrich Nietzsche's famously untimely meditation of 1874 "On the Uses and Disadvantages of History for Life." There Nietzsche extols the value of the "animal consciousness," the ability to divide oneself from the burden of historical memory:

> Consider the cattle, grazing as they pass you by: they do not know what is meant by yesterday or today, they leap about, eat, rest, digest, leap about again, and so from morn till night and from day to day, fettered

to the moment and its pleasure or displeasure, and thus neither melancholy nor bored.... A human being may well ask an animal: "Why do you not speak to me of your happiness but only stand and gaze at me?" The animal would like to answer, and say: "The reason is I always forget what I was going to say"—but then he forgot his answer too, and stayed silent: so that the human being was left wondering.... Thus the animal lives *unhistorically*: for it is contained in the present ... in blissful blindness between the hedges of past and future.[15]

Nietzsche's account of the animal's ability to forget, to live free from the weight of history—no matter how much that account might diverge from contemporary understandings of animal memory, down to even the most elemental single-cell organisms—celebrates the animal's purported ability to draw a horizon around itself. Without such a horizon, Nietzsche contends, the facility for human action (however paradoxically) becomes impossible, man becoming trapped by a historical sensibility. For these reasons, Margot Norris places Nietzsche among writers she terms "biocentric ... artists who create *as* the animal—not *like* the animal—but with their animality speaking."[16] If, as Norris contends, "the animal is truly autotelic, living from and by and for itself in an oblivion of the 'other,' beyond the reach of the consciousness, recognition, and judgment of the 'other,' then Nietzsche as a creatural writer and philosopher must negate his audience and rehabilitate his own polemical motives to purely self-reflexive ends."[17] Much as Nietzsche will famously seek to upend the expectations of human morality later in his writings, the animal here becomes a way for Nietzsche to evade both history and audience—those twin modernist urges—and in the process access what he celebrates as "life," putatively freeing himself from the consequences of temporality.

Nietzsche's claims in "On the Uses and Disadvantages of History for Life" were perhaps most memorably taken up by Paul de Man is his essay "Literary History and Literary Modernity," which contends for the very impossibility of the animal consciousness. Nietzsche's quintessentially modern claims for "moments of genuine humanity," de Man states, "are moments at which all anteriority vanishes, annihilated by the power of an absolute forgetting."[18] Yet de Man convincingly claims that Nietzsche overshoots his mark in order to reach it, discovering that the desire for an authentic and entire break from history is itself an oft-repeated, quintessentially historical claim: "as modernism becomes conscious of its own strategies ... it discovers itself to be a generative power that not only engenders history, but is part of a generative scheme that extends far back into the past."[19] Michael North, in his even more recent treatment of this theme, *Novelty: A History of the New*, expands this contention by unraveling the paradox that "novelty is not itself by any means new, being one of the first ideas to trouble the consciousness of humankind." In North's compelling account,

> Novelty is not the simplest but rather one of the most complex features of aesthetic modernism, and the desire for the new did not always bring clarity of purpose to the movement but often complexity and ambivalence. Most of all, concentration on the new tended to reveal the inherent impossibility of ever finding it in a pure state, uncompromised by a return to the old, unadulterated by pastiche and rearrangement.[20]

The Nietzschean animal consciousness is thus simultaneously a zone of possibility and never an achievable state, always a projection of an unrealizable human desire to create singly *and* the means by which such creation is made available.

To read Herriman as a modernist is to view him as a consummate chronicler of exactly these creative paradoxes. That is to say, *Krazy Kat* enacts and in many ways anticipates these philosophical and theoretical contentions about modernity and their relationship to time as relentlessly as any text of the high modernist canon. The Sunday strips of *Krazy Kat* are replete with jokes about the frustrated passage of time; these jokes are themselves almost invariably premised upon the work of repetition. Repeated gags about boomerangs, echoes, the progression of time, or clocks used as missiles litter Herriman's Sunday compositions. Indeed, many of these jokes themselves are repetitions from earlier setups in *The Family Upstairs* and other strips. Frequently jokes turn on the literal repetition of dialogue or entire scenes—a synecdoche for the brick-throwing at the heart of the strip—as iteration takes the place of narrative in *Krazy Kat*.[21]

Take, as one example among many, the November 25, 1923, Sunday strip that depicts Ignatz and Offissa Pupp both buying bells to track their respective quarry (figure 4.2).[22] In many respects this composition exemplifies the core elements of a *Krazy Kat* Sunday strip, delivering a brick directly to Krazy's head in ways not always allowed in the strip's formal and generic involutions. Herriman's conspicuous, metacomical narrator acknowledges as much, disavowing (as he frequently does) the essential plot structure of the strip itself in order to advance its aims. This forgetting is of a piece with the duplication that constitutes the humor located in the dialogue, repeated word for word, in the third and fourth panels. The joke works precisely because we remember the previous panel, are pointed to that memory by the narrative caption, and then are allowed to forget it. "If not quite a *mise en abyme*," Ben Novotny Owen writes about a separate, deeply resonant episode, "the strip at least conveys a sense of versions proliferating—quotations requoted, reframed, and repeated. The idea of an original becomes travestied through repeat performance."[23]

Figure 4.2. George Herriman, *Krazy Kat*, first published November 25, 1923.

The bell that rings here isn't one that sounds as a call to memory, but rather forgetting, as figured in both Krazy's wide-eyed surprise and Offissa Pupp's oblivion in the final panel.

Such temporal disorientation and reversal are the watermarks of Herriman's art, and the strip is careful not to collapse this play with repetition into a mere return of the same. While the plot and dialogue loop in upon themselves, Herriman's customarily changing landscape ramifies with kaleidoscopic consequences for the reader's eye and comprehension. The sawtooth horizon of

Figure 4.3. George Herriman, *Krazy Kat*, first published February 4, 1922.

the upper right-hand panel might possibly be taken as identical to the one in the bottom two tiers of the composition, but here as elsewhere mesas and potted palms kinetically emerge and disappear at will (note the vanished tree in the fifth panel), and the billowing fog (or is it clouds, or smoke?) at the bottom of the page becomes a figure for the reader's own epistemological vertigo by composition's end. The effect is of extreme movement in stasis, of change amidst repetition, the sense that even with the repeated ringing of Herriman's bell, Krazy's "Tinkel" is not identical to Ignatz's and Pupp's "Tinkle."

Another masterful *Krazy Kat* composition in this regard is the page from February 4, 1922 (figure 4.3),[24] where repetition is even more closely aligned with the Nietzschean animal consciousness when taken as a harbinger of modernist novelty. Here Herriman's customary chase gives way to multiple anaesthetized oblivions—the joke, on its most literal level, is to the increased consumption of ether during prohibition, the resistance to which might be taken as *Krazy Kat* at its most politically engaged—an oblivion that nonetheless can't arrest the continued drama of mouse, cat, and brick.[25] In what is a formally inventive panel structure even by his medium-defining and -defying standards, Herriman stacks panoramic bleeds one on top of another in five tiers, all interspersed with panel divisions of varying constellations. The bleeds both dilate the passage of time—McCloud convincingly argues that, in the bleed, "time is no longer contained by the familiar icon of the closed panel, but instead hemorrhages and escapes into timeless space"—and perform the very oceanic state experienced by Herriman's anesthetized characters.[26] This temporal flow is interrupted, literally arrested in the first instance by Offissa Pupp's "HALT!!" and the closed panels superimposed on these bleeding tiers, operating not so much as scenes within scenes as they are discrete moments within the larger variations of Coconino's variegated scroll. Bum Bill Bee's hailing from Oljeto—the heart of Monument Valley—here becomes an occasion to ostensibly draw every monument in that iconic landscape, his itinerant wanderings the dramatic inverse of Mouse's, Kat's, and Pupp's stillness-in-motion. The straight line Bum Bill Bee walks in the first panel, indeed his direct and final move off the page of the composition entirely, is replaced by the circle of the second panel and the larger circular composition of panels amid the bottom three tiers, an anticipation of the circular movement of Herriman's protagonists on every page he drew. Amid these visual acrobatics, however, comes the unaccustomed grounding of the line of trees repeated in both the top and bottom tiers, establishing a reference point from which to measure precisely the ways in which Herriman unmoors figure and ground in these involutions. Indeed, it may well be the insouciant humor with which Herriman treats the temporal paradoxes of modernist novelty—the bottle of ether his animal consciousnesses repeatedly open—that best explains modernists' affinity for *Krazy Kat* and how that Kat itself is thoroughly modern.[27]

All of the comics reproduced here draw our attention to repetition as both a structural necessity and a thematic lynchpin inherent in the medium of comics. In order to convey motion, the passage of time, and a sense of narrative, comics artists must redraw serial images with only minor alterations, allowing the reader to make the mental leaps between these concatenated differences.

Comics theorists following McCloud have termed this process closure, positing an implied or explicit seriality as the very engine of meaning in the comics medium. Much like the falling calendar pages of early film informed early audiences of the passage of time, Herriman's numbering of panels in this last example offers explicit instructions for his readers about comics conventions at the same moment he is experimenting with, and often flouting, those very expectations.[28] Ignatz and Krazy's perpetual dance in search of one another—Ignatz's final pursuit of Krazy in the bottom right-hand corner of the third figure goes unnumbered, bleeding into the next twenty years of this ongoing chase—further cements the felt presence of seriality throughout. Much of the pleasure of reading *Krazy Kat* occurs both with the repetition and alteration of set narrative and aesthetic formulas and with the constitutive repetition of comics' structure as a medium; Herriman makes those repetitions themselves the subject of his life's work. When viewed against some of the most salient modernist preoccupations, *Krazy Kat* would seem to participate fully in our renewed sense of the interpenetration of popular culture and modernist production while laughingly giving the lie to modernist claims of radical, wholly authentic newness: Herriman demonstrates how the modernist desire for a radical and complete break from the past is a perpetually frustrated desire. *Krazy Kat* thus offers us an entry point into thinking critically about *comics modernism* and how a mutual regard of the histories of comics and of modernism are imbricated into a third narrative that incorporates them both, reconfiguring our expectations of all three.

Notes

1. For a thoughtful treatment of McCay with regard to my concerns with artistic and literary modernism, see Katherine Roeder, *Wide Awake in Slumberland: Fantasy, Mass Culture, and Modernism in the Art of Winsor McCay* (Jackson: University Press of Mississippi, 2014).

2. Remarkably, the characters Dirks created for *The Katzenjammer Kids* lived their parallel lives in competing strips for well over six decades. Perhaps the greatest study in uncanny repetition, *The Katzenjammer Kids* itself ranks as the longest continuously running comic strip, where the exploits of Hans and Fritz could be read up until 2006 in the work of Hy Eisman. As a parallel study, see also Art Spiegelman's reprinting of early twentieth-century newspaper comics as a means to contend with the trauma of 9/11 in his *In the Shadow of No Towers* (New York: Pantheon, 2004).

3. See Kevin Cooley, "Picasso, Comics, and Cultural Divides: Why *Krazy Kat* Is a Kubist Kat," *Modernism/modernity* 26, no. 3 (2019): 600.

4. See Paul Peppis, "Popular Modernism in the Late *Krazy Kat* Comics: Industry and Innovation in the Color Sundays," *Journal of Modern Periodical Studies* 9, no. 2 (2019): 158. Herriman went so far as to acknowledge and playfully dismiss this regard in his October 1, 1922, Sunday strip—describing Ignatz "as a mouse of no mean intellectualism as sir Gilbert Seldes the sage of 'The Dial' would say"—in what might be regarded as one of his few direct

comments on the critical reception of his comics. See George Herriman, *Krazy and Ignatz: 1922–1924*, ed. Bill Blackbeard (Seattle: Fantagraphics Books, 2012), 81.

5. Herriman, with many of the leading comics artists of his generation, circled around the creative center of John and Louisa Wetherill in Kayenta, Arizona. For the fullest picture of the American Southwest's impact upon Herriman's life and art, see Michael Tisserand's field-shifting biography of Herriman, *Krazy: George Herriman, a Life in Black and White* (New York: Harper, 2016), especially 312ff.

6. See Gertrude Stein, *The Autobiography of Alice B. Toklas* (New York: Vintage, 1990), 23. Indeed, some of the first stand-alone *Krazy Kat* strips were published vertically in direct response to the modernist provocation of the 1913 Armory Show, where Krazy and Ignatz parody—along with a number of other cartoonists—the exhibition's most celebrated and derided painting, Marcel Duchamp's *Nude Descending a Staircase (No. 2)*. See Tisserand, *Krazy*, 237ff. and Ben Novotny Owen, "A Touch of Irony and Pity: *Krazy Kat* in the Breaks," in *Comics Studies Here and Now*, ed. Frederick Luis Aldama (New York: Routledge, 2018), 9–30. For a catalogue of comics artists' varying responses to the Armory Show, see Sarah Burns, "Cubist Comedy and Futurist Follies: The Visual Culture of the Armory Show," in *The Armory Show at 100: Modernism and Revolution*, ed. Marilyn Satin Kushner, Kimberly Orcutt, and Casey Nelson Blake (London: Giles, 2013), 345–59. See also Katherine Roeder's essay in this volume, "Modernism for the Masses: The Armory Show in Comics."

7. Barbara Haskell, *Lyonel Feininger: At the Edge of the World* (New Haven, CT: Yale University Press, 2011); Lynd Ward, *Six Novels in Woodcuts*, ed. Art Spiegelman (New York: Library of America, 2010). For an analysis of Lynd Ward in these terms, see David M. Ball, "Lynd Ward's Modernist 'Novels in Woodcuts': Graphic Narratives Lost Between Art History and Literature," *Journal of Modern Literature* 39, no. 2 (Winter 2016): 126–43.

8. Comics scholars are now undertaking this long-neglected project of considering comics in the broader trajectory of aesthetic modernism. In addition to the essays in this collection and other works cited here, see M. Thomas Inge, *Comics as Culture* (Jackson: University Press of Mississippi, 1990); Jared Gardner, *Projections: Comics and the History of Twenty-First-Century Storytelling* (Stanford, CA: Stanford University Press, 2012); and Scott Bukatman, *The Poetics of Slumberland: Animated Spirits and the Animated Spirit* (Berkeley: University of California Press, 2012). A special cluster on comics and modernism edited by Jackson Ayers can be found in the winter 2016 issue of *Journal of Modern Literature*, and penetrating analyses of comics and popular modernism can be found in Daniel Worden, "The Politics of Comics: Popular Modernism, Abstraction, and Experimentation," *Literature Compass* 12, no. 2 (2015): 59–71.

9. For a more detailed examination of American modernism in these terms, see David M. Ball, *False Starts: The Rhetoric of Failure and the Making of American Modernism* (Evanston, IL: Northwestern University Press, 2015). Glenn Willmott, in his essay "Cat People," compellingly claims that "of all animal icons, the felinomorphic trickster seems uniquely invented to express the tremendous desire simultaneously with the fear associated with the plasticity to which these modernist imaginations responded in their search for new structures of feeling for social kinship." *Modernism/modernity* 17, no. 4 (2010): 854. See also Willmott, *Modern Animalism: Habitats of Scarcity and Wealth in Comics and Literature* (Toronto, ON: University of Toronto Press, 2012).

10. Doing so ratifies the now well-established links between high modernist productions and popular culture first established in the "New Modernist" studies of more than two decades ago in exemplary works such as Michael North, *Reading 1922: A Return to the Scene of the Modern*

(New York: Oxford University Press, 1999), and Lawrence Rainey, *Institutions of Modernism: Literary Elites and Public Culture* (New Haven, CT: Yale University Press, 1999). Given these longstanding connections in modernist scholarship more broadly, the focus of a volume like this on comics and modernism can only be said to be long overdue.

11. The title of *The Family Upstairs* fluctuated during its run, often appearing as *The Dingbats*. For the most thoroughgoing description of the outgrowth of *Krazy* Kat from earlier strips, see Tisserand, *Krazy*, 216ff.

12. We might see a first glimpse of *Krazy Kat*'s relentless self-reflexivity here—the quality most universally recognized by critics as its modernist signature—as the "family upstairs" literally dwells above these new creations.

13. See Umberto Eco, "The Myth of Superman," *Diacritics* 2, no. 1 (1972): 17.

14. José Alaniz, "Animals in Graphic Narrative," in *The Oxford Handbook of Comic Studies*, ed. Frederick Luis Aldama (Oxford: Oxford University Press, 2020), 327.

15. Friedrich Nietzsche, "On the Uses and Disadvantages of History for Life," in *Untimely Meditations*, ed. Daniel Breazeale, trans. R. J. Hollingdale (Cambridge: Cambridge University Press, 1997), 60–61.

16. Margot Norris, *Beasts of the Imagination: Darwin, Nietzsche, Kafka, Ernst, and Lawrence* (Baltimore: Johns Hopkins University Press, 1985), 1.

17. Norris, *Beasts of the Imagination*, 73.

18. Paul de Man, "Literary History and Literary Modernity," in *Blindness and Insight: Essays in the Rhetoric of Contemporary Criticism* (Minneapolis: University of Minnesota Press, 1983), 147.

19. de Man, "Literary History," 150.

20. Michael North, *Novelty: A History of the New* (Chicago: University of Chicago Press, 2014), 5, 161–62.

21. Indeed, there is only a single extended storyline in the over thirty years of *Krazy Kat*'s daily run—the story of Krazy discovering the psychedelic powers of "tiger tea" in trying to save a cousin's struggling catnip business—collected in Craig Yoe, ed., *George Herriman's Krazy + Ignatz in "Tiger Tea,"* introd. Paul Krassner (Santa Ana, CA: IDW, 2010).

22. Herriman, *Krazy and Ignatz: 1922–1924*, 142.

23. Owen, "A Touch of Irony and Pity," 19.

24. Herriman, *Krazy and Ignatz: 1922–1924*, 41.

25. Herriman, it should be said, seems less interested in the notion of revolution in the political or anticapitalist terms posited by William Solomon in his formulation of the notion of slapstick modernism, "in which a series of willfully undisciplined acts of cultural improvisation defied the priorities governing large-scale capitalist manufacture." "Slapstick Modernism: Charley Bowers and Industrial Modernity," *Modernist Cultures* 2, no. 2 (2006): 171. Herriman had no compunctions about putting Ignatz and Krazy on everything from tin toys to the Broadway stage, and buying and selling are present everywhere in his comics.

26. Scott McCloud, *Understanding Comics: The Invisible Art* (1993; repr., New York: Harper Perennial, 1994), 103.

27. The revelation that Herriman passed as white for all of his adult life, limned most powerfully and persuasively in Michael Tisserand's encyclopedic biography of the cartoonist, has provided a resonant grounding for the themes of forgetting and erasure that appear throughout *Krazy Kat*'s more than thirty-year run. "Herriman's comic representations of race—but also of gender—as quintessentially modernist engagements with questions of identity," Daniel Stein

writes, "suggest a shift from an essentialist conception of racial, sexual, and social belonging to a modern understanding of identity as something contextual and performative." "The Comic Modernism of George Herriman," in *Crossing Boundaries in Graphic Narrative: Essays on Forms, Series and Genres*, ed. Jake Jakaitis and James F. Wurtz (New York: McFarland, 2012), 46. This could be said to be the now-dominant reading of *Krazy Kat*, for very good historical reasons. Among the compelling analyses of the comics' figurations of race and color not otherwise cited here, see Jeet Heer, "Krazy Kat's Colors: The Shadings of George Herriman's Black-and-White World," *Lingua Franca* 11, no. 6 (September 2001): 53–58; Eyal Amiran, "George Herriman's Black Sentence: The Legibility of Race in *Krazy Kat*," *Mosaic: An Interdisciplinary Critical Journal* 33, no. 3 (September 2000): 57–79; and Jean Lee Cole, "The Black Comic Sensibility," in *How the Other Half Laughs* (Jackson: University Press of Mississippi, 2020), 119–48. Jan Baetens examines color as both a formal quality and a marker of identity in "From Black & White to Color and Back: What Does It Mean (not) to Use Color?" *College Literature* 38, no. 3 (Summer 2011): 111–28. To these compelling accounts of Herriman's distinctly modern treatment of identity, I would add that his fascination with genealogy and kinship also remains a fascination with time as much as ancestry. "The thematic elements of passing," Henry Louis Gates Jr. reminds us, "fragmentation, alienation, liminality, self-fashioning—echo the great themes of modernism." See "White Like Me: Anatole Broyard, *The New Yorker*," in *The Henry Louis Gates, Jr. Reader*, ed. Abby Wolf (New York: Basic Civitas Books, 2012), 348.

28. While William Randolph Hearst was enough of an enthusiast of *Krazy Kat* to give Herriman the artistic freedom of his enduring support, the editors of Hearst's regional papers often refused to include *Krazy Kat*, one famously calling it "this weird stuff nobody can understand." See Bill Blackbeard, "The Kat's Kreation," in Herriman, *Krazy and Ignatz: 1916–1918*, ed. R. J. Casey (Seattle: Fantagraphics Books, 2019), 10.

Section II
PRINT, EPHEMERA, CIRCULATION

FOUR REPULSIVE WOMEN

Marjorie Organ, Nell Brinkley, Kate Carew, Djuna Barnes

JEAN LEE COLE

The experimental fiction of Djuna Barnes seems radically removed from the world of comics art. Yet she engaged in both early in her career. Her early writings for the yellow press are frequently dismissed as the byproduct of an understandable if unseemly attraction for mass culture; Barnes, after all, was just a teenager at the time and had recently moved to New York City. Others rationalize her early output as hack work done simply to ingratiate herself in New York's social intellectual scene and to pay the bills; Barnes's biographer Phillip Herring writes that these works simply "gave readers what they wanted."[1] The fact remains, however, that Barnes was not the only modern woman with artistic aspirations to plunge into the murky world of newsprint, and the idea that she "gave readers what they wanted" indicates her ability to characterize modern subjectivities in these forms as much as in her experimental fiction.[2]

For a writer known for using obscure diction and complex syntax, Barnes's engagement with the early twentieth-century cultural scene was surprisingly sensual and embodied. Her best-known piece of journalism, "How It Feels to be Forcibly Fed" (1914), was accompanied by a series of lurid photos of the young Barnes subjecting herself willingly to force-feeding, the painful, dehumanizing treatment suffered by recalcitrant suffragettes when they embarked on hunger strikes in prison. In the early 1910s, she interviewed dancers, actors, and celebrities in backstage dressing rooms or at home en déshabillé. And her depictions of these activities remained grounded in the language and rhythms of contemporary, popular speech, directed at the general masses of newspaper and magazine readers.

Editors and scholars of Barnes have taken pains to defend the "literary worth" of Barnes's popular journalism and to show its importance in her development as a capital-M modernist.³ Yet as discordant as these activities might be with the rest of Barnes's career, in and of themselves they were not unusual. Her work very clearly follows in the footsteps of other enterprising women artists who emerged during the first decade of the twentieth century.⁴ Here, I situate Barnes alongside three of these artists. Marjorie Organ was almost certainly the first female staff comic-strip artist at William Randolph Hearst's *New York Journal* in the first decade of the twentieth century, while Kate Carew drew comic strips and caricatures for the *New York World* and the *New-York Tribune* beginning in 1900 and became widely known as a celebrity interviewer in the subsequent decades. Nell Brinkley, meanwhile, entered the scene in 1907, and her thoroughly modern "Brinkley Girls," appearing almost daily in the pages of the Hearst syndicate newspapers nationwide, superseded Charles Dana Gibson's "Gibson Girls" by the time Barnes was ten years old. The works of women artists like these lay the groundwork for Barnes's early work, including her single-panel newspaper comic "Types Seen in Odd Corners Round About Brooklyn" (July–September 1913), her illustrated celebrity interviews, and her first book publication, *The Book of Repulsive Women* (1915). In all of these women's works, grotesque transformations of bodies, especially female ones, seemed required by patriarchal modernity: women were expected to project themselves as hypersexualized objects of desire while simultaneously conforming to a sleek, affectless machine-age aesthetic. Taken collectively, we can see how these women indulged and resisted these expectations, alternately and simultaneously catering to the whims of their editors and audiences, engaging in satirical play, and expressing both anguish and delight.

OF PREDECESSORS: MARJORIE ORGAN

Marjorie Organ was born in 1886 in Ireland and immigrated to the US in her early teens. At the age of fourteen she apprenticed with cartoonist Dan McCarthy, whose complex full-page cartoons frequently graced the front page of the comics section of Joseph Pulitzer's *New York World*. She was hired at Hearst's *New York Journal*, working under editor Arthur Brisbane, before she turned twenty. Newspaper offices of the time were no place for "ladies," much less teenage girls,⁵ and though Organ was not the first woman artist to publish a comic strip, she was likely the first to become a staff artist and publish a continuing strip for a major newspaper.⁶ At the *Journal*, the artists occupied the eighth floor of the Rhinelander building, a former grain warehouse, in a space filled with smoke from cigars, pipes, and cigarettes. Molten lead, meanwhile, dripped through the cracks between the floorboards from the linotype department upstairs. Michael Tisserand describes the scene: "They worked in

> STRANGE WHAT A DIFFERENCE A MERE MAN MAKES.

Figure 5.1. Marjorie Organ, *Strange What Difference a Mere Man Makes*, Fort Wayne (IL) Sentinel, April 12, 1905.

a filthy room stuffed with desks and tables. . . . Panties hung in the windows instead of curtains. ('There is no fun in such things,' Brisbane had objected. 'No, the fun has been taken out of them,' replied cartoonist T. E. Powers.)"[7] Organ must have endured these conditions with great forbearance. Yet for nearly four years, she produced both daily and Sunday strips that appeared in the *Journal* and nationwide through the Hearst newspaper syndicate.

Organ's strips highlighted the anxious conventionality of modern men and women and the means by which patriarchy transformed women into grotesques. In the appropriately titled *The Wrangle Sisters*, she depicted the perfectly coiffed, stylishly dressed sisters Jess and Bess exchanging petty insults and engaging in other undignified behavior as they competed for male attention. Elsewhere, Organ's exaggeration of bosom and bustle exemplified the distortions wrought by modernity on female behavior. In strips such as *Strange What a Difference a Mere Man Makes* (1905) and *The Man Haters' Club* (1907), she repeatedly depicted groups of women who contort themselves en masse in their desperation to attract the approval of "mere men." The women's unified group posture, learned, one assumes, from the pages of mass-market magazines and from advertisements, grotesquely exaggerates female physiological markers—breasts, buttocks, and lips—that ostensibly would attract the male target. In one installment of *Strange What a Difference a Mere Man Makes*, students at the Elite Ladies Seminary "object most strenuously" to receiving a vaccine when it is offered by a bespectacled, middle-aged female physician; "vaccination was barbarous and unhygienic," the caption reads, "and . . . they would never, NEVER submit to it" (figure 5.1). But when a square-shouldered young doctor is sent to try again, they are perfectly willing to accept "that their prejudices were absurd," clamoring, in fact, to bare their shapely arms to the prick of the needle. In this strip, Organ effectively employs composition and contrast to show the behaviors and attitudes cultivated by these "pupils" of Elite Ladyhood: moral indignation, fainting acquiescence to patriarchal authority, and the mentality of the herd. While many of Organ's drawings mimic the effervescent and unapologetic femininity of contemporary advertisements and women's pages, their appearance on the comics pages resituates them as satire and critique.

Within a few years, Organ left the chaos of the Rhinelander offices; she took up painting under the instruction of Robert Henri, leader of the so-called Ashcan School painters, and she married him in 1910. A talented painter in her own right, she exhibited at the 1913 Armory Show, but she eventually became better known as Henri's model.[8] In paintings such as *Lady in Black with Scarf* (1910), with her striking red hair and strawberries-and-cream complexion, she appeared glamorous and desirable, both a model of modern womanhood and tightly controlled by the male gaze. As a model, usually clothed but sometimes not, she is subsumed in what art historian Griselda Pollack describes as the sites of sexual exchange "across which men artists claim their modernity and compete for leadership of the avant-garde": cafés, brothels, and artists' studios.[9] This image belies the more even partnership that actually existed between Organ and her much older husband. Henri, who championed "progress, freedom, experiment," and individuality in his teaching, encouraged her along with other women artists throughout his career; he included numerous women artists, for example, in the antiestablishment Exhibition of Independent Artists he organized in New York in 1910, and he exhibited alongside Organ throughout their marriage.

MODELS: NELL BRINKLEY AND KATE CAREW

At about the same time Organ ended her career as a comics artist, Hearst and Brisbane discovered Nell Brinkley's work in the *Denver Post* and convinced her parents to allow her to move to New York City to take a job as an illustrator. Just twenty-one years old, Brinkley initially lived in a convent and met with *Journal* editors under the watchful eyes of resident nuns. But she quickly escaped the convent walls. Her art debuted on the comics page in late November 1907 but almost immediately shifted to the women's page, then—ostensibly due to positive responses from readers—to a prominent place on page two.[10] A few weeks later, she got her big break: she was sent to court to sketch the scandalous "Trial of the Century," where Harry K. Thaw was accused and convicted of murdering renowned architect Stanford White after Thaw's wife, Evelyn Nesbit,

Figure 5.2. Nell Brinkley, drawing of Evelyn Nesbit Thaw, *New York Journal*, January 8, 1908.

revealed that she had been raped by White prior to their marriage. Nesbit had modeled for Gibson and became one of the living prototypes of the Gibson Girl—featuring demure, long lashes; a rosebud mouth; upswept hairdo; and a trim, modest shirtwaist. Brinkley's drawings emphasize these characteristics but take Nesbit's hair up a few notches, making it her dominant feature and providing a visual correlate to the twists and turns of the testimony (figure 5.2). Contributing to the scopophilic pleasures of the celebrity trial—the beautiful teenaged victim; the wealthy, imposing, middle-aged architect/rapist; and the even wealthier young husband seeking revenge—Brinkley's illustrations rocketed her to fame. Her daily syndicated comic/column appeared for years afterward in newspapers nationwide.

Brinkley's full-page, full-color Sunday newspaper illustrations have received the bulk of what little attention she has received from present-day collectors and scholars.[11] But it is really her daily newspaper work—which I am calling a comic strip, for reasons I will explain below—that is most culturally significant and a model for Barnes. Brinkley was almost inconceivably prolific, and her visual style soon became ubiquitous. The "Brinkley Girl" was featured in the Ziegfield Follies in 1908 and 1909[12] and in newspaper advertisements from Spokane, Washington, to Fort Wayne, Indiana. This image was defined, developed, and perpetuated in Brinkley's daily syndicated comic/column, which featured a large panel illustration (frequently a single image, but sometimes broken up into multiple panels or images) accompanied by several column inches of text. The text could take the form of a short, often surreal narrative, a stanza or two of verse, first-person commentary, or a combination of these forms. They are clearly an adaptation of the text comic form, one of many popular subgenres of the early newspaper comic strip, which paired drawn panels with rhymed verse or prose captions and was also used by Marjorie Organ, above, as well as many other comics artists of the time.[13]

The comics revolved around the courtship and marital dramas of "Bettys" and "Billys," drawn in different situations and grappling with common dilemmas: How to choose a wife? Is marriage a failure? Do dreams come true? When do you know you're in love? At first glance, Brinkley's Bettys, like Marjorie Organ's crowds of women, seem equally undifferentiated, flocking around any eligible bachelor in the vicinity and collapsing in sighs. The accompanying text, however, frequently reveals Brinkley's satirical intent. In a strip appearing in December 1908, for example, she takes as her text the well-known nursery rhyme:

> Monday's child is fair of face,
> Tuesday's child is full of grace,
> Wednesday's child is loving and giving,
> Thursday's child must work for a living,
> Friday's child has far to go,
> Saturday's child is full of woe,
> The child that is born on the Sabbath day
> Is blythe and bonny and good and gay.

And she accompanies the verse with drawings of their respective "Bettys" (figure 5.3). But then she writes:

> It would be bullee [sic], you Billys, if you could get the Bettys doped out by that. If the old rhyme that mothers tell you when you were very little about really and truly fairies that make folks what they are on the day

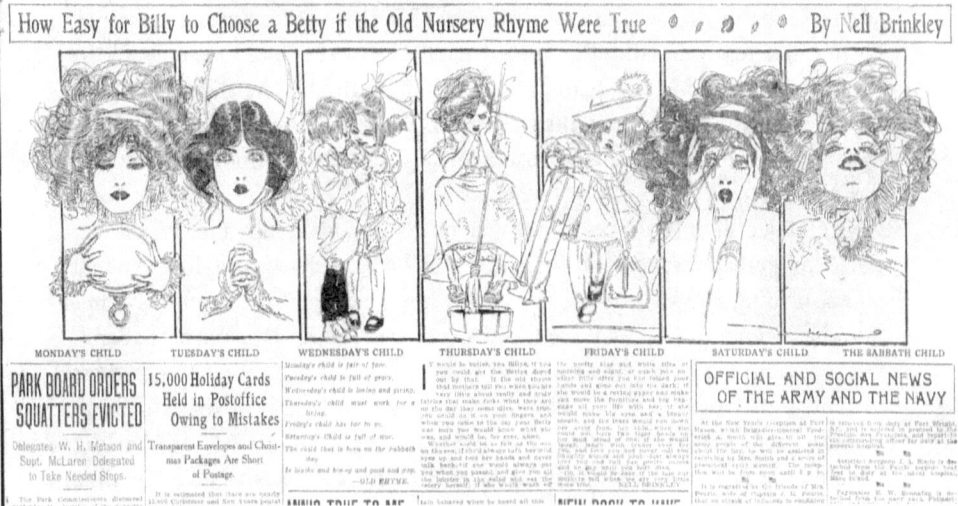

Figure 5.3. Nell Brinkley, *How Easy for a Billy to Choose a Betty if the Old Nursery Rhyme Were True*, San Francisco *Examiner*, December 31, 1908.

they come alive, were true, you could do it on your fingers, and when you came to the day your Betty was born you would know what she was, and would be, for ever, amen.

Whether she'd be as fair as the sun on the sea; if she'd always turn her mild eyes up and fold her hands and never talk back; if she would always pat you when you passed and give you all the lobster in the salad and eat the celery herself; . . . if she would laugh, laugh with tender eyes for you, and love you and never call you naughty names and pout—just always love you and call you pretty names and be gay until you both died.

Oh, it would be easy if the tale our mothers tell when we are very little were true.[14]

Elsewhere, she displays the wide-ranging ambitions and desires that animate more "Up-to-Date" Bettys, showing women in college, on the job, and engaging in athletic pursuits.[15] Heather Brooke Adams argues that unlike Gibson, Howard Chandler Christie, and other better-remembered creators of the female image, Brinkley depicted modern womanhood in all its varied forms, from debutante to shopgirl, from harried young mother to portly matron. She also showed women engaging with other women—an early example of art that passes, even while it predates, the Bechdel test.[16]

Perhaps through her savvy negotiation of the contemporary scene, perhaps simply through chance, Brinkley became a celebrity herself. Adopting a convention of the day, Brinkley depicted herself in her illustrations, pen in hand

and fashionably dressed, and photographs of her also appeared in magazines. During the year following the Thaw trial, the "Brinkley look" became all the rage; the Brinkley coat, the Brinkley hat, even the Brinkley "waist" and petticoat were featured in advertisements from clothiers and department stores across the nation. Some of these advertisements claimed that Brinkley herself had designed them.

Brinkley, unlike Gibson, was forgotten by cultural historians after World War II.[17] Why? Perhaps, writes Paul Gravett, it was "because she was too independent and disturbing a sex symbol for the stay-at-home Fifties."[18] The simple assumption that women could not be reduced to a single type, and the more challenging assertion that all women could be independent actors in society regardless of type, may have been so threatening to male historians of the American cultural scene that Brinkley was doomed to historical obscurity. Nevertheless, it would have been impossible for the young Djuna Barnes, sixteen at the time of the Thaw trial, not to be aware of Brinkley in some fashion. And it is more than likely, given the widespread syndication of her daily comics, that Brinkley was a significant influence on Barnes's early work for the periodical press.

Kate Carew (1869–1961) provided another model for Barnes. Born Mary Williams in Oakland, California, she was a student at the San Francisco School of Design when her work came under the notice of Ambrose Bierce. Bierce got her a place at the *San Francisco Examiner* in 1889, and in 1900, she relocated to New York City, "with a single eye to serious work—art with a capital 'A.'"[19] Instead, she published her first caricature in the *New York World*, under a pseudonym she claimed to have chosen "at random": Kate Carew.[20] This was the start of a long and prolific career as a caricaturist, comic-strip artist, and celebrity interviewer on both sides of the Atlantic.

Carew interviewed figures including Mark Twain, William Butler Yeats, and Sarah Bernhardt in a droll, self-deprecatory style. She also developed a visual brand in her interview features that included caricatures of herself as an old-maidish "Aunt Kate," with huge owlish glasses; an enormous, wide-brimmed hat with a question-mark-shaped ostrich feather perched on top; and a large portfolio, in which she ostensibly took down copious notes and visual impressions that she transformed into her full-page feature interviews (see Carew's self-caricature in figure 5.4).

In these interviews, her negotiations with her subject are as much the attraction as the prospect of learning private details about public figures. In one example, she pitched her own witty volubility against that of actor and playwright Charles Rann Kennedy (figure 5.4). Going in, she is determined to discuss socialism with Kennedy and plans "to begin with the Old Testament patriarchal system, [then] steeplechase through the early and middle ages down to our troublous times, where coal and wood, butter and eggs, spring

Figure 5.4. Kate Carew, "C. Rann Kennedy Interviewed Himself Enthusiastically While Kate Carew Gasped," *New-York Tribune*, March 31, 1912, section 2:3.

lamb and green peas and strikes are of daily occurrence, the result of a heinous economic system which either should or should not be abolished." Instead of Carew controlling the discussion, however, Kennedy does; within minutes, "it began to rain words, sentences, phrases, paragraphs, books, libraries, British museums. Sometimes they spluttered, sometimes splashed, sometimes merely rippled." Beating a fast retreat, Carew wryly writes,

> Beside his Niagara of eloquence the thin, purling line of talk of the usual interview is as a tiny brook to a mighty river, bred in mountain fastnesses, fed by roaring streams, bursting all limitations of space and strength....
>
> There was not a moment granted me to tell what I knew about the system of Karl Marx, Fourier, John Stuart Mills [sic], Plato, H. G. Wells, Ricardo. Actually, I didn't even have a second to say that no man who designed such a lovely easy chair as did William Morris could be wrong in his political views.[21]

While Carew acquiesces to Kennedy in their war of words, she nevertheless prevails with her pen. The images appearing with her interview effectively skewer Kennedy, representing him in a series of poses, talking, talking, talking, while seated, while standing, while smoking, in silhouette. (The symmetrical arrangement of the poses in the shape of a crucifix enhance the irony, but it's not clear whether Carew or an editor at the *World* would have been responsible for that masterstroke of newspaper page design.) Meanwhile, the solitary figure of Carew remains seated, sketching; the question mark implied by the feather in her hat broadcasts her skepticism rather than awe of her subject. And the flourish of her signature in the center of the page, finally, marks her ownership: of the images, of the page, and of Kennedy himself.

Carew's drawings function as what Charles Hatfield, in *Alternative Comics*, calls synchronistic images, which convey the passage of time and narrative sequence.[22] And while the newspaper interview is obviously different in many ways from what we might think of as a comic, it shares many of its characteristics—in particular in the way it is read. As we see in this instance, the accompanying images are not simply illustrations, nor are they portraits of the interview subject. They participate interactively with the written text to produce the *story* of the interview, which in the case of Carew was produced serially, with a different subject from week to week but consistent in its narrative trajectory. One might even call it a repeating gag: Awkward Woman Reporter Faces Vaunted Celebrity—and Comes Out on Top.

Carew also produced a semiregular comic strip called *The Angel Child*, which was published in the *World*'s Sunday comics supplement at roughly the same time that Marjorie Organ was publishing her strips in the *Journal*. While Organ's strips focused on the absurd situations facing women in the marriage market, Carew's revealed the grotesque realities of modern family life. Her "Angel Child" is an oversized toddler who unwittingly upends the lives of the rest of her family, especially her mother, who is resigned to having to punish her with a spanking at the end of every strip—a distinct contrast with customarily sentimental depictions of maternal love.

Carew was already in her thirties when she became established as "the *World*'s caricaturist," and as her career flourished, she increasingly emphasized the incongruity between her age and experience, on the one hand, and the role of the wide-eyed innocent that she was expected to play as a female journalist. In the 1910s, following her divorce from husband Henry Kellett Chambers, she frequently referred to herself in distinctly desexualized terms, as "Aunt Kate" or even "your female relative." In interview after interview, her subjects expect her to be "a frivolous person who cared for useless things." But she then demonstrates in both image and text how their tendency to underestimate and diminish her enables her to "penetrate beneath the crust" of her almost-always male subject and reveal their foolishness, their arrogance, and at times, "something almost human about them."[23] She frequently depicts herself wedged in the corner or at the bottom of her illustrations, at a scale fully a quarter or a fifth of that used for her subject; but the headlines of her full-page pieces always led with her name, not that of her ostensible subject. Carew became known as "the *World*'s caricaturist" in both senses of the word: her interviews and comic strips, like the work of her colleague R. F. Outcault (creator of the Yellow Kid), were proprietary to the *World* but also became known worldwide. In 1911, she was lured away from the *World* to London, where her interviews appeared in publications including *Tattler*; her work also continued to be published stateside, under the masthead of the *New-York Tribune*.

ENTER DJUNA

Djuna Barnes was in her early twenties when she was brought on board the *Brooklyn Daily Eagle* in 1913. Like Brinkley, Carew, and other female journalists of the day, Barnes was hired as much for the fact that she was a woman as she was for her qualifications as either an artist or a journalist. Hiring an attractive young woman to engage in the world of rough-and-tumble yellow journalism created endless opportunities to tantalize readers with voyeuristic accounts of scenes otherwise barred from upstanding members of the female sex: actors' living rooms, yes, and also betting parlors, sporting events, court proceedings, and political rallies.

Barnes was not the *Brooklyn Daily Eagle*'s first woman reporter; not by a long shot. Laura C. Holloway had joined the staff of the *Eagle* in 1873, where she worked as a reporter and eventually edited the women's page for some years.[24] Barnes, in contrast, was featured on the "sporting" pages, where she covered local events such as football games and bicycle races. In "The Tingling, Tangling Tango as 'Tis Tripped at Coney Isle" (August 31, 1913),[25] she chronicled—as she would on several occasions during her early career—the tango craze as it took hold in New York City. The piece was accompanied by a series of drawings corresponding to vignettes presented in the text; the evocative way in which she depicted these scenes points to the style she developed in her fiction. After describing the scene, the dancers, and the dance itself, she turns to the "late arrivals," "who have done the vulgar end of Coney and have been done by Coney in the end." One couple, she writes,

> drop into chairs, and say something about "Oh, my, I'm fagged out!" Fumbling for matches follows. . . . The light flutters, and smoke issues from a mouth already drooping from fatigue. "I could blow pillows instead of rings," he murmurs, and she orders soup. She is almost too weary to take interest in the gowns on show, but not too weary to notice one or two of the most startling ones. The purple crepe with the red sash and the red-heeled slippers catches her eye; she is being soothed, without knowing it; fashion is reviving her spirits, and his too. He crosses his legs, leans back and watches the dancers. It is the logical end of a day that has been too full.

The piece documents the latest fad, but it is also an elegy to Coney Island itself. The weariness of the fun-seekers, "soothed" more than scandalized by the fiery sexuality of the dance, becomes symbolic of Coney Island's slow fading away as a center of dazzling spectacle. The accompanying drawings, clippings of which are held in the Djuna Barnes papers at the University of Maryland and viewable online, underscore the dreamy, impressionistic imagery of Barnes's textual vignette, while the strong blacks ground the images on the page.[26]

Barnes was especially fascinated by the tango, a dance that took both Europe and the United States by storm in the 1910s. An exotic, aggressive, probably exhilaratingly improper dance form, tango provided a distinct contrast to the sleek, coolly impenetrable forms of modern femininity exemplified in Barnes's *Nightwood* character Nora Vote. The "audaciously physical dimension" of the dance, as Kristina Köhler has described it, clearly appealed to the sexually adventurous Barnes. She stresses its fluid, mobile forms in several other works, including a drawing, *Tangoism*;[27] in one of her first short stories, "The Terrible Peacock" (*All Story Cavalier Weekly*, October 24, 1914), she described one such dancer as "light and sinuous as a wreath of green mist," "the very poetry of motion," whose "close-fitting, silken dress . . . undulated like troubled, weed-filled water as she moved."[28]

Barnes employed a similar drawing style throughout all her newspaper work, including her newspaper comic *Types Found in Odd Corners Round About Brooklyn*, a dozen or so installments of which appeared in the weekday

Figure 5.5. Djuna Barnes, "To-Morrow Assured," *Types Found in Odd Corners Round About Brooklyn, Brooklyn Daily Eagle*, August 26, 1913.

Figure 5.6. Djuna Barnes, "The Pay," *Types Found in Odd Corners Round About Brooklyn, Brooklyn Daily Eagle*, July 28, 1913.

edition in the latter half of 1913. Barnes scholars have given little note to this short-lived series and have never read them as comics. They appeared on the front page of the feature section (which was rather cheekily subtitled, alternately, "Pictures and Sporting" or "Pictures and Sermons"),[29] appearing in one of the bottom corners of the first page, underneath an image-dominated feature that frequently highlighted local goings-on in Brooklyn, "Current Events from the Viewpoint of the Cartoonists," and so on. The bottom corners of the page featured a variety of humorous image-based content, including single-panel newspaper comics and captioned photographs, indicating that the *Eagle*'s editor classified *Types* as being generically aligned with them.

Many of the strips convey a warmly humorous gaze. In "To-Morrow Assured" (August 26, 1913), a rather windblown-looking man is depicted with arms full of books and packages of bread—intimating that despite the buffets of fortune, he has all he really needs for sustenance (figure 5.5). But not all of Barnes's comics were amusing. "The Pay" (July 28, 1913; figure 5.6) depicts a raggedly dressed woman, her face downcast and obscured by an unkempt, dark mass of hair, with hand outstretched as if seeking alms. And some are humorous in a distinctly melancholic way. "The Joke in the Tragedy of the Other Man's Life" (September 1, 1913; figure 5.7) remains untold, but one is inclined to chuckle at these two down-and-outers laughing at another even less fortunate than they. Taken as a whole, the impression given by *Types* is that of a critical but loving observer of Brooklyn street life, instances of what Daniel Wickberg has described as "subjective humor," and what I have described elsewhere as the "comic sensibility," a shared sense of the wryly laughable incongruities of lived experience.[30] Their placement in this section of the *Eagle* and the generally comic tone of surrounding elements indicates that the *Daily*'s editorship, as well as the newspaper's readership, read *Types Found in Odd Corners* as a comic feature analogous to single-panel strips such as *The Far Side* and *Dennis the Menace*. While *Types* lacks the speech bubbles and dialogue that we identify with later examples of the single-panel strip, it shares a number of its characteristics. Both "To-Morrow Assured" and "The Pay" establish a setting that launches a narrative in the reader's mind. The man carrying bread and books, juxtaposed with the caption, defines a character with an optimistic outlook and an intellectual bent, sustained not just by bread but ideas, and working to assure the existence of both. The story behind "The Pay" is less clearly defined. The woman, who is presented as a "type" encountered in an "odd corner" of Brooklyn, is dressed in rags, but she also adopts the iconography of blind Justice: the hair obscuring her face could be read as a blindfold, and the position of her outstretched hand echoes that of Justice holding out her scale. Is the woman demanding justice in the form of alms? Or is she actually expecting "pay," as indicated by the caption? And if the latter, payment for what? Reparation for past injustices, or perhaps something more sordid—payment for an illicit sort of "services rendered"? Barnes leaves these questions unanswered, in a brilliant example of what might be called comic synchronism.

Barnes eventually found her métier during this early period as a celebrity interviewer and as a stunt girl reporter in the mold of Nellie Bly, subjecting herself to force feeding, as we have already seen, dangling from a building to be rescued by firemen, playing with a baby gorilla, and the like.[31] As Jean Marie Lutes writes, Barnes's work, like that of other female "stunt reporters," involved "turning herself into an object of her own commentary, stressing her personal performance, [and] narrating the process of her own objectification."[32]

The genre of the interview, as undertaken by Barnes, Kate Carew, and others, could be viewed as a form of stunt journalism, where the female interviewer subjects herself to the risk of social castigation and intellectual humiliation at the hands of a powerful subject (usually a man). Because the interviews

Figure 5.7. Djuna Barnes, "The Joke in the Tragedy of the Other Man's Life," *Brooklyn Daily Eagle*, September 1, 1913.

frequently took place in the homes of their subjects, the interview could also take on a sexually charged atmosphere, where the lone woman reporter enters the domestic space of a public and powerful figure and thus willingly puts herself in his hands, come what may. The verbal sparring and cajoling, the provocation and flattery exchanged between interviewer and subject, resembles nothing more than flirtation. The satisfaction in reading these interviews is in seeing the female interviewer emerge triumphant, notes (and portrait—or caricature) safely tucked away in her notebook.

In her own interview of Charles Rann Kennedy (figure 5.8), Barnes acknowledges her readers' expectations: "It is the usual and natural thing—the cornering of a man, the pelting with impertinent questions, of going away and telling the world that he raises his feet and rests them easily upon the fender of fame . . . to say that when he smiles he lays bare a white, quivering ultra-personality. . . . Printers' ink was made to run the rim of the halo and printers' lead was made to hold down Venus." But she immediately reveals that she is not intimidated in the least by her subject. She writes,

> He took to himself the stature of a man who should walk in No. 8 Romeos. Instead he succumbed to fate, which gave him the eyes of a dreamer, the hair of the caveman, the smile of a humorist and the hands and feet of a woman.
>
> Like some elastic cherub, gone old for want of better understanding, Kennedy's large face looks out at you from a haven of hair as the heron from the sedge of the marsh. I told him that I was thinking of him as "Cherub Kennedy" and he laughed a little.

The illustrations accompanying the interview provide a visual analogue to the modest view of Kennedy expressed by Barnes: the grotesque figure of the elastic "Cherub Kennedy," while perhaps not exactly resembling a heron in a marsh, nevertheless takes up quadruple the column inches as the image of Kennedy-as-Romeo that Kennedy believes he projects. Barnes continues, "Kennedy is human, even terribly human. Sometimes reaching for an epigram he picks a plum; sometimes reaching for a plum his wide, sweeping hands grow amazed at the emptiness. And yet Kennedy says things."[33] The majority of the interview is, indeed, Charles Rann Kennedy "saying things"—one self-satisfied pronouncement after another, with little if any comment from Barnes. She lets him hoist himself with his own petard, in effect, though she also grants that he is "a nice man," possibly "a genius . . . as well as charming."

As the interviewer and caricaturist for the *New York Press*, Barnes published an interview about once every other week between December 1913 and August 1914. During the rest of her career, she published dozens of interviews in the

Figure 5.8. Djuna Barnes, "Kennedy Explains Meaning of Tangoism," *New York Press*, March 29, 1914. The interview and the illustration captioned "Sometimes I Play Romeo" are reprinted in *Djuna Barnes: Interviews*, ed. Alyce Barry, 29–36.

Press, the *New York Morning Telegraph*, *New York Sun*, and *New-York Tribune* Sunday magazines, as well as in magazines such as *Theater Guild* and the *Dial*. She interviewed both international and local celebrities including Lillian Russell, Mother Jones, Flo Ziegfield, Billy Sunday, and Diamond Jim Brady.

The imagery in Barnes's journalism might be less conventional, her diction more startling, than Carew's; Barnes's editor Alyce Barry, for one, remarked upon "the fantastical statements and musings" in Barnes's interviews that, to her mind, "resound . . . strikingly off the air and, so often, off the soul as well."[34] But this retroactive view would have been inaccessible to Barnes's readers. A present-day reader engaging in a side-by-side comparison of the two writers might easily identify a fantastical strain in Barnes, or a cynical, languid affect on her part in contrast with the bright cleverness of Carew. A casual reader of the daily newspaper, however, would read these interviews generically. If anything, they likely would have interpreted Barnes as simply derivative of Carew, since Carew's work was widely known and had been for over a decade before Barnes entered the scene. Even Barnes's drawings, which strike the contemporary eye as highly unusual newspaper fare, were unlikely to have done more than raise an eyebrow during this period. Newspapers of the time were capacious and eclectic in both form and content, publishing fiction and poetry as well as "straight news," stock figures, children's games, sheet music, and sports scores. Photography was in the process of becoming the dominant visual medium in newspapers, but photoengraved line art was still frequently used on the news pages as well as in the comics section.

One might also compare Barnes's work to that of Brinkley, appearing half a decade before in the *New York Journal*. Like "The Tingling, Tangling Tango," Brinkley's single-panel comics were accompanied by evocative, sometimes surreal text. In *A Popular Sport in Every Age* (figure 5.9), Brinkley presents a rather horrifying image: a young couple throwing brickbats at a naked baby—a Cupid, perhaps?—hanging from a tree. The macabre image is confirmed by the accompanying text. "It's the gentle game of killing Love," Brinkley writes:

> Stop in the world's great black woods once and watch the pitiful fun. They lug the pink-kneed little elf with his sun-netted hair and his carnation mouth out into a little cleared space.
>
> Maybe he's but a month old with them—this love. Maybe he has blossomed in their garden twenty long years and made it a paradise with his singing and his pretty ways.
>
> High up to the side of a rough-barked old tree they hoist him and by the pretty iridescent butterfly wings they tack him. And the sport is on.
>
> Any old thing they can lay their hands on is fair. There are no rules in the game.

Figure 5.9. Nell Brinkley, *A Popular Sport in Every Age*, St. Louis Star and Times, May 7, 1910.

Daniela Caselli writes that even Barnes's earliest work is governed by a "still unacknowledged poetics of impropriety" that eventually "permeates all aspects of her work and her figure as a modernist author."[35] But this poetics of impropriety was not the purview of Barnes alone. The work of all the women I have treated here—Barnes, Carew, Brinkley, and Organ—are consistent with a mode I describe elsewhere as the "comic grotesque": the use of caricature, exaggeration, and depictions of the grotesque and even the repulsive to elicit sympathetic, common feeling.[36] It is a modern—and I would argue, *modernist*—form of the old Bakhtinian carnivalesque, where class, gender, and racial identities are reversed and masqueraded as a communal recognition of shared frustration or shared desire.[37] In a generic sense, here it also applies to these women's experiments with language, subject matter, and media forms as apparently divergent as newspaper journalism, illustration, comic strip, and novel, a cross-fertilization of popular forms that is a hallmark of vernacular modernism.

MODERN WOMANHOOD, REPULSIVELY DEFINED

The embarrassed acknowledgment of Barnes within the canon of modernism may, in fact, be attributable to her embrace of the grotesque, which was not only unseemly for a woman but also for critics and scholars invested in a high-art definition of modernism that is untainted by any hint of the popular.[38] Nowhere is this more apparent than in Barnes's first book publication, *The Book of Repulsive Women*.[39] "If one truly cared for Djuna Barnes, one would say very little indeed about *The Book of Repulsive Women*," writes biographer Herring, noting that it portrays lesbianism "in the most horribly negative terms imaginable" and "life in general as a dirty, mean trick."[40] Barnes herself disavowed this production later in her life, refusing to give permission for its republication and referring to it simply as "that book of repulsive women," uncapitalized and untitled.[41] Yet in many ways it constitutes Barnes's most direct expression of the comic grotesque, merging the forms of popular sentimental poetry and modern advertising style with the more discomfiting aspects of modern womanhood.

The book, published in Guido Bruno's "Chap Books" series, consists of eight poems, or "rhythms," followed by five black-and-white ink drawings. Meghan C. Fox notes that in its visual presentation, Bruno "insists on positioning Barnes's artistic output in terms of decadent aesthetics";[42] in another instance, he credited her drawing "The Spring, the Poet, the Flower" to "Djuna Barnes, the American Beardsley" and published it alongside a poem by Charles Baudelaire.[43] It's not clear if Barnes intended the *Book*'s drawings to illustrate the poems, or if she intended them to be published in separate sections, as they appeared.[44] To readers familiar with the conventional Sunday funnies page of panels separated by gutters with text bubbles, they might not seem much like comics at all, but as with the newspaper interviews we have examined, they function in analogous ways. Several of the poems correspond with individual drawings, and their simple "rhythms" echo the text comics drawn by Organ and Brinkley.[45] For example, the first drawing of a person walking a dog immediately calls to mind the opening lines of "From Third Avenue On": "And now she walks on out turned feet / beside the litter in the street" (1–2), and the second drawing shows a woman looking upward "beneath some hard / Capricious star," as described in "From Fifth Avenue Up" (1–2). Other drawings have less obvious parallels with the poems they accompany. For example, the fifth drawing of a stylized woman wearing a hoop skirt and showing her petticoat underneath appears to correspond to the poem "To a Cabaret Dancer," but the lighthearted tone of the drawing seems ill suited, unless in a highly ironic sense, to the poem's depiction of a woman who "came with laughter wide and calm" (5) to the world of the theater, finds "Life only passion wide / Twixt mouth and wine" (9–10), and eventually becomes a "songless soul" (41) who contemplates suicide and has sex for money.

The third drawing (figure 5.10) contains images corresponding to several of the poems. In the last quatrain of "Fifth Avenue Up," Barnes describes a woman "Naked—female—baby / In grimace. / With your belly bulging stately / Into

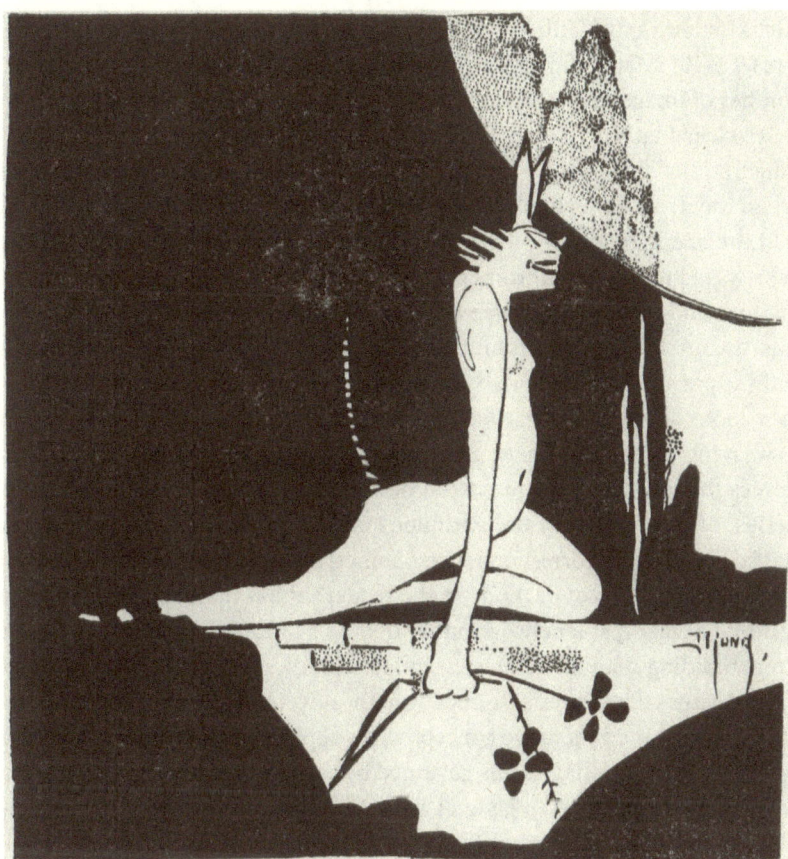

Figure 5.10. Third drawing from Djuna Barnes's *The Book of Repulsive Women* (New York: Bruno Chap Books, 1915). University of Maryland Libraries Digital Collections: https://hdl.handle.net/1903.1/8267ene

space," calling to mind the naked woman in the drawing, with belly thrust forward in profile. The last stanza of "From Third Avenue On" remarks that "those who have their blooms in jars / no longer stare into the stars," unlike the woman in the image, who tightly grasps a bunch of flowers in her hand and has the moon, or a planetary body of some sort, as a backdrop. In his edition of *The Book of Repulisve Women*, Douglas Messerli includes the drawing as a kind of frontispiece to the poem "Twilight of the Illicit," likely responding to the lines in the second stanza, which describe "your knees set far apart like / Heavy spheres; / With discs upon your eyes like / Husks of tears." The woman in the drawing certainly has her knees set far apart and appears to have her eyes closed, perhaps weeping. Likewise, the puzzling fourth drawing, featuring an odalisque across the top of the composition; a mustachioed Asianesque man with the tail of a carp on the left side of the page; and an amorphous, androgynous figure in the center, might be depicting the "lang'rous / Length of thighs" (stanza 3) of "Fifth Avenue Up," or the "spotted linen and your slack'ning arms. / With satiated fingers" of "Twilight of the Illicit" (stanza 1), or any of a number of images in "Seen from the 'L.'"

It's clear that the drawings are not intended to function as conventional "illustrations" but rather to represent visual correlatives to the "rhythms" of urban life depicted textually in the poems. As one reads, one is compelled to read the poetic rhythms against the drawings, animating both into a series of intertwined narratives of women in the modern city. Organized by repeating rhythms and echoes rather than a linear narrative or discrete thematic groupings, the images present a mulitfaceted, synchronistic, tragicomic impression of these purportedly repulsive women and their own self-revulsion. The book, then, looks toward T. S. Eliot's statement of the objective correlative in 1919. In its weaving together of image and text it also constitutes an example of what comics theorist Thierry Groensteen describes as *tressage* (braiding): a set or "series" of "continuous or discontinuous images linked by a system of iconic, plastic or semantic correspondences." Functioning in tandem and in tension with narrative, the connections in the reader's mind that take place through braiding function as a network rather than as a linear sequence.[46] For Groensteen, braiding is an affordance essential to comics as a genre and one of the characteristics that makes it distinct from the novel and other wholly text-based genres. It is also a generative concept when applied to works like *The Book of Repulsive Women*, which is less governed by a single narrative than by a group of narrative trajectories: a general aspiration upward (to stars, moon, fame, love) and gradual abasement (through processes of violation, confinement, self-abandonment, and suicide).

Fox writes that Barnes's *Book* "exposes the denigration of women's bodies and forms of expression that appears within Western philosophy and the literary canon . . . by inverting these representations, transvaluing dominant accounts of perversity, and endorsing forms of radical alterity."[47] Adopting the disguise of sentimental verse, Barnes depicts the dark side of modern female existence, ranging from the cabaret singer to the street walker to the suicide. The poems present an odd combination of clinical distance and tender sympathy. The contrast is most noticeable in the last of the eight poems, "Suicide." In the first stanza, "Corpse A" is evocatively described as

>   a shattered small
> Cocoon,
> With a little bruised body like
> A startled moon;
> And all the subtle symphonies of her
> A twilight rune.

Corpse B, in contrast, lays on the coroner's slab "like some small mug / Of beer gone flat." Despite the gruesomeness of the imagery, *The Book of Repulsive Women* conveys more than a whiff of the ridiculous. To describe the body of a suicide victim as a "small mug / Of beer gone flat"—and to have these lines be the end of the book itself—transgresses the boundaries of good taste, in the same way that the farcical highlighting of women's foibles in the marriage market or the domestic sphere, or the grotesque assertions of poverty on the comics page, transgressed the boundaries of acceptable female behavior. Barnes risks even more by asserting such an image as poetic.

The Book of Repulsive Women demonstrates that being a modern woman—a woman *in* modernity—was risky business. In the third poem, "Seen from the 'L,'" Barnes writes:

> Still her clothing is less risky
> Than her body in its prime.
> . . .
> Though her lips are vague as fancy
> In her youth—
> They bloom vivid and repulsive
> As the truth.
> Even vases in the making
> > Are uncouth.[48]

Barnes, Brinkley, Carew, and Organ, in transgressing the boundaries of both Victorian femininity and what was considered feminine print culture, adopted uncouth, even grotesque positions as poets, artists, and writers. The interplay of text and image, use of synchronistic images, and the form of the comic strip itself in their work was no less aesthetically risky than avant-garde painting or Dadaist manifesto. And they used those forms to express vivid and perhaps even repulsive truths about women's place and experience in modernity. As women, they subjected themselves to daily indignities and actual assaults on their womanhood—not to mention showers of molten lead and force-feeding. The grotesqueries of courtship, sex, and childbearing loomed persistent. Yet the indignities to which women were subjected were not simply to be borne but became the material for their art.

Notes

1. Phillip Herring, *Djuna: The Life and Work of Djuna Barnes* (New York: Viking, 1995), 77.

2. Through a process of writing, review, and revision that was interrupted, attenuated, and complicated by the COVID-19 pandemic, this essay became hopelessly intertwined with another, titled "Comic and Repulsive Women in the American Periodical Press, 1910–1915,"

appearing in a *Modernism/modernity* cluster titled "Modernism and Comics" (2024), edited by Matthew Levay. This essay includes discussion of the work of Nell Brinkley, who is absent from the *Modernism/modernity* essay, as well as additional discussion of works by the other artists. I would like to thank both Jonathan Najarian and Matthew Levay for their forbearance and creativity in working toward the viable publication of both essays, as well as the anonymous readers for *Modernism/modernity*, whose comments significantly strengthened this one as well.

3. Alyce Barry, "Foreword," *Djuna Barnes: Interviews*, ed. Alyce Barry (Washington, DC: Sun and Moon, 1985), 4; also see Douglas Messerli, "The Newspaper Tales of Djuna Barnes," in *Smoke and Other Early Stories*, ed. Douglas Messerli (Washington, DC: Sun and Moon, 1982), 7–19; and Daniela Caselli, *Improper Modernism: Djuna Barnes's Bewildering Corpus* (Farnham, Surrey: Ashgate, 2009), ch. 1.

4. This essay makes no attempt at a comprehensive survey of women comics artists from this period. Additional works to consult include Trina Robbins, *Pretty in Ink: North American Women Cartoonists 1896–2013* (Seattle: Fantagraphics Books, 2013); Martha H. Kennedy, *Drawn to Purpose: American Women Illustrators and Cartoonists* (Jackson: University Press of Mississippi, 2018); and Clémence Sfadj's essay in this volume.

5. According to historian Alice Fahs, newspapers that hired women as staff reporters segregated them into separate offices or only hired them for the "women's pages," supposedly to preserve "women's 'privacy.'" Fahs, *Out on Assignment: Newspaper Women and the Making of Modern Space* (Chapel Hill: University of North Carolina Press, 2011), 31–32. The vast majority of women who published work in the newspaper press before World War I did so as "space rate" contributors rather than as on-site staff reporters.

6. Rose O'Neill's strip *The Old Subscriber Calls* was published in the weekly humor magazine *Truth* on September 19, 1896. O'Neill produced a large number of single-panel cartoons and cover illustrations for the magazine through the early 1900s.

7. Michael Tisserand, *Krazy: George Herriman, a Life in Black and White* (New York: HarperCollins, 2016), 213–14.

8. For more on cartoonists' involvement in the Armory Show, see Katherine Roeder's essay in this volume.

9. Griselda Pollock, "Modernity and the Spaces of Femininity," in *Vision and Difference: Femininity, Feminism and the Histories of Art* (London: Routledge, 1988), 54.

10. Trina Robbins, *Nell Brinkley and the New Woman in the Early 20th Century* (Jefferson, NC: McFarland, 2001), 11.

11. Trina Robbins has led the charge to restore Brinkley to the annals of American cultural history, publishing a biography, *Nell Brinkley and the New Woman in the Early 20th Century* (Jefferson, NC: McFarland, 2001); including her in her survey of women comics artists *Pretty in Ink: North American Women Cartoonists, 1896–2013* (Seattle: Fantagraphics Books, 2013); and using her work as bookends to her survey of women comics artists of the 1920s and 1930s, *The Flapper Queens: Women Cartoonists of the Jazz Age* (Seattle: Fantagraphics Books, 2020). Despite Robbins's efforts, Brinkley's recuperation has been slow and remains incomplete.

12. Robbins, *Nell Brinkley and the New Woman*, 22, 39. Robbins includes a photographic reproduction of a line of Ziegfeld Follies chorus girls dressed as Brinkley in the Follies of 1908, with huge, flamboyant hats, plunging necklines, and fashionable walking sticks.

13. Robbins writes that Brinkley "strongly objected to 'making comics,'" but her work continued to appear on the comics page: the text comic "Love Will Find a Way" appeared in the

Washington Post on May 3, and the *Spokane (WA) Spokesman-Review* on May 10, 1908, and likely elsewhere, alongside other Hearst syndicated comic strips. Robbins, *The Flapper Queens*, 2.

14. Nell Brinkley, *How Easy for a Billy to Choose a Betty if the Old Nursery Rhyme Were True*, *San Francisco Examiner*, December 31, 1908, 9.

15. For example, see "The Up-to-Date Girl: The Strong-Bodied Betty of Wind and Sea," *San Francisco Examiner*, April 14, 1908, 7; and "The Up-to-Date Girl: The College Betty and the Business Betty," *San Francisco Examiner*, April 21, 1908, 6. Robbins suggests that Brinkley even parodied Gibson; Brinkley's 1914 drawing "Coming and Going" echoes Gibson's well-known 1900 illustration "Picturesque America," showing several young women in dark bathing costumes on a beach, but actively surfing instead of sitting demurely at water's edge. Robbins, *Nell Brinkley and the New Woman*, 38.

16. Heather Brooke Adams, "Visual Style and the Looking Subject: Nell Brinkley's Illustrations of Modern Womanhood," *Women's Studies in Communication* 37 (2014): 90–110. The so-called "Bechdel test" derives from Alison Bechdel's 1985 comic strip *Dykes to Watch Out For*, where a female character proposes restricting movie viewership to films that 1) "have at least two women" in them who 2) "*talk* to each other about" 3) "something besides a *man*" (emphasis original). The criteria have proved persistently difficult for the Hollywood film industry to meet.

17. Paul Gravett, review of *Nell Brinkley: A New Woman in the Early 20th Century*, by Trina Robbins, PaulGravett.com, posted March 25, 2007, http://www.paulgravett.com/articles/article/nell_brinkley/. Originally published in *Comics Journal*, 2002.

18. Gravett, review of *Nell Brinkley*.

19. Kate Carew (Mary Williams), "Confessions of an Interviewer," twainquotes.com, accessed July 23, 2021, http://www.twainquotes.com/interviews/confessions.html. Originally published in *Pearson's Magazine*, December 1904.

20. Carew, "Confessions of an Interviewer."

21. Kate Carew, "C. Rann Kennedy Interviewed Himself Enthusiastically While Kate Carew Gasped," *New-York Tribune*, March 31, 1912, 19.

22. Charles Hatfield, *Alternative Comics: An Emerging Literature* (Jackson: University Press of Mississippi, 2005), 52.

23. Carew, "Confessions of an Interviewer." Carew's self-deprecatory self-representation certainly was the inspiration for cartoonist Fay King, who frequently depicted herself as a rail-thin, wide-eyed naif with pad and pen at the ready and clumsy work boots beneath her shapeless, calf-length black dress. See examples in Robbins, *The Flapper Queens*, 104–13.

24. Diana Sasson, *Yearning for the New Age: Laura Holloway-Langford and Late Victorian Spirituality* (Bloomington: Indiana University Press, 2012), 63.

25. Reprinted under the title "The Tingling, Tangling Tango" in Djuna Barnes, *New York*, ed. Alyce Barry (Los Angeles: Sun and Moon, 1989).

26. Clipping of "The Tingling, Tangling Tango" is viewable at University of Maryland Libraries Digital Collections, https://hdl.handle.net/1903.1/14701.

27. Clipping of *Tangoism* (n.d.) is viewable at University of Maryland Libraries Digital Collections, https://hdl.handle.net/1903.1/9075. The publication from which the clipping was taken has not been identified.

28. Kristina Köhler, "Tango Mad and Affected by Cinematographitis: Rhythmic 'Contagions' Between Screens and Audiences in the 1910s," in *Performing New Media, 1890–1915*, ed. Kaveh Askari et al. (Bloomington, IL: John Libbey, 2014), 203; Barnes, "The Terrible Peacock," reprinted in Messerli, *Smoke and Other Early Stories*, 29, 25.

29. The *Brooklyn Daily Eagle* archive is available through the Brooklyn Public Library, bklynlibrary.org.

30. Daniel Wickberg, *The Senses of Humor: Self and Laughter in Modern America* (Ithaca, NY: Cornell University Press, 1998); Jean Lee Cole, *How the Other Half Laughs: The Comic Sensibility in American Culture, 1895–1920* (Jackson: University Press of Mississippi, 2021), 6–7.

31. Djuna Barnes, "My Adventures Being Rescued," *New York World Magazine*, November 15, 1914, and "The Girl and the Gorilla," *New York World Magazine*, October 1914.

32. Jean Marie Lutes, *Front Page Girls: Women Journalists in American Culture and Fiction, 1880–1930* (Ithaca, NY: Cornell University Press, 2006), 150. Alice Fahs writes that female stunt journalists beginning in the early 1890s "became performative public figures." *Out on Assignment*, 7.

33. Djuna Barnes, "Kennedy Explains the Meaning of Tangoism" (*New York Press*, March 29, 1914, 5:3, reprinted in Barry, *Djuna Barnes: Interviews*, 30–31.

34. Alyce Barry, "Editor's Preface," *Djuna Barnes: Interviews*, 10.

35. Daniela Caselli, *Improper Modernism*, 2.

36. Jean Lee Cole, *How the Other Half Laughs*, introduction and chapter 1.

37. James Goodwin writes that by transgressing "logical boundaries" the grotesque "functions as a method ultimately for disclosing a deep, shared structure among political, spiritual, and aesthetic domains." James Goodwin, *Modern American Grotesque: Literature and Photography* (Columbus: Ohio State University Press, 2009), 3.

38. Matthew Levay, introduction to "Comics and Modernism," in *Modernism/modernity* (2024).

39. A digital surrogate of the 1915 edition of *The Book of Repulsive Women* can be accessed through the University of Maryland's University Libraries Digital Collections: https://hdl.handle.net/1903.1/8267. All subsequent references are to this text unless noted.

40. Herring, *Djuna: The Life*, 88.

41. Melissa J. Hardie writes that it was a book that "Barnes specifically wished to repress within her writing career." Melissa J. Hardie, "Repulsive Modernism: Djuna Barnes' *The Book of Repulsive Women*," *Journal of Modern Literature* 29, no.1 (Autumn 2005): 120.

42. Meghan C. Fox, "'Vivid and Repulsive as the Truth': Hybridity and Sexual Difference in Djuna Barnes's *The Book of Repulsive Women*," *Space Between: Literature and Culture 1914–1945* 12 (2016).

43. "The Spring, the Poet, the Flower," *Bruno's Weekly*, July 22, 1916, 66.

44. Later editors, including Douglas Messerli, have rearranged the poems and drawings to appear together.

45. Modernist painters seemed drawn to the versified form of the text comic. William Glackens's short-lived comic strip *The Merry-Go-Rounders*, for example, paired Glackens's fantastic illustrations with rhymed doggerel by *Puck* editor Richard K. Munkittrick (1898); a decade later Walt Kuhn's strip *Whisk* (1909) used rhymed couplets of varying line lengths in several installments.

46. Thierry Groensteen, *The System of Comics*, trans. Bart Beaty and Nick Nguyen (Jackson: University Press of Mississippi, 2007). Originally published as *Système de la bande dessinée* (Paris: Presses Universitaires de France, 1999).

47. Fox, "'Vivid and Repulsive as the Truth.'"

48. Djuna Barnes, "Seen From the 'L,'" in *The Book of Modern Women* (New York: Bruno, 1915), 95.

JACKIE ORMES'S *TORCHY BROWN* IN *"DIXIE TO HARLEM"*

Modernism in the African American Funny Pages

CLÉMENCE SFADJ

In 1948, Langston Hughes wrote in the *Chicago Defender*: "If I were marooned on a desert island, . . . I would miss . . . Jackie Ormes's cute drawings."[1] One might wonder, as Henry Louis Gates Jr. does in his introduction to the *Encyclopedia of Black Comics*, how an artist praised by the Poet Laureate of Harlem could have slipped out of popular culture.[2] But on second thought, one might stumble on the qualifying adjective "cute"—and, moreover, on the very definition of comics in Hughes's praise. While Jackie Ormes favored attractive heroines with fashionable outfits and witty attitudes, "cute drawings" is out of tune with the sharp sociopolitical issues her comics tackle and the modernist themes she incorporates. Hughes's description of newspaper comics as "cute drawings" reveals a general attitude toward early newspaper comics that has historically excluded them from scholarly discourse on modernism; the comment also elides the disruptively suggestive political work that Ormes's comics achieve. This essay situates Ormes's comic strips, and in particular *Torchy Brown in "Dixie to Harlem,"* in the canon of modernist literature, revealing how her depiction of the daily struggles of single African American women adapting to city life complicates and expands our ever-growing map of modernism.

Comic strips and cartoons published in African American newspapers have been doubly concealed amid what Celia Marshik and Allison Pease have called the "palimpsest" of modernist literary history.[3] As works that fall outside of "the Eliot and Leavis models of the great tradition"—which is overwhelmingly white and male, and excludes ephemera and other forms of "low art" like comic strips—Black comics artists do not yet benefit from the same critical attention as their white counterparts. (Ormes, it's worth mentioning, is triply concealed:

by race, gender, and form.) Studying these works as pieces of modernist literature widens the scope of modernist studies and uncovers a complex episode of US comics history. This essay focuses on *Torchy Brown in "Dixie to Harlem"* (1937–1938), a comic strip by Ormes, the first syndicated African American woman cartoonist.[4] *"Dixie to Harlem"* follows the adventure of Torchy Brown, a young Black woman who moves from Mississippi to Harlem to pursue her dream of performing at the Cotton Club. Set in the rural South and then in Harlem during its Renaissance, *"Dixie to Harlem"* displays its heroine's intimate thoughts, her anxieties and ambitions, and the private spaces of her life. In issue after issue, Ormes weaves realism—when Torchy feels estrangement toward her family in Mississippi or when she faces financial difficulties—with dreamlike sequences in which the heroine fantasizes about new horizons.

A single woman living in the city with a roommate, working to support herself, and nurturing dreams of cabaret performances, Torchy is an example of the modern women whose lives Saidiya Hartman writes back into history in *Wayward Lives, Beautiful Experiments* (2019).[5] In a collection of fictional stories based on archival materials, Hartman recreates "the voices . . . of [African American] young women . . . [and] the intimate dimensions of their lives."[6] Her characters share many characteristics with Torchy Brown: most of them are young Black women who move from rural to urban settings, live in small apartments with roommates, and face unprecedented urban challenges. The completely new lives of these women generated what Hartman calls "a fierce and expanded sense of what might be possible" and "were part of a larger ensemble of intimate acts that were transforming social life and inaugurating the modern."[7] Hartman sketches fictional portraits of these women whose "sexuality, intimacy, affiliation, and kinship taking place in the black quarter of northern cities might be labeled *the revolution before Gatsby*."[8] In *"Dixie to Harlem,"* Ormes depicts this modern revolution as it's taking place in the 1930s, leaving a compelling visual and verbal portrait of the type of heroine *Wayward Lives* aims to recover. As recent scholarship like Hartman's has made clear, there is no complete understanding of modernity that does not take into account the perspective of African American women experiencing completely new living conditions in northern cities.

The stereotypically lowbrow status of newspaper comics partially explains their exclusion from literary canons. *"Dixie to Harlem"* ran in the *Pittsburgh Courier*, one of the most widely read African American newspapers of the twentieth century.[9] Compared to literary journals such as *Crisis* or *FIRE!!!*, newspapers were considered middle- or lowbrow, merely "popular." But African American newspapers were not disconnected from the Harlem Renaissance or modernism at large. Not only did authors like Hughes write columns in their pages, but these newspapers also shared the goal of the New Negro movement of promoting social advancement for the African American middle class.[10] As Ayanna Dozier explains in an article about one of Ormes's later comics series, the newspapers in which early African American cartoonists published their work also aimed to present models of respectability and widen the spectrum of representation for African American subjects in public media.[11] In the pages of the African American press, writers and cartoonists benefited from more representational freedom than their counterparts who collaborated with white publishers and patrons. Thirteen years after Ormes created *"Dixie to Harlem,"* Zora Neale Hurston published "What White Publishers Won't Print" (1950) in *Negro Digest*, expressing in the very first line her amazement at "the Anglo-Saxon's lack of curiosity about the internal lives and emotions of the Negroes."[12] The African American press, edited by African Americans for an African American readership, was fertile ground for the "incisive and intimate stories from the inside" that Hurston calls for.[13] The glimpses into the private life and dreams of Torchy Brown making up *"Dixie to Harlem"* offer a rich and nuanced example of such stories.

As Dozier points out, Ormes makes innovating use of the newspaper comic strip in *"Dixie to Harlem"* when she utilizes this medium to write a long-serialized story rather than disconnected gags without chronological continuity, a narrative approach that participates in the transformation of sequential art into long-form narratives in the early twentieth century.[14] Compared to most contemporaneous comic strips, the content of *"Dixie to Harlem"* stands out just as much as its form. In *Writing through Jane Crow: Race and Gender Politics in African American Literature* (2016), Ayesha K. Hardison identifies the representational issues at stake for African American women authors in the twentieth century, a context in which Black women faced the "double jeopardy" of racism and sexism and that Hardison terms "Jane Crow."[15] In an epilogue dedicated to Ormes, Hardison argues that throughout her entire career, the cartoonist challenged the conventions of both comics publication and literary expression by "visualizing black women's lives, activism, and art in spite of their Jane Crow oppression."[16] *"Dixie to Harlem"* disrupts the notion that newspaper comic strips were simply funnies targeting family audiences, disconnected from contemporary literary movements due to their lack of seriousness—or that they were merely "cute drawings." Using a comic-strip series to represent a Black woman's modern urban experience, and thus challenging what Hardison terms "Jane Crow oppression," Ormes hints at a counterhistory of US comics in which introspection and political content invest the form long before the appearance of the graphic novel. In this sense, incorporating *"Dixie to Harlem"* (and early African American newspaper comic strips in general) into our conversations about modernism also uncovers a forgotten layer of comics history.[17]

TORCHY BROWN'S EXPERIENCE OF MODERNITY

In *"Dixie to Harlem,"* Ormes depicts a heroine whose experience of modernity challenges racist and gendered stereotypes. The series eschews simplified readings and forces readers to attest to the complexity of its heroine. In *Black Women in Sequence: Re-inking Comics, Graphic Novels, and Anime* (2016), Deborah Elizabeth Whaley explains that *"Dixie to Harlem"* was published in "a society in which single, laboring, and freely moving women caused gender norm confusion, fear of their financial independence, and a variety of sexual suspicions (e.g., promiscuity, deviance, and lesbianism) among the population at large."[18] Torchy Brown falls into this category: She is a single Black woman living in the city with a roommate and working to support herself. She is an attractive performer with a flamboyant personality, but she is never depicted as immoral or unfit for society. Rather, she shares her struggles and anxieties in recurring moments of fragility. Torchy is a complex character who both aims to become a provocative figure (a cabaret performer) and tries her best to keep herself out of immoral and dangerous situations (a point we will linger on later). Refusing both extremes and fitting into no stereotype, Torchy exists as a kind of composite of Joanna Marshall and Maggie Ellersley from Jessie Fauset's *There Is Confusion* (1924) or, to borrow from a later author, a composite of Sadie and Maud from Gwendolyn Brooks's poem.[19]

From her rural origin and migration to New York City, to the formative experiences she has in an urban setting, Torchy's story arc is characteristically modern, even modernist. The move from rural town to big city is also an event Hartman chooses as a narrative starting point to retrace forgotten histories of middle-class African American modern women in *Wayward Lives*. Hartman outlines the historical importance of domestic migration as both an intimate impulse, or "the resolute, stubborn desire for an elsewhere and an otherwise that had yet to emerge clearly, a notion of the possible whose outlines were fuzzy and amorphous," and as a sociopolitical event, or "acts of flight [that would later] be recognized as a general strike against slavery in its new guises."[20] And, indeed, many narratives in Harlem Renaissance literature start from a rural-to-urban migration backstory, like Fauset's *There Is Confusion*, Hughes's *Not Without Laughter*, or Rudolph Fisher's "City of Refuge" to name a few.

In *"Dixie to Harlem,"* Torchy's southern origin and her relocation are more than a threshold into an urban tale. The series ran in the *Pittsburgh Courier* from May 1, 1937, until April 30, 1938, and Torchy's life in Mississippi on Aunt Clemmie and Uncle Jeff's farm spans almost half of the issues (from May 1, 1937, to September 4, 1937). When Torchy is still living on the family farm, Ormes juxtaposes fantasy episodes with almost naturalistic scenes of southern life. We see, for instance, in the issue from June 12, 1937, Torchy bargaining with

Figure 6.1. Jackie Ormes, *Torchy Brown in "Dixie to Harlem,"* first published July 17, 1937, *Pittsburgh Courier.*

farmers to sell animals in order to finance her migration to New York.[21] A few weeks later, in the July 24 strip, we see Torchy try on elaborate outfits to "look like a smart New Yorker," only to find out in the final panel that it was all "a nice dream" and that "next week comes the awakening."[22] Fantasizing about what Hartman calls an "amorphous" possible future, Torchy is animated by the "stubborn desire for an elsewhere and an otherwise" that soon turns into her dream of moving to New York City.[23] Taking advantage of the comic strip's short serialized format, Ormes recreates a longing for urban migration and a modernist feeling of unbelonging by juxtaposing episodes showing the technicalities of her rural life against other ones displaying her sophisticated urban fantasies.

Furthermore, Ormes uses modernist narrative techniques to represent her character's reveries, dedicating entire strips to Torchy's dreams, as we see for example in the issue from July 17, 1937 (figure 6.1). Unlike the shopping fantasy strip that ended with the revelation that it was all Torchy's dream, this episode begins with a dream; a box of text announces that the heroine has fallen asleep and "dreamed she had private passage on a sky rocket" to New York. Torchy explores the streets of New York in a state of wonder, first looking at crowds from the top of a building, then finding herself at street level, and eventually reversing her perspective and looking up at tall buildings from the sidewalk. The medium of comics allows Ormes to depict an urban experience that, from the perspective of this heroine from the rural South, is defamiliarizing and shocking to all her senses. She is not only surprised by the business of the crowds, as she exclaims in the second panel, or in awe at the fashionable outfits of "New Yawk gals," as she says in the fifth panel. She is also physically taken aback when cars zoom by her on the sidewalk. Speed lines allow Ormes to recreate Torchy's physical shock as she encounters modern technology. A simple question mark above her head encapsulates the modern, and modernist, defamiliarization the heroine experiences as she feels for the first time the speed of an automobile on a city street. In the final panel, Ormes uses the comics format to represent the overwhelming soundscape of the city, surrounding a hectic Torchy, who's holding her head and skipping on one leg in the middle of the frame, with speed lines and onomatopoeias of car honks and other clanking noises.

Ormes lets Torchy's dreamscape fill panels and even entire issues, letting her heroine wander from panel to panel in vivid fantasies that become reminiscent of modernist stream of consciousness writing. While the long story arc is linear from one issue to the next, Ormes doesn't stick to a unified narrative mode: rather, she creates, week after week, a mosaic weaving the heroine's dream sequences with realistic scenes of southern life in the first half of the series and, in the second half, of urban adaptation.

The comic strip achieves more than just telling the heroine's coming-of-age story, and more than offering readers amusing gags and pretty woman characters to look at. Thanks to Ormes's emphasis on Torchy's dreams and on her perspective, readers experience the heroine's fantasies, concerns, and dilemmas as her story progresses. The series is always faithful to comic-strip expectations to some extent, mostly in the way that the comic strip remains lighthearted even when it shows her moments of alienation or when she faces considerable obstacles. Torchy always displays charming wit, a quality that allows Ormes to include themes like segregation and prostitution while still aligning with newspaper comics expectations. In this series, incorporating Black modernism in the funnies is a balancing act that relies on Torchy's jovial nature and slapstick humor. Wrapped in traditional comic-strip humor and championed by a character whose quick wit and charisma readers recognize as typical of the funnies, sensitive sociopolitical topics make their way to the Sunday pages in Ormes's work.

In the strip published on September 4, 1937, for instance, Torchy's trip from Mississippi to New York shows her dealing with segregation in a Jim Crow train. Torchy refuses to segregate.[24] When she sees the train controller approach, Torchy quickly decides to pretend she can't read and starts joking with the white men in the car to avoid being removed by force. Ormes here invokes the anxiety and violence of racial segregation and then quietly deflects those political realities by couching them within the slapstick conventions of the humorous newspaper comic. The humor expected from this genre and its publication context becomes a device for foiling simplified—and simplifying—readings of Torchy's experience of modernity. Humor, then, serves a dual purpose: it allows Torchy to survive in the hostile Jim Crow world that surrounds her, and it allows Ormes to explore these issues within the framework of the serialized comic strip.

The comic strip remains fully realistic and serious while maintaining elements of comic-strip humor. In the strips from September 25 and October 9, 1937, Torchy sets foot in Grand Central Station, and an unknown woman picks

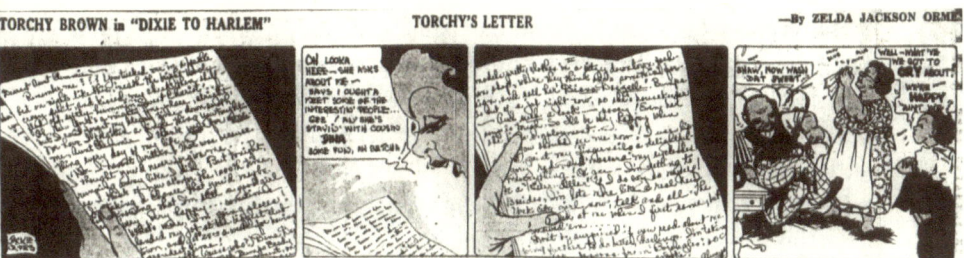

Figure 6.2. Jackie Ormes, *Torchy Brown in "Dixie to Harlem,"* first published February 5, 1938, *Pittsburgh Courier*.

her up upon arrival and invites the heroine to stay with her.[25] One issue later, Torchy overhears a phone conversation in which the same woman sells Torchy's services—which are implied to be sexual—to a client. Torchy immediately understands the trap she's about to fall into and swiftly escapes. This episode is representative of Ormes's effort to create a complex character who is neither destined to succumb to stereotypical promiscuity nor as comically gullible as typical characters from the funnies. And yet stock funnies humor constantly tempers the gravity of racial tension, which would otherwise risk making the strip too bleak for mainstream publication—and therefore unable to reach a wide audience. A similar tension holds Torchy in equilibrium: she is at once a funny comic-strip character in a fantasy world and a realistic portrait of a woman capable of adapting to modern challenges.

Most importantly, Ormes presents such events directly from Torchy's perspective, displaying her thoughts and how she processes the modern challenges she encounters. Once Torchy settles in New York, her alienation focuses on her relationship with her family in Mississippi. The strip published on February 5, 1938 (figure 6.2), includes a handwritten letter to her Aunt Clemmie and Uncle Jeff—an innovative formal experiment that takes readers aback and subverts their expectations for a comic strip. The letter gives readers a direct view into the heart and mind of Torchy, who, in the previous strip, had expressed fear and anxiety at the idea of reaching out to her family, aware of a divide between country and city, between South and North. Using the space of the comic-strip panel to insert a handwritten account of a character's deepest feelings is a bold move in 1938, an innovative use of sequential art that prefigures modern practices in the graphic novel (one can compare, for instance, Torchy's letter to Alison Bechdel's frequent use of epistolary documents in *Fun Home*). Reading Ormes's strip alongside the entire comics section of the *Pittsburgh Courier* from February 5, 1938, we see the contrast between the block of dense, cursive text of the letter and the more formally conventional strips that fill the rest of the page.

The status of the letter is ambiguous: while the reader can read its contents, it is presented at an angle, with the hand holding it covering part of the text.

It also zooms out of sight in the second panel, becoming a simple prop in the story, then back into the foreground, regaining its semiotically double quality of text and in-story object. In a newspaper page full of panels busy with characters, this block of text surprises the reader and attracts the eye, much like the reception of the letter in the story, which surprises, and even perhaps confuses, Torchy's family. While the letter is not fully disclosed, readers can peek at its content and try to decipher it.

Indeed, the reader's surprise at the sight of this unusual strip recreates that of the letter's addressees: Torchy's aunt and uncle are taken aback by this unexpected letter from New York. Their reaction is hard to interpret: Uncle Jeff is animated, with legs crossed in a movement that could be twisting or stomping, as he exclaims, "Now was'n dat sweet"; but Aunt Clemmie's reaction is more ambiguous. She is crying and holding a handkerchief to her face, her hands joined in a stance that evokes praying. The family friend who had been reading them the letter expresses her confusion and asks, "What've we got to CRY about? We're HAPPY aren't we?"

The strip ends on this question, which is left hanging in the air, unanswered. Ormes explores the conflict inherent to the themes of identity and family in the context of urban migration. Subverting the expectations of comics readers and experimenting with the use of text in the comic-strip format, she generates the emotional turmoil experienced by both her heroine and her family in the rural South as they attempt to reconnect after her abrupt departure. Under the guise of a funny comic-strip series with a pinup-style heroine, *"Dixie to Harlem"* offers *Pittsburgh Courier* readers a modern experience of constant alienation. When she is still living in Mississippi, Torchy feels out of place due to her desire to move to the city. Once she has settled in New York, the feeling of rupture from her origins and family keeps her sense of alienation present in her life. The comic strip with the letter performs the feat of simultaneously displaying the heroine's most intimate thoughts—her heartfelt attempt to reconnect with her family—as well as the family (and general urban/rural) schism that she tries to mitigate by sending this letter. Her aunt and uncle literally cannot understand the letter: they do not know how to read, but they also cannot understand Torchy and her decision to live in the city. Through this unexpected magnifying glass into Torchy's family relationships, the readers find themselves caught in the characters' difficult efforts to bridge the gap between their contrasting living experiences.

TORCHY'S ROOM: ERASED SPACES IN THE COMIC

Ormes's depiction of Torchy's modernist coming-of-age focuses on making readers experience her heroine's perspective, sharing with them her most private thoughts and moments. These essential themes of perspective and intimacy are catalyzed by Ormes's repeated efforts to visualize Torchy's private, domestic spaces. And, significantly, the medium of comics allows Ormes to depict the private spaces inhabited by her character as public spaces, visible to all in the pages of the *Pittsburgh Courier*. This tension between private and public as experienced by African American women belongs to a wider sociopolitical context that Hardison articulates in *Writing through Jane Crow*. In *Private Bodies, Public Texts* (2011), Karla F. C. Holloway points to the "compromised relationship to privacy" of Black and woman bodies that, as paraphrased by Hardison, "white patriarchal culture—always and already—depicts . . . as Other in the public sphere."[26] This issue goes hand in hand with the lack of interest for and consequential erasure of Black private life and psyche that Hurston decries in "What the White Publisher Won't Print." In a context of white patriarchy, the intimate lives of Black women are systematically erased from public view, pushed to the sides of representation. *"Dixie to Harlem"* resists this erasure. Published in 1938, in a public platform like the *Pittsburgh Courier*, Ormes's depiction of the private spaces of Torchy's life—her apartment, her bedroom—is an act of rebellion against Jane Crow oppression, dissenting against the strict rules, both legally formal and socially informal, that delimit representation and expression.

The focus on private spaces and moments in *"Dixie to Harlem,"* and in particular the exchanges between Torchy and her friends, foregrounds the intimate life of African American women within narratives of early twentieth-century urban experience. Space, privacy, openness: for many Black women authors, these topics provide central points of tension. Building on the work of Yi-Fu Tuan, Thadious M. Davis reads "space as freedom" and "place as security," and points out that "black women modernists . . . struggled to achieve the openness and freedom of space." Writing—that is, representation and expression—became a way of imagining, if not achieving, a "vantage point of security and stability which for too long and too often were not components of black life," which in turn becomes "a desire to be seen and represented within the public sphere." Black women authors such as Fauset, Nella Larsen, and Hurston (and, we might add, Ormes) "sought enabling space within the close quarters, whether familiar, societal, or geographical, in which they functioned."[27] To represent the private, domestic spaces of Black social life is to insist on the reality of Black experience, and to enter into a public sphere that has been hostile and unwelcoming.

How does the medium of comics influence the representation of space, privacy, and domestic life? What does modernity look like from the perspective of a Black woman, and how does the power of the image participate in questions about public versus private spaces? How does an artist like Ormes deploy the grammar of sequential art to claim visibility and representation in the context of erasure and Jane Crow oppression?

An important difference between spaces in comics and in nonsequential visual arts lies in the act of participatory, interactive reading. Commentators on the comics form have long observed the interactive aspects of comics art; the most famous example is the concept of "closure" as defined by Scott McCloud in *Understanding Comics*, which describes the active process by which comics readers fill the gap between the action depicted in panels.[28] Comics studies scholars have since developed the concept of closure, revealing how the diegetic world of the narrative "extends outwards from the printed page . . . into . . . the reader's space" and "pulls us *into*" the world of the story.[29] This idea of "spatial closure," in which the reader animates and explores the diegetic space of the narrative, links the material page of the comic with the lived, embodied experience of its readers. As part of the complex process of closure, reading a visual narrative (as opposed to a text) invites the audience into a shared, communal interaction, extending the space of the comic outward and, simultaneously, expanding the reader's own space by inviting them into the world of the comic.

When Ormes draws Torchy's bedroom in *"Dixie to Harlem,"* her work isn't mere preservation or exhibition of a hidden space: reading comic strips that take place in these locations is an active, participatory experience. *Pittsburgh Courier* readers see bits and pieces of Torchy's bedroom through different angles; between each panel the readers perform closure, and sequential reading fills the missing parts of this space, animating the world of the page and bringing it into contact with their own daily lives. Readers not only see a private space that would otherwise be invisible to them, but they also come to feel that world press itself against their own experiences.

Given the limited possibilities for publishing stories about Black characters' emotions, and given the centrality of African American women's intimate lives to modernity, Ormes's work is doubly relevant. Through closure, comics readers of *"Dixie to Harlem"* are active participants who give life to the modern world of Torchy Brown. In the strip from April 23, 1938 (figure 6.3), Ormes plays with the simultaneity of visual, physical, and emotional transportation. The comic strip associates the reader's eyes' left-to-right progression from panel to panel with Torchy walking through the apartment and into her bedroom, thus emphasizing the reader's embodied simulation. As the reader follows Torchy's progression through the strip, her continuous movement animates the space of her bedroom, making the storyworld wider than individual panels. The

Figure 6.3. Jackie Ormes, *Torchy Brown in "Dixie to Harlem,"* first published April 23, 1938, *Pittsburgh Courier*.

graphic sequence creates a spatiotemporal bubble in the newspaper page that the reader enters through the window of the comic-strip frame.

In a public platform unrestricted by white publishers, Ormes inscribes and preserves a space—the single woman's room in the city—which would have been kept out of white, mainstream representation. The rooms are dotted with details that suggest ornamentation and attention to interior decoration. With a female bust in a panel and textiles covering an armchair and Torchy's bed echoing her and her friend's own patterned dresses, the apartment is imbued with intimacy, revealing its inhabitants' personal touch and their taste. It is of the same fabric—almost literally, one could quip—as the women who call it home. And within the storyworld, the roommates' intimacy is itself preserved too, as we see them chat while Torchy is lying on her bed in the last panel. The comic strip readers therefore find themselves gradually guided and transported, panel after panel, into the heart of this apartment and into the middle of a space and relationship that would otherwise have been kept out of public representation.

As Whaley reminds us in *Black Women in Sequence*, the comic strip *"Dixie to Harlem"* was published in a wider social and cultural context, beyond the limited world of the publishing industry, in which "single, laboring, and freely moving women caused gender norm confusion, fear of their financial independence, and a variety of sexual suspicions."[30] Through the comics reading process, readers find themselves inhabiting the intimate spaces of a character who would otherwise cause such "confusion," "fear," or "suspicions," and they come to experience Torchy's viewpoints and intimate thoughts. Moreover, Ormes carefully resists the voyeurism that inheres in visualizing the private, domestic spaces of Torchy's life, and that some readers might expect while casually flipping the pages of a newspaper and happening across a beautiful woman character. The grammar of comics narrative and the process of sequential reading allow Ormes to turn voyeurism into empathy and to challenge oppressive stereotypes that would make Torchy an object of consumption without depth. The tension at the heart of *"Dixie to Harlem"* resides in proving that

Figure 6.4. Jackie Ormes, *Torchy Brown in "Dixie to Harlem,"* first published June 26, 1937, *Pittsburgh Courier*.

such a subversive demonstration is not incompatible with Torchy's exuberant personality, her pinup-like physique, and her status as a performer.

Visual narrative offers readers a perspective that challenges their preconceived bias. The comic-strip format provides Ormes with efficient ways to represent her character's own social anxiety, her experience of the very prejudice and oppression that Ormes subverts. A striking example is found in the issue from June 26, 1937 (figure 6.4): the first panel introduces Torchy from over her shoulder while she is reading a magazine in the private space of her bedroom. Seeing that her family is out of the house (she is still in Mississippi at this point of the story), she turns to performance and starts practicing her tap dance routine. We see her dancing but, while Torchy may seem to be performing in front of us, she is actually in front of a tall mirror in her room, which we can see on the edge of the second panel and pans out on the third panel. In the last panel, we finally see Torchy against a bare background. We are watching her perform for herself, from the perspective of her mirror. The mirror achieves two tasks: it extends the three-dimensional space beyond the apparent scope of panel frames, and it situates the act of self-reflection at the heart of this strip. Through this carefully crafted use of setting and sequential action, Ormes puts readers inside the fictional world and asks them to see Torchy as she (literally) sees herself, effectively short-circuiting societal expectations or stereotypes that might otherwise influence their gaze.

Indeed, Ormes frequently employs irony and ambiguity—characteristically modernist literary strategies—to generate multiple layers of interpretation, situating *"Dixie to Harlem"* within the expectations of the funnies genre without losing track of its politically salient explorations of racial discrimination. In the strip published on February 19, 1938, "Torch Song and Torchy!" (figure 6.5), the reader sees Torchy perform on stage from the viewpoint of the audience as she sings: "I'LL PLEAD GUILTY . . . LORD JUDGE WON'T BE TOO HARSH . . . IT'S THE **PAGAN** IN ME."[31] With this song, Torchy addresses societal prejudice toward single women who were perceived as promiscuous. Once

Figure 6.5. Jackie Ormes, *Torchy Brown in "Dixie to Harlem,"* first published February 19, 1938.

again, she offers her own perspective on the matter and shares *how it feels* to be in her position. But to what extent is this "pleading guilty" her true feeling? Does the song reveal her true emotions, or is it merely performative? The scene is suspended in ambiguous irony. Is Torchy expressing sincere anxiety about her social status as a single woman? Is the song meant to be ironic? Reading this strip, *Pittsburgh Courier* readers would have remembered scenes in which Torchy overtly pretends to be what she's not (as in the train episode in which she acts like she can't read to avoid segregation) as well as multiple scenes in which she expresses sincere anxieties (such as the strip that shows her writing the letter to her family). What, then, should readers think of this scene, which is a literal performance? If at first glance Torchy possesses traits of typical comic-strip characters and pinup girls, readers eventually find themselves navigating multiple layers of interpretation, unable to decisively pin down this heroine. The comic strip allows Ormes to superimpose portraits of her heroine as a performer over more intimate portraits of Torchy as a vulnerable character and a trickster, suspending the reader's ability to categorize Torchy and simplify her perspective. Recreating the lived experience of the early twentieth century and positioning the private lives of single Black women as a locus of modernity, *"Dixie to Harlem"* becomes a striking example of modernist literature.

CONCLUSION

The humoristic expectations inherent to the funny pages easily lend themselves to satire and sociopolitical discourse, allowing a cartoonist like Jackie Ormes to repurpose comic-strip comedy as a prismatic modernist device and to generate complex and subversive modes of interpretation. The form of the comic strip is precisely what positions *Torchy Brown in "Dixie to Harlem"* as modernist literature. Ormes uses the weekly short strip format to weave a long story arc in a fragmented, discontinuous mode that allows her to juxtapose dream sequences with realism. Emphasis on the heroine's inner turmoil remains a common thread throughout the entire series. Her inner thoughts and her sense of alienation evolve as she experiences modernity and goes from out-of-place farm girl with dreams of the city to successful Harlemite anxious that her ties with her family in the South might be beyond repair.

In *Black Women in Sequence*, Whaley reads Ormes's work as an early occurrence of "Black cultural front comics," which she defines as "comic strip art that carries a politically progressive message with the intent to contribute to and inform about broad-based social-justice struggles of the early twentieth century, draws on Black vernacular idioms and performance for the strategic purpose of political subversion through humor and signifyin(g) or Black speech patterns, and presents the diverse aspects of Black, everyday life, including gender, sexuality, and class diversity."[32] In light of Hurston's "What the White Publisher Won't Print" or Hughes's "The Negro Artist and the Racial Mountain" (1926),[33] reading early twentieth-century comics as modernist literature entails attending to their broader sociopolitical contexts. In his *Dark Laughter* series (which started in 1935 and ran throughout the 1940s), Ollie Harrington shows scenes of daily Harlem life in a satirical tone. In the *(Seeing Ourselves) As Others See Us* cartoon series (1928–1935), Jay P. Jackson invites readers to "Revel In This Amazing Picture Of How The New Yorkers Actually Live."[34] Much like Ormes's *"Dixie to Harlem,"* these comics add depth and nuance to our understanding of modernism while satirically rejecting the erasure they had to work against. Studying early African American newspaper comics isn't a mere act of scholarly inclusion. Reading these cartoonists' work closely reveals the complex intersection of modernist aesthetics, political urgency, satire, and humor that characterizes Black comics.

Notes

1. Langston Hughes. "Colored and Colorful," *Chicago Defender*, June 16, 1948, 14.

2. Gates asks: "Pam Grier's star-turn in the 1974 Blaxploitation classic, *Foxy Brown*, is a cultural touchstone . . . But who still remembers 'Torchy Brown'?" in his introduction to Sheena C. Howard, Henry Louis Gates Jr., and Christopher J. Priest, *Encyclopedia of Black Comics* (Wheat Ridge, CO: Fulcrum, 2017), vii.

3. Celia Marshik and Allison Pease, eds. *Modernism, Sex, and Gender* (New York: Bloomsbury Academic, 2019), 7.

4. For more information on Ormes's career, the success of her different series, her rise on the Chicago cultural stage, and her political engagement, see her biography by Nancy Goldstein, *Jackie Ormes: The First African American Woman Cartoonist* (Ann Arbor: University of Michigan Press, 2008).

5. Saidiya Hartman, *Wayward Lives, Beautiful Experiments: Intimate Histories of Social Upheaval* (New York: W. W. Norton, 2019).

6. Hartman, xiii.

7. Hartman, 59.

8. Hartman, 61.

9. Jackie Ormes's career and her impressive readership attest to the popularity and reach of the newspapers in which she was published. Her career spans multiple series: *Torchy Brown in "Dixie to Harlem"* was followed by the cartoon *Candy* (1945), then by her longest-running series, the cartoon *Patty-Jo 'n' Ginger*, which ran for eleven years (1945–1956). Ormes then published *Torchy in Heartbeats* (1950–1954), a series of romance and adventure comics in color denouncing the environmental consequences of capitalism. In an article by Maxine Thompson entitled "Woman Cartoonist Turns to Doll Designing" published in the November 1947 issue of *Toys and Novelties*, Ormes's readership was estimated at a million readers. Also in 1947, one of Ormes's characters was turned into a Terri Lee doll.

10. Thomas Hamilton, the editor of the *New York Weekly Anglo-African*, wrote in the first issue of his periodical, "We need a Press—a press of our own. . . . The powerful and influential journals around us certainly have but little especial interest in, nor can they present our case as it should be presented—surely as we can present it ourselves." Thomas Hamilton, "Our Paper," *New York Weekly Anglo-African*, July 23, 1859. Similarly, the founder of the *Chicago Defender*, Robert Abbott, expressed his goal "to fight the enemy on his own ground." Quoted in Roi Ottley, *The Lonely Warrior: The Life and Times of Robert S. Abbott* (Washington, DC: Regnery, 1955), 86. See also Ella Strother, "The Race-Advocacy Function of the Black Press," *Black American Literature Forum* 12, no. 3 (1978): 92. Using data she gathered by combing every issue of the *Chicago Defender*, Strother provides statistical evidence that the newspaper promoted social advancement and positive self-representation by publishing stories of successful African Americans.

11. Ayanna Dozier, "Wayward Travels: Racial Uplift, Black Women, and the Pursuit of Love and Travel in *Torchy in Heartbeats* by Jackie Ormes," *Feminist Media Histories* 4, no. 3 (July 2018): 12–29.

12. Zora Neale Hurston, "What the White Publisher Won't Print," in *You Don't Know Us Negroes and Other Essays*, ed. Henry Louise Gates Jr. and Genevieve West (New York: HarperCollins, 2022), 143.

13. Hurston, 147.

14. Dozier, "Wayward Travels," 17.

15. Ayesha K. Hardison, *Writing through Jane Crow: Race and Gender Politics in African American Literature* (Charlottesville: University of Virginia Press, 2014), 204.

16. Hardison, 220.

17. For an account of the underrepresentation of early African American comic strips in comics studies, even while the field of Black comics expands, see Sheena C. Howard, "Brief History of the Black Comic Strip: Past and Present," in *Black Comics: Politics of Race and Representation*, ed. Sheena C. Howard and Ronald L. Jackson (New York: Bloomsbury Academic, 2013), 11–22.

18. Deborah Elizabeth Whaley, *Black Women in Sequence: Re-Inking Comics, Graphic Novels, and Anime* (Seattle: University of Washington Press, 2016), 40.

19. Gwendolyn Brooks, "Sadie and Maud," in *The Essential Gwendolyn Brooks* (Boone, IA: Library of America, 2006), 57.

20. Hartman, *Wayward Lives*, 48.

21. Ormes, *"Dixie to Harlem," Pittsburgh Courier*, June 12, 1937.

22. Ormes, *"Dixie to Harlem," Pittsburgh Courier*, July 24, 1937.

23. Hartman, *Wayward Lives*, 48

24. Ormes, *"Dixie to Harlem,"* *Pittsburgh Courier*, September 4, 1937.

25. Ormes, *"Dixie to Harlem,"* *Pittsburgh Courier*, September 25, 1937, and October 9, 1937. A similar scenario is found in the chapter "An Intimate History of Slavery and Freedom," in Hartman's *Wayward Lives* (45–76).

26. Karla F. C. Holloway, *Private Bodies, Public Texts: Race, Gender, and a Cultural Bioethics* (Durham, NC: Duke University Press, 2011), 9. Hardison, *Writing through Jane Crow*, 2.

27. See Thadious M. Davis, "Black Women's Modernist Literature," in *Cambridge Companion to Modernist Women Writers*, ed. Maren Tova Linett (Cambridge: Cambridge University Press, 2010), 96–97.

28. Scott McCloud, *Understanding Comics: The Invisible Art* (1993; repr., New York: Harper Perennial, 1994).

29. Steve Braund, "The Itinerant Illustration: Creating Storyworlds in the Reader's Space," *Journal of Illustration*, no. 2 (2015): 267, 269. Similarly, in *Mise en Scène, Acting, and Space in Comics*, Geraint D'Arcy argues that the comics panel should be seen as both a frame and a window that "indicates greater space than is depicted." Geraint D'Arcy, *Mise En Scène, Acting, and Space in Comics* (New York: Palgrave Macmillan, 2020), 105. Yi-Fu Tuan offers definitions of space and place relying on subjective experience in *Space and Place: The Perspective of Experience* (1977; repr., Minneapolis: University of Minnesota Press, 2001). Tuan defines experience as "a cover-all term for the various modes through which a person knows and constructs a reality" and places "experiential perspective" at the heart of the human sense of space (8). In alignment with Yi-Fu Tuan's experiential definition of space, Karin Kukkonen builds upon theories of cognitive psychology and transmedial narratology and applies the concept of embodied simulation to comics in her essay "Space, Time, and Causality in Graphic Narrative: An Embodied Approach," in *From Comic Strips to Graphic Novels: Contributions to the Theory and History of Graphic Narrative*, ed. Daniel Stein (Boston: De Gruyter, 2013), 49–66. Kukkonen develops a theory of comics reading in which the bodies on the page transport the reader in three different ways: they "evoke . . . embodied simulations of being in the storyworld," they transport readers emotionally, and they "guide them across the face of the page" (55).

30. Whaley, *Black Women*, 40.

31. Ormes, *"Dixie to Harlem,"* *Pittsburgh Courier*, February 19, 1938.

32. Whaley, *Black Women*, 36.

33. See the recent edition of Langston Hughes's writings: *Let America Be America Again: Conversations with Langston Hughes*, ed. Christopher C. De Santis (Oxford: Oxford University Press, 2022), 20–23.

34. See *Dark Laughter: The Satiric Art of Oliver W. Harrington*, ed. Thomas M. Inge (Jackson: University Press of Mississippi, 1993). A *(Seeing Ourselves) As Others See Us* cartoon is reprinted in Tim Jackson's crucial *Pioneering Cartoonists of Color* (Jackson: University Press of Mississippi, 2016), 30.

IN DIALOGUE AND DEBATE

Comics, Little Magazines, World Literature

LOUISE KANE

In 1921, Jorge Luis Borges returned to Argentina from Europe and started an experimental literary magazine, *Prisma*. The magazine appeared only for two issues, both of which were pasted onto the walls of shops and cafes in Buenos Aires. As Borges himself would later recollect, part of the magazine's uniqueness was its format. It was not a magazine in the usual sense of a printed, bound, book-like construction with several pages; nor was it a traditional wall mural. Instead, *Prisma* existed as a unique experiment, a "mural magazine" consisting of "a large single sheet" that "contained a manifesto and some six or eight short, laconic poems printed with plenty of white space around them."[1] With its experimental form and appearance, limited readership, and short lifespan, *Prisma* exemplifies the genre that we now recognize as the "little magazine." A much debated and slightly confusingly titled form—the "little" refers to the magazine's deliberate appeal to a narrow group of readers who were expected to be intellectually curious and aware of the latest developments across literature and other disciplines—the little magazine emerged over the course of the first few decades of the 1900s as a periodical form synonymous with formal and textual experimentation, a production made by avant-garde writers and artists for likeminded individuals. Yet *Prisma*, with its white spaces and illustrated poems, seems to possess many of the hallmarks of another then emergent genre: comics. Like little magazines, comics are formally innovative productions whose impact depends largely on interplay between images, text, and the "white space" Borges references.

Prisma is one of many early twentieth-century publications that possess the qualities of both magazine and comic, but attempts to study this sort of "genre hybridity" remain limited. Scholarship on little modernist magazines and comics has followed parallel trajectories. In their now seminal article "The

Rise of Periodical Studies," published in 2006, Sean Latham and Robert Scholes argued that magazines have only recently become recognized as "autonomous objects of study."[2] This sentiment is echoed by comic book scholars, who assert that the historical marginalization of comics "as quality texts and significant mediums for study" is something that has only been challenged in relatively recent years.[3] However, the little magazine's links to the comic strip and/or comic book remain generally overlooked.[4] Most scholarship continues to present literary or artistic magazines as forms that operate separately to "a host of other categories," including "comic books," along with "motion picture fan titles, sports and recreation magazines, and travel publications."[5]

This chapter explores some examples of convergence and similarity between the magazine and comics forms. The first part examines the shared evolution of comics and the little modernist magazine; it explores their mutual status as texts that are frustratingly hard to pin down in terms of definition and disciplinary remit. The second part argues that the little magazine anticipated comics in its use of text and images that interacted or "blurred" together. The final part of the chapter connects the magazine and comics in a broader sense: in their ability to transcend national and linguistic boundaries, both forms function as progenitors of world literature, their emergence occurring at a time when the concept of literature as a global or "world" phenomenon was undeveloped. Examples from the *Mandrake the Magician* series illustrate how, like the little magazine—and often working in tandem with it—comic strips are by their very nature inherently global. Their movement across geographic regions via syndication and translation into numerous languages forged early forms of a world literary network in which texts clashed as much as they converged. Periodicals were essential to this network: it was in little magazines and newspapers, after all, that comic strips appeared, often taking up a regular space in the magazine's contents and providing light-hearted amusement to readers who looked forward to catching up with the exploits of their favorite comic characters.

DEFINITIONS

Tracing the history and definition of the comic book requires us to take a path inevitably trodden not just by comics studies scholars but by scholars of any sort of periodical publication. Sean Latham and Robert Scholes may have heralded the rise of periodical studies around fifteen years ago, but debates about what exactly periodical forms constitute, and how they should be studied, have been circling since the late nineteenth century. Both the terms "comic" and "magazine" act as umbrella nomenclatures embracing a wide variety of textual genres and subgenres. When many scholars discuss comics, they refer to both the comic strip (printed as part of periodicals such as newspapers and magazines) and the comic book (a text composed only of comic strips). As Matthew Levay has noted, "The term 'comics' can signify a wide range of things: monthly or biweekly comic book magazines, trade paperbacks collecting multiple issues of those magazines, standalone graphic novels, daily newspaper comic strips, and webcomics, to name only a few."[6] Similarly, "magazine" encompasses a vast mesh of cultural products: little magazines that propelled modernist literature in the early 1900s; big magazines like the *Atlantic Monthly* and *Vogue* or *Good Housekeeping*; newspapers that had components of magazines such as recurring columns about literature, homemaking, and book reviews; college magazines; literary supplements; penny dreadfuls (magazines known for their sensational fiction); so-called pulp magazines; and upmarket literary reviews like *Blackwood's* or the *Smart Set*. Comics and the magazine are complex and often interlinked, overlapping forms (it was, of course, magazines and newspapers in which the first comic strips appeared) that resist easy definition in terms of appearance, content, and readership.

Scholars have often tried to define both comics and magazines through their formal or functional properties. David Kunzle's two-volume *History of the Comic Strip* (1973) argues that the comics form is driven by a narrative function: in a comic, the purpose is to tell a story sequentially through pictures. A comic is therefore comprised of "a sequence of separate images," with a "preponderance of image over text."[7] According to this definition, "Any strip in which the captions occupy a larger space than the picture" is excluded on the condition that the images must carry "the burden of the narrative."[8] In more recent years, scholars have continued to privilege the sequential nature of a comic as essential to its definition, but with nuances and alterations that adapt Kunzle's original definition. For Will Eisner, comics must present images that constitute "sequential art," whereas for Scott McCloud, the sequence of images must achieve a particular purpose: to "convey information and/or produce an aesthetic response from the viewer."[9] Aaron Meskin has argued that comics do not always tell a sequential story; instead, he points to the fact that "there appear to be extant examples of nonnarrative comics," such as Robert Crumb's *Comical Comics* series.[10]

Questions of form—or, more specifically, how we navigate the form of the magazine—are also key to definitions of the little magazine, with scholars often describing it as a text with a hodgepodge of contents that produce a highly interactive, and often nonlinear, reading experience. As Kristin McLeod argues, magazines offer a "vast archive of disparate content" that means the reader is forever confronted by the "challenge" of "how to read them," and the order in which such reading should commence.[11] Over the past two decades, scholars have proposed various approaches to reading magazines: from theorizing magazines "as media"[12] to considering them as "databases" containing a "miscellany of textual objects."[13] Similarly, scholars have also contemplated new ways for reading and interpreting comics. Henry Jenkins has argued that "being able to think across media comparatively" is essential for developing an effective framework for reading comics. There is a need "to read these comics in relation to a broad array of other art practices that involve managing or depicting a relationship to stuff," he posits.[14]

Just as the question of how they should be read is often central to attempts to define comics and magazines, so too is the question of their relationship to commercial culture. Since Ezra Pound defined little magazines—"small magazines," he called them—as a type of periodical "unconditioned by considerations as to whether a given idea or a given trend in art will 'git ads' from the leading corset companies," definitions of the little magazine have tended to focus on its aversion to commercial culture and mainstream tastes.[15] These definitions have often stressed the little magazine's relationships to literary modernism as its primary defining quality. Defining modernism is, of course, a contentious business, but it is generally possible to view literary modernism as the period of intense artistic, intellectual, and ideological experimentation and newness that flourished in the first few decades of the 1900s. Suzanne Churchill and Adam McKible's definition of little magazines implicitly stresses their links to nascent modernist cultures. Little magazines are "non-commercial enterprises founded by individuals or small groups intent upon publishing the experimental works or radical opinions of untried, unpopular, or under-represented writers."[16] This is similar to the focus on noncommerciality and alterity that has shaped recent attempts to define the comic book. Take, for example, Charles Hatfield's recent discussion of a special subset of comics he terms "alternative comics," comic books that—much like the little magazine—"have breached the limits of the traditional comic book on every level, including packaging, publication, narrative form, and thematic content."[17]

Comics and magazines are textual forms with a shared history. First, they emerged and gained popularity during the same period (the late 1800s and early 1900s). Second, the magazine, as stated above, was often the "book" in which comic strips first appeared. *Famous Funnies*, a thirty-six-page magazine specializing in reprints of existing newspaper comic strips, is often cited as the first comic book, but by the late 1800s, several periodicals had already begun to include comic strips in their pages; some newspapers almost *became* comic books in their privileging of the strips and their characters.[18] Take, for example, the *Ally Sloper* comic strips. Featuring the hapless but affable Ally Sloper, so named because he "sloped" from one lodging to the next, the strips first appeared in the British entertainment magazine *Judy* in 1867, before becoming recurring features of other periodicals like the satirical *Punch*. In 1884, such was the success of the *Sloper* strips that the Dalziel Brothers, then a renowned publishing firm, decided to capitalize on *Sloper*'s success and create *Ally Sloper's Half Holiday*, an entire magazine that made the strips its primary, rather than secondary, content. As Roger Sabin has argued, *Ally Sloper's Half Holiday* thus represents "the first modern comic," even though it appeared fifty years before *Famous Funnies* shook up the North American periodical publishing scene in 1934.[19] Images from the first issue of *Ally Sloper's Half Holiday* (figure 7.1) show how the periodical did not always use the panel format now synonymous with comics but certainly anticipated key formal features of the comic book genre, such as the use of brief snatches of text and the use of recurring characters to induce audience rapport.

In the early 1900s, the commencement of bestselling illustrated weeklies like the cheap two-penny *T. P.'s Weekly* drove further demand for illustrated text that continued to anticipate the comic-strip form. The British reading public, enlarged by the success of board schools and the ready availability of affordable newspapers and penny magazines, and enlivened by growing debates about the value of literature and role of art in society, had changed, with more working-class and lower-middle-class readers than ever before seeking material that was easy to read and as entertaining as it was didactic. Publishers began to capitalize on the inclusion of illustrations as a means of appealing to this changed readership. Often inserted to aid communication, the number of illustrations in a magazine like *T. P.'s Weekly* or *The Graphic* meant that the image/text divide became increasingly hard to decipher, a blurring of visual and verbal form that anticipated and prepared readers for the comic book phenomenon. The late 1800s saw several other British magazines like *The Strand* utilize cartoons to the extent that recurring characters acquired a folkloric status later ascribed to comic book heroes, with Sherlock Holmes functioning as the most obvious example.

The question of how, exactly, a comic like *Ally Sloper's Half Holiday* differs from an illustrated magazine like *The Strand* remains a tricky one; this is one of the definitional blurrings that connects comics to wider periodical print networks and their various products, such as the literary magazine and the pamphlet. *Ally Sloper's Half Holiday* was a comic, but as it also printed other contents—short stories, poems, and essays on current affairs all mingled with the humorous and increasingly farcical *Sloper* escapades—it functioned as a literary magazine. Yet the first issue of *The Strand*, a literary magazine, contained more illustrations than the first issue of *Ally Sloper's Half Holiday*. Does this mean that *The Strand* functions, at least partially, as a comic? The differentiating factor, one could argue, is the absence of a key component of the comic: the use of text boxes and captions beneath the illustrations. For many scholars,

Figure 7.1. First issue of *Ally Sloper's Half Holiday*, May 1884.

this is the defining feature of comics, as opposed to other periodical and print forms. As David Carrier has argued, it is not just a set of illustrations that makes a comic but "a narrative sequence [of illustrations] with speech balloons."[20] While *Ally Sloper's Half Holiday* often used this format, the Sherlock Holmes stories contained illustrations that rarely used captions. In *The Strand*, the link between image and text is a complementary one; the illustrations aid the reader in understanding the lengthy paragraphs of text that comprised the Sherlock stories. In a comic, one could argue that it is instead the small text boxes that aid the reader in understanding the illustrations. In a comic, illustrations are the primary focus, whereas in a literary magazine the actual words of the text are the main content, the illustrations supplementary to it.

MODERNIST MAGAZINES: ANTICIPATING THE COMIC BOOK

This brief outline of the late nineteenth-century evolution of periodicals shows that the idea comics, magazines, and newspapers can be neatly separated into discrete textual categories with little overlap is a flawed one. As early as the first few decades of the nineteenth century, magazines like the *Glasgow Looking Glass* (which appeared in the 1820s) presented image and text in such a way as to anticipate the form of modern comics. In other words, many magazines *looked* like comics, even when they did not bill themselves by this label. While the interaction between illustrations and text in a magazine like *The Strand* might seem to be limited to a sort of supplementary function—the images of Holmes and Watson supplement each story and perform its contents—the advent of the little modernist magazine in the early 1900s saw the beginning of a hybrid form that aimed to present images that interacted with surrounding text. It is this sustained and deliberate intersection of image and text that would come to dominate and define the comic book.

The modernist magazine was a global form. In Britain, periodicals like *The Egoist*, for which T. S. Eliot served as literary editor from 1917, and the *English Review*, edited for a year by Ford Madox Ford, drove a culture that saw the little magazine emerge as a significant propagator of literary and aesthetic taste. Its remit was by no means restricted to Western metropoles. In Mexico, poetry magazines like Idella Purnell's *Palms* connected readers in Latin America with the work of well-known North American poets, evidenced in the magazine's "Negro Poets" edition, which featured several Harlem Renaissance poets. In Kolkata, India, the *Modern Review* published work by Rabindranath Tagore and Ezra Pound; and in China, magazines like *Fiction Monthly* and *New Youth* captured the imagination of a newly emboldened generation of young writers and readers influenced by the New Culture Movement that unfolded from the early 1910s. John Middleton Murry's *Rhythm*, which first appeared in London in 1911, was one of the first little modernist magazines to deliberately blur visual art and text, asking readers to make unconscious connections between the two forms. The image in figure 7.2 reflects this.

The page in question depicts *Rhythm*'s manifesto—titled "Aims and Ideals." This manifesto appeared in the magazine's very first issue in winter 1911. The magazine's definition of art praises "drawing, literature or criticism" as disciplines of equal value. This is evident if we look at the layout of the "Aims and Ideals" page. Jessica Dismorr's woodcuts, depicting figures looking straight at the reader, one of whom is in a state of semiundress, are almost as confrontational as they are arresting, their presence indicating the sort of challenging content and implicit connections to the avant-garde Left Bank Parisian art scene in which both Dismorr and *Rhythm*, through its championing of artists like Picasso and J. D. Fergusson, were firmly engrained.[21] In its blurring of art and text, the magazine operates almost as an early comic book. As M. R. Ivasyshyn has argued, "A comic book as a multimodal text consists of verbal and visual-graphic components that are interconnected and complement each other."[22] This is exactly what we see here in *Rhythm*; the magazine's manifesto is complemented by and interconnected with the illustrations interspersed throughout the text, which were selected to represent the magazine's commitment to interdisciplinary content and forward-thinking artists and writers. The magazine and its editors—Murry was originally assisted by his university friend Michael Sadleir, who would soon be replaced by Murry's partner, Katherine Mansfield—were entirely conscious of its multimodal status: it was, after all, a magazine designed to promote "the ideal of a new art" that would transcend disciplinary and regional boundaries.[23]

In the early 1910s, other magazines used strikingly interactive image/text combinations that we now associate with the comic book, though often in explicitly political contexts. The strips in figure 7.3 first appeared in the German satirical magazine *Simplicissimus* in 1909 and 1911 respectively but were reprinted in the Dada magazine *Die Pleite* some years later in 1919. The cartoons are critical of the (then) German Empire, but *Die Pleite* has reprinted them as a comment on the Social Democratic Party's increasingly militaristic stance against the more radical forms of communism that represented an apparent threat to the stability of the Weimar Republic, which was established in 1919 after the German Revolution of 1918–1919. *Simplicimuss* was always satirical, and generally sympathetic to left-wing ideals, but in 1917 its editor, Ludwig Thomas, had suddenly become a nationalist and renounced his former penchant for satire.

Die Pleite's reprinting of these comic strips is an ironic comment upon the general feeling that the working classes were being deserted, even by their former protectors. The bottom strip depicts a helpless man on the street begging

36
AIMS AND IDEALS.

RHYTHM is a magazine with a purpose. Its title is the ideal of a new art, to which it will endeavour to give expression in England. Æstheticism has had its day and done its work. Based on a reaction, on a foundation essentially negative, it could not endure; with a vision that saw, exquisitely, it may be, but unsteadily and in part, it has been inevitably submerged by the surge of the life that lay beyond its sphere. We need an art that strikes deeper, that touches a profounder reality, that passes outside the bounds of a narrow æstheticism, cramping and choking itself, drawing its inspiration from aversion, to a humaner and a broader field.

Humanity in art in the true sense needs humanity in criticism. To treat what is being done to-day as something vital in the progress of art, which cannot fix its eyes on yesterday and live; to see that the present is pregnant for the future, rather than a revolt against the past; in creation to give expression to an art that seeks out the strong things of life; in criticism to seek out the strong things of that art—such is the aim of RHYTHM.

"Before art can be human it must learn to be brutal." Our intention is to provide art, be it drawing, literature or criticism, which shall be vigorous, determined, which shall have its roots below the surface, and be the rhythmical echo of the life with which it is in touch. Both in its pity and its brutality it shall be real. There are many aspects of life's victory, and the aspects of the new art are manifold.

To leave protest for progress, and to find art in the strong things of life, is the meaning of RHYTHM. The endeavour of art to touch reality, to come to grips with life is the triumph of sanity and reason. "What is exalted and tender in art is not made of feeble blood."

DISMORR

Figure 7.2. "Aims and Ideals," *Rhythm*, June 1911.

the government to "protect our lives." Upon receiving no help, he decides that "We'll help ourselves!" The final caption—"The rebellious mob has proven itself unworthy of our good will—Fire!"—reflects the increasing mistrust with which the general public, especially industrial workers and left-leaning progressives, had begun to view the Weimar Republic.[24] The illustrations not only interact with their captions but have been placed alongside another text, a letter (seen on the far right of the page) "from a former subscriber to *Simplicimuss*."[25] The letter writer describes their frustrations with the Social Democratic Party (SDP) and their feeling that the party had become a "servant" to power and authority, rather than a challenger. The title of *Die Pleite* ("The Bankruptcy") is itself a comment on this general feeling of mistrust and despair: there was, for many, a sense that the SDP had become morally bankrupt in its treatment

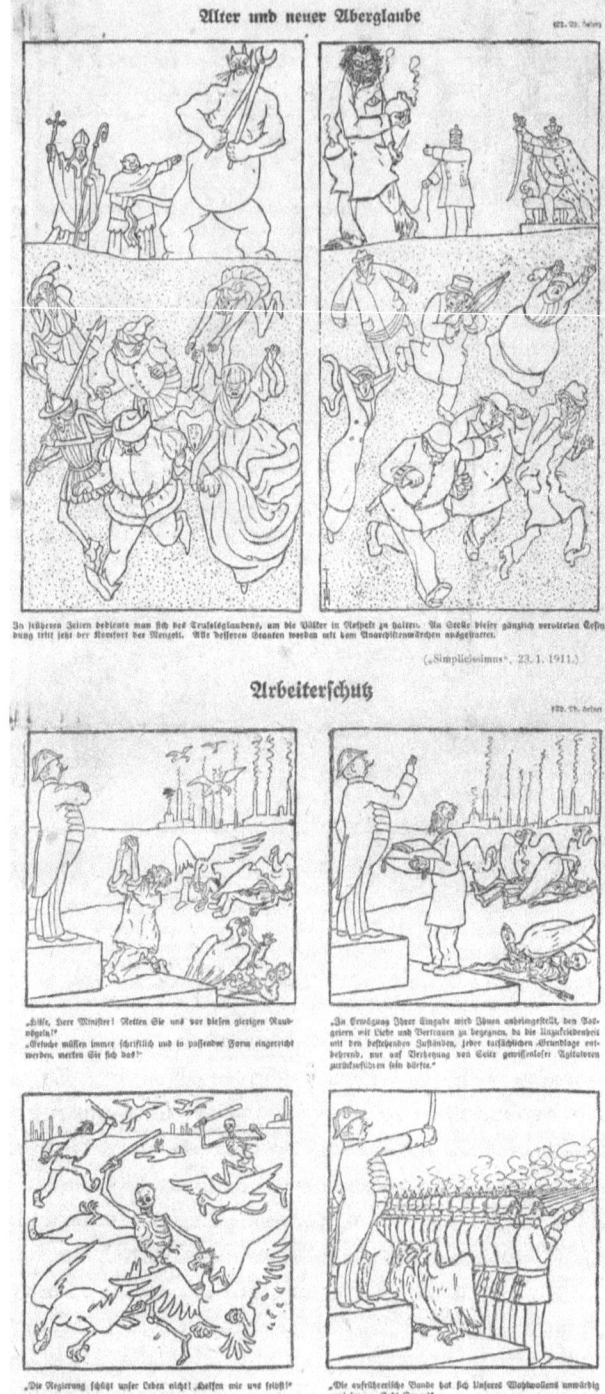

Figure 7.3. *Die Pleite*, no. 4, May 1, 1919.

of individuals who, desiring protection from the larger cogs of the state, were treated as communists or extremists, and, literally, fired upon by a government they had believed would support their needs. When the editors of *Die Pleite*—the avid Marxist, avant-gardists Wieland Herzfelde, George Grosz, and John Heartfield—decided to reprint this particular comic strip, they were making a controversial point: not only were they being heavily critical of the Weimar Republic; they were giving praise to Soviet Russia and the Communist Party. Indeed, the first issue of *Die Pleite*, however playfully, encouraged readers to attend the First Congress of the Communist International in Moscow.

Clearly, then, little magazine editors, just as later comic-strip artists would do, used conjunctions of text and image for a variety of artistic and political reasons. The blending of text and image produced and reinforced *Rhythm*'s reputation as a magazine devoted to newness in art and literature. The editors of *Die Pleite* (and *Simplicisimuss* before it) invoked comic strips to score political points and announce their magazines' statuses as apart from, or in accordance with, certain ideologies or worldviews. There is, in both magazines, an expectation that the reader will need to step in, to close the interpretive gap between the illustrations—whether it be the cartoons of *Die Pleite*, or the hand-drawn artworks in *Rhythm*—and the texts alongside which they appear. This is a technique that many magazines would continue to use. In the 1930s, the Chinese periodical *Modern Sketch* deployed image/text conjunctions that used visual art to create narratives that were easy to understand. *Modern Sketch* is an example of a Chinese *manhua*. Translated literally as "impromptu sketches," the term *manhua* denotes a sort of pictorial hybrid comic-magazine form that flourished from the early 1900s. *Modern Sketch*'s artists soon began to develop the sequential cartoon into the form we now recognize as the comic strip: narrative images accompanied beneath by captions. As John Crespi has argued, these cartoons used a variety of techniques to ensure that readers achieved "closure"—the closing of the epistemological gap of seeing the image and understanding its relevance.[26] This is, of course, an echo of Scott McCloud's assertion that "closure" in comics is the "phenomenon of observing the parts but perceiving the whole."[27]

This editorial prompting of readerly "closure" is a key similarity between comics and magazine forms, and one that does not occur so apparently in other literary forms. This idea of seeing the parts but perceiving them as an interactive whole is the central component of comics form. As Gabriele Ripp and Lukas Etter have noted, in "comic strips and comic books," a sense of narrative often depends on "readers' ability and constant activity to bridge the gutters that divide the single static pictures." This "helps to create narrativity."[28] In this sense, magazines like *Die Pleite* are multimodal: their cartoons and text say different things and readers have to piece together their relation to one another.

Other magazines also use image/text conjunctions designed to challenge or complicate readers' perceptive and hermeneutic abilities. The beginning of this chapter briefly discussed how Borges's *Prisma* looked like a magazine/comic hybrid with its strange balance of text, image, and white space. Even though *Prisma* is not a comic, when we look at it as a whole, the fragmented page layout and decorative visual designs invoke the aesthetics of a comic book. Borges was always influenced, perhaps unconsciously, by the emergent form of the comic strip. When he was made coeditor of the literary supplement to the popular daily newspaper *Crítica de la Argentina*, with Ulises Petit de Murat, he chose to issue the supplement as a part-magazine, part-comic hybrid. The supplement, titled *La Revista Multicolor de los Sábados* (the *Multicolor Magazine on Saturdays*), appeared every Saturday in the back pages of *Crítica* for just a year (1933–1934) but made an immediate impact. *Crítica*'s editor, the Uruguayan journalist Natalio Botana, had been keen to make the magazine a forerunner of all things new: its pages often covered exciting innovations in technology, medicine, and industry, and Borges was encouraged to transplant this commitment to newness into the pages of the *Revista Multicolor*.

The *Revista Multicolor* contained short stories and reviews by writers including Santiago Dabove and César Tiempo, but it was not so much its verbal as its visual contents that elicited widespread admiration and excitement. Its frequent full-page images consisted of hand-drawn cartoons and comic strips that accompanied literary content including short stories, poetry, and book reviews. Sometimes, the comic strips and other contents engaged in a satirical lampooning of contemporary political and current affairs. Brief, humorous captions narrated the events defining each set of illustrations. The magazine acted as a platform for cartoonists including Andrés Guevara, Pascual Güida, Lorenzo Molas, Arístides Rechain, Pedro Rojas, and Juan Sorazábal. Many of these cartoonists were involved with Argentina's fledgling comic book scene. Pedro Rojas, for example, served as *Crítica*'s artistic director and was also the editor of *Tit-Bits*, another Argentine magazine that provided Spanish-language translations of popular comic strips. *Tit-Bits* tended to favor reprinting North American comic strips. In the Golden Age of comics—the period stretching approximately from the late 1930s to mid-1950s—strips such as *Kevin the Bold*, *Big Ben Bolt*, and *Rusty Riley* were all translated into Spanish in *Tit-Bits*, appearing as *Kevin el Denodado*, *Ben Bolt Campeón*, and *Rusty Riley, Aprendiz de Jockey*. If *Prisma* was inspired partly by comic strips, *Revista Multicolor* was an extension of this inspiration: the *Revista Multicolor* printed so many comic strips that, as we have seen with other magazines, the magazine seemed to become a comic in itself. As Nora C. Benedict has noted, "What we find in this periodical and its literary supplement is nothing short of a spectacle."[29]

GOING GLOBAL:
MAGAZINES AND COMICS AS WORLD LITERATURE

Comics exist in most countries and cultures, and the longstanding tradition of comics in some countries such as Japan cannot possibly be adequately covered in this chapter alone. The examples this chapter discusses—from Europe, Latin America, and China—give a brief but suggestive snapshot of the universal appeal of the comic strip, and of how the periodicals that either incorporated comic strips or gestured toward the comic-strip form in their blending of art and text pioneered early types of world literature. Of course, the question of what constitutes world literature—like those similarly tricky questions of what constitutes a comic or a magazine—is contentious. Definitions of world literature tend to fall into two main camps. Scholars like David Damrosch argue that world literature operates in a sort of global network and denotes "all literary works that circulate beyond their culture of origin, either in translation or in their original language."[30] On the contrary, scholars like Pascale Casanova and Franco Moretti argue that this circulation can rarely be democratic: authors in "periphery" countries, they argue, are permanently striving to achieve prominence within cities that comprise the world's "leading capitals."[31] While the idea of world literature as a cooperative global network seems to imply all texts *can* be part of this network, some scholars have argued that it is only those considered "greats" or "classics" that are admitted to the "canon" of world literature. For example, Longxi Zhang contends that "world literature is the integrated body of canonical works of the world's literary traditions."[32]

Perhaps because of their links to commercial culture, comics' contributions to world literature have been overlooked. It has been three decades since Scott McCloud's *Understanding Comics* (1993) debunked comics' perennial association with commercialism and lowbrow culture, but the problem of aesthetic value still looms large in periodical studies. Little magazines' contributions to world literature, or the beginnings of a world literary network, have been similarly overlooked as attention is instead paid to how "modernist" the magazine question is; this is a problem given that our ideas of what modernism is are in turned defined by what David Earle has described as "the prejudice of form," meaning that "our understanding of literary modernism is still reductively based upon the material forms that those early literary historians thought worthy of archiving."[33] While some little magazines and literary reviews make it in to the archives, comics, often lumped together with pulp magazines and commercial or middlebrow publications—think *Vanity Fair* or *Good Housekeeping*—do not. Several scholars have attempted to replace approaches to periodicals that center on their bigness or littleness with more balanced discussion of how they straddle low and high cultural forms.[34] Faye Hammill and Karen Leick have shown how the big magazines— "sometimes identified as 'quality,' 'slick,' or 'sophisticated'" on account of their better paper quality and expensively produced color covers—were important progenitors of a new type of literary modernism that blended highbrow ideals with mass culture.[35] As part of their commitment to publishing content that did not necessarily have mass market appeal, the big magazines often dabbled in experimental, modernist literature. For example, the *Smart Set* published short stories by James Joyce and D. H. Lawrence. *Vogue* published contributions from Gertrude Stein.

Turning instead to how comics, little magazines, and more commercial periodicals—the so-called "big" magazines—contain examples of literary transnationalism and intertextuality synonymous with the beginnings of world literature offers a different approach, one which places less focus on periodicals' adherence to the cultures of modernism or commerce. Recent work in comics studies has started to examine the "worlding" of the form. A special issue of *World Literature Today* published an "international comics" number in 2016. Monika Schmitz-Emans has explored how Albert Kanter's *Classic Comics* series, which began in the late 1940s and saw a variety of classic novels adapted into comics form, furthered a type of "world literature" in its determination to bring "'classics' from other national literatures" to American readers.[36]

The cartoons and comic strips of the British illustrator Anne Harriet Fish demonstrate how comic strips, or more specifically their inclusion in transatlantic periodicals, forged literary networks that transcended national boundaries. Fish was born in Bristol, England, and began working as an illustrator for Conde Nast from the late 1800s. One of her popular early comic strips, *The Letters of Eve*, appeared in the British high society magazine *Tatler*. As figure 7.4 shows, *The Letters of Eve* appeared as part comic strip (albeit not in the usual square format) and part epistolary column, and tapped into the magazine's focus on English high society, fashion, and its largely affluent, upper-class readership's interest in the life of an imaginary debutante in London.

Fish's work certainly straddles the mass/modernist divide. If we look at figure 7.5, we can see how, even when publishing in a commercial magazine like *Vanity Fair*, her work is influenced by experimental art forms: cubist lines blend with minimalist shapes. However, it is the transatlantic publication of Fish's illustrations that deserves more focus than their style. The continued success of *The Letters of Eve* soon led to Fish's work appearing across the pond in American monthlies; by the early 1920s, her illustrations were well-known features not only in *Vanity Fair*, but in other large-circulation monthlies like *Harper's Bazaar*. Her front covers for *Vanity Fair*, together with her "Sweet Simplicity and Her Social Success" column, which also appeared in *Vanity Fair* in the early 1920s, made her a sought-after figure in the American publishing

Figure 7.4. Anne Harriet Fish, *The Letters of Eve*, Tatler, July 1915.

industry. Ever international, Fish's work also appeared in French magazines like *La Vie Parisienne*, which published her illustrated advertisements for the Abdulla cigarette company. Titled "Mélisande a Monte-Carlo," these advertisements were more like a recurring comic strip as they featured different scenes depicting the socialite, Mélisande, popping up at various international parties and balls, cigarette firmly in hand.

Fish's work shows how, by the early 1910s, the comic strip was going global via the pages of periodicals. The comic strip is thus contrapuntal; it pops up in different contexts in magazines from different parts of the world. However, it is true that work's appearance in global periodicals could be said to represent the inevitable circulation of a successful illustrator's work, rather than any global aspirations on the part of magazine editors. In addition, the fact that Fish's work was most popular and well known in Britain and America implies that the circulation of her illustrations does not truly represent a global "worlding" of the comic strip but instead constitutes what Jonathan Arac has described as "Anglo-globalism," a less transformative form of partial literary "worlding" that encompasses a few English-language speaking countries, rather than several countries whose languages and cultures are more varied.[37]

While Fish's work evinces a sort of burgeoning transatlanticism that occasionally incorporated periodicals from European capitals, other comic strips such as *Mandrake the Magician* evidence how periodicals transported the comic strip beyond Anglocentric, Western European cultures, transforming it into a medium through which artists, editors, and readers participated in a more diverse world literary network. David Damrosch defines world literature as "literary works that circulate beyond their culture of origin, either in translation or in their original language," and the *Mandrake the Magician* comic strips exemplify this definition. Featuring Mandrake and his friend Lothar, an African prince, who travel around the world fighting crime, the strip first appeared in a variety of American newspapers on June 11, 1934, having been syndicated by the King Features Syndicate. One of the first newspapers in which the strip appeared was New York's *Rome Sentinel*, a weekly newspaper with an estimated circulation of twenty thousand readers. The strip was quickly syndicated internationally; between 1934 and 2014, the first *Mandrake* episode, titled "The Cobra," appeared in newspapers and magazines in Australia, Argentina, Brazil, France, French Polynesia, Italy, Norway, Portugal, Spain, Turkey, the UK, and the USA.

Indicating the role mass-market periodicals played in bringing the comic strip to global audiences, one of the more prolific homes for the strip was the *Australian Women's Weekly*, which began syndicating the strip on Saturday, December 1, 1934. The *Australian Women's Weekly* was a weekly magazine that straddled the high/low, modernist/mass culture divides. As Diane Ottley

GREAT MOMENTS AT THE MOVIES

How the Bitter Taste of Life Can Be Sweetened by a Little Dash of Cinema

THE FILLUMS BY FISH

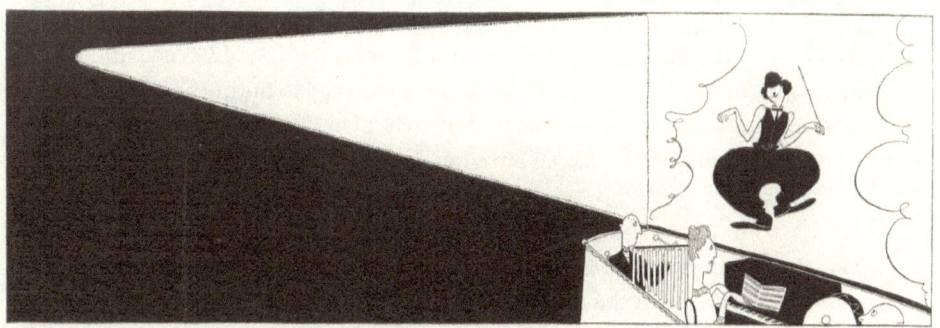

THE SCREEN AS A MARRIAGE PROMOTER

SOLOMON, who—because of his wisdom—was known as the Woodrow Wilson of his time, aptly remarked (with that unfailing *flair* for uttering a platitude so ponderously that people were persuaded it was a part of prophetic prescience) that it was not good for man to be alone—at the movies. Ah! How true that is. How beautifully, poignantly, true. For, without a maiden beside one—a ravishing and sympathetic maiden—what possible use is a movie show to a well-balanced man? A movie, by itself, registers, in the realm of human delight, zero. A maiden, by *herself*, registers precisely the same figure. A gentleman, however rich and proud, is likewise a wholly negligible agent in registering rapture. But combine them! Ah, how quickly we arrive at ardent and passionate happiness! Some philosophers even insist that the movies were only invented to check the falling marriage rate. Why, Charlie Chaplin alone has led to well over two million marriages, and that in a world in which the demand for marriages had waned, waxed, and become absolutely sluggish.

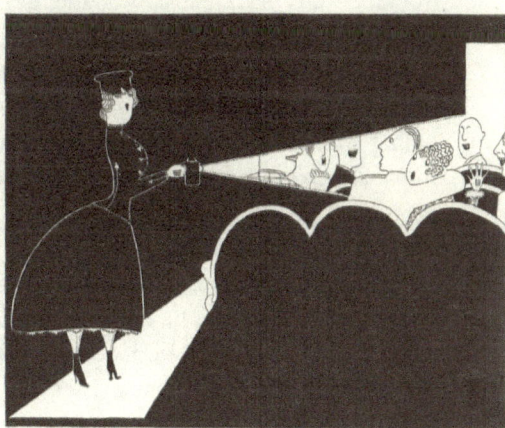

THE TYPICAL AMERICAN FILLUM

THE Rockies. Victor De La Mar, the cruel, rich mining king. Little Lina, the virtuous fiancé of Red Ike, the ranch owner—the gentleman bearing a whip in the background. Lina's baby sister—the one going down, in a simple lace nightgown. Lina, will die, you say? Die, to save her virtue? Oh, not at all. She will land safely in the top of a tall tree, after falling only two thousand feet in the air. And why the cheeild, you ask? Why, simply because no self-respecting cinema artiste ever jumps from a cliff without taking a baby along.

OH, THOSE CRUEL USHERS

THE proud and lately elected President of these here United States ought to start right out by making one or two really sensible laws. Why, in Heaven's name, can't he let the old tariff alone and begin on those super Huns, the lady ushers at the movies. A female firefly is all very well in her place—say in a garden or at the grave of a dead love—but really, *not* in the aisles of a movie palace. They all wear rubber soles, and they just dot on snooping along until they see their chance to light up little Lottie, lately a lady presidin' at the ribbons, or at the toilet goods, or the marked-down notions—and her gentleman frie who was only protecting her, anyway, just because she was so frightfully afraid in the dar'

Figure 7.5. Anne Harriet Fish, "Great Moments at the Movies," *Vanity Fair*, December 1916.

has noted, from the mid-1930s, the magazine's audience consisted of "a large number of women interested in modernity," with the work of modern artists like Mary Alice appearing in its pages.[38] That the magazine serialized *Mandrake the Magician* is interesting for several reasons; it was not the obvious choice for a magazine whose other contents in the same issue included a piece titled "Brilliant Scenes for Royal Wedding," which provided coverage of the recent wedding of England's Prince George and Princess Marina of Greece, and the magazine's recurring "Homemakers" column, "devoted to the interests of home-lovers."[39] The comic strip was introduced as "a splendid addition to the amusement side of the paper" and "an amazing creation of fiction."[40]

Comparing how *Mandrake the Magician* appeared in the *Australian Women's Weekly* to how it was then syndicated and translated in a magazine from Turkey, *1001 Roman*, demonstrates how comic strips and their global dissemination raise questions about the translatability of certain ideas. The syndication of comic strips means that, inevitably, the format and contexts in which strips appear, along with the precise ways in which captions are translated, reflect the values of different countries and cultures: public tastes, national histories, social norms. When "The Cobra" appeared in the *Australia Women's Weekly*, the main characters were introduced as follows: Inspector Sheldon "of the United States Secret Service," his daughter, Barbara, and Tommy Lord, Inspector Sheldon's assistant. They are tasked with investigating the disappearance of some papers from the study of Ambassador Vandergriff, who tells Inspector Sheldon that if the papers are revealed, "four nations will rise in a worldwide revolt that will smash civilization."[41] In panel fourteen, Lothar appears at the door of the house with the intention of investigating the possible crime with Mandrake. When Lothar appears, Inspector Sheldon and Ambassador Vandergriff are alarmed. In panel fifteen, Vandergriff asks, "What does he want? How did he get into the house?" Inspector Sheldon gets out his gun and demands, "Who are you? Put up your hands. You're under arrest." In panel sixteen, Vandergriff again asks, "How did you get into my house?" before adding, "Who is your master?" Lothar announces that he has come "not to harm you, but to announce the coming of my master."[42] In panel seventeen, Mandrake appears, with Lothar again referring to him as "my master."[43]

When in November 1939 the exact same *Mandrake* comic strip was reprinted in *1001 Roman*, a popular Turkish magazine, the racist assumption that Lothar must have a "master" on account of his being Black is absent from the captions. Here, instead, Lothar is titled Aptullah (Abdullah), a common name in Turkey that, translated from Arabic, means "servant of God." The strip in *1001 Roman* has been abbreviated and consists of only ten panels, rather than seventeen. As in the *Australian Women's Weekly* version, Lothar is described as standing at the door silently as Inspector Sheldon and Ambassador Vandergriff question him.

Crucially, though, the Ambassador does not assume Aptullah has a "master," and his manner is considerably more polite. He says, "What does he want? How did he come to this house? Please ask."[44] In panel ten, Lothar introduces Mandrake as his "bayim," a word which translates as "sir" rather than "master."[45] There seems to be a racially charged element to the Australian comic strip that is not present in the Turkish version of the same strip. The *Australian Women's Weekly* version was a direct reprint of the original King Features strip that appeared in American newspapers. It is not inconceivable that North American and Australian readers, existing as they did in countries whose histories were particularly fraught by segregation, colonialism, and the specter of the slave trade, may have been expected to view the references to Lothar's apparent "master" as de rigueur. The contrasting versions of *Mandrake* remind us that comics, being globally syndicated, have a unique ability to expose different countries' different attitudes towards things like race and class. As Charles Hatfield and Bart Beaty have noted, "Even what we have called 'Anglophone comics' is a cluster of traditions rather than a single one, a complex field in which multiple national histories overlap and sometimes compete."[46] When we add a non-Anglophone magazine like *1001 Roman* to the mix, the difference in global traditions becomes even more apparent. Comparing the Australian and Turkish versions of *Mandrake* exposes how Australia's history of white settler colonization of its indigenous population may here play a role in the inherently racist portrayal of Lothar's Blackness.

That the Turkish version of *Mandrake* is different from the Australian version seems to demonstrate, anachronistically, what Emily Apter has since termed "untranslatability." In one of the central challenges to the concept of world literature as a harmonious, equal network, Apter argues that some definitions of world literature have remained "oblivious" to linguistic, political, and cultural differences that simply do not translate and cannot be reconciled. In short, world literature can never truly constitute a fully cooperative set of equal exchanges on account of the processes of "non-translation, mistranslation, incomparability and untranslatability" that accompany the global transmission of a text.[47] Some ideas, she posits, are simply "untranslatables,"[48] an idea Katherine Kelp-Stebbins supports in her recent deconstruction of the notion that comics are an inherently universal form.[49] The presentation of Lothar in the *Australian Women's Weekly*'s *Mandrake* strips simply does not (and, arguably, should not) translate for the Turkish readers of the more avant-garde *1001 Roman*.

However, in some cases, it is true that the universal format of the comic at least transcends linguistic barriers, if not cultural ones. As figure 7.6 proves, it is not necessarily the case that readers of *Modern Sketch* need to understand Chinese to understand the comic strip. The captions aid in providing the reader

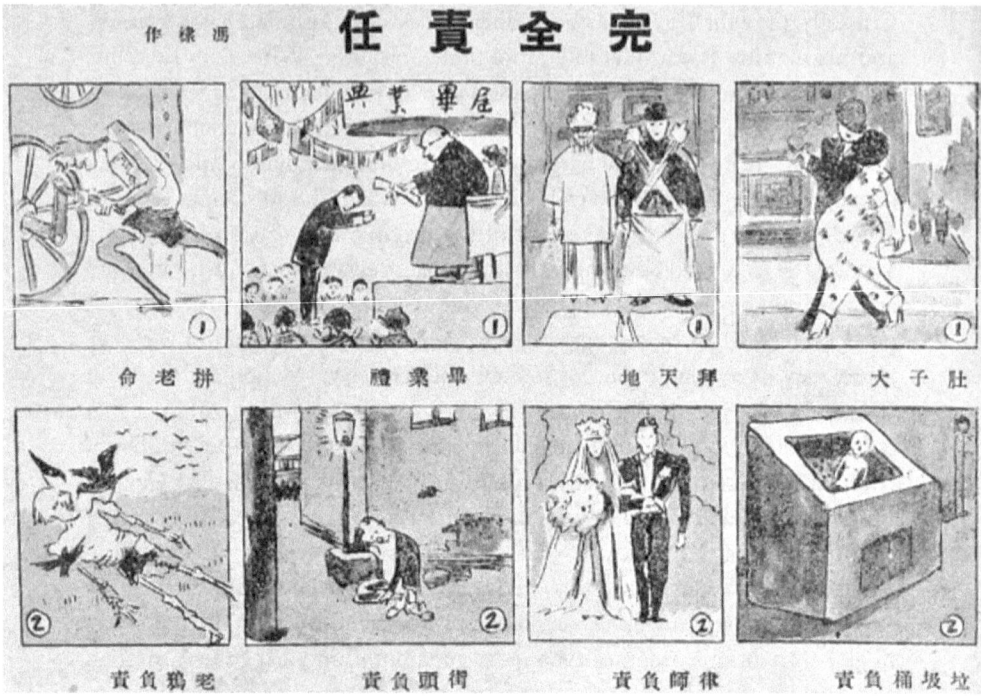

Figure 7.6. Feng Di, "Taking Full Charge," *Modern Sketch*, July 1936.

with narrative closure, but there is also a pleasure in trying to work out what the narrative means for readers who cannot understand the language in which the captions are written.

CONCLUSION

This chapter has explored magazines and comics as dialogic textual forms that were relatively new in the early 1900s. While magazines and comics are literary forms in their own right, with their own distinct histories, they also share important qualities: a reputation for experimental content, a privileging of interactions between visual art and text, a desire to publish or reprint work by artists from around the globe, a commitment to promoting readerly interpretation, and an affiliation with movements and people that are avant-garde or alternative in their cultural, political, and artistic ideals. Their shared qualities mean that the comic and the little magazine—and their contributions to world literature—must be considered in tandem; they are forms that define one another.

As Anne Fish's comics in *Vanity Fair* and the successful syndication of the *Mandrake* series in the *Australian Women's Weekly* and *1001 Roman* show, the comic strip was, literally, part of the magazine form. While little magazines created text and image conjunctions that anticipated the comic book's emergence as a medium in its own right, it is also true that in some cases comic strips occupied large portions of magazines—to the extent that their forms blurred. For example, by the end of its run, the *Revista Multicolor* looked more like a comic than a literary magazine. This exposes the arbitrary nature of using terms like "comics" or "little magazine" to separate periodicals into neat boxes: their dialogism blurs the line between the two genres.

Both the comic strip and magazine are inherently global forms. From its earliest incarnations, the little magazine functioned as a transnational text. It was, after all, to quote T. S. Eliot, a form designed to enable contributors to catch "the attention of writers and of readers . . . in other countries."[50] Magazines like *Rhythm* positioned themselves as publications designed to attract and represent voices and readers from around the globe. The worldwide circulation and syndication of comics is a major factor in their transnationalism. As Hatfield and Beaty have observed, that "certain comics cultures—take for instance Japanese manga, Franco-Belgian BD [*bandes dessinées*], and US comics—have been exported widely and influenced the comics of other cultures" is just one of many "templates" that exemplify "how comics are made worldwide."[51] To consider how these two forms work in dialogue—how comic strips fit into magazines, for example, and how the transmission of a comic strip is affected in turn by the cultural, social, and historical traditions that backdrop any magazine—is to consider the transformative potential of the periodical form as a vehicle for the construction of world literature. Magazines facilitated this construction of world literature both as system (they reprinted and/or translated comics from other countries) and ideal (the fact that audiences *wanted* these comic strips translated suggests readers' and editors' willingness to engage with literary products from foreign countries and cultures).

These dialogues bear intriguing implications for ongoing debates about what world literature is and means. The transnational nature of comic strips that circulated in magazines suggests the presence of a democratic literary network in which magazines published comic strips from different countries because they were popular with readers and translated, for the most part, across cultures, regardless of their nation of origin. However, it can also be said that maybe editors merely recognized the economic potential of reprinting popular strips, rather than feeling any particular desire to bring the comic strips of another country to their readers for any perceived cultural value. We could argue that there is an inherent bias to the global transmission of the comic strip: the fact that many comic strips originated in North America before being translated into the pages of periodicals in places like Latin America (as was the case with the Argentine *Tit-Bits*) or Turkey (*1001 Roman*) suggests an uncomfortable imbalance in which the transmission and circulation of the comics form seems to operate along the core/periphery model Casanova and Moretti describe. This is supported by the fact that editors of mass-market American magazines like *Vanity Fair* looked primarily to artists like Fish and quintessentially Anglophone periodicals such as *Tatler* for their comic–strip content, rather than to illustrators like the Latin American artists who contributed to Borges's *Revista Multicolor*. One of the conclusions we might draw is that editors of North American magazines simply may not have been as familiar with contributors to non-English-language periodicals, but this in itself seems to confirm that writers and editors operating in what were considered to be "peripheral" countries were often overlooked by those writers and editors operating in "core" metropoles.

Another conclusion we can make is that, to a degree, the early twentieth-century comic strip's ability to circulate as world literature was conditioned by the magazines in which it was published. Comic strips' visual aspects almost always translated. However, the cultural and historical nuances of the country of origin of the magazine in which they appeared often served to implicitly nationalize or politicize what viewers saw when they looked at these apparently universal images. No comic translates perfectly, and these translational "glitches" often expose—rather than bridge—cultural differences, as we saw with the *Mandrake* series. While some of the examples we have seen challenge the idea of comics and periodicals as world literature, the twin advents of the graphic novel and digital comics continue to offer further possibilities for the transmission of comic strips in ways that transcend national boundaries. Additionally, thanks to the internet, readers can view comics from practically any country, their attempts to engage with *manhua* or *manga* or *bandes dessinées* no longer requiring trips to comic shops or antique bookstores, but simply the brief click of a mouse button.

While comic strips and books are now ubiquitous, globally popular forms, their emergence, popularity, and transmission around the world would not have been possible without the periodicals that printed them. Little modernist magazines such as *Prisma* or *Rhythm* helped to anticipate the comic book format, and their influence still looms large. For example, in their handmade, alternative appearance, the Zines and underground comics that were borne out of punk and hardcore scenes of the late 1970s and 1980s and flourished in the 1990s and 2000s certainly possess qualities of the little modernist magazines that appeared almost one hundred years before. It is interesting to note that while the modernist magazine no longer exists in the way that it did in its 1910s–1930s glory years, the much-maligned commercial periodicals—the big magazines—still do. And they still maintain an interest in comics. In 2015, for example, the British *GQ Magazine*, a men's fashion and lifestyle monthly originally published by Condé Nast in New York in 1931, included an article titled "Why Comic Books Are Helping Us Process Human Rights Issues," which reprinted strips by the contemporary graphic novelist Jon Sacks.

Perhaps comic strips "outgrew" little magazines because commercial magazines had the funding to pay for their repeat syndication and translation, thus enabling their freer movement from one country to another, a movement which led to worldwide audiences, increased popularity, and enduring longevity. The evolution of the comic strip reminds us that the modernism with which magazines, both small and big, were indelibly associated was, and still remains, a complex and contradictory aesthetic and temporal category.[52] The diversity of the periodicals in which comic strips appeared reinforces the notion that modernism cannot be bisected into neat "highbrow" (little magazines) and "lowbrow" (commercial magazines) components, and instead functioned as a movement that saw elements of the popular mingle with the niche or alternative. The emergence of the comic strip was influenced, if not defined, by this popular/niche dichotomy. Comic strips could be "big" or "small"; they could gain mass readerships or could dwindle after just a few issues if their characters were not popular enough; they could—and still do—have a wide appeal or only a cult following. As Daniel Worden has argued, comic books were "rooted in the material and temporal conditions of periodicals."[53] Studying the material and temporal convergences between comic strips and magazines reveals the truly dialogic nature of both forms and their sometimes unexpected, if imperfect, constructions of global cultural exchange.

Notes

1. Jorge Luis Borges, "Autobiographical Notes," *New Yorker*, September 19, 1970, 75.

2. Sean Latham and Robert Scholes, "The Rise of Periodical Studies," *PMLA* 121, no. 2 (2006): 517.

3. P. L. Thomas, "Adventures in Genre!: Rethinking Genre Through Comics/Graphic Novels," *Journal of Graphic Novels and Comics* 2, no. 2 (2011): 188.

4. Scholarship has only recently begun to explore the links between modernism and comics. In 2018, Paul Peppis argued that comic strips such as George Herriman's *Krazy Kat* series appeared in the pages of magazines as forms of "popular modernism"; their content "works from inside a popular medium to make it new." Paul Peppis, "Popular Modernism in the Late *Krazy Kat* Comics: Industry and Innovation in the Color Sundays," *Journal of Modern Periodical Studies* 9, no. 2 (2018): 157.

5. Brooks E. Hefner and Edward Timke, "Beyond Little and Big: Circulation, Data, and American Magazine History," in "Investigating Big Magazines," special issue, *Journal of Modern Periodical Studies* 11, no. 1 (2021): 27.

6. Matthew Levay, "Repetition, Recapitulation, Routine: Dick Tracy and the Temporality of Daily Newspaper Comics," in "Seriality," special issue, *Journal of Modern Periodical Studies* 9, no. 1 (2018): 102.

7. David Kunzle, *The Early Comic Strip: Narrative Strips and Picture Stories in the European Broadsheet from 1450 to 1825* (Berkeley: University of California Press, 1973), 2.

8. Kunzle, 2.

9. Will Eisner, *Comics and Sequential Art* (Tamarac, FL: Poorhouse, 1985), 3. Scott McCloud, *Understanding Comics: The Invisible Art* (1993; repr., New York: Harper Perennial, 1994), 9.

10. Aaron Meskin, "Defining Comics," *Journal of Aesthetics and Art Criticism* 65, no. 4 (2007): 372.

11. Kirsten MacLeod, introduction to *American Little Magazines of the Fin de Siècle: Art, Protest, and Cultural Transformation* (Toronto, ON: University of Toronto Press, 2018), 4.

12. Faye Hammill, Paul Hjartarson, and Hannah McGregor, "Introducing Magazines and/as Media: The Aesthetics and Politics of Serial Form," *ESC: English Studies in Canada* 41, no. 1 (2015): 6.

13. Robert Scholes and Clifford Wulfman, *Modernism in the Magazines* (New Haven, CT: Yale University Press, 2010), 46.

14. Henry Jenkins et al., "Roundtable: Comics and Methodology," *Inks: The Journal of the Comics Studies Society* 1, no.1 (2017): 60.

15. Ezra Pound, "Small Magazines," *English Journal* 19, no. 9 (November 1930): 699. See also Hoffmann, Allen, and Ulrich's assertion that the little magazine is "non-commercial by intent" and designed "to print artistic work which for reasons of commercial expediency is not acceptable to the money-minded periodicals or presses" in Frederick Hoffman, Charles Allen and Carolyn F. Ulrich, eds., *The Little Magazine: A History and a Bibliography* (Princeton, NJ: Princeton University Press, 1946), 2.

16. Suzanne Churchill and Adam McKible, "Little Magazines and Modernism: An Introduction," *American Periodicals: A Journal of History, Criticism, and Biography* 15, no. 1 (2005): 2.

17. Charles Hatfield, *Alternative Comics: An Emerging Literature* (Jackson: University Press of Mississippi, 2005), x.

18. Paul Lopes, *Demanding Respect: The Evolution of the American Comic Book* (Philadelphia: Temple University Press, 2009), 17.

19. Roger Sabin, *Adult Comics* (London: Routledge, 2013), 18.

20. David Carrier, *The Aesthetics of Comics* (University Park, PA: Penn State University Press, 2000), 4.

21. Murry gained the inspiration for *Rhythm* from the time he spent on Paris's Left Bank in 1910.

22. M. R. Ivasyshyn, "Implementation of Verbal and Visual-graphic Means of Multimodality in *Captain America* Comic Book," *Science and Education a New Dimension. Philology* 48, no. 161 (2018): 27.

23. John Middleton Murry, "Aims and Ideals," *Rhythm* 1, no.1 (June 1911): 36.

24. *Die Pleite*, no. 4, May 1, 1919, 4.

25. *Die Pleite*, 4.

26. John A. Crespi, "China's *Modern Sketch*: The Golden Era of Cartoon Art, 1934–1937," MIT Visualizing Cultures, https://visualizingcultures.mit.edu/modern_sketch/ms_essay_03.pdf

27. McCloud, *Understanding Comics*, 63.

28. Gabriele Ripp and Lukas Etter, "Intermediality, Transmediality, and Graphic Narrative," in *From Comic Strips to Graphic Novels: Contributions to the Theory and History of Graphic Narrative*, ed. Daniel Stein Jan-Noel Thon (Berlin: De Gruyter, 2013), 191–92.

29. Nora C. Benedict, *Borges and the Literary Marketplace: How Editorial Practices Shaped Cosmopolitan Reading* (New Haven, CT: Yale University Press, 2021), 17.

30. David Damrosch, *What Is World Literature?* (Princeton, NJ: Princeton University Press, 2003), 4.

31. Pascale Casanova, *The World Republic of Letters* (London: Verso, 2004), 3, 163.

32. Longxi Zhang, "Canon and World Literature," *Journal of World Literature* 1, no. 1 (2020): 123.

33. David Earle, *Re-Covering Modernism: Pulps, Paperbacks, and the Prejudice of Form* (London: Routledge, 2016), 3.

34. See for example, Mark S. Morrison, *The Public Face of Modernism: Little Magazines, Audiences, and Reception, 1905–1920*. (Madison: University of Wisconsin Press, 2000).

35. Faye Hammill and Karen Leick, "Modernism and the Quality Magazines: *Vanity Fair, American Mercury, New Yorker, Esquire*," in *The Oxford Critical and Cultural History of Modernist Magazines*, ed. Peter Brooker and Andrew Thacker, vol. 2, *North America*, (Oxford: Oxford University Press, 2012), 178.

36. Monika Schmitz-Emans, *Literatur-Comics: Adaptionen und Transformationen der Weltliteratur* (Berlin: De Gruyter, 2012), 3.

37. Jonathan Arac, "Anglo-Globalism?" *NLR* 16 (July/August 2002): 35.

38. Dianne Ottley, *Grace Crowley's Contribution to Australian Modernism and Geometric Abstraction* (Newcastle, UK: Cambridge Scholars, 2010), 78.

39. "Homemakers," *Australian Women's Weekly*, December 1, 1934, 23.

40. *Mandrake the Magician, Australian Women's Weekly*, December 1, 1934, 3.

41. *Mandrake the Magician*, 3.

42. *Mandrake the Magician*, 3.

43. *Mandrake the Magician*, 3.

44. *Mandrake, 1001 Roman*, November 6, 1939, 42.

45. *Mandrake*, 42.

46. Charles Hatfield and Bart Beaty, introduction to *Comic Studies: A Guidebook*, ed. Charles Hatfield and Bart Beaty (New Brunswick, NJ: Rutgers University Press, 2020), 3.

47. Emily Apter, *Against World Literature: On the Politics of Untranslatability* (New York: Verso, 2013), 4.

48. Apter, 20.

49. See Katherine Kelp-Stebbins, *How Comics Travel: Publication, Translation, Radical Literacies* (Columbus: Ohio State University Press, 2022).

50. T. S. Eliot, "A Message," *London Magazine* 1, no. 1 (February 1954): 16.

51. Hatfield and Beaty, introduction, 6.

52. Scholars continue to connect comics to modernism's relationship with popular, commercial cultures. For example, Paul Peppis posits that comic strips such as George Herriman's *Krazy Kat* series were forms of "popular modernism" that "a mass cultural product that works from inside a popular medium to make it new." See Paul Peppis, "Popular Modernism," 157.

53. Daniel Worden, "Reading, Looking, Feeling: Comix after Legitimacy," in *The Comics of R. Crumb. Underground in the Art Museum* (Jackson: University Press of Mississippi, 2021), 62.

Section III

POP/ART: COMICS LOW AND HIGH

TELLING DETAILS

Feminine Flourish in Midcentury Illustration and Comics

SCOTT BUKATMAN

When I was growing up, there were some comic strips that I avoided with every fiber of my being: strips like *The Heart of Juliet Jones*, written by Elliot Caplin with art by Stan Drake, and *On Stage* (later, *Mary Perkins: On Stage*) written and drawn by Leonard Starr. These comics were steeped in details of decor and gesture, which owed much, I later learned, to illustrated fiction and advertisements in postwar magazines (primarily women's magazines). *Juliet Jones* was a soap opera strip, explicitly modeled on such shows as *These Are My Children* and *Search For Tomorrow*. It makes a lot of sense: newspapers could deliver daily installments just as television was doing, and the various features in newspapers could be targeted to different demographics.[1] *On Stage* was less beholden to its initial conceit—a would-be actress (who sees some success over the decades) coming to New York—and featured more adventure (often courtesy of Mary's husband's job as a photojournalist) than *Juliet Jones*, which rarely moved too far from Juliet's small-town setting.

I avoided these strips for all kinds of terrible reasons: I was uninterested as a kid because the stories were about grown-ups *(girl* grown-ups); I avoided them as an adolescent because they weren't about superheroes or the Fabulous Furry Freak Brothers. And I continued to avoid them as an adult comics scholar because of what I saw as their bland realism, which eschewed so many compelling attributes that were unique to comics, including motion lines, emanata, and sound effects. They weren't cosmic and they weren't comical. And they came packed with what were, to me, superfluous details.

That was a lifetime ago: I've come to not only appreciate but to veritably swoon (affectively and intellectually) over this work and the illustration styles that influenced it. And so this essay explores and celebrates the expressive and material details that proliferated though "lifestyle" magazine illustration (both fiction and advertising illustration), "soap opera" comic strips, and romance comics of the 1950s and '60s: together these media constitute an archive of images that, through their attention to midcentury American clothing, design, and domestic space, spoke to the aspirations and mild anxieties of an ideal, mostly middle-class and mostly white, female reader.

Scott McCloud and any number of Gestalt psychologists have noted that we have a predilection for seeing faces in the vaguest conjunction of the proper number of dots (two or three, depending on whether or not we need a nose) and lines (one, preferably straightish, for a mouth). In comics, McCloud argues, the simpler and more generic the face—a Mickey Mouse, a Charlie Brown—the more it can serve as a vehicle for "universal identification": "The cartoon is a *vacuum* into which our *identity* and *awareness* are *pulled* . . . an *empty shell* that we inhabit which *enables* us to travel in *another realm*. We don't just *observe* the cartoon, we *become* it!"[2]

Some shells, though, are less empty than others; not all comics art aspires to the condition of the universal. Some of it works toward a greater realism through, among other things, a specificity of detail. Such styles get a lot less love from comics scholars than do cartoony and abstract approaches.[3] As far back as 1944, the great Manny Farber lamented that "comic strips are not what they used to be . . . The old style in comic strips was to trip everything—drawing, dialogue, place, action—for laughs. The new style is almost never concerned with being funny; rather it tries to be as much like a soap opera as possible."[4]

Lifestyle illustration and soap opera strips often relied on photo-reference, and photographic realism is antithetical to the universal identification highlighted by McCloud. "When you look at a photo or realistic drawing of a face," he writes, "you see it as the face of *another*."[5] But, of course, there are virtues in the act of seeing another to whom one can nevertheless relate in some special, even secret, way, just as it can be flattering to encounter a telling detail and know just what it *tells*.

Fiction imported the detail from historical narrative to achieve the aesthetic verisimilitude that Roland Barthes called the "reality effect." It's not the specific details that matter, but their general presence, for "it is the *category* of 'the real' (and not its contingent contents) which is then signified."[6] The details Stan Drake and Leonard Starr provide have this effect of coordinating the world of the comic strip with the lived worlds of their readers, but they do more than that; the emphatic details of gesture and mise-en-scène also manifest a heightened reality that articulates some of the fantasies and fears percolating through a postwar culture venerating youth, style, and abundance.

These illustrations and comics drawings would seem to be the epitome of a self-evident transparency, and yet I find them surprisingly, almost inexhaustibly dense, with a richness difficult to fully unpack. I've tried, in this essay, to begin with simpler details and move out to greater complexities. I begin by reviewing two categories of detail: performative details of gesture and expression, and material details of decor and costume. If even the most cartoony comics styles can convey subtle emotional states through simple gesture, then what's to be gained by greater realism? Material details, too, can appear superfluous, even ornamental, and they kind of sort of are. But details of performance and setting ground the image in a particular world and address an ideal reader for whom the *right* details can communicate volumes about, say, character, taste, or class position. Lifestyle illustration reveled in ornamental and theatrical artifice, even as it traded in a snapshot spontaneity of expression and gesture. Images were packed with scenic detail and vivacious characters, each of whom seemed to inhabit their own story. Though "illustrations" by definition, they were never entirely beholden to what they illustrated, and they often possessed a satisfying self-sufficiency. Romance comics, which soared in popularity in the same period, shared much with lifestyle illustration, despite lower pay rates, cheap paper, crude printing, and an implicitly younger readership. Some of the best romance artists imbued their short narratives with judicious detail, augmented by techniques also found in Hollywood melodramas, further enworlding readers through varied compositions, changing locations, color, and narrative resolution.

EXPRESSION AND GESTURE

The work of Stan Drake is rich with telling gesture and facial expression, performative details less central to my beloved superhero comics. Consider a *Captain America* panel from a 1973 comic book (figure 8.1) penciled by Sal Buscema and scripted by Steve Engelhart. Cap (if I may) has returned home to find a note from his girl (and Shield agent) Sharon Carter; she's leaving him. The image is medium close: we can see Captain America's torso and the hand holding the note. But the emphasis is on his face. "You've **read** the note," instructs the caption atop the panel, "now read Cap's **face**."[7] Okay, let's.

He's clearly stunned. Only part of his face is visible, the upper part masked and cowled. But his eyes are widened, his mouth is open, his teeth separated. The mouth is turned down a bit at the sides. The colors of the background are replaced by pure white, and black emanata form a halo of shock. The emotion of the scene is very legible.

But do we truly *feel* Captain America's shock, or do we *recognize* it through a shorthand set of symbols that *connote* shock? Nothing individuates this face, and the image simply presents this frozen moment of surprise. There's one nice

Figure 8.1. Sal Buscema and Steve Engelhar, *Captain America*, first published 1973.

detail: some lines and coloring variation suggest crinkles in the paper he holds, signaling the tightness of his grip.

The caption tells us to *read* this face: so semiotics, rather than affect, is the proper mode of engagement. And the reader is given clues: the panel doesn't exist on its own but is part of a page comprised of six panels. The third highlights the note from Sharon; Cap is in the background. We read it before he does, and so can infer what he must be feeling in the next panel, moments later, as his knowledge catches up to ours. Assuming a modicum of empathy on our part, we do indeed know how he feels.[8] So what does it matter whether Buscema rendered Captain America's shock and grief in all its physical detail, since his audience could project their own response onto the scene?

Telling Details: Feminine Flourish in Illustration and Comics   161

Figure 8.2. Stan Drake, *Juliet Jones*, first published 1957.

But other approaches aspire to something more spontaneous and affective. In a daily *Juliet Jones* strip by Stan Drake from 1957 (figure 8.2), comprised of three panels from varied perspectives, feisty and fabulous Eve Jones is berating herself for something as her perseverating sister Juliet calmly listens.[9] Eve's frustration is evident in the dialogue, but also in her "acting." In the first panel her torso is thrust forward in what would be an awkward pose, but which clearly conveys angry pacing. Her face is the focus of the tightly cropped center panel, and her expression is charmingly asymmetrical, expressive of this performance of self-critical wallowing: she wallops her hand with her fist in an all-too-human gesture that neatly connotes self-abnegation and self-consciousness at once.

The final panel has her in a chair, her body semirecumbent. The context—her volatility in the scene, the rapidity of her movement—suggests that she has perhaps thrown herself into the chair. But wait! The case can be made that she's actually doing it as we watch. There are no motion lines, but her arms and the flow of her skirt about her knees imbue the image with motion. Her body isn't quite settled. Her hair is subtly forward, suggesting that she's still moving back. This implied motion is in keeping with what we know about Eve: she's a self-performative, good-hearted drama queen given to grand gestures, who *flings* herself into a chair in resigned frustration. There's *character* in this flourish—the reader takes pleasure from Eve's company, her *presence*.

One might posit a dichotomy, then, between affective face (Eve) and semiotic face (Cap). David Apatoff does something like this in a blog post comparing Drake's art with Ivan Brunetti's.[10] Drake provides a nuanced verisimilitude, while Brunetti's entire mission has been to strip his work of extraneous elements. His characters perform stock gestures not unlike those in nineteenth-century guides to melodramatic acting, while Drake's perform naturalistically, soliciting identification in ways familiar to moviegoers, TV watchers, and magazine readers. Brunetti is *semiotics*, Drake is *affect*, and the difference is measured in the degree of illustrative realism.

Except, no. Affect and meaning just aren't as dichotomous as this. Hordes of cartoony cartoonists, Brunetti included, have endowed their simply limned characters with great expressive range. A small line, an eyebrow, say, disported in a different direction, shifts the emotional valence. Audience inference, aided by narrative context and personal experience, fills in unseen details. Not "fills in" as in Scott McCloud's gutter, but fills in from a knowledge of the world, of relationships, of faces.

Comics, after all, has its roots in caricature, an abstraction of the real that combined overall simplification with selective exaggeration. The art historian E. H. Gombrich saw caricature as belonging to a history of art that eschewed the mimetic in favor of simpler methods of generating an impression of the real.[11] The ephemerality of facial expression, physiognomy, and posture are difficult to capture through laborious and meticulous mimicry. To demonstrate how minimal cues can convey a great sense of expression, Gombrich looked to children's literature, cartoons, and comics.

Caricature emphasized distortion and simplification for comic effect; in the nineteenth century, Rodolphe Töpffer began innovating a new kind of picture story that built upon caricature's speed and exaggeration. His faster, sketchier line, panel after panel, page after page, encouraged a fast-paced reading of his breakneck, frenetic tales. Töpffer's emphasis was on body, gesture, and setting, rather than nuances of facial expression. He was also an amateur actor, and his interest in the grandness and legibility of stock theatrical gestures was everywhere evident in his "paper pantomimes" (Thierry Smolderen's phrase).[12] It's in this sense that drawing in comics is akin to writing. Caricature and paper pantomimes demonstrate that comics characters needn't be overrich in detail to have affective power.

Nevertheless, there is phenomenological and affective power in the details of facial expression, comportment, gesture, and settings, abetted by compositional techniques that bind details into something more perceptually mimetic that enworlds its readers differently.[13] In considering how *works enworld*, Eric Hayot notes that both words speak to a condition of totality: "The work and the world name a self-enclosing, self-organizing, self-grounding process. This process is neither act nor event, subject nor object; it is the ground of activity, eventfulness, subject- and object-hood, and of procession." And there is "no common word for what the work and the world share, unless it is 'world' itself."[14] An aesthetic work shows us worlds, but it also constitutes a world of its own—and this is true whether that world is limned by the semiotic strategies of Sal Buscema or the mimetic performativity of Stan Drake. An encounter with the aesthetics of a comic poses and answers questions at once. Is this world like my world? What kind of consequences will actions have? Should I laugh?

Empathize? Thrill? Ponder? The parameters of the universe are established; horizons of expectation emerge as the reader is enworlded.

And that reader brings something to bear as well. Phenomenologically, Peter Mendelsund writes, "reading mirrors the procedure by which we acquaint ourselves with the world.... The practice of reading feels like, and is like, consciousness itself: imperfect, partial; hazy, co-creative."[15] Comics and illustrations like Stan Drake's solicit a particular cocreativity through particular details and by the realism with which they're presented. Details, for example, of expression and gesture, or of decor, or clothing—perhaps the details of a nice coat.

FASHION AND FLOURISH

There's a really, *really* nice coat that appears in a Sunday *Mary Perkins* from 1966 (figure 8.3). In the broad title panel that tops the strip, a character, Cathy Verna, is opening her door, and she's wearing this **coat**.[16] A magnificent, checkered affair with a large pattern typical of its time, broad black checks alternating with white. The coat itself has a design that ornaments the texture of the fabric, which seems to be a nubby tweed or wool—detail is literally "woven in."[17] The squares bend into other shapes as the coat gathers and drapes over her leaning body. We see the coat only twice more, without the same emphasis.

What's up with the coat? It adds nothing to the narrative, and it must have been a bear to render. Yet, dead center at the top of the strip, right next to the splashy overlaid title, it is by far the most attention-grabbing element of a page that includes lots of other effective details.

Its narrative insignificance is borne out by its placement. Newspaper editors could run *Mary Perkins* in its original three-tier layout as a half-page feature; they could lop off the top and run it on one-third of a page; they could even wrestle it into two tiers on one-quarter of a page by shrinking the art and adjusting the layout. The coat-as-ornament is *only* emphasized in that top tier, which itself is often ornamental. The virtuosic flourish that *is* the coat would never even have been seen by much of the *Mary Perkins* readership.[18]

So far I've mentioned "feminine" details of coats and performance, but Naomi Schor has famously wondered whether the detail itself is feminine. Her work tracks the history of gender-based dismissal of the detail. True art, as defined by such eighteenth-century figures as Joshua Reynolds, was to be understood at the level of the *whole*, with details selectively deployed to serve its singular meaning.[19] What Reynolds called "detailism" failed on two levels: its particularity privileged the material over the Ideal, and its proliferation distracted and thereby blocked access to the Sublime.[20] Schor argued that

Figure 8.3. Leonard Starr, *Mary Perkins*, first published 1966.

Reynolds "implicitly re-inscribes the sexual stereotypes of Western philosophy ... forging a durable link between maleness and form (*eidos*), femaleness and formless matter."[21]

The next century saw "the invasion of the arts by an anarchic mass of details" that eroded distinctions between significant and insignificant details, and between realism's judiciousness and naturalism's profligacy.[22] Detail was ornamental, and ornament was decidedly Not Art. Styles marked by an excess of detail betokened a feminine or effeminate sensibility. Gombrich, on the other hand, has posited ornament as soliciting a different mode of viewing.[23] Rather than a gaze that must encompass everything, the ornamental permits the gaze to wander where it will and rest where it might.

And so what Schor winningly calls the *insubordinate detail* is "feminine" in that it posed a threat to a masculine "hierarchic order which ... subordinates the periphery to the center, the accessory to the principal, the foreground to the background."[24] Cathy's coat in *Mary Perkins* might be just this kind of "insubordinate detail": not only feminine in its status as women's fashion but subordinated to neither narrative nor a hierarchical scopic regime. This monumental coat, despite its centrality, is ornamental rather than meaningful; a virtuosic, but presumably irrelevant, flourish. It draws the eye that lets itself be drawn, the eye that's willing to partake of incidental, rather than teleological, pleasures.

Unimportant and expendable though it may be, however, the coat tells us *something*—something about Cathy (her taste, her affluence) but also something about the readers of *Mary Perkins*. It signals the strip's midcentury modernity—it looks to be on trend, as does Cathy's coiffure and the short-sleeved ensemble she sports beneath the coat. As a signal, it floats above the narrative (physically as well as connotatively) and communicates with, even flatters, the au courant reader adept at decoding its fashion-forward signals.

To understand fashion is to know something of modern culture. To understand how fabrics drape is to know something of how bodies behave: how they inhabit and navigate the world, even how they actually sit. There's an anecdote about a cartooning instructor discouraging his students from drawing a woman on a couch with a leg tucked beneath her because, natural as the pose was in life, on paper "it always came out looking freakish, like the woman was missing one leg from the knee down." Someone brought him a *Mary Perkins* where Mary is seated just that way, casually and naturally.[25] Starr has learned from photography's snapshot realism a way of situating bodies more spontaneous than conventional.

Adolf Loos fully recognized, in the early twentieth century, a kind of degenerate power in the "ornamental and colorful effects" associated with ladies' fashion: a corruption taken still further by the imperatives of commodity culture; we no longer put so poisonous a spin on these things. Roland Barthes regarded the detail as something of a "luxurious extra" (Schor's phrase) in art and literature: never just boringly necessary, but something sensual, eroticized, and desublimated.[26] Schor adds, "Eros resides in the detail, because the detail is always at least partially sited in a real body."[27] Such details as Cathy's meticulously rendered coat, Eve's spontaneous performance, and Mary's natural comportment ground the work of these artists in tactile, sensual realities, building worlds that may have been contrived or ideal, but that were also firmly connected to the lived experience and aspirational dreams of middle- and working-class women.[28]

THEATRICALITY AND LIFESTYLE

If unnecessary detail could be regarded as ornamental, even fussy, it could also leave a comics artist open to the charge of being an *illustrator*—a term used as a pejorative by cartoonists, artists, and art historians alike. The commercialism of illustration put it at odds with the ostensible purity of the fine arts, as did its emphasis on production over inspiration. Alexander Nemerov writes of N. C. Wyeth's increasing dissatisfaction with the mandate of the job: "More and more he disagreed, sometimes vehemently, with his mentor's [Howard Pyle's] conviction that illustration could dramatize and clarify an action on the one hand and subtly illuminate a kind of essential truth on the other."[29] Illustration was, by definition, theatrical, and unalterably possessed of theater's artifice. The nineteenth-century aesthetician Frances Wey aligned "the abuse, the profusion of details" with "decadent literatures," and artifice with the falsity and superficiality of "painted women."[30]

Theatricality and ornament abound in the work of the commercial illustrators associated with such postwar magazines (and particularly women's magazines) as the *Ladies Home Journal, Good Housekeeping,* and *McCall's,* which were radically redefining their look. Such European émigré art directors as Mehemed Fehmy Agha and Alexey Brodovitch brought to *Vogue* and *Harper's Bazaar* deeply modernist sensibilities that incorporated typography and photography into bold graphic design, ideas that trickled down to less edgy publications. These magazines published plenty of fiction (until magazine fiction essentially vanished with the advent of television), and the artifice of illustration lent itself to fiction; fashion demanded the documentary power of photography.

Earlier magazine illustration was often executed in slow-drying oil paint and was printed as either a full page or an inset image. The postwar period saw a shift to media, like gouache and watercolor, that dried more quickly. These also yielded a flatter image, which illustrators turned to their advantage: they could layer their work, combine line drawings with painted elements, or mix media. Their work could also be more easily incorporated into page design; and some, like Al Parker, began to design pages—beautifully.

Illustrators at the powerful Charles E. Cooper studio in New York produced work that was "photographic" in two ways: photo-reference was used for everything from expression and posture to lighting, fashion, and composition; and it was an art of the "instant," often capturing what Armando Mendez calls "a single moment of telling expression."[31] The face—the woman's face—augmented by the proper accessories and appropriate pose, took on new graphic power (those critical of the striking work of Coby Whitmore, Jon Whitcomb, and others dubbed it "big head" illustration). Steeped in theatricality and artifice, these images nevertheless trafficked in all kinds of realistic detail.

Beyond illustrating their respective fictions or products, the task of this work was to reflect contemporary life and fashion in exciting ways—the best was strikingly modern, indeed modern*ist*, in its treatment of word and image, color, picture plane, and heterogeneity (famously, Al Parker illustrated all the fiction in one issue of *Cosmopolitan* using five pseudonyms and five different styles).[32] If this lifestyle illustration was less avant-garde than the work on

Figure 8.4. Columbia Records, *Music for Gracious Living*, 1955.

display in the tonier fashion magazines, it was nevertheless new, and deeply invested in the aesthetics of midcentury modernism.

The vivacity of these illustrations is put into high relief when compared to the photographed album covers for the *Music for Gracious Living* series released in 1955 by Columbia Records (figure 8.4): "bright photographs from the Hedrich Blessing architectural photography studio . . . [offer] subtly instructive pictured scenarios to answer the uncertainties of gracious living."[33] These images share much with lifestyle illustration—attention to the details of milieu, decor, and costume; staged settings of interpersonal interaction. And yet they couldn't be more different. The models gaze in each other's direction, look at a book, stare wistfully, and perhaps a bit alluringly, into an off-LP space, but nothing moves. Only the most generic of expressions hint at some form of emotion, but there is no life behind the eyes, and no connection of gazes. There is no point of imaginative entry to these glossy but inert Stepford-suburb images.

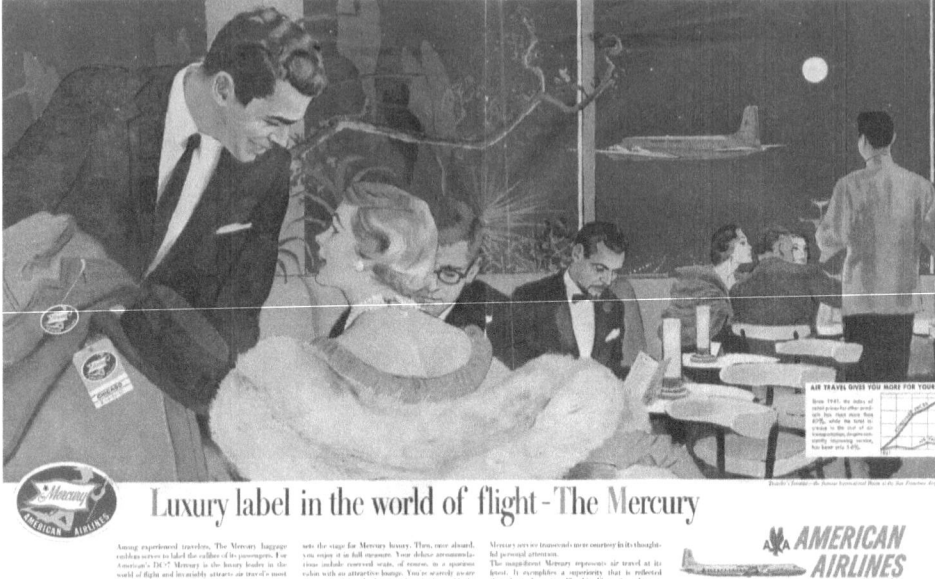

Figure 8.5. Al Parker, advertisement for American Airlines, 1957.

Compare the embalmed scene on the cover of the "Barbecue" edition with an upscale airline advertisement from 1957 by Al Parker, one of the deans of lifestyle illustration (figure 8.5). First, the barbecue, where a cheerful grandpa manning the white-brick grill gives his wife (a tad overdressed in pearls) over by the table a friendly look; she returns a thin smile. An overalled kid whose face isn't visible eyes a watermelon in the lower foreground. A young man, the couple's son I suppose, is perched next to the grill, looking expressionlessly at the food. There are a few fields of action, but it's mostly staged in the middle distance and photographed with the smallest of elevated angles. It's a family barbecue—nothing to see here, no story, no characters.[34]

Things are different over at Parker's airport lounge—here the hustle and bustle of people coming and going suggests a myriad of momentarily intersecting narratives. A woman in the foreground, sporting what could be a mink stole, a dress with a lowish back, and three strings of (more appropriate) pearls is chatting up a suited young man holding a natty fedora and some luggage—a vastly more interesting narrative is unfolding here. His head tilts down as hers looks up—they're on intimate terms for sure. He's on his way elsewhere and has only turned briefly back toward the woman; when he stands, he will exit both frame and story. As it is, he's almost, but not yet, gone. Perhaps he'll stay? Meanwhile, a tuxedoed gent at the next table peruses a drinks menu, while behind *him* a table of three—an older man with two more minked women—are being served what simply must be martinis. In the background, beyond the picture window, a DC-7 settles in for what looks to be the smoothest of landings as a benign full moon overlooks all.

The difference is more than one of milieu (though having said that, give me the airport lounge every time). The comics artist Joëlle Jones, who channeled lifestyle illustration styles and motifs into her period *Lady Killer* stories, appreciates the emphasis that illustrators placed on performative detail: "With only a single image a larger story had to be hinted at."[35] *Everyone* in Parker's illustration has an implied story, a reason to be there and an attitude toward their situation. The photo on the album cover tells us that a multigenerational middle-class family is about to have a barbecue; everything, and everyone, is almost literally nondescript. The gentry in the illustration have places to go, people to see, secrets to share, martinis to drink.

It's striking how lifeless the photograph is, and how lively the illustration. The photograph is more posed, more still; if photography is the medium of the instant, none of that power is evident here. And no single snapshot of an airport lounge could capture so many simultaneously telling expressions, gestures, and interactions. Both images are contrived, but only the illustration "contrives" to generate a modern sense of energy, narrative, spontaneity, and simultaneity.

Readers didn't need to identify their *own* faces, fashions, or furniture in the images they perused, but they surely recognized themselves in a class position, a narrative dilemma, an aspiration, a gesture. They might appreciate that women are neither generic nor "universal"; they might, in fact, feel something more like solidarity with the position of *this* woman in *that* space, in *this* predicament. Implied female readers and viewers might share an investment in the particulars of class position, social constraints or social opportunities, the desire for a well-appointed home, a yearning to be fashionable. All of these positions of identification would depend upon the display of details neither broadly iconic nor universally accessible. A world of taste—a lifestyle—could be conveyed through the "telling" details of decoration and adornment, coiffures and coats. A vague sense of "fashion" was not enough. These postwar illustrators, whether dramatizing a moment in a story or the pleasures of finding the right toothpaste, glory in selective detail.

Al Parker wrote of the wartime and postwar moment in the history of his craft. Wartime shortages put limits on what should be depicted and on what materials were available, but Parker remembers that "while this hardly created a climate for discovery, the young artist gratified his creative impulse by concentrating on adornment, design and layout of pages. Further, the wartime shortage of art supplies became an asset by inducing him to experiment with substitute materials, adding unusual techniques to his endeavors."[36] He points to the powerful rapport that obtained between artist and reader: "Chic accessories with which he peppered his pictures provided a sustained involvement for the reader. Each illustration that featured these props produced letters from near and far. A chair covered in needlepoint, placed in a composition because of its interesting texture, brought inquiries about the availability of its pattern."[37]

The double-page Coby Whitmore illustration for Nelia Gardner White's "End of a Marriage" masterfully deploys composition, white space, and alienated chic (figure 8.6).[38] The left page provides the title (in a "fun" serif font more appropriate to a Doris Day comedy than the downbeat tale on offer), three columns of story, and a brief caption floating above all. A line of blue pillows stretches to the right-hand page, where a woman in a coolly colored, close-fitting bodysuit sits cross-legged, her body turned outward, her expression serious but undramatic. She clutches her hair, more in puzzlement than anguish. Her feet are bare; a modestly painted toe is visible, its soft pink matching her fingernails and lipstick. She wears a wedding band and several beaded necklaces of varying lengths and shades of blue. The necklaces sit atop the blue and olive stripes of the bodysuit, providing pops of color and graphic boldness. Behind her stands a man in a dark business suit, jacket open, hands on hips. The top of the page cuts him off just below the shoulders—he has no head, no face. His posture suggests that the woman before him is an enigma, a problem he cannot solve. There is a small caption to the side: "They'd quarreled. They'd had a honey of a quarrel." In the back, a vase of deepest blue-black holds flowers of blue and off-white, punctuated by green leaves. The vase seems almost free floating in a field of white, but a few wrinkles hint at the presence of a tablecloth and the table beneath. The white of the cloth matches the white of the background and the white of the page, all flattening the space into uninhabitability.

The illustration may center on the woman, but the gaze is hardly male (a literal male gaze has actually been sliced from the page). She's the object of our regard but also a possible point of identification. The flesh tones of her face and bare arms and legs are the warmest elements of the drawing. It might be interesting to learn her story, so we, perhaps, begin to read.

"End of a Marriage" is narrated in the first person, but from the *husband's* perspective. His marriage is marked by a cool reserve. He commutes to work, and a recent entrant to his carpool group, Mark Brewster, is newly, passionately, playfully married to an effervescent young woman, Kathie. The story would seem to write itself: our narrator is smitten by this feminine life force, so different from the wife he comes home to each night. The enervating whiteness of Whitmore's tablecloth and background add to the chilly flatness of the scene, telling of a love not just dead but embalmed.

Figure 8.6. Coby Whitmore, illustration for "End of a Marriage," by Nelia Gardner, April 13, 1957.

Except—it's the newlyweds whose marriage disintegrates. So *they're* the couple in the picture. Or not: we learn that Kathie tends toward "comfortable and gay" clothes—besides, her marriage doesn't cool, it flames out. At story's end, the narrator ruminates on the safety his marriage offers; it will neither soar like a rocket nor crash like one. He wants to tell her so, "But I can't say any of it. We are quiet people and we just don't talk much." So the illustration has a peculiar, almost ironic, relationship to the story it ostensibly illustrates.

While the narrative is light on lifestyle details—the ones it provides are pretty generic—the illustration has a specificity that speaks to photo-reference and at least a cursory familiarity with contemporary fashion (or fashion magazines, anyway). Its measured chilliness also offers something more cosmopolitan, more arty, than the story's textbook suburbia of carpools and cookouts.

Images like these, following Schor, could be seen as decorative at their core. The fiction doesn't depend upon the illustration for its meaning: for one thing, the image represents a collaboration between illustrator and art director; the author wouldn't have been in the loop and the artist probably wouldn't have read the story. And when stories were reprinted in books, magazine illustrations would be left behind. And where a book or magazine cover needed to attract buyers, interior illustrations had more latitude. In this sense, then, these illustrations really weren't especially "illustrative"; they were ornamental, providing bursts of color, visual variety, and aesthetic pleasure throughout the magazine—in this sense, it's the *story* that's ancillary to the image.

Magazine readers were "unpredictable," Jennifer Greenhill tells us, "with layout and the distribution of contents catering to and encouraging flitting methods of perusal."[39] Her term for the consumers of magazines, who by turns view, read, and handle them, is "beholders." While this kind of illustration might be understood to have a specific function—their allure designed to encourage a beholder to become a reader—I'd wager that more often than not, a compelling illustration was appreciated simply for itself, for whatever chunk of time it was beheld.[40]

Many comics artists moved into illustration when the bottom fell out of the comic book market in the later 1950s.[41] Some moved back to comics when they could; others harnessed the rhetoric of comics for advertisements. Drake, Leonard Starr, Alex Kotzky, and others brought some of the techniques of lifestyle illustration to comics. They have come to be called "photorealists," which is confusing to anyone versed in art history. Their work was *not* meant to mimic the surfaces of the world with photographic precision, but their use of photo-reference did open onto a fresh aesthetic, a realism different from the earlier work of Hal Foster (*Prince Valiant*) or Alex Raymond (*Rip Kirby*). Drake moved to comics from advertising, where he created some alluring comics-ads for Ipana toothpaste. He was a firm Raymond acolyte but modernized his own approach to realism by using the then-new Polaroid camera to capture facial expression and posture with new accuracy and facility (but note that pre-"photorealists" often drew from life, whether working with models or rehearsing expressions in a mirror). These carefully rendered people were firmly situated in particular places and contemporary times with a matter-of-factness that rivaled television's. Drake's work was instantly distinguished by the spontaneous liveliness of his characters, and the soap-opera setting of *Juliet Jones* provided ample opportunities for emoting.

One can see how a devil-may-care character like Eve Jones could emerge only in the wake of this snapshot realism. The cartoonist Dave Sim writes, "Photorealism captured a moment and was, therefore, structurally 'unbalanced' a lot of the time.... Every other element of non-stylized realism, fixed tableaux, was diametrically opposed to photorealism, snapshot reality."[42] A great comics character is always *animated*, but these comic strips gave us characters that were *vivacious* in the ways that the people in lifestyle illustration were vivacious—they were unrehearsed and of their moment in posture, attire, and setting.[43] The immediacy of an inked line, combined with the clarity and spontaneity of the snapped photo, gives the figures a *life* that more schematic or abstracted approaches might not. They seem to elude, or perhaps *exceed* would be the better word, the control of the artist and the flatness of the medium, emerging as figures that belong to the *world* rather than just the page.

The snapshot realism of Austin Briggs and Stan Drake sought to capture the ephemerality and spontaneity of expression and posture, an artistic goal from well before the invention of photography. Linda Nochlin wrote of the Barbizon school of painters that they emphasized "the momentary effects of nature—the play of light, the effect of changing seasons, the instantaneously observed and the haphazardly recorded phenomena—conveyed in freer, sketchier and more open and responsive brushwork than that of any landscape painters hitherto"—an approach that accelerated in the latter decades of the nineteenth century.[44] She refers to a "contemporary immediacy," an "unbuttoned intimacy, caught as if unawares," and a "plenitude of incident and charm of detail."[45]

Cinema, too, even at its most Hollywoody, captures the spontaneity of an actor's expression and comportment. Heightened performance—abetted by costume and decor as well as florid musical scores—was melodrama's stock in trade, and postwar America saw, in tandem with lifestyle illustration, an efflorescence of the family melodrama (also known, remember, as the "woman's film").[46] In *Some Came Running* (Minnelli, 1957), the uncontrolled, exuberant body language of Ginny (Shirley MacLaine) and her blowsy pink dress attracts the viewer in ways that Martha Hyer's tightly withheld and deeply beige schoolteacher just doesn't. Photography freezes an expression in place, but cinema restages and presents it as process; moreover, as Jean Epstein emphasizes, it magnifies and heightens it. "Waiting for the moment when 1000 meters of intrigue converge in a muscular denouement," Epstein writes, "satisfies me more than the rest of the film."[47] The "big head" has profound power. Barthes, of course, contrasted the masklike face of Garbo, appearing "when the cinema is about to draw an existential from an essential beauty," with that of Audrey Hepburn, whose face "has nothing of the essence left in it, but is constituted by an infinite complexity of morphological functions."[48] A face, that is, that communicates through animated detail; a face that belongs squarely to American modernity. The poster for *Breakfast at Tiffany's* was by Robert McGinnis, one of the most prolific of commercial illustrators.

COMIC BOOK ROMANCE

Romance comics belonged to comic books, and comic *books* had nowhere near the cachet of comic *strips*, not for the cartoonists and not for their readers. Comic-strip creators often became celebrities with high public profiles; comic book artists often labored in anonymity within a "shop" system based on the division of labor. But comic books were tremendously popular through the mid-1950s, and the established genres of superheroes and funny animals shared rack space with comics devoted to war, western, teen humor, science fiction, horror, crime, and romance.

Joe Simon and Jack Kirby's *Young Romance* kicked off the genre in 1947. These young journeymen were hardly prescient: romance pulp fiction, true confession magazines, radio soap operas, and newspaper strips all emphasized ongoing sagas of domestic life. *Young Romance*, like many another comic trying to attract older readers, was text heavy but also suffered from a lack of variety in composition and facial expression—delicacy of expression wasn't a particular strength of Jack Kirby's (neither was "chic"). Within two years, however, there were over a hundred romance titles on the stands, outselling every other genre and even cannibalizing sales of confessions magazines.

Romance comics hammered on the ideas that a woman needs a man, marriage beats career (for women), quiet solidarity (eventually) triumphs over flashy romantic thrills, and husbands like neither ambitious women nor uncommitted housekeepers. The protagonists were uniformly young— just-starting-out career girls and high schoolers seemed especially beset with romantic challenges. Stories delivered closure and stability in a handful of pages: their self-contained nature aligned them with Hollywood melodrama more than the continuity strips rooted in the soap opera's open-serial form. Conservative though they were, romance comics were the one genre that presented realistic people in contemporary, everyday settings. They explored a range of settings, from working-class homes to posh penthouses, ski resorts to skid rows (and while there were some period stories, most were set in the here and the now).

Like most genre comics, romance comics were formulaic, but formula has virtues that can thrive within its proscribed limits. Philip Furia argues that those looking for "original insight, sincerely expressed," in Tin Pan Alley love songs may miss "the cleverness, the inventiveness and, in the best sense of the word, artifice, that displays itself by ringing endless changes upon what are indeed the tiredest clichés."[49] As for love songs, so, too, for love stories. Here and there, a romance comic will offer a refreshingly unexpected twist or satisfying visual flourish that works its comics magic, invigorating genre and formula.[50]

Romance comics offered an alternative to the action-oriented bodies that dominated all other comics genres (including superheroes *and* funny animals). John Benson notes that "facial expression and body posture were the most significant story-telling tools" that romance comics had at their disposal; further, characters limned by such luminaries as Matt Baker "have *personality*, which is the essential ingredient needed to bring the scripts to life."[51] Photo-reference was less evident in romance comics than in either illustration or comic strips, but

Figure 8.7. Alex Toth, "Working Girl's Romance," first published 1955.

Naomi Scott points out that "artists drew their wives, sisters, mothers, neighbors and friends."[52] The images were often replete with quotidian detail and gesture. At their best, romance comics could be vivacious as well as modern.

A single panel from "Working Girl's Romance" (1955) illustrated by Alex Toth is exemplary (figure 8.7).[53] The character's psychological conflict (is she willing to keep working after marriage?) has engendered a physical exhaustion, which Toth conveys with telling details. Her body language could hardly be more legible: her coat is draped over the chair arm; this was her first stop upon getting home. Her eyes are closed, head fully reclined, legs stretched before her with ankles crossed. She has fabulous taste in midcentury fashion and decor. Behind her a tripod table lamp casts light above and below the shade; on the left a chest of drawers with asymmetrical pulls peeks in. The chair into which she has clearly collapsed has a lovely Populuxe profile, and her full skirt, heels, sleeveless blouse, and bold earrings all look, for want of a better word, cool. It's a perfect lifestyle illustration, really: it depicts its upscale milieu with as much detail as its limited space can manage; decor and costume command at least as much attention as the narrative events. The illustrators were a big influence on Toth: "Emotional drama, as opposed to physical, suddenly was center-stage, and I wanted to do it right. Plus, I enjoyed doing the stylish thing, well-dressed men and women. Inspired by Parker, Whitcomb, plus fashion magazines to bone-up on the latest thing, to smartly dress men and women; it was fun!"[54]

Toth also brings it to the art for "I Do" (1955), a story about Alice, whose desperate upward mobility estranges her from two social circles.[55] The art is an assemblage of immaculate compositions, each change of scene, angle, and proximity telling us more than the script about the worlds the protagonist oscillates between. One particularly dazzling page depicts her self-inflicted dilemma: the panels on the left situate Alice in public spaces; those on the right emphasize her isolation (figure 8.8). Feeling out of place, she "turned and fled" from an upper-class dance—Toth frames her in close-up, head tilted down, a fugitive tear on her cheek. Behind her, bewildered guests wonder at her behavior. In the panel to the right we look down upon Alice, alone in her darkened bedroom, packing a suitcase. The next tier returns her to the unsmiling world of her untuxedoed working-class friends: "I soon found that they no longer accepted me." The adjacent panel views her from below as she leaves the club, lonely ovals of tasteful recessed lighting against a dead, black background framing her face ("I don't belong here anymore!"). At the bottom, Alice is seen in close profile, intruding into the left foreground, where she espies happy, chatty, Congo Room clubgoers. The final panel is split in two: on the left we look over her shoulder at a necking couple; on the right, a tight closeup of an eye, an eyebrow, and two fingers raised to a cheek as she realizes, "There's no place for me to go!" The small, regularly arrayed panels don't allow for a surfeit of detail—and detail was never Toth's thing—but each panel provides at least one striking element: a carefully observed hairstyle, lamp, wallpaper, makeup, and several lonely tears. The text is entirely generic, but the illustrations enworld us with affective intimacy.

The compositions of every panel are positively Sirkian, surprising, perhaps, from an avowed he-man like Toth, who seemed happiest with swashbuckling adventure. The framing and compositions again and again situate Alice as at the same time in a world and separate from it; her experience and emotion structure the page. Toth enjoyed working with genres and forms that allowed for a variety of faces and bodies: "I found the [romance] scripts of that time to be a cut above the gimmicky stuff of my superhero output. Thus, I welcomed illustrating somewhat more 'realistic' situations, . . . it forced me to study, to reach, to analyze, to open up and feel more, sense more from the writer's copy and intent, than I'd ever done before!"[56]

"I Do" demonstrates that it's more than narrative closure that aligns romance comics more with movies than TV serials: it's also the artist's ability to employ such "cinematic" elements as varied compositions, big budget locations, and vivid color. In place of the strong *seriality* of strips and soaps, romance comics (and comic books in general) offered a strong *sequentiality*, enabled by the increased page count as well as the expanded space of the page. While there are plenty of differences between storyboards and comics pages, it's easy to see Toth's work on "I Do" as something of a protostoryboard (and indeed Toth would go on to design and storyboard a host of TV cartoons in the 1960s and '70s).

Telling Details: Feminine Flourish in Illustration and Comics 177

Figure 8.8. Alex Toth, "I Do," first published 1955.

CONCLUSION

The fashion-photo features in many a postwar magazine can often seem oddly unconcerned with the display of actual clothing. Soft focus, elaborate and fantastical settings, odd croppings, and near nudity all make perception strangely difficult. Such features speak the language of fantasy more than literal truth; Elizabeth A. Kessler has compared them to the liminality of half-dreams.[57] Lifestyle illustration was less evidently "arty": legibility and bright clarity align the work more easily with the waking world of the reverie. I've elsewhere discussed reverie in relation to the brevity of the comic strip—a momentary pause in one's day, a detour from productivity.[58] The magazine, with its aesthetic and ethos of browsing, offers many opportunities for such commodified reveries, including these deeply appealing illustrations. Beyond the humdrum accumulation of accurate details that ground the action in a believable world, these distilled and insistent displays, decorative and ornamental, generate something more wondrous than mundane.

Is the detail feminine? In this case, at least, they are.

Although they were aimed at a working- and middle-class female readership of the midcentury, I find the flourishes of lifestyle illustration, soap opera strips, and romance comics terribly compelling. They carry the charge of "the real" more than most comics images yet rather less than photographs; as drawings, I can view them at a more casual remove. In their fusion of contrived narrative and heightened detail, they seem to aspire to the condition of the Hollywood melodrama. The more I gaze, the more I realize that, for me, they draw together many of the pleasures of all those other media.

I was, as a teen, more familiar with this sort of detail than I realized. Stan Drake's influence is strongly felt in the work of Neal Adams—*the* superhero artist of the 1970s. More realistic musculature and attention to the nuances of facial expression marked a break with past tradition. Adams had followed a path similar to Drake's—after working as a gag artist for *Archie* comics, he went into commercial illustration, turning out comic-strip advertisements before getting his own soap opera strip, *Ben Casey* (later, he briefly ghosted for *Juliet Jones*). In the mid-1960s he began doing superhero comics. This was the start of the *first* period in comics history when people began chattering about how comic books were "growing up": Marvel was wooing the college crowd with its neurotic heroes, though DC was still cranking out its white-bread superhero product. Adams's work hit big, and a few years later, when even DC was becoming "relevant," his photo-realist approach, new to superhero comics, proved deeply suitable.

Figure 8.9. Neal Adams and Denny O'Neil, *Green Lantern/Green Arrow*, vol. 2, no. 86, 1971.

Adams's collaborations with writer Denny O'Neil privileged a new emotionalism, perhaps on strongest display in their *Green Lantern/Green Arrow* series (you know, the one where they drive off in a pickup truck to look for America). The story that centered upon the drug addiction of Green Arrow's young sidekick provided rich opportunities for expressive physiognomy and intense, affecting close-ups (figure 8.9). Adams, I now see, managed to sneak a melodramatic, "soap opera" visual sensibility into superhero comics—a mashup of genres and aesthetic styles typically gendered in different directions. Back then, I drooled over my Neal Adams comics at the very same time as I disdained *Mary Perkins: On Stage* and the other girl/grown-up strips with which it actually shared so much.

I once wrote that superheroes don't wear costumes to fight crime, they fight crime in order to wear costumes. One could equally say of lifestyle illustration, photorealist comic strips, and romance comics that the characters aren't fashionable to serve a narrative, but that the contrivances of narrative frame and license their emphatic stylishness. The phenomenologically rich worlds this art opens onto is recognizably proximate to my own, but highlighted and heightened. I'm captivated by the just-so perfection of the gestures and attitudes of its people, the precision of these bodies and spaces, the implied narratives in which every element and every character is in its perfect place. They present a gloriously theatrical realm of animated gesture and fashions, as real as it was artificial, as artificial as it was real: a world of decorative images, feminine flourishes, and the vivacity of the modern.

Notes

1. Although as Jared Gardner points out, radio and television took the idea of the open-ended serial from earlier continuity comic strips. See "Serial Pleasures, 1907–1938," in *Projections: Comics and the History of Twenty-First-Century Storytelling* (Stanford, CA: Stanford University Press, 2012), chap. 2.

2. Scott McCloud, *Understanding Comics: The Invisible Art* (1993; repr., New York: Harper Perennial, 1994), 36 (emphasis and ellipsis original).

3. Andrei Molotiu, writing about *Juliet Jones*, has defined what he calls "cartoonism": "the privileging, in some critical rhetoric, of more simplified, cartoony art, which is seen as inherently more appropriate to sequential narrative than more detailed or 'realistic' art." Molotiu, "How to Read *Juliet Jones*" (paper presented at the First Annual Conference of the Comics Studies Society, Urbana-Champaign, IL, August 10, 2018). See also Andrei Molotiu, "Cartooning," in *Comics Studies: A Guidebook*, ed. Charles Hatfield and Bart Beaty (New Brunswick, NJ: Rutgers University Press, 2020): 153–71. This essay is *deeply* indebted to Andrei's work and ongoing, incisive critique.

4. Manny Farber, "Comic Strips," *New Republic*, September 4, 1944, 279.

5. McCloud, *Understanding Comics*, 36 (emphasis original).

6. Roland Barthes, *The Rustle of Language*, trans. Richard Howard (Berkeley: University of California Press, 1989), 148 (emphasis added).

7. Steve Englehart (w), Sal Buscema (p), and John Verpooten (i), *Captain America*, vol. 1 #161 (Marvel, 1973) (emphasis original).

8. Pavle Levi pointed out in conversation that the sequence works as a classic Kuleshov effect.

9. April 13, 1957. Molotiu notes that humor strips are inevitably framed in medium shot (which, I'd add, derives from theatrical, even vaudeville, convention); realistic strips experiment

with such cinematic devices as varied shot distances and compositions. This is even more true of romance comics, as I discuss later in this essay. Molotiu, "How to Read *Juliet Jones*."

10. David Apatoff, "Stan Drake," *Illustration Art* (blog), November 9, 2014, https://illustrationart.blogspot.com/2014/11/stan-drake.html.

11. E. H. Gombrich, *Art and Illusion: A Study in the Psychology of Pictorial Representation* (Princeton, NJ: Princeton University Press, 2000), chap. 10.

12. Thierry Smolderen, *The Origins of Comics: From William Hogarth to Winsor McCay*, trans. Bart Beaty and Nick Nguyen (Jackson: University Press of Mississippi, 2014), 43.

13. See Molotiu, "How to Read *Juliet Jones*." Molotiu links their compositional variety as "not simply resulting from the influence of cinema, but from the demands of illustration when put to narrative purposes."

14. Eric Hayot, *On Literary Worlds* (Oxford: Oxford University Press, 2012), 24–25. For more on this, see my *Hellboy's World: Comics and Monsters on the Margins* (Berkeley: University of California Press, 2016).

15. Peter Mendelsund, *What We See When We Read* (New York: Vintage Books, 2014), 403. This aligns intriguingly with André Bazin's championing of such filmic techniques as the shot in depth and the long take, both of which privilege ambiguity and incomplete knowledge.

16. Leonard Starr, "Mary Perkins On Stage," November 13, 1966. Reprinted in *Leonard Starr's "Mary Perkins On Stage,"* vol. 8 (Chicago: Classics Comics, 2011).

17. Thanks to Beth Kessler for the fashion info!

18. The quarter-page format would further reduce its size.

19. Naomi Schor, *Reading in Detail: Aesthetics and the Feminine* (New York: Routledge, 2007), 5.

20. Schor, 8.

21. Schor, 9–10.

22. Schor, 46.

23. "Critics who feel overwhelmed by the assault on their senses made by the profusion of ornament and have therefore condemned it as tasteless and barbaric may have misunderstood what was expected of them." E. H. Gombrich, *The Sense of Order: A Study in the Psychology of Decorative Art* (Ithaca, NY: Cornell University Press, 1984), 116.

24. Schor, *Detail*, 15.

25. Kurt Busiek, introduction to *Leonard Starr's "Mary Perkins On Stage,"* ed. Charles Pelto, vol. 2 (River Forest, IL: Classic Comics, 2006).

26. Schor, *Detail*, 109.

27. Schor, 115.

28. In Schor's reading of Barthes's reading of photography, "the detail becomes the privileged point of contact between reader and text: the discursive *punctum* is the hook onto which the reader may hitch her own fantasies." *Detail*, 114. I find no punctum in these illustrations—every detail is carefully placed, there is no insubordinate accident of image-making that allows the real to enter, to "puncture" the illusory space.

29. Alexander Nemerov, "N. C. Wyeth's Theater of Illustration," *American Art* 6, no. 2 (1992): 47.

30. Schor, *Detail*, 47.

31. Armando Mendez, "Something Cool: Alex Raymond, Rip Kirby, and the Rise and Fall of the Photorealistic Comic Strip," *Comic Art* 2, (2003): 56.

32. Manuel Auad, ed., *Al Parker: Illustrator, Innovator* (San Francisco: Auad Publishing, 2014), 96–99.

33. Janet Borgerson and Jonathan Schroeder, *Designed for Hi-Fi Living: The Vinyl LP in Midcentury America* (Cambridge, MA: MIT Press, 2017), 97.

34. I haven't even mentioned the stuffed dog in the foreground.

35. Joëlle Jones, "Joëlle Jones Talks *Lady Killer*—An Amazing Upcoming Comic," interview by Comic Vine, updated December 8, 2014, https://comicvine.gamespot.com/articles/interview-joelle-jones-talks-lady-killer-an-amazin/1100-150626/.

36. Al Parker, "The Decade: 1940–1950," in *The Illustrator in America, 1880–1980: A Century of Illustration*, ed. Walt Reed and Roger Reed (New York: Madison Square, 1993), 206–7.

37. Parker, 206.

38. Nelia Gardner White, "End of a Marriage," *Saturday Evening Post*, April 13, 1957.

39. Jennifer Greenhill, "Flip, Linger, Glide: Coles Phillips and the Movements of Magazine Pictures," *Art History* 40, no. 3 (2017): 589.

40. In the same way, advertising illustration was "meant" to generate consumption, but most of those who encountered the advertisements just enjoyed the art.

41. Mendez, "Something Cool," 53.

42. Dave Sim, *Glamourpuss* #12 (Aardvark-Vanaheim, 2010), 20.

43. Farber would disagree. Comic strips, he wrote, "have learned the advantage of variegated views of a subject and scenes packed with decor, people and shadows to *simulate* liveliness." "Comic Strips," 279 (emphasis added).

44. Linda Nochlin, *Realism* (New York: Penguin, 1971), 138.

45. Nochlin, respectively, 143, 145, 150. There are many resonances between Nochlin's take on impressionism and the lifestyle illustrators but the differences are important to note: Many illustrated figures are very posed, albeit not in formal postures. The images are anything but antinarrative, but are, rather, pregnant with implied narrative (that's their purpose).

46. Farber: "The major influence on the new strips seems to be the movies, and anything that influences movies." "Comic Strips," 279.

47. Jean Epstein, "Magnification and Other Writings," trans. Stuart Liebman, *October* 3 (1977): 9.

48. Roland Barthes, "The Face of Garbo," in *Mythologies*, trans. Annette Lavers (New York: Noonday, 1991), 56–57.

49. Philip Furia, *The Poets of Tin Pan Alley* (Oxford: Oxford University Press, 1992), 15.

50. Look at, for instance, Ogden Whitney's romance comics, recently collected in *Return to Romance: The Strange Love Stories of Ogden Whitney*, ed. Dan Nadel and Frank Santoro (New York: New York Review Books, 2019).

51. John Benson, "Matt Baker & St. John Romance Comics: An Aesthetic Appreciation," *Alter Ego* 47 (2005): 37 (emphasis original).

52. From the introduction to *Heart Throbs: The Best of DC Romance Comics* (New York: Simon and Schuster, 1979), cited in Michelle Nolan, *Love on the Racks: A History of American Romance Comics* (Jefferson, NC: McFarland, 2008), 195.

53. Alex Toth (p) and Michael Peppe (i), "Working Girl Romance," *Love Romances* #53 (Atlas Comics, 1955).

54. "A Talk With Alex Toth," *Comic Book Artist* #11 (January 2001), 14. Greg Sedowski further notes of his splash pages that "Toth embraced the opportunity to do a large illustration

as it allowed him to emulate the magazine illustrators he admired," including Al Parker. See Alex Toth, *Setting the Standard: Comics by Alex Toth 1952–1954*, ed. Greg Sedowski (Seattle: Fantagraphics Books, 2011), 410. Here and elsewhere Toth also praises Hollywood genre films for their dynamic storytelling and way with dialogue. See Dean Mullaney and Bruce Canwell, *The Life and Art of Alex Toth: Genius Isolated* (San Diego: IDW, 2017), 100.

55. Alex Toth (p) and Michael Peppe (i), "I Do," *Lovers* #67 (Atlas Comics, 1955).

56. Mullaney and Canwell, *Genius, Isolated*, 100.

57. In conversation, May 2019.

58. Scott Bukatman, *The Poetics of Slumberland: Animated Spirits and the Animating Spirit* (Berkeley: University of California Press, 2011), 1–26.

SPEED LINES

Futurism and Superheroes

DANIEL WORDEN

The years 1913 and 1922 are widely used as benchmarks for the gradual emergence of modernism in the United States. In 1913, the Armory Show introduced European modernism to a New York City audience, and in 1922, works like T. S. Eliot's *The Waste Land*, James Joyce's *Ulysses*, and Virginia Woolf's *Jacob's Room* were published.[1] We should remember, of course, as Susan Stanford Friedman and many other scholars have argued, that there are multiple modernisms;[2] the years 1913 and 1922 are critical shorthand for thinking about what we now call "transatlantic modernism," especially as New York becomes a major node of a formerly Eurocentric avant-garde. Yet transatlantic modernism of the early twentieth century is merely one form of modernism. Other forms of modernism may come into clarity with other benchmark years for contextual shorthand, and it is understandable that a category like "popular modernism" would have different benchmark years and other artistic, historical, and stylistic priorities.

While our traditional periodizations for modernism privilege fine arts and "literary" publications, it is now common to acknowledge that other forms of modernism, both in particular regional or national contexts and in other media environments, emerged at different moments. Superheroes, for example, are just as much a product of modernism as the other genre types that thrived in modernity, such as the femme fatale, the hard-boiled detective, the traumatized veteran, and more. A product of popular modernism emerging from the newsstand, comic books in the United States circulated as periodicals and were sold alongside the magazines that have been the subject of so much scholarship in the New Modernist Studies. "Popular modernism" names, in part, the broad swath of genre-based art and literature that proliferated in print, radio, and film in the twentieth century. From *Krazy Kat*'s Dadaist landscapes to *Flash*

Gordon's totalitarian dictators, the texts of popular modernism blend commercial forms with modernist styles. One of popular modernism's recurrent genre tropes is the superhero, a genre trope that is spectacularly popular in our present moment, too. The superhero trope helps me to understand the contours of a different historical and political horizon for modernism—and to more fully conceptualize how the superhero works in our culture today, as a dual figure of both fascist and socialist ideologies. In this chapter, I will consider the superhero as a modernist genre trope and chart its connections both to more traditional forms of modernism and to the political ideologies carried forward by those modernist forms.

While traditional modernism might be inaugurated by the years 1913 and 1922, the American superhero's benchmark years are later, 1938 and 1956.[3] In 1938, *Action Comics* #1 introduced Superman in the "Golden Age" of comics. An iconic superhero, Superman is an orphan from the planet Krypton who becomes a "champion of the oppressed." In 1956, *Showcase* #4 introduced the "Silver Age" Flash, a forensic scientist named Barry Allen with superspeed. Just as the 1913 Armory Show presented avant-garde art to the American public, the superhero would synthesize avant-garde aesthetics with the popular genres of the American mass media. 1938's Superman was a hybrid figure, yoking together concepts from literature, newspapers, mythology, pulp magazines, scripture, and the circus, and he is more notable as a paradigm, a formative example of the superhero trope, than he is as a singular character. The Flash of 1956 was a revision of an older version of the speedster character, redesigned and reframed for a newly regulated comic book industry. Superman, of course, would remain the archetypal superhero throughout the many shifts in early comic book publishing and retains significant purchase over our cultural imagination even today.[4]

As one of the new media forms to flourish during modernism, alongside film, magazines, newspapers, and photography, comics have both historical and ideological connections to the aesthetic theories that would propel formal and narrative experimentation in the twentieth century. *Action Comics* #1, published in 1938, introduces Superman as an impossibly strong figure (figure 9.1). Attributed to Joe Shuster and Jack Adler, the cover illustration itself documents the influence of modernist aesthetics on superhero comics. Superman is depicted lifting up an automobile and smashing it into a boulder; as the "champion of the oppressed," Superman here seems to be fighting modernity and technology itself. He is more than human, terrifying the fleeing bystanders. While armchair comparisons of Superman to the notion of the übermensch, from Nietzsche and/or the Nazi regime, abound, it strikes me that a more immediate context for Superman is modernist visual culture, as the character assumed poses and powers that had been well established by 1938. Superman's heroic pose partakes of a modernist visual iconography evident in the futurist artist

Figure 9.1. *Action Comics* #1 (DC Comics, 1938). Cover art by Joe Shuster and Jack Adler.

Umberto Boccioni's sculpture *Unique Forms of Continuity in Space* (figure 9.2). As Caroline Tisdall and Angelo Bozzolla explain, Boccioni's sculpture realizes the futurist ideal of bodily transformation:

> More than any other image of Futurist art *Unique Forms of Continuity in Space* embodies the aggressive energy of the statement: "We are the primitives of a new sensibility." Human features made way for a synthesis of every kind of machine the Futurists ever depicted, his chest swelled out into the shape of the "non-human model" envisioned by Marinetti in "War, Sole Hygiene of the World": "endowed with unexpected organs adapted to the exigencies of unexpected shocks . . . a prow-like development of the breast-bone which will increase in size as the future man becomes a better flier." And, as if in flight, the thigh

Figure 9.2. Umberto Boccioni. *Unique Forms of Continuity in Space*. 1913, cast in 1950. Courtesy of the Metropolitan Museum of Art.

and calf muscles of this monstrous mechanized mannikin, all the more alarming for being half-size, are pushed back as if by the pressure of air as it cuts through space.[5]

What Boccioni figures as aggressive, futuristic, and mechanized armor in *Unique Forms*, Siegel and Shuster fashion as a superhero costume, the "S" signifying his status as "the future man."

Superman's resemblance to Boccioni's *Unique Forms of Continuity in Space* is just one visual connotation at work in the cover image. *Action Comics* #1's cover illustration has a background filled with lines that radiate from a yellow center. These lines and colors create a sense of explosive action. The bright center of the composition radiates in a way that evokes another futurist work, Giacomo Balla's *Street Light* (figure 9.3). In *Street Light*, Balla seeks to capture luminescent energy, an electric streetlamp, and in the painting, he renders not just light's movement through space but the burst of light occasioned by the modern fossil fuel industry. On the cover of *Action Comics* #1, Superman creates the same visual effect as the electric streetlamp, producing energy and light that radiates outward as power. While Balla's *Street Light* wasn't acquired by the Museum of Modern Art until 1954 and therefore might not have been a direct inspiration—though Boccioni could indeed have been a direct influence on the young Siegel and Shuster in the 1930s, as noted below—Balla's painting is significant, in part, because of how it distills not just a futurist but also a more generally modernist interest in both the "machine" and nature. The light bulb competes with the moon to illuminate the bulb itself, staging a tension that Amelia Jones has identified as central to the Dadaist movement in New York earlier, in the 1910s. The "machine works" of modernists like Marcel Duchamp, Jones argues, "are extremely complex and can most productively be viewed as incomplete negotiations of the violent challenges to the masculine subject in urban industrialism."[6] While Balla's *Street Light* itself may offer either a sense of masculine virility—the power of electricity!—or a sense of loss—the moon pales in comparison!—the luminous, explosive energy in the painting becomes background for Superman's own assertion of masculine power in *Action Comics* #1.

Superman's costume also has notable overlap with futurist art, and Balla himself would turn to making textiles and other outfits. "Considered the father of Futurist fashion," Emily Braun writes, "Balla began designing textiles and suits in 1912–1913. With asymmetrical cuts and diagonal surface patterns, the brightly colored outfits were a direct translation of the dynamic 'force-lines' of his painted canvases."[7] The brightly colored, simple outfits of futurism were meant to facilitate dynamic, bodily action, and in the cotton, latex, leather, and spandex outfits of superheroes, futurist ideas of fashion's form brightly announcing its function are continued. Balla's fashions strive for the functionality of the leotard and the iconicity of abstraction. As Scott Bukatman has argued, the urban superhero is, in keeping with this modernist lineage, very much a dandy, taking to the night in a flamboyant costume:

> Alongside the image of an idealized, classical self, superheroes further embody a male fantasy of flamboyant, performative intemperance, something blocked by the pragmatic, self-controlled economy of a historically constructed masculine cultural identity signified by the visual drabness of his closet. But many of those closets have secret doors opening onto a broader sense of what is appropriate for the boy or man. Our costumed vigilante is perhaps something more a dandy, a flamboyant, flamboyantly powered, urban male, who, if not for his never-ending battle for truth, justice, and the American Way, would probably be ordered to "just move it along." What battles against "crime" and "corruption" really do, it seems, is license the donning of the superhero garb,

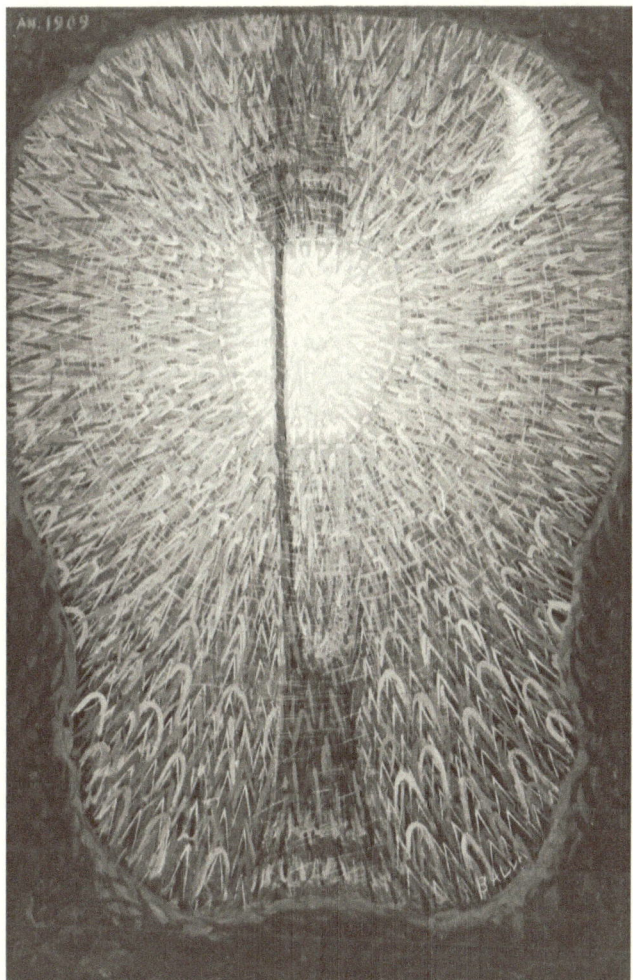

Figure 9.3. Giacomo Balla. *Street Light*. c. 1910–1911 (dated on painting 1909). © 2023 Artists Rights Society (ARS), New York / SIAE, Rome. Digital Image © The Museum of Modern Art / Licensed by SCALA / Art Resource, NY.

legitimate the movement out of the home, through the window, and into the secret magic of the urban night. The fantasy, then, is one of dressing up—superheroes don't wear costumes in order to fight crime, they fight crime in order to wear the costumes.[8]

Not unlike a futurist suiting up for a war that is both aesthetic and military, the superhero dons a costume that enacts identity in a fictional world.

In addition to Superman's pose, the light, and the costume, the damaged car on *Action Comics* #1 has a futurist backstory. In his "Foundation and Manifesto of Futurism," F. T. Marinetti details how a car wreck inspired his futurist ideas. In his car, Marinetti "sped on, squashing beneath our scorching tires the snarling guard dogs at the steps of their houses, like crumpled collars under a hot iron."[9] Marinetti then describes how he makes an irrational U-turn, almost hits some cyclists, and crashes in a ditch. Everyone thinks the car is totaled, but it turns out that Marinetti's "gorgeous shark" of a car comes "back from the dead, darting along with its powerful fins!"[10] Marinetti's fetishistic shark-car is just part of the transformation occasioned by the car crash. Marinetti himself is also transformed, "with my face covered in repair-shop grime—a fine mixture of metallic flakes, profuse sweat, and pale-blue soot—with my arms all bruised and bandaged, yet quite undaunted."[11] Marinetti's transformation might be familiar to fans of superhero comics; he becomes, in a sense, a working-class superhero, costumed, shiny blue, covered in semimysterious substances, battle-tested, and stronger than ever. Clark Kent's meek journalist persona is preceded here by the avant-garde poet, both of whom have a secret life of explosive action. And for both Marinetti and Kent, the automobile has become a symbol of technological advance, mechanized speed, and human potential.

Comic book superheroes often have more in common with the futurists' ideas about the human body than with Nietzsche's übermensch. In "Against Academic Teachers," Marinetti criticizes Nietzsche's idea of the Superman and posits a distinctively futurist vision of the figure:

> [Nietzsche's] Superman is a product of the Greek imagination, spawned from the three great stinking corpses of Apollo, Mars, and Bacchus. He is a mixture of elegant Beauty, the warrior's strength, and Dionysian ecstasy, which are manifested in the greatest classical art. We are opposed to this Greek Superman, begat from the dust of libraries, and against him we set the Man who is extended by his own labors, the enemy of books, the friend of personal experience, the pupil of the Machine, relentless cultivator of his own will, clear in this flash of his own inspiration, endowed with the feline power of scenting out, with the ability to make split-second judgments, possessing those instincts typical of the wild—intuition, cunning, and boldness.[12]

Marinetti's gloss on the futurist superhero might be a blueprint for the later comic-book superhero, from its anti-intellectual cultural cache and its embrace of technological motifs, to its relentless individuality and its emphasis on explosive action. For Marinetti, these futurist visions were "like preliminary sketches of the extended man we are preparing," figuring futurist artworks themselves as partial, fragmentary, or serial works in and of themselves, much like the superhero narratives, whose partial, fragmentary, and serial narratives were determined by the system of the periodical newsstand.[13] The works of both the futurists and the US comic book industry were, in both effect and presentation, spontaneous productions. The futurists staged theatrical interventions that sought to overturn conventional boundaries of time and space, and comic book readers entered into a serial narrative, one on which they could exert control through letters to the editor, participation in fan culture, and even future employment as creative talent. In both art scenes, aesthetics seeped beyond the individual work of art, fomenting an arts culture with deep connections to political and social currents.

Given the immense geographic and cultural difference between the Italian futurist avant-garde of the 1910s and the American newsstand of the 1930s, what are the chances that the cocreators of Superman, Joe Shuster and Jerry Siegel, had seen the work of Boccioni or Balla, let alone the Dadaists, cubists, imagists, surrealists, or other members of the modernist avant-garde? The odds are actually not that bad. Joe Shuster attended the Cleveland School of Art in the early 1930s, so he was likely exposed to modernist art before creating Superman. Moreover, Boccioni's *Unique Forms of Continuity in Space* was one of many futurist works included in the Museum of Modern Art's *Cubism and Abstract Art* exhibit in 1936.[14] It is plausible to read a popular renaissance of futurist aesthetics in 1930s American comic books, even if that revival was less an intentional return than an effect of modern style. But perhaps more important than any avant-garde ideology was Shuster and Siegel's involvement in print culture of the 1930s. They actively published and contributed to science fiction fanzines in the 1930s and set out to get work for hire as a freelance comic book team. The visual markers of modernism evident on the cover of *Action Comics* #1 are not necessarily emblems of direct influence or self-aware referencing, as we may expect of postmodern artists who often signal or cite their influences, but are instead signs of modernism's transformation into a series of tropes that trigger in a viewer a sense of explosive action and iconic meaning. Futurism's idealistic heroism is visible in *Action Comics* #1 immediately, in part because, by the late 1930s, futurism as an aesthetic style had entered the popular lexicon of visual iconography. Modernism had become familiar.

Inside of *Action Comics* #1, Superman's story is twelve pages long, and he exonerates a death row prisoner set for execution, beats up a domestic abuser, rescues Lois Lane from a kidnapper, and travels to Washington, DC, where he uncovers a corrupt lobbyist promoting a war for profit in South America. In and of itself, this is a lot of plot to cover in twelve pages by contemporary storytelling standards in the comics medium. Yet, in this early moment in comic book history, this Superman story was only one feature story in a sixty-eight-page comic book. While we speak of *Action Comics* #1 in hushed tones—it is even covered by major news outlets whenever a copy of this comic book comes up for auction—we must remember as scholars that *Action Comics* #1 has the same storied, mythologized iconicity as the Armory Show. Both *Action* and Armory are routinely invoked to signal the "beginning" of aesthetic movements in the United States, and I posit here that both *Action* and Armory in fact represent the gradual emergence and normalization of modernist aesthetics in the United States. If the Armory Show consolidated and defined "high modernism" in the United States, then *Action Comics* #1 also consolidated and defined "popular modernism" later in the century. In what follows, I offer a selection of case studies and explore how the aesthetic of US superhero comics extends the modernist framework of futurism further into the mid- and late twentieth century. I argue, ultimately, that if we take superheroes seriously as an element and outgrowth of the modernist avant-garde, we can begin to understand both the artistic experimentation and the populist nationalism so evident in the superhero genre today.

THE VISUAL POLITICS OF SUPERHERO COMICS

As Jared Gardner, Charles Hatfield, and Shawna Kidman have documented, American comics have been shaped by many of the same aesthetic, industrial, and social forces as film, literature, and television. Moreover, the work of comics studies scholars has uncovered the deep ties between particular comics artists and other artists of more established media forms; it is hard for me to think of World War I now, for example, without thinking of George Herriman's *Krazy Kat* comic strip, whose comics about trench warfare between a brick-throwing mouse and a cat capture the idiocy of state-supported violence just as Dada and surrealism also exhibited an absurdist response to the conditions of modernity. In a later genre of comics art that carries along the populist ideology of the early twentieth-century American newsstand, the Superman stories that appeared in the early years of *Action Comics* (the title is still in print and reached its thousandth issue in 2018) featured a hero who has the gruff, powerful confidence of a futurist ideal. He is a threat not just to criminals and gangsters but also to lobbyists and government officials.

Famously, Superman's early status as a working-class hero would give way to overt nationalism in the 1940s, as the superhero in the United States came to be equated with the war effort. Symbolically bolstered by the fact that the American flag's red, white, and blue print easily in the four-color process used for comics in this period, Superman, Captain America, Wonder Woman, and many other superheroes fought against fascism throughout, and even before, the United States' involvement in World War II. Earlier, for the Italian futurists to whom Superman owes an aesthetic debt, putting their aesthetic into practice was infamously disastrous. After advocating for World War I, some Italian futurists marched off to battle, only to be injured, killed, and then yoked to Mussolini's emerging fascist regime. Yet, as Enda Duffy, Amelia Jones, Christine Poggi, and others have elaborated in different ways, avant-grade art practices exceed the discreet "-isms" that we often use to separate the overlapping movements from one another, especially when we think of avant-garde art through alternative categories rather than through those refined traditionally in art history and English.[15] A figure like Superman, then, represents the popular trajectory of futurist aesthetics, from within New York's modernist-leaning culture industry. A genre type derived from modernism, Superman and his superheroic kin symbolize American ideals during World War II and, more importantly, in its long aftermath.

By 1956, comics had shifted considerably as a popular medium in the United States. After a publishing boom in the 1930s and 1940s, a postwar downturn pushed many comics publishers out of the marketplace, and many remaining comics publishers shored up their place on American newsstands by forming the Comics Code Authority, which ensured that comic books stamped with the CCA seal were appropriate for children. Under these new conditions, the superhero's previous ties to real-world political events, such as warfare in Germany or Japan, recede, and a new level of often goofy abstraction enters into comics narratives. On the cover of *Showcase* #4, the Flash races out of a film strip, surpassing the speed of projection through his immediate, explosive presence on the comics page. This "Silver Age" Flash aims to surpass the limits of media itself, to jump out of the moving picture and the page, to merge art into life. The cover suggests an avant-garde aspiration, the destruction of the barrier between art and everyday life.

Showcase #4 introduced the character Barry Allen, who becomes the Flash when Allen is soaked in chemicals and struck by lightning. When drawing the Flash, Carmine Infantino uses generous amounts of "speed lines," sometimes referred to as "motion lines," to signal the superhero's impossibly fast movements across the page. As other comics historians have noted, it is hard not to see the similarity between the speed lines that are ubiquitous in comics illustration and the representation of motion and movement in Marcel Duchamp's *Nude Descending a Staircase (No. 2)* (figure 9.4). Notable, in part, because it was a part of the Armory Show, Duchamp's well-known painting introduces time into the static space of the painting. Comics introduce time into the fixed space of the printed page, too, and while comics also use panels, text, and other elements to convey sequence, the representation of a single figure in motion, in a single illustration, is a common practice. In *Showcase* #4, for example, the Flash races down the side of a skyscraper, his fleet movement represented by speed lines (figure 9.5).[16]

Figure 9.4. Marcel Duchamp. *Nude Descending a Staircase (No. 2)*. 1912. © Association Marcel Duchamp / ADAGP, Paris / Artists Rights Society (ARS), New York 2023. The Philadelphia Museum of Art / Art Resource, NY.

The speed lines that denote the Flash's superheroic movement trail behind the figure, though they have the visual effect of also propelling the figure forward, as well as connecting him to the past. The Flash's speed line panels represent the epitome of comics form, which consolidates the insertion of time into the space of the image. As the cover of *Showcase* #4 itself demonstrates, the Flash captures the movement we associate with film, but in a print culture form (figure 9.6). As Stephen Kern has noted, Duchamp's *Nude Descending a Staircase* is part of a broader modernist interest in motion, inspired by

Figure 9.5. Interior page from "Mystery of the Human Thunderbolt!" in *Showcase* #4 (DC Comics, 1956). Robert Kanigher (writer), Carmine Infantino (penciler), Joe Kubert (inker), Gaspar Saladino (letterer).

Figure 9.6. *Showcase* #4 (DC Comics, 1956). Cover art by Carmine Infantino and Joe Kubert.

developments in media technology. Kern writes, "Marcel Duchamp observed that 'the whole idea of movement, of speed, was in the air,' and acknowledged that his *Nude Descending a Staircase* was inspired by chronophotographs and motion pictures. The cinema reproduced the mechanization, jerkiness, and rush of modern times."[17] With the Flash, this aesthetic interest in speed becomes a narrative theme as well as a formal structure for image making. Less about speed itself than about heroic fantasy, the Flash embodies the speed and fragmentation occasioned by modernity in an individual, heroic icon. In the 1910s, Duchamp's figuration of modern speed distorts and disfigures the human figure, rendering it a series of lines and shapes cascading across the image. This interest in speed was also prevalent among the futurists, in works such as Giacomo Balla's *Dynamism of a Dog on a Leash* or Anton Bragaglia's works of photodynamism. In *Showcase* #4, Carmine Infantino prioritizes the individual figure; at the end of every speed line is a heroic individual, not a blur of shape and color. The Flash is just one example of how modernist ideas are revised and reworked to shore up tradition.

THE FANTASTIC FOUR VERSUS THE FUTURIST

In *Action Comics* #1, Superman is faster and stronger than machines. An alien from another planet, his blue and red leotard as well as his alter ego Clark Kent confirms his status as an "ideal" American individual. This humanist logic is a hallmark of popular modernism, which in the pages of middlebrow magazines, pulps, and comic books adopted modernist styles while reinforcing the humanistic social norms that many modernists bristled against. The same structure is evident in *Showcase* #4, in which the Flash retains his individuality even as he traverses the boundaries of time and space. The modernist visions articulated by the futurists earlier in the twentieth century often read like superhero stories, yet they emphasize more thorough transformations of the individual than Superman or the Flash. As Marinetti wrote in another of his futurist manifestoes, "Extended Man and the Kingdom of the Machine" (1915):

> We believe in the possibility of an incalculable number of human transformations, and we are not joking when we declare that in human flesh wings lie dormant.
> The day when it will be possible for man to externalize his will so that, like a huge invisible arm, it can extend beyond him, then his Dream and his Desire, which today are merely idle words, will rule supreme over conquered Space and Time.
> This nonhuman, mechanical species, built for constant speed, will quite naturally be cruel, omniscient, and warlike.
> It will possess the most unusual organs; organs adapted to the needs of an environment in which there are continuous clashes.
> Even now we can predict a development of the external protrusion of the sternum, resembling a prow, which will have great significance, given that man, in the future, will become an increasingly better aviator.[18]

As I've suggested briefly above, Marinetti's descriptions of bodily transformation read like a rubric for creating your own superhero—from winged heroes like the Justice Society's Hawkman or the X-Men's Angel, to the invisible, stretchy, indestructible, or fiery bodies of Marvel's iconic superhero team, the Fantastic Four. Reading Marinetti's vision of human transformation alongside the Fantastic Four provides some insight into how modernist ideologies were adapted into the contexts of both American superhero comics and postwar American liberalism.

Created by Jack Kirby and Stan Lee and published in 1961, *Fantastic Four* #1 introduced the superhero team, composed originally of Mister Fantastic (Reed Richards), the Invisible Girl (Sue Storm), the Human Torch (Johnny Storm), and the Thing (Ben Grimm). Endowed with superpowers when they were exposed to "cosmic rays," the Fantastic Four are a group of do-gooders who operate out of the top floors of the Baxter Building in Manhattan. The Fantastic Four's earliest adventures include struggles against the world-domineering plans of the Mole Man, Doctor Doom, the Puppeteer, and other villains, and the stories typically involve travel to other planets, dimensions, and temporal realms, in a hodgepodge of mystical and pseudoscientific settings. These adventures might seem at odds with the often nonnarrative art produced by Marinetti and other futurist artists, yet as Richard Humphreys has argued, "Futurism seems to come with Darwinian evolution, evoking a sci-fi fantasy of 'Things to Come,' with intergalactic travel, alien encounters and extraordinary transformations of the human mind and body."[19] Indeed, the transformation of the Fantastic Four is an emblem of the futurist notion that "movement and light destroy the materiality of bodies."[20] The comic series explores what could happen in a world of heroic dematerialization, where heroes wear "unstable molecules" to cover their unstable bodies. The Fantastic Four make literal the avant-garde aspirations of the futurists, rendering acceleration, evolution, and technological progress into humanoid forms.

Futurism itself would eventually be directly invoked by a *Fantastic Four* character, the Futurist, who appeared in a two-issue storyline in 1980. In *Fantastic Four* #215, a scientist named Randolph James is assaulted by a "gang of thugs" looking for money. Suffering from his injuries, Professor James uses his experimental "evolution-accelerator" on himself, hoping that it will heal him. In a typical scientific, superheroic twist, the "evolution-accelerator" turns the scientist into the Futurist, an advanced humanoid with immense powers and a neoclassical outfit (figure 9.7).

By the next issue of *Fantastic Four*, the Futurist has teamed up with the villain Blastaar, who entered Earth through an interdimensional portal. They fight the Fantastic Four, and the Futurist inevitably realizes that the Fantastic Four are not his enemies after all. Blastaar gets sent back through the

Figure 9.7. Interior page from *Fantastic Four* #215 (Marvel Comics, 1980). Marv Wolfman (writer/editor), John Byrne and Joe Sinnott (artists), Joe Rosen (letterer), Carl Gafford (colorist), Jim Shooter (consulting editor).

Figure 9.8. Interior page from *Fantastic Four* #216 (Marvel Comics, 1980). Marv Wolfman and Bill Mantlo (writers), John Byrne and Pablo Marcos (artists), Irv Watanabe and Michael Higgins (letterers), Carl Gafford (colorist), Mark Gruenwald (editor), Jim Shooter (consulting editor).

interdimensional portal, and the Futurist journeys into the cosmos, where he will explore "the supreme vastness of the universe." It is notable, and perhaps indicative of the allegorical honesty of the comics medium, that Reed and Sue Richards's son, Franklin Richards, saves the day by defeating Blastaar. As the anchor of the normative family unit symbolized by the Fantastic Four's own version of the literally "nuclear" family, Franklin plays an instrumental role in ultimately redeeming the Futurist in the comic book. The Futurist leaves Earth to roam the universe, after ending his partnership with the warlike Blastaar. The avant-garde is personified and reworked into a popular shape (figure 9.8).

On the one hand, the *Fantastic Four*'s Futurist story is emblematic of the speed of superhero comics—both the speed of narrative pacing, as a character like the scientist Randolph James undergoes a rapid series of transitions in mere pages of a comic book, and the speeds available to superheroes and villains through speculative technologies and energy forms. The fittingly named "Futurist" character makes apparent an aesthetic allegiance that runs throughout many superhero comics, beginning even with the superhero's predecessors in newspaper science fiction comic strips like *Buck Rogers* and *Flash Gordon* and early comic book characters such as the original Human Torch, an android created in a lab. In their late modernist incarnation in Marvel Comics, characters like the Futurist represent the aesthetic possibilities of technology as a disruptive and expansive force, with the same tropes of bodily transformation, inhuman violence, and technological utopianism that the Italian futurists employed in the early twentieth century. Yet, as Alan Nadel has argued about Cold War American culture generally, these tropes are "contained" in superhero narratives that reaffirm the moral righteousness of United States liberalism and the sanctity of the normative white American family.[21] Just as futurism was a mode for the articulation and expression of political ideology, superhero comics have remained an ideological medium, from the overtly propagandistic phase during World War II to the present.

FURNISHED MAN, THE MODERNIST SUPERHERO

By connecting superhero comics to the deep influence of futurism on what we generally regard as modernism, I have extrapolated how modernist tropes appeared in American superhero comics, a periodical-based form that engaged in both the aesthetic experimentation and the patriotic nationalism characteristic of much late modernism. While the comics themselves provide plenty of evidence of modernism's influence on superhero aesthetics—this isn't particularly surprising given the insights of the New Modernist Studies—there is a more political element to this aesthetic lineage. This political edge is often dulled by modernist scholars, from Hugh Kenner forward, who have been invested in rescuing modernist traditions from their complicity with the fascist regimes of World War II. Yet, as Walter Benjamin made clear in his 1936 essay "The Work of Art in the Age of its Technological Reproducibility," the futurists and other modernists produced images of heroic, European males marching into horrible battle, aimed at rallying the masses to an ethnic nationalist cause. This reality, which links fascist aesthetics to American comic books, should inform our understanding of contemporary phenomena like trolling, wherein aggrieved male comic book readers associated with "comicsgate" target and harass comic book creators associated with bringing much-needed diversity to the comics industry.

Modernism cannot wash the blood of fascism from its hands; better to openly acknowledge the murderous colonialism, misogyny, nationalism, and racism that are at the core of modernism to move beyond deadly tropes. And indeed, modernist ideological impulses are not evacuated from, but instead reworked by, the US superhero comics that adopt futurist ideas and styles. To return to Walter Benjamin, it can be useful to think about comics as part of the kitsch or "folk art" that flourished in the late nineteenth and twentieth century, as amateur artists and writers (like Jerry Siegel and Joe Shuster, creators of Superman) could gain access to mass circulation due to the social and technological changes that define modernity. In his writings about kitsch and folk art, Benjamin makes a distinction between "high art" and "low art" that is informative: "Art teaches us to see into things. / Folk art and kitsch allow us to see outward from within things."[22] What we witness by reading superhero comics is the gradual revision of modernist forms into a popular culture that relies on idealized archetypes to allegorize complex realities. Superhero comics are allegorical, much like the folktales, myths, and popular images out of which its major intellectual properties were forged.

In order to understand how we can read superhero comics as more than a passive receptacle of modernist ideas, for better or worse, I posit that Walter Benjamin created an early superhero figure in his 1925 essay "Dream Kitsch." We might call the superhero that Benjamin imagines the "Furnished Man." Reshaped by the forces of modernity, "Furnished Man" has the ability to rewire his brain so that he dreams, thinks, and sees the world itself as a work of modernist art:

> What we used to call art begins at a distance of two meters from the body. But now, in kitsch, the world of things advances on the human being; it yields to his uncertain grasp and ultimately fashions its figures in his interior. The new man bears within himself the very quintessence of the old forms, and what evolves in the confrontation with a particular

milieu from the second half of the nineteenth century—in the dreams, as well as the words and images of certain artists—is a creature who deserves the name of "furnished man."[23]

Like Jake Barnes, Stephen Daedalus, Bigger Thomas, and other heroes of modernist literature, the Furnished Man is reshaped by modernity, caught in a perpetual struggle between the "old forms" of society and the mechanizations of modernity. Yet in comics, these struggles themselves become tropes, serialized and recirculated on the periodical newsstand.

In the 1950s, Theodor Adorno returned to the concept of the "Furnished Man" when he considered the role that new media forms have played in building a cultural world that was starkly different from reality:

> The gap between private existence and the culture industry, which had remained as long as the latter did not omnipresently dominate all dimensions of the visible, is now being plugged. Just as it is hardly possible to take a step outside of working hours without stumbling across some proclamation of the culture industry, so too are the various media it utilizes so seamlessly intermeshed that reflection can no longer catch its breath between them in order to realize that their world is not the world.[24]

Adorno goes on to note that this saturation of reality has been accomplished by "cinema, radio, magazines, and in America especially, *funnies* and *comic books*."[25] In Marvel Comics' 2014 series *Ms. Marvel*, for example, the teenage Kamala Khan writes *Avengers* fan fiction and then becomes a superhero herself, realizing her popular culture fandom in the "real world" of the Marvel universe. *Ms. Marvel* is a Furnished Man, emblematic of the collapse between fantasy and reality, the culture industry and history. Contemporary superhero universes reflect our mediated environment, wherein superhero cosplay is not just at comics conventions and political rallies but also in everyday life. According to so many advertisements, stories, and slogans, we are all superheroes in our own way now. The ubiquity of comics and superheroes in the culture industry today make it even more urgent that we take seriously the legacies of modernist ideologies. As for Furnished Man and for us, these ideologies fuse popular modernism to everyday life.

Notes

1. See Marilyn Satin Kushner, Kimberly Orcutt, and Casey Nelson Blake, *The Armory Show at 100: Modernism and Revolution* (London: Giles, 2013) and Michael North, *Reading 1922: A Return to the Scene of the Modern* (Oxford: Oxford University Press, 2002).

2. See Susan Stanford Friedman, *Planetary Modernisms: Provocations on Modernity Across Time* (New York: Columbia University Press, 2015). The methodological implications of the New Modernist Studies have made the kinds of comparisons between comics and modernism that I undertake in this essay possible. For another good summary of New Modernist methodology, see Paul K. Saint-Amour, "Weak Theory, Weak Modernism," *Modernism/modernity* 24, no. 3 (September 2018): 437–59.

3. For histories of US comic books, see Jean-Paul Gabilliet, *Of Comics and Men: A Cultural History of American Comic Books*, trans. Bart Beaty and Nick Nguyen (Jackson: University Press of Mississippi, 2010); Charles Hatfield and Bart Beaty, eds., *Comics Studies: A Guidebook* (New Brunswick, NJ: Rutgers University Press, 2020); and Shawna Kidman, *Comic Books Incorporated: How the Business of Comics Became the Business of Hollywood* (Oakland: University of California Press, 2019). An insightful reflection on historical periodization and comic books is Benjamin Woo, "An Age-Old Problem: Problematics of Comic Book Historiography," *International Journal of Comic Art* 10, no. 1 (2008): 268–79.

4. For a recent survey of Superman across culture and media, see Ian Gordon, *Superman: The Persistence of an American Icon* (New Brunswick, NJ: Rutgers University Press, 2017).

5. Caroline Tisdall and Angelo Bozzolla, *Futurism* (Oxford: Oxford University Press, 1978), 81 (ellipsis original).

6. Amelia Jones, *Irrational Modernism: A Neurasthenic History of New York Dada* (Cambridge, MA: MIT Press, 2004), 125.

7. Emily Braun, "Futurist Fashion: Three Manifestoes," *Art Journal* 54, no. 1 (Spring 1995): 36.

8. Scott Bukatman, *Matters of Gravity: Special Effects and Supermen in the 20th Century* (Durham, NC: Duke University Press, 2003), 216. Thanks to Jon Najarian for this reference.

9. F. T. Marinetti, "The Foundation and Manifesto of Futurism," in *Critical Writings*, ed. Günter Berghaus, trans. Doug Thompson (New York: Farrar, Strauss and Giroux, 2006), 12.

10. Marinetti, 13.

11. Marinetti, 13.

12. F. T. Marinetti, "Against Academic Teachers," trans. Doug Thompson, in Berghaus, *Critical Writings*, 81.

13. Marinetti, 82.

14. See "Cubism and Abstract Art," MoMA, The Museum of Modern Art, accessed June 12, 2023, https://www.moma.org/calendar/exhibitions/2748.

15. Enda Duffy, *The Speed Handbook: Velocity, Pleasure, Modernism* (Durham, NC: Duke University Press, 2009); Jones, *Irrational Modernism*; and Christine Poggi, *In Defiance of Painting: Cubism, Futurism, and the Invention of Collage* (New Haven, CT: Yale University Press, 1992).

16. Comics have varied potential connections to a figure like Duchamp, whose well-known readymade *Fountain* bears a reference to Bud Fisher's comic strip *Mutt and Jeff*.

17. Stephen Kern, *The Culture of Time and Space, 1880–1918* (Cambridge, MA: Harvard University Press, 2003), 117.

18. F. T. Marinetti, "Extended Man and the Kingdom of the Machine," trans. Doug Thompson, in Berghaus, *Critical Writings*, 86.

19. Robert Humphreys, "Futurism: May the Force Be With You," in *Futurist Manifestoes*, ed. Umbro Apollonio (Boston: MFA, 2001), 222.

20. Umberto Boccioni, Carlo Carrà, Luigi Russolo, Giacomo Balla, and Gino Severini, "Futurist Painting: Technical Manifesto 1910," trans. Robert Brain, in Apollonio, *Futurist Manifestoes*, 30.

21. See Alan Nadel, *Containment Culture: American Narratives, Postmodernism, and the Atomic Age* (Durham, NC: Duke University Press, 1995).

22. Walter Benjamin, "Some Remarks on Folk Art," trans. Rodney Livingstone, in *The Work of Art in the Age of its Technological Reproducibility and Other Writings on Media*, ed. Michael W. Jennings, Brigid Doherty, and Thomas Y. Levin (Cambridge, MA: Belknap Press of Harvard University Press, 2008), 255.

23. Walter Benjamin, "Dream Kitsch," trans. Howard Eiland, in Jennings, Doherty, and Levin, *The Work of Art*, 238.

24. Theodor W. Adorno, *Critical Models: Interventions and Catchwords*, trans. Henry W. Pickford (New York: Columbia University Press, 1998), 49–50.

25. Adorno, 50 (emphasis original).

"OUR FIRST LITERATURE"

The Poetics Underground of Joe Brainard's New York School Comics

NICK STURM

Accounts of the history of underground comix generally agree that the first issue of R. Crumb's *Zap Comix*, released in 1968, formally inaugurated the rise of the alternative comics movement. In the foreword to *Rebel Visions: The Underground Comix Revolution, 1963–1975*, Patrick Rosenkranz reiterates the foundational stature of *Zap* while also gesturing toward a prehistory that played out in more ephemeral publications. Looking to earlier comics by Joel Beck, Gilbert Shelton, and Rick Griffin, Rosenkranz performatively wonders how to determine the actual origins of the comix movement. "It was underground," he coolly quips, "so who knows?"[1] The subterranean mixture that generated experimentation in comics certainly has roots in the satirical pages of *Mad* magazine, founded in 1952, which is often cited by comix artists from Crumb to Spiegelman and beyond as a formative influence. However, the leap from *Mad* to a dispersed comics counterculture that then solidified around *Zap* offers an abbreviated lineage that minimizes, and often erases, how other genres and adjacent media shaped the nascent comix underground. Comics scholars tend to hint at these other influences, most often referring to the literary impact of Beat writers "to whom many comix artists looked for inspiration."[2] Roger Sabin also points to what is "less well documented" in the narratives of underground comix, particularly the influence of "Beat publications, literary magazines, and especially college magazines."[3]

While acknowledging important aesthetic precedents and alternative mediums, it is difficult to glean much from such observations. Who are these unnamed writers and publications? What medium-specific associations can we trace between comic books and literary magazines? If popular yet controversial Beat writers from the late 1950s influenced comics artists, did underground comix have any reciprocal influence on avant-garde poets in the late 1960s? What role did poets and other avant-garde artists play in shaping the rise of alternative comics? If "academically, the underground has been a period under near-erasure," as Charles Hatfield notes, then mapping the unaccounted-for connections between alternative comics and literary movements will begin to populate these lines of inquiry, generating a robust and specific history of the experimentation that fueled artists in both disciplines.[4]

One such artist is Joe Brainard, whose engagement with poets and merging of comics forms with avant-garde visual aesthetics constitutes a major intervention in alternative comics. In 1964 and 1965, Brainard published two issues of *C Comics*, an idiosyncratic variation on the comic book medium composed mostly of comics made in collaboration with poets.[5] Brainard also published over a dozen comic strips in the underground newspaper the *East Village Other* from 1966 to 1967, including collaborations with poets such as Ted Berrigan, Kenward Elmslie, and Ron Padgett. Associated with the New York School, a provisional network of transgenerational artists that includes poets, painters, novelists, and filmmakers, Brainard's work as a writer and visual artist, as well as his extensive collaborations with poets in the form of drawings, collages, and comics, makes him an integral interdisciplinary figure. In addition to the *East Village Other* and *C Comics*, Brainard contributed comics and cover illustrations to little magazines like the mimeographed *The World* and to establishment literary magazines like the *Paris Review*, while continuing to collaborate on long-form comics with poets into the 1970s.

One of the most frequently observed features in Brainard's comics, paintings, and other works is his incorporation of the well-known comics character Nancy.[6] A profile in *People* magazine, written after his show at Fischbach Gallery in 1975, describes his serial appropriation of Ernie Bushmiller's protagonist as "one of his great obsessions."[7] He was particularly keen on collaging or drawing Nancy into unexpected aesthetic lineages that magnify his nonhierarchical commitment to forms inclusive of the traditional, avant-garde, and popular. As the *People* reviewer notes, "He has painted her in a variety of imitated art styles: Nancy as a sensuous de Kooning woman, Nancy as Duchamp's *Nude Descending a Staircase* and even Nancy as *Mona Lisa*."[8] The publication in 2008 of *The Nancy Book*, an edited collection of Brainard's Nancy-related works, sparked a revival of critical interest in Brainard's humorous and complex appropriations.[9]

While Brainard's Nancy is a prominent and compelling serial feature of his work, his interventions among comics forms reach far beyond his appropriation of Bushmiller's Nancy. Indeed, much of Brainard's comics work remains "absent from growing scholarship in comics studies."[10] *C Comics* in particular has remained obscured, due in part to the insular aesthetic categorizations that have tended to isolate the study of avant-garde literature and alternative comics."[11] Even a literary critic sympathetic to Brainard's work, Nathan Kernan, observes that *C Comics* "exhibit something of the irreverence and energy of an underground 'zine' put together by a bunch of high-school students."[12] Rather than tacitly judging comics as merely adolescent, we should see Brainard's work as establishing a legitimate and sophisticated role for comics as a critical and imaginative form that engages both visual art and literature. As Daniel Worden notes, "Brainard's comics draw attention not to how comics can be molded into an already established discourse—not, in other words, because they can be read as novels or approached like paintings—but to how comics can bear their own aesthetic ideology."[13]

It is not a coincidence that *C Comics* emerged within the New York School, a constellation of artists who had a deep appreciation for the aesthetics of popular forms like comics. Many New York School poets grew up in the so-called "Golden Age" of comic books and absorbed those visual and textual influences into their wide-ranging and eclectic extraliterary interests.[14] The poet Bill Berkson, who frequently collaborated with Brainard on comics, describes their presence as organic and originary: "Comics were very natural. We had a feeling for how they worked. They were our first art and, in many respects, our first literature."[15] This familiarity with comics' formal qualities and recognition of their interdisciplinary aesthetic value is on display throughout both issues of *C Comics* in the ways that Brainard and his collaborators subvert the standard principles of comics' form and content. As a 1969 article in the alternative newspaper *Kaleidoscope Chicago* describes: "'C' comics were as heavy and as 'far out' (in a different way) as what gets published today (Joe Brainard did all the drawings and New York poets finished the texts), this up to 4–5 years ago, when there weren't no 'underground' comix happening yet."[16] Attending to how New York School poets and artists experimented with comics not only offers a renewed prehistory of the comix underground; it also helps us to see how New York School comics constitute their own subgenre of alternative comics.

DRAWING OUT THE INTERDISCIPLINARY COMIX UNDERGROUND

In fact, the existence of a collaborative community of comics artists and poets is constitutive of underground comix as a movement. Crumb's catalytic *Zap Comix* No. 1 was printed in San Francisco by the poet Charles Plymell in early 1968. Plymell's affiliations across the New American poetry—shorthand for the networks of avant-garde writers collected in Donald Allen's influential anthology *The New American Poetry 1945–1960*—made him a significant hinge between East and West Coast communities of poets, including the San

Francisco Renaissance, Beats, and New York School. An early emissary of radical aesthetics in San Francisco's Haight-Ashbury, Plymell's friendships with Beat writers Allen Ginsberg, William Burroughs, and Neal Cassady, as well as his support of comix artists like Crumb, facilitated his unique merger of the literary and comix undergrounds. Plymell first published Crumb's work in exactly this avant-garde crucible, reprinting Crumb's comics alongside prose and poetry by Burroughs, Ginsberg, d. a. levy, and Bob Kaufman in his underground newspaper the *Last Times*.[17] Not only did Plymell situate Crumb's work in the radical context of the *Last Times*, he also advocated for Crumb's art in influential literary circles. "I had been attending parties at Don Allen's, the West Coast editor for Grove," Plymell writes. "I was trying to get both him and [Lawrence] Ferlinghetti to publish Crumb.... The literary publishers seemed uninterested at the time."[18] Though Plymell's attempt to breach the disciplinary divisions between literature and comics among leading publishers was unsuccessful, the effort reveals an active fellowship between poets and comics artists working to reimagine the connections between their shared aesthetics and audiences.

Despite the lack of endorsement from avant-garde bastions Grove and City Lights, underground newspapers—from the ephemeral *Last Times* to well-established alternative papers—had been operating as a generative proving ground for new comics by offering regular publication to young artists. Trina Robbins describes the *East Village Other*, founded in October 1965 on Manhattan's Lower East Side, as a magnet for underground comix artists.[19] The paper published comic strips such as Bill Beckman's *Captain High!*, Kim Deitch's *Sunshine Girl*, and Nancy Kalish's *Gentle's Trip Out* as well as Spain Rodriguez's "comic newspaper" *Zodiac Mindwarp*, all of which predated the release of *Zap*. As Rosenkranz notes, "Crumb stated that Bill Beckman's 'Captain High' strips in the *East Village Other* were 'the first underground or hippie-type comic strip I ever saw.'"[20] Young poets influenced by *The New American Poetry* anthology also flocked to the paper, including Berrigan, Ishmael Reed, Jim Brodey, David Henderson, and Allen Katzman, all of whom were variously involved as founding editors or early contributors. The afterlives of the New American poetry and the future of underground comix were bound together in the *East Village Other*.

The first year and a half of the paper's publication—from late 1965 to early 1967—offers a particularly rich history of how poets and comics artists thrived side by side in the interdisciplinary underground of the Lower East Side. Beckman, the author of *Captain High!* and a close friend of the poets, established a pivotal precedent for Crumb's work and is an important figure in this interdisciplinary publishing context. As the paper's art editor, Beckman gave the *East Village Other* a Dadaesque design that matched the literary edge brought to the paper by its poet contributors. Early articles like Reed's "Poetry Place Protest" and Berrigan's "Get the Money!" made the *East Village Other* the de facto poetry newsletter of the Lower East Side. Poetry even featured in the inaugural adventure of Beckman's *Captain High!* strip, the first comic ever published in the *East Village Other*, as we meet the stoned hero "on the Lower East Side, higher than Edgar Allen Poe." Peering into a trash can, "Captain High searches for new meaning" before disguising himself in a scarf for The Fugs, the local avant-garde rock 'n' roll band newly formed by poets Tuli Kupferberg and Ed Sanders.[21]

At the intersection of avant-garde poetry, taboo-breaking rock music, and satirical drug-culture comics, Beckman and Sanders were close confidants.[22] It was Beckman who designed the sign for Sanders's infamous Peace Eye Bookstore, "the nerve center for extreme literature in New York."[23] Comics art was even celebrated as its own distinct aesthetic practice at the Peace Eye. In November 1968, Sanders's bookstore hosted "the first underground comic art show" exhibiting "pages from R. Crumb's notebooks, and original strips by Crumb, Art Spiegelman, Kim Deitch, Bill Beckman and Spain Rodriguez (who drew the invitation)." The press release for the show, *Ape Rape: An Exhibition of Lower Eastside Comic Art*, notes that "these artists live & work together, constantly comparing a million ideas and anecdotes, cackling & chortling over the pushy violence of the world." The "immediate energy" of their comics is given a literary equivalence, generating "profound sensations of mirth, anarch, [and] poetry" in viewers. Sanders's recognition of comics artists as a movement brought the provocative aesthetic innovations of comix into conversation with a capacious avant-garde lineage. As he describes the show's opening, "Peace Eye was packed that night—even Robert Frank showed up!"[24] Like the *East Village Other*, the Peace Eye was a crucial hub for comics artists where their work thrived in a broad countercultural milieu.

THE RADICAL INTERVENTIONS OF *C COMICS*

But before *Captain High!* and the *East Village Other*, before *Zap*, and before the anarchic interdisciplinarity hosted by the Peace Eye, Brainard's *C Comics* made an unprecedented and radical intervention into comics forms. In *C Comics* No. 1, Brainard and his poet collaborators adopt a range of formal approaches to reimagine the comics form, often integrating aesthetic features consummate with their avant-garde interests. Some of these retain the panel form of the traditional comic strip, like Brainard and Berrigan's "Stamp Out the Family Plan!" (figure 10.1), while transforming the narrative sequencing suggested by the panel's progression into an associative collage of disparate words, images, and graphic features. Beginning with differently designed iterations of the word "Stamp!" the comic then shows a featureless nude figure

"Our First Literature": The Poetics of New York School Comics

Figure 10.1. Joe Brainard, "Stamp Out the Family Plan!" with Ted Berrigan. *C Comics* No. 1, 1964.

shouting "Tetelestai!"—Greek for "it is completed," Jesus's last word on the cross, according to St. John. An arrow pointing toward the figure's waist is marked by the word "here." This is followed by a panel filled with a large glimmering diamond ring, suggesting an abbreviated narrative of a consummated marriage in reverse. Continuing with the titular "family plan," the next panel jumps ahead to "DEATH" written vertically in thick letters, a humorous subversion of the supposed joys of wedlock. The penultimate panels depart from this loose narrative completely, presenting two cut-out pieces of lined notebook paper with Berrigan's handwritten text on them.

These fragments are striking for how they concretize the comic panel into a material form rather a narrative frame, as if pieces from a William Burroughs-style cut up, an experimental process that Berrigan also adopted, had been pasted into the comic.[25] Formal idiosyncrasies appear across the strip, such as images that spill into gutters, crossed out or misspelled (and corrected) words, small arrows that point out stray lines and dots, and a mixture of graphic design features reminiscent of both comics and advertisements. Teetering between a skeletal narrative and the momentum of non sequitur irrationality, forgoing plot and character for an associative assemblage of text and image, "Stamp Out the Family Plan!" transforms the one-page comic strip into a raucous avant-garde grid. In Brainard and Berrigan's collaborative hands, each panel is its own miniature canvas open to whatever might appear in the compositional process.

Other comics forgo such visual density and variety for minimalistic forms. Brainard's collaboration with Padgett, "Cézanne," presents four panels containing a thought bubble, a brief caption, the word "paint" written in cursive, and a scratched-out phrase, suggesting that artistic composition is, like the strip itself, mostly an iterative process supported by failure and empty space. Brainard also folds literary genres into his comics, such as in his collaboration with James Schuyler, "What To Do?," whose text is the entirety of a one-act play by Schuyler. Absent any panels, the seven-page comic features three characters—a wife, husband, and a man named Egbert with whom both of them are in love—who are represented by three faces lifted from a standard soap opera comic. Recreating the play's script in a pared-back visual medium, Brainard assigns each character's repeating face, without any changes to their expressions, the speech balloons containing their lines. Like fragmented mannequins frozen in emotional situations they are not able to register, the faces repeat as the lines of the play cascade down each page. The comic quickly becomes laden with text as an extended dialogue between the wife and husband leads to piles of speech balloons stacked on top of one another. Egbert's entrance into the comic introduces a queer subtext amplified by Schuyler's campy variations on the narrative tensions of their ménage à trois. Lines like "You smell so fresh" and "I was just kissing your wife" become pleasurably absurd as the comic-play toys with the gendered sexual tensions between the characters. The collaboration ends with the wife offering a euphemistic invitation to her husband and Egbert to begin their own affair: "I know you men like to sit up all night and talk, but I need my rest." With her eyes closed and head titled upward, the woman literally clutches the pearls around her neck as the comic cleverly entangles the heteronormative and homoerotic subtexts of Schuyler's play. "What To Do?" is doubly interdisciplinary for adapting Schuyler's piece of poets theater, an avant-garde subgenre common to the New York School, into a comics form. Like the cut-up fragments in "Stamp Out the Family Plan!" and playful depictions in "Cézanne," Brainard's adaptation of Schuyler's play breaks open comics forms to an influx of avant-garde experiments.

Brainard's comics did not simply illustrate existing poems. Rather, his collaborations with New York School poets incorporated literary techniques and genres, and appropriated from a range of nonliterary sources, to create an entirely new kind of interdisciplinary experiment. Seeing one of Brainard's comics hardly prepares a reader for the content and form of another. For example, an associative, darkly humorous comic like "Skree" with Padgett features a suicidal dinosaur while playing with the flexibility of comic panels as postmodern frames; "I-Spy" with Elmslie includes a cast of hard-scrabbled agents spouting coded gibberish; and another comic with Elmslie features a crying woman running out of the panel grid behind her, which seems to be exploding with a "Whosh! Crackle! Pop! Bang!" Above the woman, who is reaching out for help, a large thought balloon is filled with a recipe for shrimp and coleslaw Jell-O salad, which cuts off halfway through the directions. Including a range of cultural citations and sources associated with everyday forms, literature, comics styles, and fine art, the inventiveness of such works prefigures the transgressive, collaborative comics produced in the decades after Brainard.

Published in June 1964, *C Comics* No. 1 can be read as Brainard's raw, initial experiment with collaborative comics. Its mimeographed stencil production, which permitted printing only on the recto and does not always allow for consistently dark lines or the retention of fine detail, created a visually complex but disposable-looking document. In 1965, the Boke Press–published *C Comics* No. 2 switched to a more expensive offset printing method that allowed for content on both verso and recto. Combined with a comic book–like, saddle-stitched format, the result is a striking magazine with an avant-garde flair. Brainard continued to refine the forms of his collaborations, opting for longer comics that regularly reach ten pages and for painterly comics that build off the graphic richness of earlier experiments. Brainard also produced interstitial advertisement content in the second issue, such as an ad for the poetry pamphlets published by John Bernard Myers's Tibor de Nagy Editions and a parodic clothing ad, written by Schuyler, that features a brawny man with an axe over his shoulder and reads "I dreamt I got my nuts off in my Dan River shirt." Other faux ads for products such as "C Cream" and "Happy Time Clocks" appear alongside promotions for books by Frank O'Hara and Edwin Denby, building a larger *C Comics* universe filled with imaginary subversive kitsch and populated by the literary avant-garde.

Figure 10.2. Joe Brainard, from "Foreheads," with Barbara Guest, *C Comics* No. 2, 1965.

Many of the comics in *C Comics* No. 2 are extraordinarily beautiful compositions that are made even more fascinating by their unexpected textual components. Brainard's collaboration with Barbara Guest, "Foreheads," is a particularly sophisticated example of this (figure 10.2). Guest's lineated text, assigned to animals like an elk and polar bear, reads like an ethereal, fragmented poem. "My antlers warm / The cold nights of the forehead / When the atom stars / Burn my scientist paws," says the elk, while the polar bear offers a litany of arctic forehead similes. Pairing elegantly drawn fauna with non sequitur meditations on the nature of foreheads, the panels are as dreamy and esoteric as they are amusing and mundane, like a mysterious children's book of bizarre talking animals. The disjointed shading around the animals adds a sketch-like quality that is reinscribed through Brainard's preservation of his own small mistakes—a misdrawn star, a squiggly line on the bear's back, and a stray mark in the corner—all of which have corresponding arrows pointing out their presence.

This is a technique that Brainard uses throughout his work, but that he first adopted when drawing comics. As he describes in an interview:

> Sometimes I do a lot of small drawing, like cartoons, and when I make mistakes I just cross them out and leave them. I like the way they look crossed out. Like in *C Comics*, I was doing the drawings on the spot in ink. I made a lot of mistakes. First I redid the drawings but finally I just started to scratch them out and I got to like the mistakes. They looked good to me.[26]

Like John Cage's aleatoric music and Berrigan's collaged sonnets, Brainard's scratch outs enact an experimental commitment to preserving the compositional process as an important part of an artwork's content. These retained mistakes appear in both issues of *C Comics*, including on the cover of the second issue and prominently in comics like "Hard Times," a collaboration with Frank O'Hara filled with scratched-out lines and ink blotches (figure 10.3). These techniques take on a representational quality when entire figures are scratched out, usually when expressing some form of doubt or insecurity. "But am I truly relating I wonder if I truly am?" asks a nude man in a modeling pose. His expression of self-consciousness is amplified by the full outline of his body and the attendant thought bubble traced over with a scratched-out line. Embracing chance and error, Brainard's willingness to highlight his mistakes for their visual appeal, which then become a part of the figurative landscape of his comics, shows him tapping into a set of contemporary avant-garde techniques as relevant for comics as for experimental music, painting, and literature.

Brainard also used his comics to defend precisely the kind of New York School aesthetics he was incorporating into *C Comics*. When *New York Times* art critic Hilton Kramer wrote dismissively about shows by Alex Katz and Jane Freilicher, describing Katz's new work as full of "cardboard emotion" and Freilicher as composing "feeble structures," Brainard pounced on the opportunity to pan Kramer in return.[27] Presented as an advertisement for "Curlee Clothes" written by James Schuyler, the comic features a repeating image of a man, Alex, and a woman, Jane, chatting discretely with one another (figure 10.4). Brainard's stand-ins for Katz and Freilicher sarcastically mime quotes from Kramer's review, tossing them back and forth like pieces of gossip. "Say,

Figure 10.3. Joe Brainard, "Hard Times," with Frank O'Hara, *C Comics* No. 2, 1965.

Jane," says the man, "I hear you're 'lacking formal resources'!" "Yes, Alex," the woman replies, "I 'faltered badly depicting interior-exterior views intersected by planes of windows'!" Mocking Kramer with his own words, the authority of the pedantic art critic is reduced to mere social patter, simply another brand of the transient "fashion" that Kramer accuses Katz and Freilicher of succumbing to. That Alex and Jane are gossiping about the review in a comic strip is all the more withering for Kramer's complaint that Katz has sunk to espousing "a taste for the blatant vulgarities of billboard color and comic-strip drawing," a reference to the burgeoning Pop aesthetic that Kramer sees as an insidious influence on "otherwise serious artists." By restaging the review in these same "vulgar" popular forms, Schuyler, who was also an adept art critic, critiques Kramer's false dichotomy between supposedly high and low aesthetics. In another advertisement, Schuyler points to the gendered divisions inscribed in

Figure 10.4. Joe Brainard, "Curlee Clothes," with James Schuyler, *C Comics* No. 2, 1965.

that hierarchy by highlighting Kramer's sexist descriptions of Freilicher's work as having a "limited compass" and "a certain lady-like charm." In the wake of Brainard and Schuyler's clever comics counterattack, Kramer's patronizing review is rendered powerless.

LITERARY EROTICS FROM BRAINARD TO CRUMB

As we have seen, Brainard's comics carve out a vivid aesthetic autonomy in the interdisciplinary art scene of the 1960s. The capaciousness of Brainard's comics also poses novel interpretative challenges for scholars who have tended to cast his work in limited terms. Worden approaches Brainard "as a comics poet" whose comics and drawings fulfill an "anti-capitalist imagining, a negation of value that preserves aesthetics while bypassing the monetized categories of fine art and literature."[28] Worden, like many critics, finds Brainard's work peculiarly elusive, claiming, for example, that his work expresses "not the proliferation of meaning but the denial of meaning."[29] Reading the comic "Poem," a collaboration by Brainard and Frank Lima from *C Comics* No. 2 that depicts a tape dispenser and inkwell, both of which have thought balloons containing the single word "Iron," Worden finds a seemingly impenetrable obscurity: "it is hard to posit any meaning." Indeed, as I have argued elsewhere, Brainard's work articulates a complicated relationship to artistic labor and aesthetic pleasure, including a deep distrust of "materialism [and] capitalistic labor as an end-in-itself."[30]

However, while "Poem" is surprising and enigmatic in the strain of "Stamp Out the Family Plan!" and "Foreheads," this focus on what is supposedly "meaningless" in such work overdetermines Brainard's critique of aesthetic values. It is not that comics like "Poem" embody "the denial of meaning," a conclusion that assumes Brainard's art acts in the negative by subtracting meaning, but that they enact exactly "the proliferation of meaning" that Worden claims they lack.[31] Brainard's comics are wonderfully overfull with associative meanings and visual-textual correspondences, offering themselves as excessive and allusive while dissembling and rearranging readers' expectations about genre, form, and compositional process.

Brainard did approach the antiestablishment politics of the *East Village Other* in one of his comic strips, though in his own distinctly Brainardesque way. In the three-panel comic "Waffles," a collaboration with Elmslie, a young man is shown at the edge of a pool during what looks like swimming practice. A coach kneels above him holding a stopwatch as he accusingly asks, "Apeshit over waffles, huh?" The second panel features the man in the pool responding, "We ate each other, honest!" In the final panel, we see a close up of a document titled "U.S. Army Application" with a large "REJECT" stamp across it. The humorous leaps from panel to panel suggest a joking and erotic gay narrative that parodies the absurdity of the supposed visibility of queer sexuality, which here is used as a litmus test for unfitness for military service.[32] Another collaborative strip with Elmslie in the *East Village Other*, "Queer Bar," depicts three men in a bar conversing in non sequiturs that are presented as humorously emasculating. "I've just bought a house in the country. Should I put a porch in front or in back?" asks one man. "Every time I throw a football it woobles [sic]," responds another. In both examples, Brainard parodies the stigma and isolation assigned to queer sexuality and mocks the conspicuousness assigned to gay men by arbitrary external markers ("Apeshit for waffles, huh?") by recalibrating those experiences in the comedic and countercultural context of the alternative press. Well before *It Ain't Me Babe*, *Wimmen's Comix*, and *Gay Comix*, these strips, along with Brainard's collaborations with Schuyler and Frank O'Hara in *C Comics* and *The World*, are important precedents for registering gay and lesbian sexuality in the heteronormative (and sometimes misogynistic) world of comics.

At the same time, Brainard also adapted the exaggerated sexuality of underground comix for his own work. In 1969, Berrigan proposed a third issue of *C Comics* that would be "about sex, absolutely straight, what we like, who's attractive (boys and girls for both), etc. I'll talk about my experiences with boys, you with girls, and vice versa. Or is that too much do you think?"[33] Though he did not take up Berrigan on the idea, Brainard had been eager to publish another *C Comics* that would focus on sex and sexuality. The popularity of underground comix served as an instigating force. As Brainard wrote in his journal on June 25, 1969: "I find the new California comics coming out now very inspiring. Especially Crumb. Not always so good, perhaps, but inspiring. Especially sex. There *is* a new freedom. And I plan (slurp) to take advantage of it."[34] Attuned to how the underground was developing in *Zap*, Brainard was working out an alternative comix aesthetic in dialogue with Crumb's liberatory erotics.

Like his appropriation of Bushmiller's Nancy, Brainard's engagement with and variation on Crumb would come through collaboration with poets. In the same journal entry, Brainard describes working on "some fuck drawings for a cartoon strip," a genre he also referred to as "fuck cartoons" that would become a regular part of Brainard's comics art. Most of Brainard's "fuck cartoons," such as one he composed with John Giorno, remain unpublished.[35] One that did make it into circulation is "Recent Visitors," a ten-page collaborative comic with Berkson that depicts Nancy and Carl Thomas Anderson's character Henry having sex surrounded by fragments of elusive, non sequitur text (figure 10.5).[36] After Nancy and Henry meet on the street, an attraction brought

Figure 10.5. Joe Brainard, from "Recent Visitors," with Bill Berkson, *Fits* No. 2, 1972. Reproduced in *The Nancy Book* (2008).

on by a spontaneous superhero-like horniness, nearly every panel shows the characters switching sexual positions in their seemingly inexhaustible lust for one another. "They went to the dark corners of the basement," reads the text stretching across eight panels, "places I didn't think were going to be used." The seemingly quaint sentence, reminiscent of a pulp novel, acts as a humorous innuendo for the "dark corners" that Nancy and Henry are discovering in one another's bodies, places that Bushmiller and Anderson likely "didn't think were going to be used" by their seemingly asexual characters. Having arrived in the proverbial basement, Nancy and Henry's pornographic descent into their own sex-crazed comix underground is complete. Even if he thought the underground cartoons themselves "not always so good," drawings such as "If Nancy Was an Underground Comic Character" (1972), which depicts a spazzed-out Nancy masturbating with a dildo plugged into the wall, confirm Brainard's ongoing dialogue with artists like Crumb.

However, like with the *East Village Other* and *C Comics*, the publishing context of Brainard's comics is an important marker of how his work acts as an intervention in the established histories of underground comix. In 1972, "Recent Visitors" appeared in the San Francisco–based comics and literary magazine *Fits*. Edited by a group of five former Columbia University students, the Fits Collective acted as a short-lived but important underground press, mixing articles on women's liberation with poems by Ginsberg, Diane di Prima, Audre Lorde, Lewis Warsh, and Alice Notley alongside comix and illustrations by Spain, Bill Griffith, Ken Greene, Kim Deitch, and Rory Hayes.[37] While work by Spain and Deitch had appeared in the *East Village Other* with Brainard's comic strips, *Fits* marks a merger of avant-garde poetry and the comix underground in ways that were not produced before or after its brief run.[38]

Complicating our received notions about the medium, Brainard's work redefines what the comic book can do, especially in relation to avant-garde literature and visual aesthetics.[39] Little magazines and other ephemeral publications acted as constitutive forces in shaping the post-1945 American literary landscape in ways that scholars are slowly coming to understand. As we begin to read rare primary sources like *C Comics* and *Fits*, new interdisciplinary subgenres will come into view. As Brainard writes in *I Remember*, "I remember thinking that comic books that weren't funny shouldn't be called 'comic books.'"[40] Though his youthful questioning should not be taken as a critique, Brainard's doubt about the stability of the medium introduces a welcome flexibility. The visual-textual collaborations that he produced from the first issue of *C Comics* up to *The Class of '47* (1973) with Robert Creeley, which is Brainard's last published long-form comic, embody this push against established comics genres. Brainard's series of Boke Press publications that began with *C Comics* No. 2 are another important set of interdisciplinary texts, especially genre-pluralistic works like *The Baby Book* (1965) with Elmslie and *100,000 Fleeing Hilda* (1967) with Padgett. Such "comic bokes" offer novel ways to revise the history of alternative comics art. In particular, Brainard's work presents a challenge to the reign of the graphic novel in comics studies. As this essay has demonstrated, some of the most aesthetically suggestive and ambitiously multimodal work has been done not in book-length comics but in little magazines and periodicals that circulated among local groups of artists and poets. Such work would also serve as examples that help to enrich and complicate significant subgenres of comics art, such as the *Abstract Comics* explored by Andrei Molotiu and *Poetry Comics* created by Dave Morice, both collected in anthologies with those titles. With scholarly attention so closely following recent reproductions of Brainard's work, bringing the entirety of his comics back into print will surely lead to important critical appraisals from new generations of scholars.

Notes

1. Patrick Rosenkranz, *Rebel Visions: The Underground Comix Revolution, 1963–1975* (Seattle: Fantagraphics Books, 2008), 13.

2. Charles Hatfield, *Alternative Comics: An Emerging Literature* (Jackson: University Press of Mississippi, 2005), 18.

3. Roger Sabin, "Underground and Alternative Comics," in *Comics Studies: A Guidebook*, ed. Charles Hatfield and Bart Beaty (New Brunswick, NJ: Rutgers University Press, 2020), 41.

4. Hatfield, *Alternative Comics*, 7.

5. *C Comics* was a spin-off of Ted Berrigan's mimeographed poetry magazine *C: A Journal of Poetry*, the primary underground publishing venue for a growing nexus of New York School poets, which appeared in thirteen issues from 1963 to 1967. Brainard contributed nine covers throughout *C*'s run, one of which features a collaborative comic with Berrigan.

6. Two of Brainard's earliest Nancy works are the collaborative comic "Personal Fancy Love" with Ted Berrigan, published in *Columbia Review* 46, no. 2 (1964), and the comic "Nancy" with Bill Berkson, published in *C Comics*, no. 1, the latter of which is not included in *The Nancy Book*.

7. Lee Wohlfert, "Joe Brainard's Collages Come in One Size—Petite," *People Weekly*, December 22, 1975, 72.

8. Wohlfert, 72.

9. Most of the scholarship on Brainard's comics explores the queer performativity of Brainard's Nancy. Examining works such as "If Nancy Was a Boy," in which Nancy lifts her skirt to reveal male genitalia, scholar Jessica Stark has focused on Brainard's transformation of "the provocative, queer affordances of the comic writ large." "*Nancy* and the Queer Adorable in the Serial Comics Form," *American Literature* 90, no. 2 (June 2018): 317. Similarly, Ramzi Fawaz has pointed out the continuity between Brainard's "exploration of Nancy's queer and gender transitive potential in the 1970s" and "her explicit use as a lesbian and genderqueer icon . . . in the 1990s." "Stripped to the Bone: Sequencing Queerness in the Comic Strip Work of Joe Brainard and David Wojnarowicz," *ASAP/Journal* 2, no. 2 (May 2017): 348. It is worth noting that Bushmiller's Nancy made frequent appearances in underground comics throughout the 1960s and 1970s; see for example Gilbert Shelton's "Dickless Tracy," signed "Clang Honk," published in the *East Village Other*, August 1–15, 1966; and Jay Lynch's "Phoebe and the Pigeon People," which appeared in the *Chicago Reader* from 1978 to 1996. Though it is arguable that Brainard's Nancy is more radical and a longer lasting feature of his work, Lynch, Shelton, and Brainard's use of the character reveals a shared appropriative gesture that situates Brainard's "obsession" with Nancy as one common to alternative comics widely.

10. Daniel Worden, "Joe Brainard's Grid, or, the Matter of Comics," in "B-Side Modernism," ed. Jennifer Ashton and Oren Izenberg, special issue, *Nonsite.org*, no. 15 (January 16, 2015), https://nonsite.org/joe-brainards-grid-or-the-matter-of-comics/.

11. Recently, scholars Daniel Worden and Jessica Stark have been begun to bridge the disciplinary divides imposed on Brainard's comics, respectively highlighting his comics' critique of traditional aesthetic value and arguing for the need to analyze his serial comic forms alongside canonical cartoonists. Another important step toward reading Brainard's writing and visual art together is the recent essay collection edited by Yasmine Shamma, *Joe Brainard's Art* (Edinburgh: Edinburgh University Press, 2019).

12. Nathan Kernan, "The Madonna of the Future," in Shamma, *Joe Brainard's Art*, 55. Alternatively, Jenni Quilter briefly and competently describes *C Comics* in *New York School Painters & Poets: Neon in Daylight* (New York: Rizzoli, 2014), 156–70.

13. Worden, "Brainard's Grid."

14. Quilter describes the range of the poets' early aesthetic interests in *New York School Painters & Poets*:

It should be noted that at Harvard, Ashbery and O'Hara had already gathered together a wide range of cultural influences, both high and low. They liked recherché literature (Ronald Firbank, Ivy Compton-Burnett), comics, Hollywood and French movies, poet John Wheelwright, author Henry Green, modern French and Russian poetry, and modern music (John Cage, Arnold Schoenberg, Erik Satie, and Francis Poulenc). Their move to New York City further widened their interest, but it did not establish the characteristic of its breadth. (310)

15. Bill Berkson, "Working with Joe," *Jacket*, March 2002, http://jacketmagazine.com/16/br-berk.html.

16. Rich Mangelsdorff, "Poetry Project at St. Mark's-in-the-Bowery," *Kaleidoscope Chicago*, March 14–27, 1969.

17. As Charles Plymell recounts, his reception of Crumb's work came out of a literary context:

I think the first strip of Crumb's I saw was in an underground newspaper from the upper Midwest. There were some poets from Cleveland associated with the poet, d. a. levy, who had come to the San Francisco scene . . . and who had given me a paper. I had a larger press in the Mission District at the time. . . . So, I put out a couple of issues of a newspaper I called *The Last Times* in which I lifted Crumb's strip from the Midwest underground paper. (Charles Plymell, "Curled in Character," Beats in Kansas, accessed November 20, 2020, http://www.vlib.us/beats/plymellrcrumb.html.)

18. Plymell.

19. Rosenkranz, *Rebel Visions*, 46–47.

20. Rosenkranz, 58. It's interesting to note that Crumb's first publication in the *East Village Other* was in October 1967, comparatively late considering his peers' earlier publications, though his influence quickly skyrocketed.

21. Beckman's *Captain High!* appeared ten times in the *East Village Other* from November 1965 to May 1966.

22. When the Peace Eye was raided by police in early 1966, the story made front page news in the *East Village Other*. The headline "POET ARRESTED ON OBSCENITY" ran above a photograph of Sanders sifting through the mess of papers left by the cops. The *Captain High!*

strip in the same issue appears to comment on Sanders's arrest, albeit for a different crime. "Meanwhile at The Department of Evil, a plot is cooking," reads the opening panel, showing the malicious Inspector Nodding-Act preparing a "pot raid" on Captain High. The strip ends in medias res as Captain High intercepts the police transmission, a superpower that Sanders likely wished he had. "INTELLECTUAL VIOLENCE!" reads a banner over the comic, a declaration that describes the Inspector's nefarious crackdown on Captain High as much as the New York Police Department's targeting of the Peace Eye.

23. Rosenkranz, *Rebel Visions*, 48. Note that Spain Rodriguez designed the second sign for the Peace Eye when it moved into the former *East Village Other* offices in early 1968.

24. Ed Sanders, *Fug You: An Informal History of the Peace Eye Bookstore, the Fuck You Press, the Fugs, and Counterculture in the Lower East Side* (Philadelphia: De Capo, 2011), 359.

25. For more on the reciprocity between Burroughs's and Berrigan's experimental composition methods in the 1960s, see my chapter "'There Are No Typographical Errors in This Edition': Burroughs's Textual Infection of the New York School," in *Burroughs Unbound: William Burroughs and the Performance of Writing*, ed. Stanley Gontarski (London: Bloomsbury Academic, 2021).

26. "An Interview with Joe Brainard" in *Bean Spasms* by Ted Berrigan, Ron Padgett, and Joe Brainard (New York: Granary Books, 2012), 24.

27. Hilton Kramer, "Art: Disciple of Pop School, or Victim," *New York Times*, November 27, 1965.

28. Kramer.

29. Worden applies a similar interpretation to a drawing in Brainard's *Some Drawings of Some Notes to Myself* that he claims "seems to have no meaning," adding that there "is no way to even begin to answer these questions" about the drawing's connotations. Worden, "Brainard's Grid."

30. Nick Sturm, "'Fuck Work': The Reciprocity of Labor and Pleasure in Joe Brainard's Writing," in Shamma, *Joe Brainard's Art*, 186.

31. Brainard refused to describe himself or his work in the oppositional terms that Worden uses. In a 1977 interview, New York School poet Tim Dlugos asked Brainard about his involvement in "the 'counter-culture' thing in the Sixties." Brainard immediately refers to his comic strips for the underground press but pushes back on being associated with any oppositional ideology: "I did cartoons for the *East Village Other*, but I was never . . . I mean I'm not anti-anything, really." Joe Brainard, "Diary 1969 (Continued)," in *The Collected Writings of Joe Brainard*, ed. Ron Padgett (New York: Library of America, 2012), 497.

32. "Waffles" might have been inspired by Brainard's own experience. In 1963, he was declared unfit for military duty after telling a psychologist at a draft induction center that he was gay. See Ron Padgett's *Joe: A Memoir of Joe Brainard* (Minneapolis: Coffee House, 2004), 63.

33. Berrigan's letter to Brainard, dated October 22, 1969, is reproduced in Quilter, *New York School Painters & Poets*, 233–35.

34. Brainard, *Collected Writings*, 241–42.

35. In *Great Demon Kings: A Memoir of Poetry, Sex, Art, Death, and Enlightenment* (New York: Farrar, Straus and Giroux, 2020), John Giorno describes "working on a collaboration with the artist Joe Brainard, a pornographic cartoon" (243).

36. "Recent Visitors" recalls the sexualization of fictional cartoon characters in "Disneyland Memorial Orgy" by Wallace Wood, published in *The Realist* (May 1967), though with an avant-garde literary edge. "I really like the whole idea of art," thinks Henry as he strolls across the comic's opening page.

37. The Fits Collective had a deep affiliation with the history of independent publishing in the New York School. At Columbia in the late 1960s, Alan Senauke and Hilton Obenzinger edited the school's student literary magazine *Columbia Review* that Padgett had helped to edit in the early 1960s. The administration's censorship of an issue of *Columbia Review* in 1963, in part because of an explicit word in a poem by Berrigan, led to Padgett and his coeditors' resignation from the magazine. In April 1963, the censored edition of *Columbia Review* was released as the *Censored Review*, the magazine that inspired Berrigan to publish the first issue of *C: A Journal of Poetry*, in May 1963. The titular C of Berrigan's magazine is a reference to the *Censored Review*. In 1969, Senauke and Obenzinger helped to edit the anthology *A Cinch: Amazing Works from the Columbia Review*, which includes work by Berrigan, Padgett, Brainard, and other poets of the New York School.

38. As was the case with Brainard's comics, the critical reception of such projects has tended to fall into an interdisciplinary no-man's-land. In his description of *Fits* on the website comixjoint.com, comics collector M. Steven Fox notes that the publication "barely qualifies as" a comic, ostensibly for its literary content. Like Brainard and *C Comics*, neither *Fits* nor its editors are referenced in *Rebel Visions* despite the unprecedented connections between comix artists and literary sources that it records. The magazine also offers a startling array of other visual-textual experiments, like cut-up style newspaper collaborations by Ron Padgett and Tom Veitch, the latter of whose close friend, Greg Irons, also had work in *Fits*. Other important interdisciplinary publications that combined poetry and comics include the mimeographed literary magazine *Meatball*, edited by Joel Deutsch in San Francisco from 1969 to 1971, which contained comics by Crumb; Bill Berkson's *Big Sky* poetry magazine, which he styled after comic book–style publications and which published Veitch's and Irons's early collaborative ecocomic "The Creature from The Bolinas Lagoon"; and the comics illustrations that Brainard would regularly publish in the *Paris Review* in the late 1960s.

39. As Hatfield notes,

> Though comix were crucially nurtured by a network of radical newspapers, such as the *East Village Other* and the *Berkeley Barb*, and early on gave rise to short-lived tabloids like *Yellow Dog* (in its first incarnation, 1968–1969) and *Gothic Blimp Works* (1969), it was Crumb's subversive appropriation of the comic book that proved to be the decisive break with the past. As Bill Griffith remarked, Crumb "reinvented the comic book. Took it over just as other people of his generation took over music" (Rosenkranz 71). *Zap* became the catalyst for a whole new field of comix publishing because Crumb took back the comic book and redefined what it could do. (*Alternative Comics*, 8)

40. Joe Brainard, *I Remember* (New York: Granary Books, 2001), 76.

Section IV
COMICS AS MODERNISM

PROFANE TRANSFIGURATIONS

On a Detail of a Painting in a Panel in an Installment of *Little Annie Fanny*, 1963, or How Harvey Kurtzman and Arthur Danto (Mostly) Agree, and Deep Down Really Disagree Too

ANDREI MOLOTIU

Pop Artists' appropriation and transformation of comic-book and comic-strip imagery has generally been discussed in art history as a maneuver in which artistic intentionality, consciousness of the image as form, and any art-theoretical awareness reside fully on the side of the appropriating gallery artist, while the comics creators are cast as having little artistic agency of their own, or even any creativity beyond the seemingly simple demands of their craft. The tone for such views was set by the Pop Artists themselves, as for example by Roy Lichtenstein, who in a January 1966 BBC interview with David Sylvester discussed the (lack of) artistic merit of his source images and how he transformed them in his paintings:

> Sometimes you get a very interesting image that would almost be good by itself except that this was not the artist's intention. I think that one needs more than pure intention to make a work of art: in other words, my intention to exhibit doesn't automatically make it a work of art. But the original cartoonist has a job to do. He gets a story out and he's very good at his craft and puts it together and it's very interesting, but it isn't really inventive and it isn't really formed. I think it's inventive only in a mass way, that it has become inventive if you suddenly sit back and look at it and say: "My God, look what's happened to this image. We take this for an eye and this for a shadow under a chin and look what it really looks like." But this has gone on from generation to generation of illustrators, each one adding a little bit to the last, and it's become a

kind of universal language. So I'm interested in what would normally be considered the worst aspects of commercial art.[1]

In response, many comics creators and fans, already in the 1960s but particularly since 1980 or so, have seen Lichtenstein and his colleagues as nothing but plagiarists, copyists devoid of any originality; David Barsalou's Internet project, "Deconstructing Lichtenstein," in its various online incarnations since 2000, has articulated a particularly vehement expression of this position.[2]

In both these views—Lichtenstein's coming from the realm of high art and Barsalou's from comics fandom—only one side is seen as aware of the other: whether they consider Pop's appropriation as a profoundly transformative act or as simple theft, neither Lichtenstein nor Barsalou mentions the possibility that comics was as aware of gallery art as vice-versa, and that therefore appropriation and commentary may have flowed in both directions. To argue for this possibility is to attempt not so much to upturn the old high/low hierarchy as to flatten it, granting agency and even theoretical self-awareness to creators on both sides of the divide. A full overview of such a "flattened" comics-and-art history of what might be called the long 1960s would take in everything from Lichtenstein and Andy Warhol to the work of Jess Collins, Joe Brainard (see Nick Sturm's chapter in this collection), Jack Kirby, and Jim Steranko. I would like here to delineate only one chapter of it: the complex relationship to modern art of Harvey Kurtzman (1927–1994), creator of *Mad* magazine, the publication for which he is still best known today.[3] I will relate the views on high art that emerge from Kurtzman's 1960s work (and from one panel of one 1963 comic in particular) to those of philosopher of art and art critic Arthur Danto (1924–2013), widely considered the foremost theorist of Pop. I will then apply Danto's views of how Pop Art functioned, particularly in relation to its display context and its art-theoretical climate, to Kurtzman's earlier work at *Mad*, which I will argue can be seen not only to have engaged in similar strategies but to afford us a critical perspective on Danto's theories that may help critique and refine them.

KURTZMAN, LICHTENSTEIN, AND *LITTLE ANNIE FANNY*

Kurtzman, after starting his career working freelance for Timely (the future Marvel) Comics, as well as for other publishers, found a home at EC Comics in 1950 and created *Mad* for them in 1952. He edited *Mad*'s first twenty-seven issues, from October 1952 to April 1956, and was the sole writer of the first twenty-three, comic book–formatted ones. After quitting EC and his editorship in 1956, he engaged in a variety of publishing ventures that led, by the early 1960s, to his editorship of *Help!* magazine (1960–1965), as well as to his work

Figure 11.1. Harvey Kurtzman, cover of *Mad* #22, "Special Art Issue" (EC Comics, 1955).

on *Little Annie Fanny*, the fully painted comic that, with his closest collaborator, Will Elder, he produced for *Playboy* from 1962 to 1988.

Kurtzman's engagement with "high art" can already be seen from the covers he designed for *Mad* #22, the "Special Art Issue" of April 1955 (figure 11.1), a burlesque on Picasso's *Girl Before a Mirror* of 1932 with the clownish face of Elder substituted for the girl's mirror reflection, and for *Mad* #14, of August 1954 (figure 11.2), which is either a typical schoolboy's prank on the *Mona Lisa* or Kurtzman's take on Duchamp's own schoolboyish prank, the *LHOOQ* of 1919.

Figure 11.2. Harvey Kurtzman, cover of *Mad* #14 (EC Comics, 1954).

(What we know of Kurtzman's awareness of the art world, including his mention of Duchamp in the aforementioned "Special Art Issue," suggests it is the latter.)

This engagement blossomed in the context of early Pop Art, in particular in the last panel of Kurtzman's and Elder's installment of *Little Annie Fanny*, drawn in collaboration with Russ Heath, which appeared in the September 1963 issue of *Playboy* (figure 11.3).[4] In this installment, Annie meets for the first time the artist Duncan Fyfe Hepplewhite, revealed by the end of the comic to be an art forger extraordinaire. While the previous three pages of the story feature jokes on Manet's *Olympia*, Whistler's *Mother*, Rembrandt, and Frans Hals, by the last panel Hepplewhite has gone full modernist, his studio chock-full of (his own

Figure 11.3. Harvey Kurtzman, Will Elder, and Russ Heath, *Little Annie Fanny*, originally published in *Playboy*, September 1963.

Figure 11.4. Roy Lichtenstein, *The Kiss*, 1962.

versions of) the crème de la crème of the period's avant-garde paintings, including Franz Kline, Mondrian, Picasso, Miró, Pollock, and Rothko. Among these paintings appears a version of Lichtenstein's 1962 painting *The Kiss* (figure 11.4), itself based on a panel from Milton Caniff's newspaper strip *Steve Canyon*. *The Kiss* had been featured in Lichtenstein's 1962 solo show at the Leo Castelli Gallery, which was the artist's first solo exhibition to include paintings based on comics panels, or indeed to include any work that we would associate with Pop Art.[5] By 1967 or so Lichtenstein was going to become a regular reference in comics from Marvel to *Archie*, but as far I can ascertain *Little Annie Fanny* is the first instance of a comics creator referencing his work. While the other paintings in the *Little Annie Fanny* panel are relatively straightforward versions of their generic models, Lichtenstein's painting has both been carefully copied and has undergone some notable changes: it has been turned ninety degrees counterclockwise, its background color has been changed from blue to red, and a speech balloon saying "Shazam!" has been added.

Figure 11.5. *Art News*, March 1962, 14, including review of Roy Lichtenstein's show at the Leo Castelli Gallery.

That speech balloon, I will show, can be read as a commentary by Kurtzman on Lichtenstein's work and perhaps on Pop in general. It is harder to read a similar intentionality to the other changes. They could easily have resulted from Kurtzman and his collaborators basing their copy of Lichtenstein on a black and white, possibly misoriented, image, for which they would have had to guess the color. Was Lichtenstein's painting ever reproduced in this manner?

As it turns out, it was. A black and white reproduction of *The Kiss*, similarly turned ninety degrees counterclockwise, appeared in the March 1962 issue of *Art News*, illustrating a review of Lichtenstein's Castelli show (figure 11.5). The similarities between the *Art News* reproduction of *The Kiss* and the version of it in *Little Annie Fanny* are too strong to leave much doubt that this was indeed the source Kurtzman, Elder, and Heath used.

Everything we know about the production process on *Little Annie Fanny*, as well as about Kurtzman's and Elder's biographies and cultural interests (Heath being only a hired hand on the strip), suggests that the choice of using *The Kiss*, as well as the other artworks, was solely Kurtzman's. The *Art News* source for the Lichtenstein is a strong indication that Kurtzman (who at the time, according to his biographer Bill Schelly, was more and more interested in socializing with the New York intelligentsia than with other cartoonists and commercial artists) was at least an occasional reader of the art press.[6] This is, of course, evidence of precisely the kind of awareness on the part of comics creators of developments in the art world that I noted is ignored both in most art-historical accounts of the Pop Art period and in fan-culture ripostes like Barsalou's. It is fascinating that, along with more established names, Kurtzman chose to use an artist who at the time constituted the cutting edge of the avant-garde, long before Lichtenstein became a popular name with the public.[7] Of course, the fact that Lichtenstein's painting was based on a comic probably strongly informed Kurtzman's choice.

It is also very likely that the *Art News* review was Kurtzman's first introduction to the Pop artist. (As, indeed, it was for Arthur Danto, according to his own testimony.[8]) Having, by the early 1960s, left the comic-book world behind in search of more prestigious and remunerative publication venues such as *Playboy*, Kurtzman, upon reading the review and seeing the (misoriented) reproduction, probably recognized in Lichtenstein his own ironic attitude toward the industry and publishing format where he had gotten his start.

So much for the color change and reorientation of Lichtenstein's painting in *Little Annie Fanny*; how about the addition of the speech balloon? The term "Shazam!" comes of course from *Captain Marvel*, the Fawcett comic about a young boy, Billy Batson, who, when speaking said word, turns into the eponymous adult superhero. *Captain Marvel* was rather unique in depicting such a transformation from child to adult; for the most part, Golden Age superheroes' heroic personae were rendered as having the same age and size as their mundane secret identities. It's hard to see how the *Captain Marvel* reference applies to *The Kiss*'s ostensible content, the kissing lovers. Rather, the added speech balloon seems to be a commentary on the "comicity," so to speak, of Lichtenstein's source, the *Steve Canyon* strip, and on the transformation undergone by the imagery from lowly comic to high-art painting.

Yet, in adding the word balloon, Kurtzman collapses two very different segments of the comics world. Within the period's hierarchization of comics, newspaper strips had significantly higher cultural prestige than comic books, and in particular than superhero ones, which were seen to be aimed exclusively at children. Within newspaper strips, realistically rendered, nonhumorous ones such as *Steve Canyon* were regarded more highly than cartoony, humorous ones, and among the creators of these "adult" strips, Milton Caniff was particularly respected. On the other hand, the storylines of *Captain Marvel*, along with C. C. Beck's gentle artwork, had been designed to appeal to even younger children than the average superhero comic-book consumer.[9] The addition of the word balloon to Lichtenstein's painting can be taken partly to signify Kurtzman's perception of how such hierarchization within the comics world was homogenized from the point of view of the high-art world, which perceived all comics indiscriminately as low art and as unworthy of cultural pretensions, and to which such intramural distinctions as those between a well-respected newspaper strip and a children's comic book became meaningless.

Distinctions based on readers' ages, however, were particularly urgent within the comic-book field, which regularly formulated its artistic and thematic ambitions in terms of appealing to older readers. Kurtzman and EC Comics had been at the forefront of this development in the 1950s, particularly with Kurtzman's war comics such as *Two-Fisted Tales* and *Frontline Combat*, as well as with other comics at EC that addressed weighty themes such as racial discrimination and the Holocaust.[10] From this perspective, Billy Batson's transformation into Captain Marvel, from child to adult, can be taken as iconic of the comic-book industry's ambitions. (The early 1960s, by the way, were a crucial period for these developments. The comic-book industry's attempts at artistic respectability, as particularly exemplified at EC Comics, had been temporarily defeated by the comic-book panic of 1954 and by the establishment of the Comics Code Authority. The code, by imposing strict morality regulations on the industry and banning any controversial subject matter or questioning of authority, had ensured that comic books remained seen as child fodder and nothing more for the remainder of the 1950s.[11] It was only by 1961 or so that the industry showed renewed artistic ambitions by—very tentatively—beginning to address again older readers.)

And yet Lichtenstein had leapfrogged the comics industry's entire tentative, gradual process of maturation by taking comics imagery, reframing it in a gallery context, and making it acceptable as high art: feted by the art world, reviewed in *Art News*, hung side by side with Pollock and Picasso. In terms of artistic prestige, this was beyond anything that the comic-book creators could have dreamed. This seems to be the principal gist of Kurtzman's addition of the "Shazam!" word balloon: that in Lichtenstein's work, comics, like the young and powerless Billy Batson, seemed to have instantly grown up, transformed into the all-powerful Captain Marvel of high art. Yet, ironically, despite this instant maturation, "untransformed" comic books and comic strips got no more respect than before—and perhaps, in being simply used by Pop Art as anonymous imagery fodder, even less.

ARTHUR DANTO, POP ART, AND THE NOTION OF "TRANSFIGURATION"

Another observer noticed at the time the power that Pop Art had to take the lowly and mundane and raise it into the empyrean precincts of the art world. Philosopher and later art critic Arthur Danto based his epoch-making 1964 article in the *Journal of Philosophy*, "The Artworld," on his experience of Andy Warhol's April 1964 show at the Stable Gallery, in which Warhol's *Brillo Box* multiples were exhibited. These *Brillo Boxes* were almost precise replicas, albeit silkscreened on wood, not cardboard, and without the joins and fold overs of the cardboard showing, of the twenty-four giant-size-package boxes that James Harvey had designed, probably the previous year, for Brillo. Yet, of course, Warhol's were valued art objects, while Harvey's were nothing but pieces of disposable packaging. From this distinction drawn between objects that (at first glance, at least) seem visually indiscernible, Danto built a complete theory of art that seemed to transcend the then-dominant formalism of Clement Greenberg and better to explain the conceptual transformations that occurred in art in the post-abstraction (or postmodern) era.

From the first, Danto referred to such transformations as "transfigurations," giving a distinctly metaphysical cast to what was supposed to be an analytic theory of art. Writing, in his 1964 article, of Warhol's operation in *Brillo Box*, he asked:

> Is this man a kind of Midas, turning whatever he touches into the gold of pure art? And the whole world consisting of latent artworks waiting, like the bread and wine of reality, to be *transfigured*, through some dark mystery, into the indiscernible flesh and blood of the sacrament? Never mind that the Brillo box may not be good, much less great art. The impressive thing is that it is art at all. But if it is, why are not the indiscernible Brillo boxes that are in the stockroom?[12]

Danto went on to answer his own question: "But then a stockroom is not an art gallery, and we cannot readily separate the Brillo cartons from the gallery they are in." It was the gallery, seen not only as a physical but as an art-theoretical space, that made the whole difference. Warhol's *Brillo Boxes* were objects infused with theory, in ways in which Harvey's utilitarian Brillo boxes weren't:

> What in the end makes the difference between a Brillo box and a work of art consisting of a Brillo Box is a certain theory of art. It is the theory that takes it up into the world of art, and keeps it from collapsing into

the real object which it is (in a sense of *is* other than that of artistic identification). Of course, without the theory, one is unlikely to see it as art, and in order to see it as part of the artworld, one must have mastered a good deal of artistic theory as well as a considerable amount of the history of recent New York painting.[13]

From this point on, the issue of visually indiscernible objects, one a work of art, one not, became the cornerstone of Danto's philosophy of art. Danto elaborated on the notion at length in his 1981 book, *The Transfiguration of the Commonplace*, whose title enshrined the notion of "transfiguration" as, metaphorically at least, what happens in the transformation of mundane object into artwork.[14] Danto returned to this point often, for example explaining in 1997: "Pop . . . transfigures into art what everybody knows: the objects and icons of common cultural experience, the common furnishings of the group mind at the current moment of history. . . . Pop celebrated the most ordinary things of the most ordinary lives—corn flakes, canned soup, soap pads, movie stars, comics. And by the process of transfiguration, it gave them an almost transcendental air."[15] Note the reference to comics. Comics themselves are "ordinary things," "banal" objects, no different from canned soup or soap pads (not to mention movie stars!).[16] They are not artworks any more than the Brillo soap pad boxes in the stockroom are, and are thus denied the metaphysical elevation of art.

Can a parallel be drawn between Danto's view of the transformation of comics into Pop Art as "transfiguration" and Kurtzman's ironic notion of this change, implied by his "Shazam!" addition, as a magical maturation? The locus classicus for the notion of transfiguration is, of course, the transfiguration of Jesus in the New Testament.[17] This is precisely Danto's reference when using the term, as made explicit in *The Transfiguration of the Commonplace*: "Peter, John, and James saw Jesus transfigured before them: 'His face did shine as the sun, and his raiment was white as the light.'"[18] The biblical quote that Danto gives is a perfect instantiation of the dictionary meaning of transfiguration as "a complete change of form or appearance into a more beautiful or spiritual state."[19] And that is precisely what happens when Billy Batson turns into Captain Marvel—or for that matter when any seemingly regular human reveals their superhero self: they become more idealized, more free of earthly constraints, more beautiful, and seemingly even more spiritual.

Kurtzman, by adding "Shazam!" to Lichtenstein's painting, seems to be agreeing with Danto, at least ironically: the change from comic to avant-garde artwork *is* a transfiguration, an elevation into a more rarefied state, while comics themselves are doomed to always be Billy Batson, not Captain Marvel, banal objects and fodder for kids but never proper grown-up art.

FORMAL INNOVATION, MEDIUM SPECIFICITY, AND SELF-REFERENTIALITY IN KURTZMAN'S EC WORK

Since, for Danto, artistic transfiguration can only be effected in an art-theoretical atmosphere, while comics are nothing but untransfigured ordinary objects, it follows that comics are, implicitly, theoryless. Yet are they? To explore this question, I would like to take here a brief detour through Danto's own view of the precursors to his philosophy of art. Generally, Danto's theory can be seen as providing a purely conceptual justification for art that is opposed to the formalist theories of critics such as Clement Greenberg, theories which it came to replace just as Pop Art and the other postmodern conceptualisms in its wake replaced the high-modernist abstract art that Greenberg championed. Given that Danto's philosophy focused on visual indiscernibles, while Greenberg emphasized the unique visual qualities of the work he favored, the distinction seems well-founded.

Yet, when Danto first formulated his theory of the "artworld," it applied equally well to formalist work such as abstract expressionism as to Pop Art. In his 1964 article, Danto discusses a hypothetical "10th street abstractionist [who] blankly insists that there is nothing here [that is to say, in his painting] but white paint and black."[20] The question then arises for Danto of what would distinguish this perspective from a philistine's position which, in describing a painting as nothing but paint, implies that any artistic quality is also absent from the canvas. Danto continues:

> The answer . . . lies in the fact that this artist has returned to the physicality of paint through an atmosphere compounded of artistic theories and the history of recent and remote painting, elements of which he is trying to refine out of his own work; and as a consequence of this his work belongs in this atmosphere and is part of this history. . . . His identification of what he has made is logically dependent upon the theories and history he rejects. . . . To see something as art requires something the eye cannot decry—an atmosphere of artistic theory, a knowledge of the history of art: an artworld.[21]

The theories that underlie the work of the "10th street abstractionist" are not conceptual but formal: they are implied to be precisely those of the champions of abstract expressionism, Greenberg or Harold Rosenberg. However, Danto doesn't suggest that the abstractionist is himself a theorist, or that his "theories" need to be verbalized by himself or by anyone else, such as a critic.[22] Rather, the abstractionist simply responds to "the history of recent and remote painting" through critical reflection on his art, and the result of that reflection is fully visible in the work he produces. This process does not require a well-articulated, verbalized theory but rather a process of self-reflection evidenced in the resulting artworks, a process that in itself can be read as theoretical.

This view is precisely that of Greenberg, who, for example in his 1960 article "Modernist Painting," argued that each art form in modernism engages in reflective self-criticism so as "purify" itself of elements shared with other arts and therefore to emphasize the medium-specific properties of its own formal devices.[23] Danto praised Greenberg as a precursor to his own theories:

> It was greatly to his credit that Greenberg worked out an entirely novel theory of modernism, according to which that movement arose when it became conscious of itself as a problem, and undertook a quasi-Kantian investigation into its own foundations. It was Greenberg's thesis that with modernism, art became the subject of art, which undertook to create foundations for itself by seeking that which was unique to each of the arts.[24]

Yet, if all it takes for an art to be perceived as functioning within a theoretical climate is self-critical reflection on the formal conditions of its own medium, what is there to keep comics out of Danto's "City of God" of the artworld?[25] After all, comics had tirelessly explored the intrinsic capabilities of its medium—essentially, had undertaken "a quasi-Kantian investigation into its own foundations"—from the very start. Such investigation had already begun with Rodolphe Töpffer, who in his 1845 "Essay on Physiognomy" analyzed the relationship of abbreviated, cartoony art to sequential narrative, using this notion to draw a distinction between the new, still-unnamed medium he had pioneered, on one hand, and both traditional art and prose narratives, on the other, thereby drawing out the specificity of comics' mediumatic procedures.[26] Similar tactics can be shown to have characterized the artistic achievements of comics' most important pioneers from Winsor McCay and George Herriman to Will Eisner and Jack Kirby (to stay only within the realm of pre-1960s creators), and it is no coincidence that they did so at the same time as modernism became the dominant mode in the more traditional arts; formed during modernity, comics has been since its inception a thoroughly modernist art.[27] However, for our current purposes let's stick with Kurtzman's own investigation of comics' medium-specific potential.

Kurtzman's war comics for EC, and in particular the ones he wrote and drew himself, were a virtual laboratory for the self-critical exploration of comics' formal properties. In stories such as "Search" (*Two-Fisted Tales* #21 [EC Comics, 1951]; figure 11.6), Kurtzman explored the tier of panels as a basic unit of comics narration, for example unifying the intrinsic discontinuity of the panel

Figure 11.6. Harvey Kurtzman, panels from "Search," *Two-Fisted Tales* #21 (EC Comics, 1951).

sequence in the bottom tier of the story's first page through continuous sound effects that spanned the whole tier, crossing the vertical gutters; at the same time, the discontinuity was reinforced by coloring (in collaboration with Marie Severin) the individual panels in monochrome. The intrinsic paradox of comics reading—the construction of continuous narratives out of discontinuous sequences of images—was thereby highlighted.

In "Kill!" (*Two-Fisted Tales* #23 [EC Comics, 1951]), Kurtzman continued to explore these issues by unifying formally the entire story, narrating similar events in the lives of his two enemy protagonists, the American soldier Abner and his Chinese counterpart Li, across similarly formatted tiers of panels placed in similar positions on corresponding pages. In "Corpse on the Imjin!" (*Two-Fisted Tales* #25 [EC Comics, 1952]), Kurtzman not only deepened his exploration into structuring a story in unified tiers but opposed the opening and closing double-page spreads, largely formed of static panel compositions, with the frenetic middle spread, with its graphically dynamic depiction of hand-to-hand combat between an American GI and an enemy soldier. The resulting work was an object lesson in sequential dynamism, which I have argued elsewhere is one of comics' foremost devices, around which the very possibility of abstraction in the comics medium coalesces.[28]

We could continue the analysis of these stories at length, and indeed the formal accomplishments of Kurtzman deserve to be highlighted as a high point of formalist comics artistry. I mention them briefly here so as to demonstrate that Kurtzman in his narrative work functions precisely like Greenberg's self-reflective artist who helps determine the "unique and irreducible" elements of the art he practices, those "effects exclusive to itself" that are "unique in the nature of its medium." Much like the black and white painting of Danto's hypothetical 10th street abstractionist, these comics are imbued with theoretical meditation.

In his work at *Mad* (for which he never drew the final art, but for which he provided detailed panel-by-panel breakdowns as well as further art direction to the artists under his command) Kurtzman continued such self-reflexive inquiry into the properties of the medium, but he combined it with a heightened self-referentiality that prefigured the ironic quotationality of Pop.[29] Indeed, when Danto discusses Lichtenstein's *Composition*, his analysis could with only a few word changes be applied to *Mad*'s parodic procedures:

> The whole work makes a number of sly artworld allusions, and is in every sense a piece of "art about art," as such work came to be known. It is like Lichtenstein's painting of large brush strokes in which he lampooned the veneration of the heavy looped swirl of paint that emblematized abstract expressionism. Mockery is one of the armaments of civilized aggression, and Lichtenstein's work is filled with internal artworld barbs.[30]

Mad was, above all, a comic about comics, "filled with internal [comics] world barbs." Based both on its formal self-reflexivity and on its ironic, quotational self-referentiality, we can see that Kurtzman's work was just as self-aware as the work that Danto and Greenberg championed. From this perspective, Danto's description of comics as theoretically untransfigured "banal objects" becomes indefensible. However, I would like to add one more piece to the puzzle of the connections between Kurtzman and Pop Art, and for this we need to close our *Mad* magazines and look closely at their covers—before we return to the *Little Annie Fanny* panel with which we started.

KURTZMAN'S *MAD* COVERS: STRATEGIES OF DECONTEXTUALIZATION AND RECONTEXTUALIZATION

Thinking back to Warhol's *Brillo Boxes*: how exactly was their "transfiguration of the commonplace" effected? The space of the gallery, an "atmosphere" in Danto's words, "compounded of artistic theories" seems to be crucial, but so are the operations of decontextualization and recontextualization—that is to say, *decontextualizing* an object by taking it away from its "proper" place (such as the place of the Harvey Brillo boxes in the stockroom) and *recontextualizing* it by resetting it in the gallery space. Along with these two maneuvers, at least in Warhol's work (as opposed to Duchamp's), the newly consecrated artwork required a subtle hint that the reconfigured object was not simply itself, but a simulacrum of itself, a faux. This was achieved in the *Brillo Boxes* by silkscreening onto wooden blocks, not cardboard, and leaving out the folded-over flaps, the visible edges of cut cardboard, and so on.

Decontextualization, recontextualization, simulation, faux: these must have seemed familiar strategies to Kurtzman. They were strategies he had practiced at *Mad* repeatedly, particularly in the second half of the magazine's run in comic-book form, and particularly in the magazine's covers. While the first ten issues had featured cartooned covers, issues #11–#23 can be seen as *Mad*'s conceptual phase. Six of the thirteen covers in this stretch were simulacra of other types of publication; three others (#14, #15, and #22) featured artwork appropriated from outside the comics realm; one (#23) featured a simple typeset word ("THINK") against a blank background, reminiscent, to the artworld-minded, of the later word paintings of On Kawara. One cover (#13) was drawn as a connect-the-dots puzzle that was hardly a puzzle at all; another (#17) consisted of primarily text, referring to the conceptual twist of the entire issue, which had been printed "upside down"; and finally there was the conceit of the issue #13 cover, which I discuss in more detail later.

Let's look at the simulacrum covers first. The trend started with the cover of issue #11 (May 1954), a parody of *Life* magazine's cover designs, featuring a grotesque drawing by Basil Wolverton superimposed over the unprepossessing skyline of the Lower East Side as photographed from a window at EC's headquarters (figure 11.7).[31] It can easily be compared with any number

Figure 11.7. Harvey Kurtzman (design), cover of *Mad* #11 (EC Comics, 1954), featuring a drawing by Basil Wolverton.

Figure 11.8. Cover of *Life* magazine, May 1, 1954.

of contemporaneous *Life* covers, such as the one of March 1, 1954—probably displayed on newsstands as the same time as *Mad* #11—featuring Rita Moreno (figure 11.8).

While the cover of *Mad* #11 was a broad parody not likely to be mistaken for its source, *Mad*'s strategies of simulation quickly became both subtler and more pointed. They began ironically to comment on the political predicament of the comic-book industry during the period: Fredric Wertham's anti-comics crusade, as formulated particularly in his 1954 book, *The Seduction of the Innocent*; the April and June 1954 hearings of the Hendrickson-Kefauver Senate Subcommittee on Juvenile Delinquency dedicated to the nefarious influence of comic books, hearings at which both Wertham and William Gaines testified; and the subsequent establishment, later that year, of the Comics Code Authority, many of whose rules seemed specifically aimed at EC.[32] More generally, they also commented on the perceived low cultural status of comics, which made this predicament both possible and potentially successful. That is to say, while the immediate target of some of these covers may have been Wertham and his ilk, the larger implications addressed the very conditions that also led to Lichtenstein treating comic-book artists as uncreative artisans (as for example in his January 1966 BBC interview, quoted above), and to Danto thinking of comic books as "ordinary," "banal" things as opposed to "transfigured" artworks.

The politically most pointed cover was that of *Mad* #16 (October 1954, figure 11.9), the first issue to go into production after the April Senatorial Subcommittee hearings. The cover looks like a newspaper, complete with trompe l'oeil rendering, along the right-hand and bottom edges, of the irregularly cut pages of a paper and greyscale renderings of "cartoons as photographs." Chronicling a barely exaggerated crackdown on comic-book artists, the faux news copy adds a "far-fetched rumor . . . that they are disguising their books to look like newspapers in order to sneak them onto the stands. However, this rumor is plainly ridiculous." Simulacrum and topicality are inextricably intertwined, and the reader is plunged into a vertiginous abyss of self-reference.

Mad #12 (June 1954) had the all-text cover of a literary journal, a "little magazine" in the parlance of the time, and came with the asterisked explanation: "This special issue is designed for people ashamed to read this comic-book in subways and like that! . . . *Mad* cover design makes people think you are reading high-class intellectual stuff instead of miserable junk." The cover was both a reference to the perceived lowbrow status of comic books and a lampooning of the highbrow pretensions of the literary press. *Mad* #19 (January 1955) looked like a racing form while describing itself as "Another Entertaining as Well as Educational Cover Design." The pushback against Wertham's notion that comic books were corrupting the youth of America, pushback achieved through the ironic confirmation and assumption of Wertham's charge, is clear.

Mad #21 looked like a page of back-of-the-comic-book ads, the paratext turned parodically into the text. *Mad* #20 (figure 11.10) looked like a school composition book ("special issue . . . designed to sneak into class") but also eerily like Lichtenstein's painting of nine years later, *Compositions I*; any causal connection between the two can only be speculated on but, knowing Lichtenstein's avid consumption of comic books, is certainly not out of the question as either a conscious allusion or, possibly more likely, as an unconscious reminiscence on the Pop artist's part. *Mad* #14 and #22 (see figures 11.1, 11.2) were the Leonardo da Vinci/Duchamp and Picasso references discussed above, in which the problematization of the high art/low art distinction is particularly clear.[33]

Perhaps subtlest of all, *Mad* #13 seems to have a relatively straightforward cover, except printed very small, in one corner of an otherwise bare orange expanse. The cover copy describes its strategy: "This cover . . . Mad's

Figure 11.9. Harvey Kurtzman, cover of *Mad* #16 (EC Comics, 1954).

Figure 11.10. Harvey Kurtzman, cover of *Mad* #20 (EC Comics, 1955).

answer to comic-book titles . . . The cover with the smallest title in the world!" (figure 11.11). I can't help but see in it an ironic response to Fredric Wertham's critique, in his alarmist anti-comics article of November 1953 in *Ladies' Home Journal*, of comics titles "in huge, eye-catching type, sharp colors."[34]

How would these issues have looked on the newsstand or in a drugstore comics rack? The only photograph I could find of a comic-book *Mad* on display unfortunately does not show one of these "conceptual" covers (figure 11.12).[35] Rather, we seem to be looking—over on the far left, about a third of the way down the image—at *Mad* #8, tucked in among other magazines. But we can use our imagination. Picture the uncanniness of a liliputian title and cover art image among the other titles, normal-sized for comics—that is to say, aggressively loud in both copy and design. The cover of *Mad* #13 carried an intrinsic

Figure 11.11. Harvey Kurtzman, cover of *Mad* #13 (EC Comics, 1954).

critique of its neighbors' earnest attempts to lure readers; on the newsstand, it acted like the asocial kid at the back of the class, sarcastically commenting on all its peers. Or else picture thinking you stumbled on a misfiled composition book, only to discover it was just another issue of *Mad*, in full simulacrum mode. Picture, among all the garish covers, coming across a Picasso—garish in its own, very different way, but as out of place on a comics rack in 1955 as, in 1962, a blown-up comic panel would have looked in a gallery. These were all uncanny objects, not fitting in, rubbing like sandpaper against their neighbors on the newsstand.

In all these imaginary encounters we see Kurtzman's own strategy of de- and recontextualization fully realized: a Picasso or a da Vinci on a newsstand; a composition book or a racing form among comic books. The subtle distinction,

Figure 11.12. Photograph of newsstand display, ca. 1953.

the Warholian clue of fauxness, is there too, not least in the presence of the various *Mad* logos on these covers. Of course, Kurtzman's strategy, as opposed to Warhol's, lacked what for Danto was the most important ingredient in the transfiguration of art: a theoretical space, an "artworld." After all a newsstand or a drugstore comics display is not a gallery, right? But then, is a gallery itself "a gallery," that hallowed space of art theory? And is that transfiguration all it's cracked up to be?

If Danto earnestly celebrated the transfiguration in art, Kurtzman in his appropriation of Lichtenstein in *Little Annie Fanny* was significantly more ironic and cynical about it. Let us return to the vehicle of Kurtzman's metaphor—the added "Shazam!" word balloon. Already in *Mad* #4, in the story

"Superduperman," drawn by Wally Wood, Kurtzman had parodied Captain Marvel as "Captain Marbles" and Superman as the title character. When Clark Bent transfigures into Superduperman or Billy Spafon into Captain Marbles, neither reaches "a more beautiful or spiritual state." They become self-important, ridiculous creatures who fall flat on their faces as soon they leap out a window. They become creatures who, like Captain Marbles (and like almost all superpowered beings in Kurtzman's oeuvre) are only in it for the money: "To heck with this Captain Marbles gimmick," says Captain Marbles himself. "The only important thing is the good ol' do, re, mi . . . Lettuce . . . Kale . . . Shekels . . . Get it? Cash!"[36]

Can we transfer Kurtzman's cynicism from his view of superheroes to his view of the art world? I would argue that we can, and that we have prime evidence for this in the *Little Annie Fanny* panel with which we started. To several of the paintings in that panel, Kurtzman and Elder have added "sold" signs. The Franz Kline has been "sold to Westport Shopping Center," the Miró "to Container Corp of Amer[.]," and the abstractish still life on the easel "to Sears Roebuck." The Pollock, on the other hand, has been "sold to Guggenheim Museum." Yet Kurtzman's and Elder's ironic tone seems to be asking, is there really a difference?

It is striking that Arthur Danto almost always refers to the transfiguration as taking place inside a *gallery*. The art gallery, even more than the museum, is for him the art-theoretical space par excellence. Kurtzman's and Elder's cynical perspective, however, awakens us to the indisputable fact that an art gallery is still a commercial space; like the newsstand and the drugstore, deep down it's just another pedlary. This vaunted transfiguration, then, is it metaphysical or economic? Is it a matter of infusing theory into a "banal" object so as to transform it into an artwork, or rather of selling something for thousands of dollars instead of a ten-cent cover price?

If a gallery is seen as yet another commercial venue, its privileged, "art-theoretical" space becomes the most disposable element of the transformation Danto chronicled. What matters is not the specific place—gallery, museum, or newsstand—where the work ends up, but the critical strategy of creating simulacra and marking their fauxness, of decontextualizing and recontexualizing. Thinking of it this way, I would argue, allows us to establish more complex parallels and avenues of communication between art and comics without falling into the trap of high and low, of upward aspiration or downward appropriation, of celebration or resentment. It allows us to stop placing all agency on one side of the equation and treating the other as fodder for either appropriation or fraudulent plagiarism, but rather to consider Kurtzman, Lichtenstein, and Warhol as engaging in similar artistic processes and as participating in the same cultural development. It further allows us better to understand what

Figure 11.13. Art Spiegelman, cover of *Raw* #7, May 1985.

happened next, better to track the cross-fertilization that led to the formation of art comics, an important part of whose DNA is the very work of Harvey Kurtzman and his collaborators at *Mad* (figure 11.13).

Notes

1. See David Sylvester, *Some Kind of Reality: Roy Lichtenstein Interviewed by David Sylvester* (London: Anthony d'Offay, 1997). This quote taken from "Roy Lichtenstein—'BBC Interview,'" ASX, posted October 13, 2013, https://americansuburbx.com/2013/10/interview-roy-lichtenstein-bbc-interview-1966.html, where the text of the 1966 interview is available in full.

2. "Deconstructing Roy Lichtenstein," https://www.flickr.com/photos/deconstructing-roy-lichtenstein/.
For an early response by comics creators to Lichtenstein's work, see Lawrence Alloway, *Six Painters and the Object* (New York: Solomon R. Guggenheim Museum, 1963), exhibition catalog: "Lichtenstein's references to comic strips have been accused, by those who only know art, of being too close to real comic strips. However, a group of professional comics artists (at National Periodical Publications) judged them as definitely not mirror images of current comics style. The professionals regarded Lichtenstein's paintings derived from comic strips as strongly 'decorative' and backward-looking." (First section of introductory text.) Alloway appears to have expressly shown Lichtenstein's work to DC/National artists in preparation for the exhibition, so as to defend Lichtenstein from accusations of plagiarism.

3. For a fuller overview, see my article "Art Comics," in *The Routledge Companion to Comics and Graphic Novels*, ed. Frank Bramlett, Roy Cook, and Aaron Meskin (New York: Routledge, 2016).

4. *Little Annie Fanny* appeared in *Playboy* from October 1962 to September 1988. As per Kurtzman's usual modus operandi, he wrote and laid out the story for the September 1963 installment in full, then supervised and corrected Elder and Heath's pencils. The pencils were then reviewed by Hugh Hefner, who, as the publisher of *Playboy* and a former would-be cartoonist, took a very close interest in the strip before Elder and Heath proceeded to render the strip in full watercolor. See Harvey Kurtzman and Will Elder, *"Playboy"'s Little Annie Fanny*, vol. 1, *1926–1970* (Milwaukie, OR: Dark Horse Comics, 2000).

5. *Roy Lichtenstein* (exhibition), Leo Castelli Gallery, 4 East 77th Street, New York City, February 10–March 3, 1962. See https://www.castelligallery.com/exhibitions/roy-lichtenstein11.

6. See Bill Schelly, *Harvey Kurtzman: The Man Who Created "Mad" and Revolutionized Humor in America* (Seattle: Fantagraphics Books, 2015), 422, for the *Help!* magazine Christmas party of 1961 to which Kurtzman invited "the movers and shakers in the city," including Tom Meehan of the *New Yorker* and "Burt Bernstein (Leonard Bernstein's younger brother)." Kurtzman's desire to leave the comic-book world and move to more high-profile magazines is mentioned repeatedly throughout the book, for example on p. 344: "Entering the world of the high-class slicks was an intoxicating moment in Harvey Kurtzman's life . . . At the age of thirty-one, he had finally hit the big time."

7. This probably happened with Dorothy Seiberling's "Is He the Worst Artist in the U.S.?," *Life* magazine's story on Lichtenstein in its issue published on January 31, 1964.

8. Arthur Danto recounts the following in *After the End of Art: Contemporary Art and the Pale of History* (Princeton, NJ: Princeton University Press, 1997):

I have the most vivid recollection of seeing my first pop work—it was in the spring of 1962. I was living in Paris . . . I stopped one day at the American Center to read some periodicals, and I saw Roy Lichtenstein's *The Kiss* (printed sideways) in *Art News*, the crucial art publication of those years. I found out about pop the way almost everyone in Europe found out about it—through art magazines, which were, then as now, the main carriers of artistic influences. And I must say I was stunned. I knew that it was an astonishing and an inevitable moment, and in my own mind I understood immediately that if it was possible to paint something like this—and have it taken seriously enough by a leading art publication to be reviewed—then everything was possible. (123)

Mutatis mutandis, Kurtzman's reaction may not have been all that dissimilar.

9. It is notable that no new Captain Marvel comics had come out for almost a decade, due to a copyright infringement suit successfully brought by DC Comics against Fawcett, claiming too close similarities between Captain Marvel and Superman. The last Captain Marvel appearance at Fawcett had been in *The Marvel Family* #89, January 1954. The other two Captain Marvel titles, *Captain Marvel Adventures* and *Whiz Comics*, had ended their runs in November 1953 and June 1953, respectively. Kurtzman was evidently banking on the *Playboy* readers' childhood memories to help them get the "Shazam!" reference.

10. This trend of equating artistic ambition with the intended age of the reader has, of course, continued all the way to the present, from Marvel in the 1960s construing its readers as teenagers as opposed to DC's supposed preteen readership, to the formation of the graphic novel format as a means of selling comics in bookstores and getting them reviewed in respected venues such as the *New York Times Book Review*.

11. For more on these developments, see David Hajdu, *The Ten-Cent Plague: The Great Comic-Book Scare and How It Changed America* (New York: Farrar, Straus and Giroux, 1999), and Amy Kiste Nyberg, *Seal of Approval: The History of the Comics Code* (Jackson: University Press of Mississippi, 1998).

12. Danto, "The Artworld," *Journal of Philosophy* 61 (1964), 580 (emphasis added).

13. Danto, 581.

14. Danto, *The Transfiguration of the Commonplace: A Philosophy of Art* (Cambridge, MA: Harvard University Press, 1981).

15. Danto, *After the End of Art*, 130.

16. Danto refers to the "banality" of such objects repeatedly in *The Transfiguration of the Commonplace*, for instance: "the events in the artworld which provoked the philosophical reflections in this book were in fact just that: transfigurations of the commonplace, banalities made art. . . . A fresh start was required, in which the transfigured objects were so sunk in banality that their potentiality for aesthetic contemplation remained beneath scrutiny even after metamorphosis." v, vi.

17. See Matthew 17:1–8, Mark 9:2–8, Luke 9:28–36.

18. Danto, *Transfiguration of the Commonplace*, vii.

19. See https://www.lexico.com/en/definition/transfiguration; this definition is widely quoted in art websites online and even became the title of a group exhibition at the Cooper Cole Gallery, Toronto, in May–June 2019. See https://coopercolegallery.com/exhibition/2019-a-complete-change-of-form-into-a-more-beautiful-or-spiritual-state/.

20. Danto, "The Artworld," 579.

21. Danto, 579–80.

22. I should stress that, in saying "he," I am using here the pronoun that Danto himself applies to his fictional abstractionist.

23. Clement Greenberg, "Modernist Painting," in *The Collected Essays and Criticism*, vol. 4 (Chicago: University of Chicago Press, 1993), 85–93.

24. Danto, *Philosophizing Art: Selected Essays* (Berkeley: University of California Press, 1999), 3–4. See also his *After the End of Art*, where Danto claims that in modernism art underwent a "shift to a new, reflective level.... For that recognition we have to turn to the writings of Clement Greenberg, who achieved, one might say, a self-consciousness of the ascent to self-consciousness." 66.

25. "The artworld stands to the real world in something like the relationship in which the City of God stands to the Earthly City. Certain objects, like certain individuals, enjoy a double citizenship, but there remains . . . a fundamental contrast between artworks and real objects." Danto, "The Artworld," 582.

26. See my discussion of Töpffer in my article "Cartooning," in *Comics Studies: A Guidebook*, ed. Charles Hatfield and Bart Beaty (New Brunswick, NJ: Rutgers University Press, 2020). I expanded on those points in my talk, "The Use-Value of Incompleteness: Rodolphe Töpffer, *Obadiah Oldbuck*, and the Birth of Comics," delivered at the *Panels on Panels* conference, Indiana University Bloomington, February 14, 2020.

27. I discuss this continuing problematic in "The Shape of the Jewel: Polyphony, Polyrhythms, and Musical Structure in *The Castafiore Emerald*," in *The Comics of Hergé*, ed. Joe Sutliff Sanders (Jackson: University Press of Mississippi, 2016), as well as in my articles "Cartooning" (see note 26) and "Abstract Form" (see note 28).

28. Andrei Molotiu, "Abstract Form: Sequential Dynamism and Iconostasis in Abstract Comics and in Steve Ditko's *Amazing Spider-Man*," in *Critical Approaches to Comics: Theories and Methods*, ed. Matthew J. Smith and Randy Duncan (New York: Routledge, 2011).

29. The two terms "self-reflexive" and "self-referentiality" are too often treated in contemporary critical language as having identical meanings. However, they denote two distinct, though at least in one sense related, qualities. *Self-referentiality* occurs when a work of art *refers* to itself, highlights what have more recently come to be known, in both critical and fan discourse, as its "meta" qualities. (A popular synonym for "self-referential" in recent critical as well as fan discourse is "meta," derived, as far as I can tell, from the notion of "metafiction" or related notions such as "metaliterature," "metacinema," etc.) *Self-reflexivity*, on the other hand, derives from Clement Greenberg's notion, discussed above, of the self-criticism in which every modernist medium needs to engage in order to "purify" itself of elements shared with other mediums. Note that, while self-referentiality leads to a multiplication of levels of representation (we have *both* fiction and metafiction superimposed, as it were; fictional characters *both* engage in the diegetic plot *and* show awareness of the medium's conventions, of the reader/viewer, etc.), self-reflexivity leads particularly to abstraction, to doing away with any representation whatsoever. From this point of view, self-referentiality and self-reflexivity are antithetical values. Furthermore, in its Greenbergian acceptance, self-reflexivity refers to a work's *formal* qualities. Self-referentiality, implying the notion of reference, of necessity refers to content, or rather to the interaction between content and form. Instructive here is the moment in the Kurtzman-written, Jack Davis–drawn story in *Mad* #1, when the character Galusha, in order not to be dragged into a haunted mansion, grabs onto the gutter between two panels: content (character)

here interacts with what is usually purely a formal, extradiegetic device (the gutter)—thereby bringing it *into* the story's diegesis and turning formal device into content.

30. Danto, *Philosophizing Art*, 69. J. Hoberman was the first to stress the modernist and media-critical potential of such quotationality in Kurtzman's *Mad* in his article, "Vulgar Modernism," originally published in *Artforum*, January 1982, and reprinted in Hoberman, *Vulgar Modernism: Writings on Movies and Other Media* (Philadephia: Temple University Press, 1991), 32–40. For his discussion of *Mad*, see 36–38.

31. Bill Schelly identifies the "photographic cityscape" as "taken through the window of the men's room at 225 Lafayette St." *Harvey Kurtzman*, 282.

32. See Hajdu, *The Ten-Cent Plague* and Nyberg, *Seal of Approval* (as in note 11).

33. In the case of *Mad* #22, the "Special Art Issue" and the most idiosyncratic of Kurtzman's editorial run, this is true of the entire book. It deserves a close reading of its own in connection with Kurtzman's treatment of the high-art/low-art distinction, but that is unfortunately outside the scope of this article.

34. Fredric Wertham, "What Parents Don't Know about Comic Books," *Ladies' Home Journal*, November 1953, 50–53. The quote comes from an image caption on p. 52.

35. I would like to thank Rodrigo Baeza, who helped me find this image in response to a query I sent to the comixscholars listserve in September 2020. Rodrigo also dated this image to late 1953, based on identifying the *Blackhawk* cover on the lower right as the December 1953 issue.

36. *Mad* #4 (EC Comics, 1953), 6.

ART SPIEGELMAN AND THE GHOST OF PICASSO

JONATHAN NAJARIAN

> It would be very interesting to preserve photographically, not the stages, but the metamorphoses of a picture. Possibly one might then discover the path followed by the brain in materializing a dream.
> —PICASSO, "STATEMENT, 1935"

In late 1990, New York's Museum of Modern Art hosted an exhibit titled *High and Low: Modern Art and Popular Culture*. Organized by Kirk Varnedoe, MoMA's chief curator of painting and sculpture, and Adam Gopnik, the *New Yorker* writer and critic, the show sought to demonstrate the complex entanglement of Art, that which gets displayed in a museum, and Not Art, that which gets left out of the museum: advertising, graffiti, caricature, comics. In the lengthy accompanying volume, Varnedoe and Gopnik clarify that the high/low divide in the title of both the exhibit and the catalog is not intended to codify the differences between "fine" and "popular" arts (words I've put in quotes to recognize their fluid, shifting, and uncertain status). "We call these areas of representation 'low,'" Varnedoe and Gopnik write, "not to denigrate them out of hand (on the contrary, we hope to show that within their realm artists can be found who made work of originality and intensity) but to recognize that they have traditionally been considered irrelevant to, or outside, any consideration of achievement in the fine arts of our time."[1] The exhibition sought to complicate the easy divide between high and low, and, perhaps, to assuage thinkers and critics, such as Theodor Adorno or José Ortega y Gasset, who were suspicious of the commingling of high and low. Varnedoe and Gopik explain their rationale as follows: "We wanted not just to chronicle and celebrate but also to understand in greater depth the dialogue between high modern art and certain aspects of popular culture, such as advertising, graffiti, comics, and caricature—to grasp the origins of that interchange, its development, and its recurring structures, in order to see what that history might tell us about modern life."[2] To transcribe what Varnedoe and Gopnik refer to as a *dialogue* between high and low, to probe these origins, the exhibit put works by Picasso, Duchamp, Juan Gris, Man Ray, and (of course) Roy Lichtenstein alongside some of the popular sources that inspired their work. The show formalized—that is, brought to the space of the museum, and hence institutionalized—informal anecdotes that had been circling for decades: the modernist avant-garde loved popular culture.

For all of the ambitious intentions of *High and Low*, at least one cartoonist remained unimpressed. In a project for *Artforum*, Art Spiegelman published a scathing review in the form of comics (or, more accurately, in the co-mixed form of words and images) titled *High Art Lowdown* (figure 12.1). "Brain teaser," one section reads. "Since art is a subset of culture, how can you compare apples and fruits?!" Spiegelman is responding to the inevitable takeaway of a show titled *High and Low* hosted by MoMA: despite the organizers' efforts to examine the distinctions between something called "art" and something else called "popular culture," despite the desire to put these two in dialogue rather than hierarchical relation, the show ended up reifying the distinctions it hoped to complicate.[3] In a two-panel sequence, Dick Tracy characters—they're partially obscured by the word balloons, both visible and not—summarize: "I've searched high and low, chief—all I *see* here is their permanent collection." "They've made myopic choices, not daring the risks that come with a 'risky' topic!" Imprinted on Dick Tracy's hat is an important qualifier, the first of many: "Warhol was here . . . Gould wasn't!" Spiegelman is particularly miffed about the principles of selection, which aren't just myopic, they're Borgesian in their illogic; the show allows *Krazy Kat*, a "safe bet, praised by everyone from e. e. cummings to Umberto Eco," to represent nearly all of the rest of comics art. Missing from the show are the likes of Harvey Kurtzman, Jim Nutt, Milt Gross, and, surprisingly, figures like Toulouse-Lautrec.

Spiegelman and "all his friends" are missing too, a slight that would have been particularly sharp, given Spiegelman's extensive efforts to curate, in *Raw* magazine (1980–1991), the best of the low. Yet *High Art Lowdown* is most suggestive to me not as a critique of the MoMA exhibit, but as an example of Spiegelman's persistent and subtle use of visual allusion and intertextuality (or perhaps "intervisuality"). The image is a collage of visual styles and themes, with characters and aesthetics from heterogeneous artistic traditions coming into contact. The collage aesthetic, which has roots in modernist movements such as cubism and Dada, is integral to the grammar of comics. *High Art Lowdown* offers collage as a visual metaphor for thinking about the comics page,

Figure 12.1. Art Spiegelman, *High Art Lowdown: Modern Art and Popular Culture*, a project for *Artforum*, December 1990.

which is itself a juxtaposition of panels and discrete images; while most comics employ a consistent visual style (for the sake of readability and legibility), the surprising or jarring juxtaposition of images remains a possibility latent in the grammar of all comics. *High Art Lowdown* is richly citational, casting styles and images from a diverse collection of artists and characters—Lichtenstein and Dick Tracy, Picasso and Bud Fisher, Herriman and Miró—into one allusive frame. Nearly all of these citations call attention to the thorough imbrication of comics and modernism, as Spiegelman presents many of the images with twists and variations: the face of the Lichtenstein woman (which appears to be allusive but not citational) melts off, revealing a cartoonish skull; Ignatz Mouse hurls a brick through a Miró painting; Duchamp's *Fountain* (1917), which was signed "R. Mutt" after the famous comics character from Bud Fisher's *Mutt and Jeff*, has been reinscribed into a comics panel (though the *R* has been altered to an *A*); Picasso's famed portrait of Gertrude Stein has been repurposed as an ad for hemorrhoids.[4]

As I'll argue, this strategy of visual allusion and parody is something Spiegelman picked up from reading Harvey Kurtzman's *Mad* in the 1950s. *Mad*'s irony took aim at the culture of the day—not just "high" culture but also popular culture, especially comic books. So much of Spiegelman's work is compelling for how it employs the naturally complicated grammar of comics to build the structures of the past into architecture of the present. Spiegelman has said that he thinks of comics as a form that materializes history. Such materialization is especially evident in a work like *Maus*—which, as critics have long pointed out—is itself both a document of and testament to a history that, for all its gravity, threatens to slip out of public recollection. As I'll argue here, Spiegelman's work materializes history in other ways as well, namely by flexing the diverse, multimodal aesthetics of comics history into an ambitious language of pictorial storytelling. Spiegelman would develop a collage aesthetic inspired by and yet distinct from both Kurtzman's *Mad* and the avant-garde. Significantly, Spiegelman would encounter *Mad* first; his original exposure to "high art" was through humor and parody, an important reversal that would set off a kind of backward-looking sensibility to his aesthetic formation. We can bring the same method of reading—backward rather than forward—to Spiegelman's comics, where we come to appreciate or understand the past differently after engaging with his work. In this chapter, I seek to demonstrate a ghostly or haunted reading of "Ace Hole, Midget Detective." Spiegelman's work enacts a kind of reversal: Spiegelman and his text are haunted by the ghost of Picasso, who had died just before Spiegelman began work on the project; but Spiegelman himself comes to haunt Picasso's ghost. Just as Spiegelman could never fully shake the parodic images of high art that he encountered in *Mad*, so too do we turn to Picasso haunted by the specter of Spiegelman.

INSIDE *MAD*: ART IN THE UNDERGROUND

Like so many of the artists who would form the comix underground, the young Spiegelman found himself enraptured by *Mad* magazine, which he first encountered in 1955. And the emotion and religious intensity that "enrapture" connotes is not hyperbole: "It was love at first sight," Spiegelman reports, in the introduction to the 2008 version of *Breakdowns*, of his first glimpse of *Mad*.[5] After convincing his mother to spend part of her grocery allowance on the magazine—we know from *Maus* that Vladek would not have approved—Spiegelman walks home in a trance: "I studied *Mad* the way some kids studied the Talmud!" The young Spiegelman has happened upon a paperback *Mad* anthology published by Ballantine Books, which began reprinting old issues of *Mad* magazine in 1954 with *The Mad Reader*; the issue Art finds in the grocery store with his mother (on a shelf of books with titles that, in sequence, read "Lotsa / Lurid / Paperbacks / And / A Few / Bland / Inspirational / Titles") is Paperback Three, *Inside Mad*, "With a Backword by Stan Freberg." The bottom half of *Inside Mad*'s cover consists of portions of twelve different issues of *Mad* magazine, and one of these covers in particular catches Spiegelman's eye: the cover of issue #11, first published in May 1954, subtitled "Beautiful Girl of the Month Reads 'Mad.'" Issue #11 of *Mad* is a parody of a May 1953 issue of *Life*, which readers would learn immediately upon opening the issue, since *Mad* has reprinted the two covers next to one another with a block-letter warning at the top, "Beware of Imitations!" (see figures 11.7 and 11.8). To suss out the imitations, the editors of *Mad* recommend rolling up and smoking first *Mad* and then "any other magazine." "Notice," the editors proclaim, "how gently [*Mad*] sets your head on fire," which you can then compare with the experience of smoking a magazine like *Life*: "Notice the oily brown poisonous coloring of the smoke ... the hotness of the melted staples on your tongue.... Yes ... once you make this test, we guarantee you will never smoke an imitation magazine again ... You will never do **nuttin'** ever again!"[6]

The appeal of *Mad* is not hard to understand. While the publication began, in 1952, as a pastiche of crime, horror, and superhero comics, it quickly expanded its satirical gaze, under the editorial guidance of Harvey Kurtzman, to American culture broadly; the irreverence of asking young readers to smoke poisonous magazines until their heads exploded was typical of the reflexive, self-aware, and darkly appealing humor that would define the publication. Rebelling against the decorum and etiquette that shaped older generations, *Mad* took aim at the contradictions of middle-class, midcentury America and spared no one—even *Mad* readers were lampooned with satirical farce, as in issue #11, when the comic depicts stereotypical readers, such as "The Young Mad Reader," who "very often used an axe on his playmates! When he read *Mad*, he realized how ugly and sordid axing his playmates was ... so now he uses a pistol!" Spiegelman sums up *Mad*'s appeal nicely in the panels depicting his first encounter with the paperback anthology: "*Mad* warped a generation. In the bland American 1950s it was saying something new! It was saying: 'The media—the whole damn adult world—is *lying* to you ... and we here at *Mad* are part of the media!'"[7] After the Comics Code Authority was widely adopted in 1955, *Mad* shifted from being a comic book to a magazine, partly to evade the censorship that was delimiting the content of other comics publications.

(The paperback anthologies reprinted the comics, but since they were technically books, they weren't subject to the CCA.) Reading *Mad*, then, was a self-conscious act of rebellion: not only did the magazine skewer conformist (and adult) values in self-referential lampoon; it also sidestepped the censorship laws that were put in place in part to try to preserve the fragile fiction of American middle-class values. Prefiguring the 1960s counterculture, *Mad* offered a vision of an alternative America, one that did not hide from the ugliness of racism, misogyny, and violence, even if it did not, in the end, provide any solutions to those social ills.

Part of *Mad*'s success was its ability to transcend the geographically dispersed but culturally like-minded community of readers who made up its early audience.[8] The counterculture that blossomed around *Mad*—fans responded to invitations to dictate the endings of strips, posted to bulletins that the magazine would acknowledge, and self-published their own parodies and imitations—quickly became an insider's game, what Michael Warner would call a "counter-public" complete with its own set of cultural expectations and unique discursive code.[9] And it was indeed the *Mad* generation that would shape American culture in the latter half of the twentieth century, both within the world of comics and beyond it. As several historians (and comedians) have suggested, without *Mad*, we might never have had *SNL* or *The Simpsons*, to say nothing of Crumb or Spiegelman or the rest of the comix underground that emerged in the 1960s and '70s.[10] *Mad* provided a template and a vernacular for postwar American satire: take aim at everyone, and especially yourself. As Kurtzman would later write, "The style I developed for *Mad* . . . was necessarily thoughtful under the rowdy surface. Satire and parody work best when what you're talking about is accurately targeted; or, to put it another way, satire and parody work only when you reveal a fundamental flaw or untruth in your subject."[11] The searching, self-critical, and even self-loathing aspect of so many underground comics (Justin Green's *Binky Brown*, Crumb's "Mr. Natural," S. Clay Wilson's "Lester Gass, The Midnight Misogynist," Spiegelman's "Prisoner on the Hell Planet") are a natural evolution of the boldness of *Mad*'s satire.

But there's another element of *Mad*'s appeal that helped to shape the comics underground: *Mad* was bound in surprising ways to the cultural divide between stereotypically "high" and "low" art. When young Spiegelman picks up the Ballantine *Mad* anthology, in 1955, the first thing he notices is the "beautiful girl" on the cover: "I saw her as soon as I walked into the store . . . In all my 7 years I'd never seen anything like her . . . she was *tiny*—even smaller than my 5-foot-tall mom—she was about an inch high . . . She was a paperback cover girl and she smelled of the illicit. I couldn't keep my hands off her!"[12] Spiegelman is describing the "Beautiful girl of the Month"—herself a *Mad* reader—on the cover of *Mad* #11, a snaggle-toothed, serpentine girl with hairy warts, unkempt eyebrows, a droopy eyelid, and a drooling, canine-esque tongue hiding the undersized chin that disappears into her neck. Spiegelman positions the beautiful girl between two distinctive aesthetic styles: "She looked a bit like the Mona Lisa and a bit like those Picasso women I'd learn to love years later." What he doesn't mention is that both the *Mona Lisa* and "those Picasso women" also appear on the cover of *Inside Mad*, as reprints of covers of previous issues; the cover of *Mad* #14, published in August 1954, is a reproduction of the *Mona Lisa*, a copy of *Mad* bent into her folded arms, while issue #22, the "Special Art Issue" from April 1955, features a reproduction of Picasso's *Girl Before a Mirror* (see figures 11.1 and 11.2). These images would have been clearly visible to the young Spiegelman, picking up the paperback *Inside Mad* (though only a portion of Picasso's *Girl* from *Mad* #22 is visible in the reproduction of the cover that Spiegelman himself reprints in his introduction to *Breakdowns*). His comment about the "beautiful girl" looking a little like the Mona Lisa and a little like Picasso women becomes a sly inside joke, pointing out the subtle triangulation of women as they appear on the cover of *Inside Mad*, from *Mad* cover girl over to a cubist woman, then diagonally down to the Mona Lisa and back up. Spiegelman professes to read the *Mad* cover girl as "the meatballs-and-spaghetti version" of the high art tradition, but the relationship between "high" and "low" that he sees in *Mad* can't be so easily reduced to mere playful mimicry. Spiegelman learns from *Mad* how ostensibly contrasting artforms intersect, and he internalizes how satire and irony can be deployed to bridge cultural divides.

Mad #22, the "Special Art Issue," is an intricate, absurd satire, part fictitious biography of *Mad* cartoonist Bill "Chicken Fat" Elder, part irreverent survey of various art-historical movements, part commentary on the economic precarity of being an artist. The issue begins with Elder's early years, when he mixed paints with chicken fat and started smearing (as young children are wont to do) handprints on—well, everything, including family towels, Uncle Louie's bald head, Aunt Brunhilda's dress, and eventually the interior of his house (age three) and the entire downtown of a city (age four). Elder's life story becomes a history of art and craft; his sculptures include an ashtray he carved "under the pen name of Benvenuto Cellini" (which is a photograph of a sculpture known as the Rospigliosi Cup, formerly thought to be produced by Cellini but now believed to be a forgery from ca. 1840–1850), a piece titled "The Thinker" (Rodin's, though Elder used "a whole jumbo plasticine set" instead of bronze), and Mount Rushmore (plasticine again, not mountain rock). The issue continues in this fashion and is relentless in reclaiming both art objects and familiar household images as part of Elder's artistic training: his "abstract paintings" include an electrical diagram, a weather map, and the king of spades; his "realist" period consists of a series of photographs; and "the most brilliant part of his career" is illustrated with reproductions of the *Mona Lisa*, Vermeer's

Woman with a Water Jug, the portrait of George Washington on the one-dollar bill, and "the ceiling of the Sixtine Chapel [*sic*]." The most amusing alternative history in issue #22 of *Mad* occurs in Elder's early life as an artist. The editors explain that, early on, Elder's visual style was not fully developed and his paintings took on an oddly surrealistic quality, yet owing to his subsequent fame, these images are today admired, if still misunderstood:

> Today his shmears, most of them shmeared at 2 years old, in his sticky little crib while sitting there cooing contentedly surrounded by his chicken-fat, his banana-pulp and clouds of green flies . . . Today those shmears (3 of which are shown below) are hung in various museums and signed with Elder's various pen names such as "Braque," "Matisse," "Picasso," etc . . . That is why very often, you can hear observers exclaim, "Why, those paintings look like they've been shmeared by a 2 year old!"[13]

The corresponding paintings reproduced (in black and white) in *Mad* #22 are Braque's *Guitar and Bottle of Marc on a Table* (1930), Matisse's *Red Interior, Still Life on a Blue Table* (1947), and Picasso's *Woman with Cockerel* (1938).

There is something compelling about *Mad*'s insistence on reprinting all these images, about putting them on the page for readers. While it's true *Mad* readers were not getting the actual history of these artworks—and while many readers, including a seven- or eight-year-old Art Spiegelman, were likely too young to know or understand the full context of works produced during the Italian Renaissance, American neoclassical, or European high-modernist periods—viewers did get to *see* these images. Although some, such as Henri Fentin-Latour's *Un atelier aux Batignolles*, have been edited (in Fentin-Latour's group portrait, Elder's smiling face has been superimposed over Monet, seated at his easel), many others, including the modernist images from Braque, Matisse, and Picasso and the reproductions of da Vinci, Vermeer, and Michelangelo, appear in roughly their original format (allowing, of course, for the variations in print size and color). Whatever else he learned from *Mad*, Spiegelman saw in its pages many of the foundational works that have shaped our understanding of art.

Mad informed the young Spiegelman's sensibilities about the relationship between fine art and comics, not by reifying the binary but by complicating it. *Mad*'s satirical reprints of high art classics are an example of what cultural critic J. Hoberman has termed "vulgar modernism." Vulgar modernism, for Hoberman, is not so much a collection of specific art objects as it is "a particular sensibility," "a popular, ironic, somewhat dehumanized mode reflexively concerned with the specific properties of its medium or the conditions of its making."[14] Indeed, Hoberman himself cites *Mad* as an example of the sensibility he has in mind:

Edited by Harvey Kurtzman and published by E. C.—the same firm whose grisly horror comics (*The Vault of Horror, The Crypt of Terror,* etc.) became the target of a national crusade complete with congressional investigation—the original *Mad* was a comic book that parodied other comic books. . . . What distinguished *Mad*'s parodies from those of various college humor magazines, or the pornographic "eight-pagers" which first appeared during the 1930s, was the highly developed self-consciousness of their characters.[15]

Mad is famous for its relentless, biting satires of well-known comics characters: Mickey Mouse becomes Mickey Rodent; Archy, Starchi; Dick Tracy, Fearless Fosdick; and Superman, Superduperman. What makes these parodies *modernism*, if vulgar modernism, for Hoberman, is the reflexive awareness of the aesthetic project; *Mad* is exposing both the formal limits of comics and the cultural framework in which they are interpreted.[16]

Spiegelman may also have learned something about visual allusion and citation. *Mad*'s Art Issue presents a mode of using art and also suggests, tacitly, a theory of reproducibility. Embracing the relatively high quality of printing allowed by the half-tone processes used to produce *Mad*, the issue insists on the reproducibility of art, projecting famous images into a narrative context that reshapes and challenges how we view them. Comics is at its core an art of reproducing images, both in drawing and redrawing the same characters in multiple panels across the page and in learning to copy or mimic the visual styles of other artists. In those early days of *Mad*, Will Elder became famous among his friends for his copies of other cartoonists; as Spiegelman himself has written, "Elder had the uncanny ability to parrot *any* cartoon style, often making it look better than the original source."[17] Just below the surface of *Mad*'s irreverent humor is a theory of—or, at least, an attitude toward—the image: images exist to be copied, manipulated, edited, and deployed in new contexts. As Spiegelman's own work evolved, it would exhibit a similar, if more serious, attitude toward the reproduction of canonical works of art, repurposing familiar images and building elaborate narrative storyworlds around them.

In his admiring, even loving, tribute to Kurtzman, published in the *New Yorker* on the occasion of Kurtzman's death in 1993, Spiegelman recounts a moment, five years earlier, when he spoke to Kurtzman's students at the School of Visual Arts in New York City. Spiegelman's talking head presents slides of Kurtzman's work, most of it from the early 1950s, when *Mad* was still a comic book and not yet a magazine. "'Mickey Rodent' changed my life," Spiegelman tells the class of Kurtzman's parody, which is attributed to "Walt Dizzy." "Something sinister was revealed below the sanitized surface of 1950s Disney America."[18] Kurtzman's appeal for the young Spiegelman was as much formal as it was satirical; he goes so far as to say that Kurtzman "*created* a precise formal grammar of comics," a comment that is powerfully revealing coming from someone like Spiegelman, who is so attentive to the rich history of comics images.[19] It's worth noting, too, that Spiegelman's tribute, presented in comics form, itself cites some of Kurtzman's most recognizable works, including Mickey Rodent, the cover of *Mad* #11, *Two-Fisted Tales*, and even, faux-accidentally, a page from *Little Annie Fanny*, with Spiegelman's avatar blushing, as if the panel appears by mistake. Spiegelman's tribute does for readers what his original lecture did for Kurtzman's students. Here, it comes with the added benefit of printing Kurtzman's images in the storied pages of the *New Yorker*.[20]

"ACE HOLE" AND THE VOICE OF PICASSO

In "Ace Hole," the titular Ace takes an assignment tracking down the "small-change underground cartoonist" Al Floogleman, a semiautobiographical avatar for Spiegelman himself (figure 12.2). "Tough porno laws," Ace tells us, "put [Floogleman] out of business," so he "stepped up into the forgery racket": the former cartoonist has been trafficking "bum Picassos," some of them through the art dealer Laurence Potatohead. Floogleman doesn't have a large role in the comic—he's found dead on page two, a bullet through his head and a note in his pocket (Ace's first clue)—but he's an important figure in situating Spiegelman's work in a historical trajectory that emerges out of Harvey Kurtzman. Spiegelman may have gotten the idea to depict a debased version of himself as an art forger from Kurtzman and Will Elder's early edition of *Little Annie Fanny*, published in September 1963 in *Playboy* magazine (see Andrei Molotiu's chapter in this volume). In that issue, Annie meets an artist with a name even more extravagantly satirical than Al Floogleman: Duncan Fyfe Hepplewhite. Hepplewhite—not to be confused with the eighteenth- and nineteenth-century cabinet makers George Hepplewhite and Duncan Phyfe—is an art forger who specializes in producing copies of artists like Picasso, Utrillo, and Pollack.[21] As Molotiu points out, we can see in the background of his studio a distorted version of Lichtenstein's *The Kiss*; the painting is tilted ninety degrees to the left and has "Shazam!" printed in a comics speech balloon over the top of the image. Hepplewhite's forgery offers commentary on the nature of comics publication: in order for him to reproduce masterpieces of painting, Kurtzman and Elder themselves have to reproduce those paintings. Lichtenstein may have been borrowing (or forging?) comics style for museum galleries, but Kurtzman and Elder were then reforging Lichtenstein's art and putting it back into comics.

The first panel of "Ace Hole" features, along the left edge of the page, three small, circular panels, each labeled with the name of one of the three central

Figure 12.2. Art Spiegelman, "Ace Hole, Midget Detective," *Breakdowns: A Portrait of the Artist as a Young %@&*!* (New York: Pantheon, 2008), 1.

characters. These introductory panels are familiar to midcentury comics publishing: they're the sort of panel we might expect from Silver Age superhero comics, introducing readers to the key players of the issue. But in Spiegelman, these images don't yet correspond, visually, to any of the characters who appear in the book; aside from the verbal label, there's no indication that the collection of lines contained within the panel will become figures in the comic. The panels are, of yet, just lines, demonstrating the varying width and textures produced by different instruments of drawing. Immediately below, a contemplative Ace reflects, "It was tough scaring up a line on Floogleman." Ace's comment can be punningly applied to the circular panels themselves: Spiegelman is scaring up a line on his characters. Our first introduction is not to the visual images of Ace, Greta, and Potatohead, but rather to the medium in which they're constructed.

Circular panels are important in Spiegelman's work. Early in *Maus*, a circular panel offers our initial glimpse into the past; a young Vladek emerges for the first time from a panel that is, in its shape, strikingly similar to the three panels at the start of "Ace Hole." The circular panel is a vehicle for transportation, though in "Ace Hole" that transportation is spatial rather than temporal: we're moved from the printed space of the comic to the imagined space of the artist's studio. Spiegelman inverts a trope of comics publishing by previewing not the characters themselves, but the utensils with which they are drawn. The utensils become a formal signature—that is, an imprint of Spiegelman's formalism, which registers on two levels. The brush, nib pen, and felt-tip highlight the material form of the comic, revealing the multimedia aspect of Spiegelman's work. (Notably, the "ghost of Picasso" image that appears later in the comic was created using an etch board technique, not any of the pens listed on the opening page.) By invoking the conventions of the Silver Age superhero comic, the circular panels situate "Ace Hole" in a tradition of genre comics even as they suggest its affiliation with modernism's characteristic attention to form and materiality.

At the end of chapter one, after Ace lets himself into Floogleman's apartment, he's ambushed by Greta and Potatohead and "[dives] down an inky pit." The inky pit is a well of classic comics; the last panel of the page is a reprint of one of Winsor McCay's *Little Nemo* comics and serves as a visual representation of Ace's gradual loss of consciousness. Spiegelman, though, playfully revises the tropes of McCay's classic. At the very bottom of the page, where Nemo is typically depicted awakening from his nighttime reveries, Ace sits passively against his bed and observes that he has just "splashed into slumberland!" Instead of awakening in that final panel, he has fully realized his entry into the hypnotic dream sequence that makes up chapter two: part surrealist fantasy, part metareflective commentary on the nature of visual representation, the chapter is a stark departure from the tongue-in-cheek pulp of the previous two pages (figure 12.3). Picasso's talking head dances through the first four

Figure 12.3. Art Spiegelman, "Ace Hole, Midget Detective," *Breakdowns: A Portrait of the Artist as a Young %@&*!* (New York: Pantheon, 2008), 3.

panels, migrating from buoyant stick figure to plump speckled rooster to trio of jungle cats. The dazed Ace, still in the same position as in that final panel on the previous page, gazes at the transmigrating artist, while the pillow against which he rests morphs into the headless torso of a naked woman. The fourth panel expands to reveal a television airing a scene from a *Katzenjammer Kids* comic that yields in later panels to Floogleman's head, first with a bullet hole puncturing the space above his left eye and, later, crying tears that escalate into an ocean swelling around Ace.

Flanking the left and right edges of the second row of panels are two mirrored images, dotted with a border that invokes a marquee movie poster, illuminated by a series of lightbulbs. In the left image, a tiny Ace rides a massive cat and reflects, "I was an ugly kid: in fact, I was so ugly, my parents would call a *proctologist* whenever I caught a head cold!" A can of coke rises from a cat-food dish and carbonates the background. In the mirrored, inverted image, Ace has become a skeleton, the cat has adopted the rigid angles of a cubist composition, and the speech balloon is filled with a metafictional quip: "(midget on a cat, telling joke!)." The two panels make literal a sentiment from a Picasso statement, dated to 1935. In remarks to Christian Zervos, Picasso reflected, "A picture used to be a sum of additions. In my case a picture is a sum of destructions. I do a picture—then I destroy it."[22] Ace's cubist somnambulism is an act of destruction, stripping the image of its representational significance and leaving only metapictorial commentary. We can think of comics style itself as a form of destruction—this is the heart of McCloud's idea that the comics icon consists of "amplification through simplification"—and Spiegelman's metaimage joke compounds the reductive tendency.[23] The cartoon icon gains purchase by reducing an image to a small collection of essential details; the Ace skeleton and cubist cat further reduce those essential details as the image threatens to dissolve into nonsense.

Most of chapter two can be read as a quiet (if bizarre) illustration—a bringing to life—of Picasso's aesthetics. We can read the metacommentary of the illuminated panels ("midget on a cat, telling joke!") as a playful, postmodern representation of another section of Picasso's 1935 statement to Zervos: "You must always start with something. Afterward you can remove all traces of reality. There's no danger then, anyway, because the idea of the object will have left an indelible mark."[24] The right side of the mirrored image removes all traces of reality from its corresponding left-side image; and we know what the image represents—and can interpret "(midget on a cat, telling joke!)"—because of the "indelible mark" the other image has left. One wonders, too, about Ace's pillow, which transforms into a female torso; are we supposed to see in the image a visual echo of Picasso's brashly masculine ideas about passion and formal composition? Picasso: "It is my misfortune—and probably my delight—to use things as my passions tell me. What a miserable fate for a painter who adores blondes to have to stop himself putting them into a picture because they don't go with the basket of fruit!"²⁵ The surrealist illogic of the page casually sidesteps the issue of whether the divergent images "go with" one another, allowing the body of a naked woman to punctuate Ace's dreams. "To use things as my passions tell me": the credo of the comics underground.

But then, we need not be so speculative about Picasso's aesthetic statements; he is, after all, quoted throughout the page, in speech balloons trailing his morphing stick figure. His arrestingly realistic face haunts and anchors the page. Spatially, the most noticeable quote comes from the large central Picasso portrait, which bears the caption "The Ghost of Picasso" and seems to emerge from the gutter between panels. "You have to have an idea of what you are going to do, but it should be a vague idea," Picasso tells us.²⁶ The "vague idea" seems related to the perplexing scenario Ace has found himself in: lying unconscious in Floogleman's apartment, his mind awash in a fantasia of surrealist comics history, Ace has only a vague idea of where he's headed or how to crack this case. More revealing than the thematic connections, though, are the textual features of Picasso's statements, all of which appear in quotation marks—a rare move for Spiegelman, who tends not to use quotation marks when quoting other people (the comics speech balloon is enough to indicate that the person is speaking).²⁷ Conventionally, the quotation marks are a form of doubling, indicating speech typographically within the pictographic speech balloon.

Unless the quotation marks and the speech balloons serve different purposes: we might be tempted to read the speech balloons to indicate speech and the quotation marks to indicate citation. We know Picasso is speaking because of the conventions of comics, and we know that the cartoon avatar is citing the actual words of Picasso because of the conventions of written language, the fact that we use quotation marks to signal when words from another context are being repurposed in a new context.²⁸ Peculiar, then, that the quotes Spiegelman provides are at times inaccurate, if only slightly so—Picasso's quotes are misquoted.

We need not read this as a sloppy editorial transcription; nor does it necessarily suggest a slip of Spiegelman's pen. Rather, the quotation marks signal the elaborate intertextuality of Spiegelman's text, positioning "Ace Hole" in conversation with other documents that have preserved Picasso's voice and presence. And indeed, *what* Picasso says on these pages is ultimately less interesting than *how* he says it: in a visual prosopopoeia, as a ghost speaking from the absence of the grave. Published in 1973, "Ace Hole" was drawn in the wake of Picasso's death, and his image haunts the comic just as his legacy haunts the careers of artists, like Spiegelman, trying to find their own place in the world of art. Picasso's scratchboard head is the most realistic image in the comic, and it anchors the page, falling directly in the middle and flanked evenly on both sides. The slightly angled vertical lines of the panel invoke a block-letter exclamation mark, or perhaps an old-fashioned keyhole, like a portal to another realm that readers can peep discreetly through. Picasso's ghost—his image in this comic—is temporally unstable, reanimating a figure who has just died. This instability is reinforced by the intricate weave of panel borders: the ghost seems to be simultaneously behind (in the top lines) and in front of (see the left and right edges) the four TV panels surrounding it. Picasso's head is framed by panels that have an indeterminate, even non-sequitur relationship to the talking head, and the ghost image vanishes into the gutters on the sides, evaporating into the timeless white space on the page. In a 1923 statement, Picasso proclaims, "To me there is no past or future in art. If a work of art cannot live always in the present it must not be considered at all."[29] Aesthetically, the idea is suggestive, claiming a timeless quality that allows art to transcend its particular historical and cultural moment.[30] But in a real, material sense, Picasso's death marks a distinct transition: the past, in which he was alive, and the present/future, where he has died, his words now relegated to the mouth of an inken ghost suspended in the eternity of the comics gutter. The material sensibility (the ink and paper, the human bodies) that motivate so much of Spiegelman's work is a temporally bounded sensibility, one that challenges or tempers the abstract and idealized idea about an eternal, perpetual present. Picasso's body is now gone; Picasso is passed and past; Picasso is no longer the future. "Reality," Ace reflects at the bottom of the page, "is not a nice place to be."[31]

The image of Picasso's ghost is also a formal device, bringing philosophical aesthetics squarely into contact with the grammar of comics. Picasso's description of how the past and future collapse into a perpetual present recalls the present of the comics page, which we read sequentially only by convention; the panels at the bottom of a page do not, in a literal sense, "occur" "after" the panels at the top.[32] As a ghost, Picasso has been released from the sequential temporality of human existence; as an image emerging from the gutter, he transcends the conventional progression of panels, from left to right and top to bottom. Picasso may haunt this comic, but he does so in a way that does not seem to cause Spiegelman any anxiety. Instead, his appearance relies on comics' uniquely bizarre temporal framing. Utilizing the present moment of the comics page to contain both past and future, Spiegelman reveals Picasso's aesthetic creeds to be a comics aesthetic. Picasso is contained within the comic; even the medium of comics offers the most convincing realization of his artistic ideal.

I'd like to propose one final preposterous reading of Picasso's ghost, preposterous in the etymological sense, meaning both before (pre) and after (post). A conventional understanding of aesthetic influence traces lines of thought from those who came before to those who came after. (These traditional channels of influence might also, perhaps implicitly, follow a centrifugal trajectory, from the center of High Art production outwards to the margins, though much recent work in comics and periodical studies has challenged this trend.) If we accept this trajectory, from past to present and from center to margin, we might read Picasso's ghost as a visual metaphor for Spiegelman's anxiety of influence: Picasso's absent presence haunts the page, reminding the cartoonist of his compromised status as a pulp-obsessed neurotic, a fringe artist fated to produce mere cartoons. My sense, though, is that influence operates on this page in a far more complex way than this linear trajectory would suggest. Picasso's image doesn't appear unannounced from the eternal void of the gutter; rather, his presence is heralded through a series of surrealist, transmogrifying stick figures—a chorus of comics characters who parade Picasso's language onto the page. The history of avant-garde modernism is fully woven into the fabric of the history of comics, such that it would be just as accurate to say that *comics* has influenced Picasso. "Ace Hole" affords no privileged status to art at the "center," as opposed to art at the "margins," of aesthetic seriousness; Ace the stock pulp stereotype stalks Greta the Picasso girl who cavorts with Potatohead in absurdist comics farce, all while Winsor McCay's dreamers dream and the Katzenjammer Kids brawl and famous paintings censor and blur the cartoonish, stylized violence of the comic. If the ghost of Picasso haunts Spiegelman, then we should add, reading preposterously, that comics likewise haunts Picasso.

"AN OCEAN OF PAIN AND DEATH": *GUERNICA*, MODERNISM, AND VIOLENCE

Chapter four of "Ace Hole" contains the narrative's violent climax, the stock trope of pulp fiction we've been anticipating since the story began (figure 12.4). In the first panel, Ace cavorts flirtatiously with Greta, the "camera" angled portentously behind the couple, anticipating Potatohead's arrival. Potatohead, the "Twisted Tuber," enters gun drawn, but Ace, initially shaken ("I was in grease up to my dimple!") is too quick: in a prolonged three-panel sequence, Ace squeezes his trigger repeatedly. "When the smoke cleared," he reports, "there wasn't enough left of Potatohead to make a decent knish!" A mound of mashed potatoes, seasoned with the facial accessories of a Potato Head doll, is all that remains for Greta to mourn. Ace coolly strikes a match to light a cigarette.

Narratively, the sequence is a standard plot device: a tense showdown between a double-crossing villain and a gritty hero ends with the villain's necessary demise. Visually, though, these panels subvert the pulp conventions that have provided structural framing for so much of the story. Potatohead's execution occurs in the largest panel on the page; this rectangular panel, located just below the exact center point, anchors the other panels, which contort

Figure 12.4. Art Spiegelman, "Ace Hole, Midget Detective," *Breakdowns: A Portrait of the Artist as a Young %@&*!* (New York: Pantheon, 2008), 6.

to accommodate it. And of course, this central panel, framed as it is by the other, smaller panels, *doesn't* actually depict the climactic violence that we understand to be occurring at this moment. Instead, the scene is replaced by a near-perfect reproduction of Picasso's 1937 masterwork, *Guernica*.[33] A large text box is interposed over the painting (without cropping the image significantly) bearing the official seal of the Comics Code Authority, the famous self-imposed censorship code adopted by many major comics publishers in the aftermath of the publication of Fredric Wertham's *Seduction of the Innocent* and subsequent senate subcommittee hearings on juvenile delinquency. The code would signal the end of subversive EC comics such as *Crime SuspenStories* and *The Vault of Horror*, and would eventually push comics exploring sex, violence, and other "adult" themes to the underground.

Guernica is Picasso's most political painting, and one that marked a pointed shift in his political engagements. For most of his early career, Picasso was a distinctively apolitical artist. A Spaniard living in self-imposed exile in Paris, Picasso remained aloof, quietly above the turmoil of early twentieth-century politics and the violent factions that would later divide Europe. That changed on April 26, 1937, when the Spanish nationalist general Francisco Franco directed the bombing of Guernica, a small, peaceful Basque town in northern Spain. The news reports reached Paris quickly, and they were shocking: in a much-lauded piece for *The Times*, George Steer wrote that "Guernica, the most ancient town of the Basques and the centre of their cultural tradition, was completely destroyed yesterday afternoon by insurgent air raiders." As Ellen Oppler has pointed out, this sort of civilian bombing would have been especially shocking in 1937; Germany's invasion of Poland was still more than two years away, and it would be another eight years before the United States would drop bombs on Hiroshima and Nagasaki.[34] The attack on Guernica struck many as particularly senseless or heinous, and motivated even the apolitical Picasso to take decisive action. The result was *Guernica*, originally exhibited as a mural at the 1937 Paris International Exhibition. In a statement Picasso issued while working on *Guernica*, the artist offered a succinct and direct statement of the political value of art: "In the panel on which I am working, which I shall call *Guernica*, and in all my recent works of art, I clearly express my abhorrence of the military caste which has sunk Spain in an ocean of pain and death."[35] Several years later, Simone Téry would confirm with Picasso a story about a Gestapo officer who showed Picasso a reproduction of *Guernica*. "Did you do that?" the officer asked, to which Picasso responded, "No, you."[36]

Reading "Ace Hole" politically, we can interpret *Guernica*'s placement as a pointed critique of the censorship rules adopted by many comics publishers in the wake of the 1954 Senate Subcommittee hearings. Articles six and seven of the infamous Comics Code Authority, which Spiegelman quotes at the top of the *Guernica* panel, read:

6) In every instance good shall triumph over evil and the criminal punished for his misdeeds.
7) Scenes of excessive violence shall be prohibited. Scenes of brutal torture, excessive and unnecessary knife and gun play, physical agony, gory and gruesome crime shall be eliminated.

Spiegelman seems indignant: are the hundreds, or even thousands, of innocent civilians killed during Franco's bombing of Guernica an instance of good triumphing over evil? Does the wailing mother clutching her dead child not count as "excessive violence" or "physical agony" or "gruesome crime"? Of course, the answers to these questions are easy to sort out, but they raise a host of other questions about the relationship between comics and "fine art": what makes *Guernica* art and comics dangerous political propaganda that promotes violence? Why are we more comfortable with images that depict real-world, politically motivated suffering than we are with scenes of fictional violence in comics? Is it *only* because of lingering and wrong-headed assumptions that one of the mediums is for kids?

But there's also a formal reading of *Guernica*'s placement in "Ace Hole" that reveals the surprising spatiotemporal overlap between the avant-garde and comics. In his famous commentary on the painting, the theorist and art historian Rudolph Arnheim points out that *Guernica* is an image that collapses time and space: "How does the subject matter of the mural compare with the facts?" Arnheim asks in his seminal book *The Genesis of a Painting: Picasso's "Guernica."* He continues, "Obviously, Picasso condensed the event in time and space. No painting can present a sequence of happenings as a film or story can."[37] Comics, too, is a medium that condenses events in time and space. In *Guernica*, the chaos of the bombing—which lasted for roughly three hours and caused civilian casualties whose numbers are being disputed today—becomes the spatial dislocation of the painting. As the eye moves around the image, the extent of the violence and horror is revealed. Picasso thus invokes a phenomenology of comics reading, intuitively understanding how to utilize the space of the image to create the illusion of time, of temporal passing. We can read *Guernica* as a series of panels—ten, twenty, one hundred—that have collapsed in on one another.

While we can deploy the conventions of pictorial narrative to make sense of the raucous composition of *Guernica*, we should also understand that sequential imagery was fundamental to its production. In January 1937, more than six months before he began work on *Guernica*, Picasso produced a sequence of images called *Sueño y mentira de Franco* (*The Dream and Lie of Franco*) (figure 12.5). The sequence owes as much to surrealist fantasy as it does to the grammar of comics.[38] Discrete images are meant to be read in conjunction, and they are carefully divided by geometric panels borders; the figures are distorted with cartoonish exaggeration; we can even sense a certain nightmarish quality that we might expect from Winsor McCay, with monsters of distorted proportion spilling across the page. The sequence may be Picasso's most political work—more so even than *Guernica* itself—in part because it was made quickly, as a work of antifascist propaganda designed to make money to support Franco's political opposition. Scholars have sometimes concocted bizarre descriptive categories to avoid calling *Sueno y mentira* comics—the art historian Herschel Chipp uses the rather haute term "etching suite"—but we should note in both the style and the grammatical sequencing of the panels how attentive Picasso is to the workings of the comics page.[39]

By including *Guernica* as a panel in "Ace Hole," Spiegelman reinscribes the painting in a context of pictorial narrative—a context, it should be clear, that was already pivotal to the painting's conception and execution. Positioning *Guernica* as a product of *Sueno y mentira*, we might read the painting as a comics image that has collapsed the discrete panels of the etching; what had been a series of moments, formally demarcated by panel boundaries, has become a cubist collage of overlapping temporalities. Suggestively, the painting functions similarly in "Ace Hole": we've been reading a sequential narrative, moving carefully between individual panels, until this moment of violent, climactic contact. Instead of revealing sequentially the outcome of the violence, Spiegelman collapses the action into one complicated, temporally unstable panel. Although the panel is visually unrelated to anything we've been reading—*Guernica* has little to do with potatohead gangsters, I think—conceptually it matches precisely with how Spiegelman is thinking about the tension between pictorial narrative and pictorial stasis. *Guernica*, as both an historical object and as a panel in Art Spiegelman's comic, presents the chaotic unfolding of violent action in one spatially and temporally suggestive frame.

There's one final element of *Guernica*'s history germane to its placement in "Ace Hole." I've said above that we can read the painting as a culmination of *Sueno y mentira*, a finale so chaotically grand the panel borders have collapsed in on themselves. In fact, though, Picasso would not actually finish *Sueno y mentira* until *after* he had completed *Guernica*; while most of *Sueno* was completed in January 1937, the last four panels weren't filled in until June 7, three days after the completion of *Guernica*. *Sueno y mentira*, then, is both a precursor and a response to *Guernica*; *Sueno y mentira* might have initially served as something of a preparatory cartoon for *Guernica*, but then so too did *Guernica* become a preparatory cartoon for *Sueno y mentira*. In the complex system of relations between painting and comics—to which Spiegelman directs our attention, and which was already there in Picasso—comics is not an unfinished or anticipatory medium for the experimental shock of the avant-garde.

Figure 12.5. Pablo Picasso, *Sueño y Mentira de Franco*, 1937.

Rather, comics engages in a mutually beneficial dialogue with the avant-garde. *Sueno y mentira* prepared Picasso for *Guernica*, and *Guernica* allowed him to finish *Sueno y mentira*; Picasso himself informs the work of Art Spiegelman, and Spiegelman's work informs and conditions how we understand Picasso.[40]

The appearance of the *Guernica* image is grammatically peculiar: as a visual allusion, it falls outside the temporal sequence of images that make up the narrative. This is a technique Spiegelman learned, of course, from his early years reading *Mad* magazine, when Kurtzman and Elder built a narrative conceit that appropriated the history of art to construct a fictional narrative world that was densely allusive. The "Special Art Issue" asks readers to suspend not disbelief but prior knowledge and familiarity, reading recognizable images and prominent artists as props in a story about Bill Elder. We can read Spiegelman's *Guernica* through a similar critical lens: not as an unexpected citation of an aesthetic tradition that exists outside the world of the comic, but as an image that has a necessary relation to the panels around it. I'm suggesting that the *Guernica* image is not an act of self-censorship, but rather a productive, meaningful representation of the violence that we understand to be taking place at this moment in the narrative. Following *Mad*'s lead, I'm asking us to read *Guernica* literally, if ironically, as an accurate and stylized representation of the assassination of Potatohead.

Does this reading feel off, deliberately provocative in a way that leads us afield from what Spiegelman is doing? If so, is that because we detect immediately, in *Mad*, an ironic, irreverent tone that conditions our expectations about how *Mad* will treat Picasso and Matisse and Michaelangelo and da Vinci? Is it because we detect in Art Spiegelman an ambition and seriousness that lies beneath his story about a midget detective who assassinates a potatohead gangster only to realize that a cubist woman has set the whole thing up? Spiegelman *doesn't* have the same attitude towards satire, humor, and burlesque as *Mad*; there are other drives at play in his work. And perhaps the most important of these drives, perhaps the most significant difference between Spiegelman and *Mad*, is the rigorously historical impulse that we see in "Ace Hole." "Ace Hole" is not merely a comic about the past; "Ace Hole" *is* the past, rendered in the medium of comics. Put slightly differently, Spiegelman embraces fragments of the history of pictorial narrative and visual culture—from Picasso and the avant-garde, from the Katzenjammer Kids and Winsor McCay and newspaper comics, from pulp detective fiction and serialized comic books—to create a new diegetic space, one that becomes the very history it represents. In an often-quoted assertion, Spiegelman has claimed that comics is a form that "materializes" history.[41] We might say that "Ace Hole" uses the space of its pages to materialize the history of twentieth-century visual culture.

Notes

1. Kirk Varnedoe and Adam Gopnik, *High & Low: Modern Art and Popular Culture* (New York: Museum of Modern Art, 1990), exhibition catalog, 16.

2. Kirk Varnedoe and Adam Gopnik, *Modern Art and Popular Culture: Readings in High & Low* (New York: Museum of Modern Art, 1990), 11.

3. This is sometimes evident in the language Varnedoe and Gopnik use to track the relations between high and low, as when they write that "popular graphic and painterly and poster styles *passed into* [emphasis added] high painting," which implicitly and subtly assumes that the purpose of "low" or popular art is to get adopted into high art, as if the popular aspires to the condition of the avant-garde. *Modern Art and Popular Culture*, 14.

4. The original *High Art Lowdown*, as it appeared in *Artforum* in 1990, had "Preparation H / Shrinks Hemorrhoids" printed over the image of Gertrude Stein. That lettering does not appear in my copy of *Co-Mix: A Retrospective of Comics, Graphics, and Scraps*, which reprints *High Art Lowdown* as one of the very first images.

5. Art Spiegelman's *Breakdowns* was originally published by Belier in 1977 with the subtitle *From Maus to Now*. Pantheon (New York) reissued the book in 2008 as *Breakdowns: Portrait of the Artist as a Young %@&*!* and with a new introduction and afterword by Spiegelman. Pantheon reissued the book again in 2022.

6. *Mad* #11, (EC Comics, 1955) (ellipses and emphasis original).

7. Spiegelman, introduction to *Breakdowns: Portrait of the Artist*.

8. *Mad* enjoyed an enduring allure and folded only in 2019.

9. As Warner writes in *Publics and Counterpublics*, "A counterpublic maintains at some level, conscious or not, an awareness of its subordinate status. The cultural horizon against which it marks itself off is not just a general or a wider public but a dominant one." See *Publics and Counterpublics* (New York: Zone Books, 2005), 119. As Jared Gardner has observed, "EC [the publishing company responsible for early *Mad* titles] created a self-referential community, winking at inside jokes and speaking with their readers in a slang likely to mystify new readers. The strategy worked, creating a loyalty to the publisher, especially among young adult readers, and the sense that EC was something apart from the standard fare blanketing the newsstands." See *Projections: Comics and the History of Twenty-First Century Storytelling* (Stanford, CA: Stanford University Press, 2012), 98.

10. For more on Kurtzman's inimitable influence, see Denis Kitchen and Paul Buhle, *The Art of Harvey Kurtzman: The Mad Genius of Comics* (New York: Abrams ComicArts, 2009). In Steven Heller's words, "Kurtzman was the spiritual father of postwar American satire and the godfather of late-twentieth-century alternative humor." "The Art of Rebellion," *New York Times*, August 6, 2009, https://www.nytimes.com/2009/08/09/books/review/Heller-t.html.

11. Harvey Kurtzman, *From Aarch! to Zap!* (New York: Prentice Hall, 1991), 41.

12. Spiegelman, introduction to *Breakdowns: Portrait of the Artist*.

13. "The Child," *Mad* #22, "Special Art Issue," (EC Comics, 1955), 3 (ellipses original).

14. J. Hoberman, *Vulgar Modernism: Writing on Movies and Other Media* (Philadelphia: Temple University Press, 1991), 33.

15. Hoberman, 36.

16. The scholar M. Thomas Inge has labeled this a "comic kind of intertextuality or self-referentiality," observing that everyone from Stan Lee to Marilyn Monroe was subject to appear,

usually in a humorously modified form, within the pages of *Mad*. See "Harvey Kurtzman and Modern American Satire," *Studies in American Humor* 30 (2014): 32.

17. Art Spiegelman, "Commix: An Idiosyncratic Historical and Aesthetic Overview," *Print*, November/December 1988, 71 (emphasis original).

18. Art Spiegelman, "H. K. (R.I.P.)," *New Yorker*, March 29, 1993, 76.

19. Spiegelman, "H. K. (R.I.P)," 77 (emphasis added).

20. Jeet Heer has referred to comics artists' tendency to collect and reproduce images as "recuperative nostalgia." Comics are an art born of technological change, and as Heer observes, "Technological change produces nostalgia." Heer writes primarily about Crumb, the inveterate collector of twentieth-century material goods and ephemera, though Heer ends his essay with a nod to Spiegelman: "The nostalgia craze left a deeper mark on comics than other forms, because comics were in greater need of a history, a usable past that could fertilize future work. With his gift for aphorism, Art Spiegelman in 2014 observed: 'the future of comics is in the past.'" See Jeet Heer, "Trash Collectors: Alternative Cartoonists as Recuperative Nostalgists," in *"Raw," "Weirdo," and Beyond: American Alternative Comics, 1980–2000*, ed. John McCoy and Andrei Molotiu (Boston: McMullen Museum of Art, Boston College, 2022), 85, 91.

21. Hepplewhite might object to the idea that he produces "copies." Annie says that she once saw a Picasso that was nearly the same as the one in Hepplewhite's studio. "EXACTLY the same," he clarifies. "I paint original Picasso!" Hepplewhite expresses a notion of creativity—exactly the same as its source and yet simultaneously original—very similar to Borges's Pierre Menard, who "re-creates" Cervantes's *Don Quixote*. Incidentally or not, "Pierre Menard, Author of the Quixote" was published in English translation in 1962, just one year before Hepplewhite appeared in the pages of *Playboy*.

22. Pablo Picasso, "Statement by Picasso: 1935," in *Picasso: Fifty Years of his Art*, by Alfred Barr (New York: Museum of Modern Art, 1946), 272.

23. Scott McCloud, *Understanding Comics: The Invisible Art* (New York: Harper Perennial, 1994), 30.

24. Picasso, "Statement by Picasso: 1935," 273.

25. Picasso, 272.

26. The quote comes originally from Daniel-Henry Kahnweiler, *Juan Gris: sa vie, son oeuvre, ses écrits* (Paris: Gallimard, 1946), 83. Spiegelman may have seen the quote in Dore Ashton, *Picasso on Art: A Selection of Views* (New York: Viking, 1972), 28, which was published just two years before "Ace Hole."

27. Joe Sacco has confessed that Art Spiegelman doesn't like when he, Sacco, uses brackets to indicate where text has been altered for clarity. In an interview with Hillary Chute, Sacco said, "I talked to Art [Spiegelman] about this, and he doesn't like the brackets. I understand his point of view. I do agree that this is not what I want to see if I'm reading a comic book, for god's sake, but on the other hand, the journalistic imperative means more to me when you're quoting someone than the 'nice comics balloon' imperative." See Hillary Chute, *Outside the Box: Interviews with Contemporary Cartoonists* (Chicago: University of Chicago Press, 2014), 149.

28. I'm invoking ideas from Jacques Derrida's famous response to J. L. Austin, "Signature Event Context." Writing, for Derrida, is a "potent means of . . . *extending* enormously, if not infinitely, the domain of oral or gestural communication"; he continues, arguing, "Every sign, linguistic or nonlinguistic, spoken or written . . ., in a small or large unit, can be *cited*, put between quotation marks; in so doing it can break with every given context, engendering an infinity

of new contexts in a manner which is absolutely illimitable." See Jacques Derrida, "Signature Event Context," in *Limited Inc* (Evanston, IL: Northwestern University Press, 1988), 3, 12. The overlap between Derrida's ideas in that essay and Spiegelman's own practices of citation and allusion would be worth explicating in more detail.

29. Pablo Picasso, "Statement by Picasso: 1923," in *Picasso: Fifty Years of His Art*, by Alfred Barr (New York: Museum of Modern Art, 1946), 270–71.

30. The idea of art that transcends historical particularity is not unique to Picasso, of course. Walt Whitman offers a similar sentiment in his famous preface to *Leaves of Grass*: "The prescient poet projects himself centuries ahead and judges performer or performance after the changes of time.... A great poem is for ages and ages in common." See Walt Whitman, *Leaves of Grass and Other Writings*, ed. Michael Moon (New York: W. W. Norton, 2002), 634.

31. In his 1935 statement, Picasso reflected, "There is no abstract art. You must always start with something. Afterward you can remove all traces of reality." Picasso, "Statement by Picasso," 273.

32. As Hillary Chute has written, "Comics offers an aesthetic system that pushes back on both progressive linear movement and the freezing of time. Comics provides an experience and view of time in which it is tensile and layered, proliferative instead of linear, dispersed rather than propulsive." *Disaster Drawn: Visual Witness, Comics, and Documentary Form* (Cambridge, MA: Belknap Press of Harvard University Press, 2016), 84.

33. The *Guernica* reproduction is preceded by a rare instance of what Scott McCloud would call a "non-sequitur" transition: we see an image of a rabbit and a deer, but have little context for how to interpret the image. Is the rabbit hunting the deer? Is this a metaphor for Ace hunting the much larger Potatohead? We know that Spiegelman would become partial to animal metaphors; and McCloud wonders whether any transition can truly be a non-sequitur transition. *Understanding Comics*, 73.

34. In her excellent scholarly compendium, *Picasso's "Guernica": Illustrations, Introductory Essay, Documents, Poetry, Criticism, Analysis* (New York: W. W. Norton, 1988), Ellen Oppler writes,

> After the destruction of Coventry, Rotterdam, Dresden, and Hiroshima, one may wonder about this universal outrage over an air raid that became 'the most notorious event of the whole war.' Fifty years ago, however, it was the first saturation bombing of a civilian center, and Guernica itself was a very special town. This ancient capital of the Basques, whose origins are shrouded in the legends of prehistory, was honored throughout Spain as the oldest center of democracy. (57)

35. Ashton, *Picasso on Art*, 143.

36. Quoted in Ashton, 149.

37. Arnheim, *The Genesis of a Painting: Picasso's "Guernica"* (Berkeley: University of California Press, 1980), 19.

38. Although André Breton made several attempts to claim Picasso as a surrealist, Picasso always rejected the label.

39. See Herschel Chipp, *Picasso's "Guernica": History, Transformations, Meanings* (Berkeley: University of California Press, 1988), 12. The artist Roland Penrose, who knew Picasso and wrote an early biography, acknowledges the debt that Picasso owes to comics. In *Picasso: His Life and Work*, first published in 1958, Penrose writes, "The story of violence and misery inflicted by the arrogant leader of the military rising reads from picture to picture like a strip cartoon or the

popular Spanish 'Alleluias' Picasso had known as a child." See Penrose, *Picasso: His Life and Work*, 3rd ed. (Berkeley: University of California Press, 1981), 297.

40. Oppler recalls the many parodies, satires, and other reproductions of *Guernica* produced by artists like Pat Conant, Eugène Mihaesco, Randall Enos, Josep Guinovart, Equipo Crónica, Peter Saul, and Tom Marioni, many from the 1970s and '80s. Spiegelman is not included, though he should be; this context situates his reproduction in a very particular historical moment, when artists were thinking about the history of art and reincorporating it—both aesthetically and politically—in their contemporary work. See *Picasso's "Guernica,"* 124–31.

41. See Joshua Brown, "Of Mice and Memory," *Oral History Review* 16, no. 1 (1988): 98.

LITTLE TOMMY LOST AND THE ANACHRONISTIC COMIC

MATTHEW LEVAY

Figure 13.1. Cole Closser, *Little Tommy Lost* (Toronto, ON: Koyama, 2013).

How are we to interpret the above image (figure 13.1)?[1] The question is alternately straightforward and, as we will see, perilous. On the one hand, any casual reader of newspaper comic strips will notice at least a few basic conventions of that medium and publication format, which provide some context for analysis: a brief, linear narrative whose movement occurs over a sequence of panels that proceeds from left to right; word balloons that, in all but one instance, emerge from the mouth of a central character; a small title box in the leftmost panel, which seems to identify that character by age (Little), name (Tommy), and situation (Lost); and of course the faded newsprint, which may well be the first clue to suggest the image as an example of a newspaper comic strip. On the other hand, a more finely attuned reader could situate the image within a thicker historical context. For instance, it is not only the image's print quality that evokes a prior era. Tommy's dialogue draws heavily upon idioms that are no longer commonplace ("gee," "feller," "golly"), expressions that find their counterpart in the unseen vendor's warning to "leggo dem fruits, kid," and thus indicate an earlier moment in American vernacular speech.

The art of the strip, meanwhile, closely resembles that of early twentieth-century American newspaper cartooning. The artist's line is thin and wavering, with cross hatching used to carve out intricate material detail while wobbly balloons and lettering effectively erase the distance between the dialogue and the action of each panel. Finally, the strip is punctuated by a black rat silently expressing an emotion of its own—puzzlement—in a comedic trope most often associated with earlier works. Taken together, these observations lead us toward what would appear to be a firm foundation for analysis: this is most likely a single episode in an early twentieth-century American newspaper comic strip, depicting a young boy who has been separated from his parents during a family outing to the big city. The situation is not played for laughs, but appears serious. Little Tommy, as the title of his strip makes plain, is lost, and he alternates between fear and despair at his plight. The strip's ending is characteristically irresolute, to be continued in the comic's next installment.

There is just one problem with this interpretation: this is not an example of an early American newspaper strip at all but rather the opening sequence of Cole Closser's *Little Tommy Lost*, a 2013 book of comics whose contents are made to resemble such predecessors. In painstaking detail, this strip and others contained in Closser's book, which charts its eponymous protagonist's struggles in and eventual escape from a workhouse for orphans, frustrate the contemporary reader's temporal orientation, adopting the guise of an earlier period in comics art so completely that it becomes difficult to discern any difference between this twenty-first-century comic and the early twentieth-century predecessors from which it draws its inspiration. Excerpted in this fashion, the image presented above becomes eminently and elaborately deceptive; even a seasoned reader of American newspaper comics could be forgiven for falling for it. And so this sleight of hand elicits some pressing questions: what is the purpose of making such temporal confusion the defining formal feature of a comic? And if Closser's comic relies upon a radical reorientation of its audience's experience of temporality, how are we to understand such manipulation of the reader's experience of time? Is this an instance of homage or experiment, an attempt to think through specific formal problems via the example of a past style of cartooning, or an effort to reconfigure the notion of a personal style altogether?

This essay attempts to answer such questions by situating Closser's work in relation to one of the most significant if seemingly paradoxical forms of experiment in contemporary comics: the deliberate adoption of visual styles unique to early twentieth-century newspaper strips and animation, whereby these popular idioms of modernism serve as a mode of critiquing past and present social attitudes, aesthetics, and material conditions. Indeed, since the early 1990s, a number of cartoonists have increasingly turned to what I term an "anachronistic aesthetic," producing work meant to appear much older than it actually is. Using *Little Tommy Lost* as a case study of this phenomenon, this essay explains how the anachronistic aesthetic functions not as simple homage but rather as a pointed critique of the social and political attitudes of early comics and their creators. By comparing Closser's book to one of its most prominent forebears—Harold Gray's *Little Orphan Annie*—we can better understand how this anachronistic comic's use of historical precedent serves a dual purpose: first, as an exercise in technical dexterity, by imitating the recognizable style of a famous cartoonist in order to make a contemporary comic connote a long-distant past, and second, as an opportunity, through the juxtaposition of old and new, to critique the conservative social and political ideologies apparent within Gray's work, particularly its indifference to children's suffering, its privileging of individual promise over collective welfare, and its disregard for social institutions as sources of camaraderie and support. In short, by studying the thoroughness by which Closser inhabits an earlier visual style in conjunction with the political valences of his decision to do so, we gain a stronger understanding of how and why the anachronistic aesthetic represents a form of innovation wholly unique in contemporary comics.

DEFINING THE ANACHRONISTIC AESTHETIC

Some of anachronism's critique emerges through forms of overt citation, and Closser's work knowingly employs the signature styles of several early twentieth-century newspaper cartoonists. Even the title of *Little Tommy Lost* puns upon many of those predecessors (Gray's *Little Orphan Annie*, along with Winsor McCay's *Little Sammy Sneeze* and *Little Nemo in Slumberland*, being the most notable). But other elements of critique come through in an even more thoroughgoing manipulation of comics' visual and material registers, which speaks not to a single predecessor or historical antecedent but to comics' early history more generally, and to our current archival practices for preserving that history. For example, just as *Little Tommy Lost* is printed on thick, glossy paper, it still gives the material illusion of aged, cheap newsprint, which makes it feel more like a scrapbook collection of daily newspaper strips than an original, twenty-first-century work. In this way it references our contemporary moment, in which archival reprint editions of early newspaper comics are widely available and handsomely produced, while also hearkening back to a time before, when the only way to obtain complete runs of those strips was to clip them from the original newspapers oneself.

Other elements of the book's panels, both visual and textual, further its evocation of past forms, and as the opening attempt to interpret a decontextualized example of the book makes plain, each element of *Little Tommy Lost* appears designed to challenge, if not outright fool, the casual reader's understanding of the book's chronological provenance by mirroring the material forms of an earlier moment in comics history. In tracing how Closser's work self-consciously draws upon the popular modernist forms of early twentieth-century comics art in such a quintessentially modernist fashion—that is, by throwing into question a reader's sense of his book's temporality—we can better perceive how the anachronistic aesthetic charts a path forward for contemporary cartoonists by inhabiting and repurposing those forms, breathing new life into apparently outmoded styles in an effort to show just how vital their critical potential can be when artists and readers question the social and political attitudes they connote.

Thanks to two concurrent trends in recent criticism—first, the continued rise of comics studies as a field of academic inquiry, and second, modernist studies' turn to popular culture as a site of significant scholarly value—it now generates no serious controversy to speak of comics and modernism in the same breath, in the way I have just proposed. As several critics have persuasively demonstrated, comics were part of modernism all along. Jared Gardner describes comics as "the first and arguably most important of the new vernacular modernisms" that came on the scene in the early twentieth century, as the medium, even in its infancy, "was dedicated to diagramming the serial complexities of modern life and fixing the fragments of modernity on the page."[2] David M. Ball, meanwhile, sees in contemporary comics a "characteristic ambivalence about their status as popular cultural productions [that] repeats modernist anxieties about literary value that reemerge precisely at the moment graphic narratives are bidding for literary respectability" and finds "the persistence of modernism in that most unlikely of places: the contemporary American graphic narrative."[3]

Here we have two methods for understanding modernism and comics in relation to one another: first, by seeing those comics that appeared during modernism's heyday, in the opening decades of the twentieth century, as popular but no less experimental efforts to engage with the conditions of modernity through serial form, and second, by observing similar efforts in contemporary comics, many of which deliberately question their status as works of art in language that echoes earlier modernist inquiries. The latter method speaks to a process that Christopher Pizzino terms "autoclasm," or cartoonists' direct engagement with comics' low cultural status in ways that are simultaneously galvanizing and self-defeating.[4] Whichever method we choose—and of course we need not choose at all and can accept both to be true simultaneously—comics and modernism, while not necessarily synonymous, are now much more readily and correctly understood in relation to one another, as coexisting and at times even mutually reinforcing in their use of aesthetic form to strategic ends.

If one accepts form as the hinge between comics and modernism, then one might expect an essay on an experimental, modernist strain in contemporary comics to follow a predictable trajectory. Recent works by authors such as Richard McGuire, Olivier Schrauwen, Eleanor Davis, Aidan Koch, and Yuichi Yokoyama display many of the stylistic elements that critics traditionally associate with modernism: stream of consciousness narration; abrupt shifts in temporality, setting, and point of view; total departure from a linear narrative; a self-conscious emphasis on the medium's conventions in order to draw attention to the constructed nature of all comics art; and a mixture of subtle and intensely rendered visuals that range from colorful abstract expressionism to a cold, geometric minimalism. But the kind of experiment we find in the anachronistic aesthetic exists in a different register, unique and undertheorized in contemporary comics and modernist studies alike. Simply put, a comic like Closser's *Little Tommy Lost*, which deliberately immerses itself in the visual culture of the early twentieth century, does not evince the same forms of experimentalism as those of these other contemporary cartoonists, nor does it immediately suggest an avant-garde sensibility.

Made to look at least several decades older than its publication date would suggest, and therefore to echo comics' history rather than signal its future, the novelty of Closser's anachronistic approach, and hence its indebtedness to and furtherance of modernism, resides somewhere else, tied to a different modernist aesthetic in which the repurposing of past forms and the temporal confusion it generates leads to a startling juxtaposition of old and new. In the anachronistic comics of Closser and others, the social and political attitudes of the past come under withering scrutiny through the connotation of earlier visual styles, at the same time that artists repudiate any easy assertion that the present is uniformly superior to what it has replaced. What these anachronistic artists create, in essence, is something akin to Charles Tung's description of modernism as a time machine, or a phenomenon in which "modernist experiments . . . sought self-consciously to question and reconceptualise time by foregrounding the ways in which their own devices, often in concert with psychological, social and historical mechanisms, structured and produced time."[5] *Little Tommy Lost*, by this formulation, displays a modernist sensibility not simply by reproducing the cartooning styles dominant during the initial, modernist moment of the early twentieth century but by using such reproduction to signal a bygone era and, more crucially, to expose that era to critique.

In referring to an anachronistic aesthetic that denotes a specific form of visual experimentation in contemporary comics, I want to take care not to suggest that such a concept simply encompasses all forms of drawing that, for lack of a better phrase, "look old." Contemporary comics are awash with overt references to comics history, from Tom Scioli's impressive imitation of Jack Kirby in *Gødland* (2005–2012) to the phenomenon of the "homage cover," in which a contemporary artist copies with only superficial changes an iconic cover image from a Golden or Silver Age superhero comic, usually for comedic or reverential effect. Such examples update their source material in some sense—they are not plagiarized, nor are they entirely predictable, lockstep remakes of an original work—but they ultimately serve as forms of veneration or pastiche, meant to honor the artists and styles that came before them.[6]

While artists who practice an aesthetic of anachronism may include some loving gestures toward the styles they adopt, and may speak admiringly of their influences in interviews, reverence is not the central condition of their work. Neither is nostalgia, or any other fondness for earlier cartooning styles that carries with it a desire for a return to bygone eras—typically the era of a reader or creator's childhood—or the social and political values that dominated them.[7] The anachronistic aesthetic is thus demonstrably different from what Jan Baetens and Hugo Frey chide as the sense of nostalgia that can permeate those contemporary comics that mine older examples of the medium for inspiration, pursuing "the otherwise predictable fashion for anything vintage" in an attempt to appeal to readers' emotions regarding their childhood media consumption or to cash in on vintage trends.[8]

Far from a nostalgic or even a necessarily admiring enterprise, the anachronistic aesthetic is fundamentally critical; artists who employ it do so in order to critique the form and ideology of comics and other artistic productions from prior eras, as well as to critique a twenty-first-century moment that either ignores the ephemeral art forms of the early twentieth century or views them in overly limited frameworks of popular entertainment, all while pursuing the technical challenge of drawing in a way that believably inhabits an earlier visual aesthetic. In this fashion, contemporary cartoonists who work in an anachronistic vein engage in a subtle but no less significant form of experimentation that uses the visual registers of early vernacular, popular modernisms to create works that, despite their apparent antiquity, are nonetheless demonstrably new. They may appreciate or even love the material from which they draw inspiration, but those affects are beside the point, foundations rather than ends unto themselves.

LITTLE ORPHANS, PAST AND PRESENT

For these reasons, Closser's work provides a productive model for how anachronistic aesthetics manifest on the page and for the critical work they perform. Unfolding over a sequence of eighty-four individually numbered "strips,"

Closser's *Little Tommy Lost* scrupulously mimics the appearance of an archival collection of early newspaper comics.[9] Most pages of the book feature two horizontal strips of three to four panels each, arranged one on top of the other, each strip a self-contained, titled sequence rendered in black and white. Some include a date, formatted numerically as a month and day, and all include Closser's signature. Every seventh strip is presented in the fashion of a Sunday newspaper strip, rendered in full color, taking up a full page, and interrupting the narrative with a one-shot sequence that relates to the storyline of the previous "daily" strips but does not directly intervene in it. Significantly, while the book is printed on thick, glossy white pages, each strip appears to have been originally printed on aged, yellowing newsprint, an effect Closser achieved by scanning pieces from a collection of old newsprint, digitally combining the paper with his line art, and finally distressing that art to mimic the impression of ink pressed onto paper by a metal plate. This effect is further enhanced by the fact that each strip appears on the page as a photograph of an original strip (a shadow running along the corners of each strip highlights this photographic quality); Closser placed a copy of each strip behind the original and then blurred the outline created. Though these effects have been achieved digitally, their verisimilitude is no less striking for that and in fact is all the more impressive given the meticulous process by which Closser effectively recreates the material qualities of an older, paper-based form through digital manipulation.[10]

In this way, *Little Tommy Lost*, in both its presentation and its style, alludes to a number of possible inspirations and predecessors, including both early strips themselves and the numerous archival reprint projects from publishers like Fantagraphics, Drawn & Quarterly, and the Library of American Comics, which have brought near-complete collections of early twentieth-century newspaper strips to twenty-first-century readers. I want to linger over one of those antecedents, however, to demonstrate why Closser's anachronistic aesthetic does more than praise its source material: Harold Gray's *Little Orphan Annie*, which premiered on August 5, 1924, and ran until 2010, well after Gray's death in 1968. Now in the process of being collected in hardback editions by the Library of American Comics, with sixteen volumes either printed or in production, Gray's comic is both a quintessential example of classic American newspaper cartooning and one of the most visible collected reprint projects of recent years, embodying the archival impulse to preserve, in high-quality productions, the history of the early American comic strip to which Closser's volume alludes in its own material conditions. Gray's strip is also a cultural touchstone, its earliest years offering a representation of determined individualism in the throes of hardship (and what would soon become the catastrophe of the Great Depression) that helped set a standard for cartoonists' depictions of child protagonists for generations. As Lara Saguisag explains in her study of childhood in early American comics, Depression-era readers "took comfort in the figure of Annie, an innocent-yet-plucky child, whose inherent goodness and vitality enabled her to survive and defeat corrupt and criminal forces," and their enthusiasm made Gray's title character "the most recognizable, beloved comic strip character of the period."[11] Thus, in its art and narrative, *Little Orphan Annie* offers a useful comparison for illustrating how Closser's anachronism functions as a contemporary rebuttal to Gray's positing of a divide between social institutions and individual will.

Gray's conservatism, and the manner in which his political positions made their way into *Little Orphan Annie*, is well known. As Michelle Ann Abate argues, Gray's comic "uses orphan-hood as a vehicle to critique not simply family ties or legal guardianship in the United States during the 1920s but also . . . the nanny state. Annie repeatedly demonstrates that she doesn't need to be protected, coddled, or taken care of by Daddy Warbucks—and she likewise doesn't need such treatment by another wealthy, paternalistic benefactor: Uncle Sam."[12] Rebellious and independent, Annie exemplifies Gray's conservatism in consistently demonstrating that even the most disadvantaged need only the force of will to overcome innumerable, structural obstacles, while characters like Daddy Warbucks assert free-market capitalism as the most beneficial solution for any number of social ills.[13]

Take, for instance, one of the earliest strips, published on September 29, 1924, when *Little Orphan Annie* was not yet two months into its run (figure 13.2). In it, Mrs. Warbucks describes to her husband Oliver—who, in the strip published two days prior, told Annie to refer to him as "Daddy," cementing his relationship to her and also giving the character the name by which audiences would come to know him—how her trial period of fostering Annie has been taxing, but that she has made such a noble, selfless commitment to the girl as a form of charity. While some aspects of her statement are true (she was indeed the person responsible for bringing Annie into their home), Daddy Warbucks immediately blasts his wife's description as incongruous with her character, joking that "if I was as full of charity as you are I'd be the most successful mortgage-loan shark outside of Sing-Sing." Crucially, however, Gray does not end the strip on the third panel, but rather moves past the joke in order to emphasize Daddy Warbucks's argument that an orphan like Annie doesn't require benefactors like him or his wife at all. "Annie doesn't need charity," he scoffs. "Just give her an even break and she'll do the rest—Charity!!—BAH!"

Here we have multiple ironies, none of which the strip acknowledges. For one, Annie's joining the Warbucks family would seem to provide her with far more than an "even break" given Daddy Warbucks's fantastic wealth. Second, while it is true that Annie may not need charity in order to survive, she certainly needed an external agent to remove her from her orphanage, and thus to have

Figure 13.2. Harold Gray, *Little Orphan Annie*, September 29, 1924.

even the possibility for individual flourishing, the "doing the rest" of which Daddy Warbucks claims she is eminently capable. And finally, the fact that Mrs. Warbucks views Annie's presence as an ordeal, to which Daddy Warbucks is quick to respond by defending Annie's character and physically removing Annie from the scene, suggests both that benevolence can only go so far and that it is absolutely necessary to protecting Annie from abuse. But the strip glosses over these inconsistencies, and instead leaves us with Daddy Warbucks's exclamation, which in a single, emphatic syllable dismisses such concerns in favor of a view that prizes the gumption and know-how of the extraordinary child. Here and elsewhere in Gray's comic, social institutions are presented as unnecessary and even offensive restrictions on individual ingenuity.

A cursory reading of *Little Tommy Lost* might well find an equally pessimistic view of social institutions. After all, its protagonist, who spends nearly the entirety of the book in an orphanage, is not actually an orphan; separated from his parents on a trip to the big city, Tommy searches for his family until a suspicious police officer apprehends him and delivers him to a workhouse for young boys. The workhouse is run by Augustus Greaves, a frightening, Dickensian figure who claims to find adoptive parents for a number of the older or injured boys, but who actually sends them to work for an equally sinister man named Cromwell, whose precise occupation is never clear, but who seems to be running a criminal operation that results in several boys' deaths. This wholly corrupt institution, which bars Tommy from reuniting with his parents, represents a place of imprisonment and misery for the lost child, placing him in a system of unproductive manual labor designed to tire him into obedience and build his strength for Cromwell's operation.

Tommy's isolation, meanwhile, presents a somber counterpoint to the wildly creative freedoms enjoyed by the child protagonists of the early twentieth-century comic strips to which Closser's style nods. In her study of Winsor McCay, Katherine Roeder notes that "images glorifying childhood as a period of unfettered creativity dominated the visual landscape of early twentieth-century

American fiction, magazines, and comics,"[14] and Scott Bukatman describes the exuberant dreamscapes of McCay's *Little Nemo in Slumberland* as "a fleeting refuge from the stolidity of the real," a "space of play and plasmatic possibility in which the stable site of reading or viewing yields to an onslaught of imaginative fantasy."[15] By contrast, Tommy's flights of fancy are few and far between, confined to the occasional small celebration for a holiday like Halloween, and always undercut by the sadness of remembering the family, and hence the freedom, he has lost.

Significantly, though, what initially appears as a critique of social institutions becomes on closer inspection a more nuanced attempt to reclaim the value of such institutions against those who, like Gray, perpetuate the stereotype that they function as unnecessary burdens on individual freedom. Closser achieves this not through the depiction of the singular individual—to do that would be to capitulate to Gray's example—but through an emphasis on the collective. Whereas Tommy is the undisputed protagonist of this narrative, *Little Tommy Lost* is also a story of its minor characters, in this case actual orphaned boys who see in one another the family they never knew, and in the institution either a benevolent actor that saves them from even more desperate poverty and isolation or a space that can help them realize their own benevolence and establish forms of solidarity necessary to their own survival. In an early strip, titled "Motherless Children," Tommy expresses his desires to escape the orphanage—a mounting refrain in the later strips, motivated by his hope of finding the parents whose existence his fellow orphans largely doubt or else rarely take seriously—only to irritate his friend and eventual enemy Pete by his apparent lack of gratitude (figure 13.3). Pete chastises Tommy for having no appreciation for Greaves's meager offerings of food and shelter, but more damningly, for suggesting that the alternative, a life of homelessness, would be preferable to the ersatz family the orphanage provides: "Gosh, bud—as ugly as it is, this place is our home! Old Man Greaves gives us food to eat, clean clothes to wear, an' a warm, safe place to sleep. Heck, Tommy, it shore beats th' street an bummin' fer scraps ev'ry day! Not knowin' where you'll end up each night!" For Pete and many of the other children, the uncertainty of isolation is far worse than the indignities of the workhouse, as Pete sees in the latter at least some provision for community and shared comfort.

The adult world outside of the orphanage, by this logic, cannot be trusted to provide for children like these (that is, poor orphans), so the workhouse represents a retreat into something more stable, an institution that will, reliably, provide. Later, an older bruiser of a boy named Clarence Pigg—who begins the book as Tommy's tormentor but, in yet another reversal, becomes his most loyal friend—makes a similar point, hinting that the orphanage can allow new family structures to emerge for those who have no relatives whatsoever.

Figure 13.3. Cole Closser, *Little Tommy Lost* (Toronto, ON: Koyama, 2013).

Lamenting that he has long responded to other boys' fear of his size by taking on the role of a bully, Clarence explains that "if my mama wuz alive, she'd shore be sore with me. She always used to tell me how proud she wuz o' me. Then she'd say, 'don't forget, baby—bein' big means yoo gotta watch out fer ev'rybody what's smaller'n yoo.'"[16] From this point onward, Clarence takes on the role of Tommy's protector, but what's crucial is that he does so not out of any maternal guilt but because he recognizes that the memory of his lost family should spur him to protect "ev'rybody" he can. Clarence here becomes both paternal and fraternal, as the responsibilities of "bein' big" necessitate his caring for a young child by providing emotional comfort and physical protection. In this sense, the orphanage becomes a site of surrogate families, its brutality softened if never alleviated by the forms of kinship and connection that emerge in response to it. *Little Tommy Lost* rebuts Gray's emphasis on extraordinary individualism in the face of danger with a collective suffering that reveals both the necessity of community and the power it can provide the weak. Closser's is a world that replaces the extraordinary wealth of Daddy Warbucks with the pathos and loyalty of Clarence; more broadly, it is a world that rejects implausible good fortune—being fostered into the uppermost echelons of society—in favor of the quiet solidity of friendship among the marginalized.

This mutual reinforcement of suffering and solidarity makes *Little Tommy Lost* a much more disquieting representation of childhood than one finds in the boom-and-bust adventures of Gray's *Little Orphan Annie*, whose protagonist regularly loses her fortune and encounters life-threatening obstacles only to triumph over such challenges by virtue of individual savvy and good sense. Gray's work offers a rosier assessment of the cruelties of the adult world as no match for the powers of the resourceful child. That assessment has had an outsized influence on comics produced in the nearly 100 years since *Little Orphan Annie* first appeared, though it also participates in an even longer history of comics' engagement with the figure of the child as a site of artists' and readers' fantasies of how American childhood functions, whether as a period of innocent mischievousness, antic play, or, as Mark Heimermann and Brittany Tullis argue, as a much broader "dialectical institution that both shapes and is shaped by cultural and social factors across time and space."[17] Bringing Closser's anachronistic comic into closer proximity to source material like Gray's thus opens up new ways for seeing how *Little Tommy Lost*'s characterization of childhood exposes the fantasy of that stage for what it is, and thereby makes the critical function of the anachronistic more legible as a way of thinking across time and space about what a popular art form like comics can and should represent.

Little Tommy Lost insists upon the violence that was always at the heart of early American cartooning, particularly violence against children and other vulnerable groups, but that was so often muted by the medium's serial form. It is easy to see how the suspense of the daily newspaper strip was always undermined by the reader's knowledge that titular characters like Gray's Annie are likely to make it out of any scrapes they encounter largely unscathed, since to kill off or irrevocably change the comic's star would go against the principles of continuity inherent in serial media itself.[18] Little Orphan Annie will never be an orphan for long, nor will she succumb to the many threats that menace her, and so Gray could cement his portrayal of Annie as the indefatigable champion of individualism through her continual evasion of the irrevocable.[19] As Michael A. Chaney agues, the figure of the child is, simply put, "the face of American comics," having been "the default actor of American comics since the commercial inception of the form."[20] And yet, he maintains, "the child of comics is no mere instrument of sentiment" but rather "a formal correlative" that provides a deeply philosophical vehicle for understanding experiences of narrative and individual temporality.[21]

This idea of temporality is crucial to understanding the narrative of *Little Tommy Lost* as an indication of how easily children can be betrayed by the dangers of the world, and of how solidarity among children becomes a vital form of protection against an adult world that can exploit them without any real consequences, which in turn helps us understand how Closser's anachronism is more than just a visual style. Though *Little Tommy Lost* is bound to different expectations for character development and stasis than a longer, daily comic strip like Gray's, it still stands in stark contrast to the assessment of *Little Orphan Annie* offered by Pamela Robertson Wojcik, who argues that Gray's strip, even as it depicts its protagonist as "unmoored from home—orphaned or displaced—and find[ing] herself on the streets," removes the sense of danger that might otherwise pervade that situation. As opposed to Tommy, who experiences the world as a combination of cruelty and loneliness that is paradoxically reinforced and assuaged through the experience of the orphanage, Annie's encounters on the street "emphasize Annie's mobility and freedom and ascribe to her significant agency to transform and improve not only her situation but also that of adults," presenting "a vision of the urban as largely benign, and of girlhood as powerful."[22]

In *Little Tommy Lost*, by contrast, childhood community is powerful, but there is nothing in the world that is benign. In this comic, a policeman who finds a child separated from his parents on a family trip will assume the boy has no family and send him to an orphanage where he will operate heavy machinery that gravely injures some of his companions, and where the promise of being released only comes with an expectation of being even more fully exploited by unscrupulous adults. Here, children can die—Clarence does, murdered by one of Greaves's henchmen who does odd jobs around the workhouse—and they have little dignity beyond that which they afford each other. In these representations, Closser renders in an anachronistic visual style some of the events that never happened in the comics upon whose example he draws, or could never happen with this kind of painful verisimilitude. Characters could die in *Little Orphan Annie*—infamously, Gray killed off Daddy Warbucks in a thinly veiled protest against the New Deal, only to bring him back in due course—but their deaths could never communicate the kind of misery that *Little Tommy Lost* emphasizes as the lot of orphaned children trapped in poverty and abuse by unfeeling adults. Closser's narrative is a bleak one, but only in the sense that it recognizes the systemic problems of the early twentieth century (and today) yet refuses to accept Gray's solution that individuals somehow overcome impossible odds through gumption and self-interest alone. Anachronism, then, renders more starkly what is implicit in its source material and offers a form of critique that blends pointed narratives with an intricate, old-fashioned style without subsuming the former into the latter.

THE NOVELTY OF THE OLD, OR THE MODERNISM OF ANACHRONISM

Cartoonists like Closser draw upon the aesthetics of anachronism to create work whose force emerges from its critical perspective on both the history of comics and the social and political mores that shaped that history. In turn, they provide an instructive example of how such engagement with the past can serve as a contemporary form of experiment by demonstrating a presentist skepticism of prior social attitudes within the visual register of early comics. To its critics, however, the anachronistic aesthetic is bound up in a kind of popular nostalgia that traffics in the comfort of old things. In the preface to an excerpt of his comic *Black Rat* published in the *New Yorker* in 2015, Closser described himself as "one of those weirdos who gets nostalgic for times I never actually lived through," and so we might describe *Little Tommy Lost* as equal parts criticism and tribute, blending political critique with a detailed and palpably affectionate rendition of the visual and dialogic tropes of early newspaper comic strips.[23] And even when a more nuanced analysis of that rendition disputes any notion of a simple affirmation of its source material, it remains hard to see how a fascination with the old can be effectively described as new, especially when much of the sameness of contemporary art—particularly corporate art and its obsession with rebooting established, successful properties—arises from its catering to familiar tastes. As Michael North has argued, "right now, at a time when most first-run movies seem to be either remakes or sequels, when the popular new singers are all expert mimics of some vocal style of the past, when period nostalgia progresses through the decades faster than time itself and threatens to catch up with the present, the status of novelty as a value would not seem to be particularly high."[24]

Closser, though, is no mimic, and the anachronistic aesthetic no straightforward exercise in period nostalgia, trading on the solace of a bygone era that contemporary readers never experienced firsthand. Instead, anachronism in comics like *Little Tommy Lost* underscores the inherent instability within notions of novelty that W. J. T. Mitchell characterizes as permeating all media, particularly media perceived as new. "When it comes to media," Mitchell argues, "the 'shock of the new' is as old as the hills, and needs to be kept in perspective. . . . That doesn't mean that these innovations are not really new, or make no difference; only that the difference they make cannot be settled by labeling them 'new' and treating all of the past as 'old.'"[25] Similarly, an anachronistic work like *Little Tommy Lost* demonstrates full awareness of its medium's age, and through its aesthetic severs any assumed connection between novelty and the contemporary. The contemporary art object does not have to announce its age or periodicity in any particular way, and that object's novelty arises in relation to mainstream fashions and tastes rather than existing as an inherent quality. The old, for Closser just as it was for the modernists of the early twentieth century, can indeed be new, depending on what one does with it.

This unorthodox method for making it new obviously brings us back to modernism. I have argued elsewhere for a broadened conception of modernism that includes those works we can productively characterize as instances of popular modernism, which purposely deliver the varieties of aesthetic experiment most commonly associated with an avant-garde within the generic mandates of a popular form.[26] Comics, and particularly the newspaper strips of the early twentieth century, are increasingly recognized as just such an instance. As Paul Peppis maintains, George Herriman's riotous challenge to the formal conventions of the newspaper comic in his 1930s-era *Krazy Kat* Sunday strips represents a telling example of popular modernism, as "a mass cultural product that works from inside a popular medium to make it new."[27] Similarly, Jackson Ayres claims that modernism and comics "served to coproduce each other," originating within the same cultural ferment.[28] But, as this essay has demonstrated, we don't need to confine our attention to the early twentieth century in order to see how modernism and comics inform one another. Through an anachronistic aesthetic, twenty-first-century cartoonists have reinterpreted their modernist predecessors, finding ways to make the past speak to the present, and vice versa, in a form of critical experiment that opens up new possibilities for understanding comics' history by interrogating many of the implicit and explicit social assumptions that underpin it. Their modernism, then, comes from a simultaneous deployment of past aesthetics and present critique, a way of making old comics new again by reminding us of their physical beauty and political limitations in equal measure.

Notes

1. Figures 1 and 3 are from Cole Closser, *Little Tommy Lost* (Toronto, ON: Koyama, 2013). Because the book is unpaginated, further references will note each strip's individual number and title. I want to thank Cole Closser for offering permission to reproduce these images here. I also thank him for his generous responses to my questions and for his willingness to discuss his methods with me.

2. Jared Gardner, *Projections: Comics and the History of Twenty-First-Century Storytelling* (Stanford, CA: Stanford University Press, 2012), 7.

3. David M. Ball, "Comics Against Themselves: Chris Ware's Graphic Narratives as Literature," in *The Rise of the American Comics Artist: Creators and Contexts*, ed. Paul Williams and James Lyons (Jackson: University Press of Mississippi, 2010), 103, 105.

4. Christopher Pizzino, *Arresting Development: Comics at the Boundaries of Literature* (Austin: University of Texas Press, 2016), 4.

5. Charles M. Tung, *Modernism and Time Machines* (Edinburgh: Edinburgh University Press, 2019), 2.

6. In an interview for *The Comics Journal*, Scioli says that his decision to emulate Kirby's style was based in admiration, but he goes on to explain that such imitation also served as a form of "unlearning what you learned and forgetting what you know"—in effect, reorienting his own approach to drawing "because there's a lot of things that Kirby does that go counter to academic drawing or go counter to natural ways of depicting things." Ian Thomas, "'As Far as Career Goes, It was One Option': The Tom Scioli Interview," *The Comics Journal*, posted July 13, 2020, http://www.tcj.com/as-far-as-career-goes-it-was-one-option-the-tom-scioli-interview/.

7. This is not to suggest that cartoonists who adopt an anachronistic aesthetic cannot admire or appreciate the comics their work imitates. Artists like Closser and others—most notably the Canadian cartoonist Seth and American cartoonists Art Spiegelman, Chris Ware, Kim Deitch, and Tim Hensley—are quite open in their love of old, print comics. I maintain, though, that their work is not solely, or even primarily, about admiration or homage but rather offers a

more critical assessment of comics history, preservation practices, cultural capital, and the contemporary production, distribution, and reception of comics art, in addition to the verbal and visual styles of that art. In other words, their comics are focused on far more than technical proficiency in imitation.

8. Jan Baetens and Hugo Frey, *The Graphic Novel: An Introduction* (Cambridge: Cambridge University Press, 2014), 218.

9. In a 2015 interview for *417 Magazine*, Closser says of his process: "I use dip pens, brush and graphite. I do all the drawing, and then I scan it.... But then I go to great lengths to imitate old production techniques. I try to make things look like they've come off of a printing press. I really like that feeling. I want them to feel like old printings that are then scanned and put into a book." Rose Marthis, "Seven Questions with Cole Closser," *417 Magazine*, December 2015, https://www.417mag.com/issues/december-2015/seven-questions-withcole-closser/.

10. Cole Closser, email to the author, March 8, 2021.

11. Lara Saguisag, *Incorrigibles and Innocents: Constructing Childhood and Citizenship in Progressive Era Comics* (New Brunswick, NJ: Rutgers University Press, 2019), 175–76.

12. Michelle Ann Abate, *Funny Girls: Guffaws, Guts, and Gender in Classic American Comics* (Jackson: University Press of Mississippi, 2019), 17.

13. For a fuller biographical sketch of Gray, which usefully complicates the cartoonist's politics, see Jeet Heer, "Jeet Heer on the Complex Origins of Little Orphan Annie," *Literary Hub*, August 3, 2020, https://lithub.com/jeet-heer-on-the-complex-origins-of-little-orphan-annie/.

14. Katherine Roeder, *Wide Awake in Slumberland: Fantasy, Mass Culture, and Modernism in the Art of Winsor McCay* (Jackson: University Press of Mississippi, 2014), 9.

15. Scott Bukatman, *The Poetics of Slumberland: Animated Spirits and the Animating Spirit* (Berkeley: University of California Press, 2012), 1.

16. Cole Closser, "Mama Tried," in *Little Tommy Lost*, 43.

17. Mark Heimermann and Brittany Tullis, "Introduction: Bridging Comics Studies and Childhood Studies," in *Picturing Childhood: Youth in Transnational Comics*, ed. Mark Heimermann and Brittany Tullis (Austin: University of Texas Press, 2017), 3.

18. On the function of seriality in the daily newspaper comic strip, see Matthew Levay, "Repetition, Recapitulation, Routine: *Dick Tracy* and the Temporality of Daily Newspaper Comics," *Journal of Modern Periodical Studies* 9, no. 1 (2018): 101–22.

19. This predictability is precisely the issue that Umberto Eco explored in his famous essay "The Myth of Superman," in which he posits that Superman must exist in a storyworld in which he completes tasks, performs actions, and potentially undergoes minor changes of character in order to satisfy audiences' expectations that something happen to justify continued reading of the serial narrative, but without aging or otherwise developing in any significant way (and in which he also noted the fundamental "comicality of the situation" made plain in strips like Gray's, where Little Orphan Annie "prolonged her disaster-ridden childhood for decades"). See Eco, "The Myth of Superman," *Diacritics* 2, no.1 (Spring 1972): 17.

20. Michael A. Chaney, *Reading Lessons in Seeing: Mirrors, Masks, and Mazes in the Autobiographical Graphic Novel* (Jackson: University Press of Mississippi, 2016), 57.

21. Chaney, 57.

22. Pamela Robertson Wojcik, "Little Orphan Annie as Streetwalker," in Heimermann and Tullis, *Picturing Childhood*, 16.

23. Françoise Mouly and Mina Kaneko, "Cole Closser's *Black Rat*," *New Yorker*, September 2, 2015, https://www.newyorker.com/culture/culture-desk/cole-clossers-black-rat.

24. Michael North, *Novelty: A History of the New* (Chicago: University of Chicago Press, 2013), 1–2.

25. W. J. T. Mitchell, *What Do Pictures Want? The Lives and Loves of Images* (Chicago: University of Chicago Press, 2005), 213.

26. See Matthew Levay, *Violent Minds: Modernism and the Criminal* (Cambridge: Cambridge University Press, 2019), especially 123–68.

27. Paul Peppis, "Popular Modernism in the Late *Krazy Kat* Comics: Industry and Innovation in the Color Sundays," *Journal of Modern Periodical Studies* 9, no. 2 (2018): 158.

28. Jackson Ayres, "Introduction: Comics and Modernism," *Journal of Modern Literature* 39, no. 2 (Winter 2016): 111.

AFTERWORD

Graphic Modernisms

HILLARY CHUTE

I first presented at the Modernist Studies Association annual conference in 2006 with a paper about Winsor McCay: the cartoonist whose dreamy and terrifying comics appear in this volume and whose work has long occupied the thinking of several of this volume's contributors—for instance, Scott Bukatman, in his brilliant 2011 study *The Poetics of Slumberland: Animating Spirits and the Animated Spirit*. McCay's fantastical, architectonic comics from the early 1900s express and model so many of modernism's central concerns, especially with spatiotemporal experimentation and the destruction of fixed perspective, along with the eruptive power of the dream and desire set against the rational logics of the social.[1] Glenn Willmott organized the panel, "Modernism and Comics," to which I had applied cold as a newly minted PhD. Willmott wrote in the public call for papers, "While contemporary graphic narratives in comic strip, book, and 'novel' form rapidly gain scholarly attention, the great age of comics, from the birth of the strip genre at the turn of the 20th century to the censorship clampdown of the 1950s, remains all but a dark continent in relation to other popular and avant-garde cultures of modernism." Writing this afterword seventeen years later, after Willmott and others' call to analyze the connection between comics and modernism, it's gratifying to note the increasing and sophisticated attention scholars across fields are turning to comics and/as modernism.

That attention was on significant display at the Modernist Studies Association conference in 2018, which touted Graphic Modernisms as its annual theme and inspired several contributors to this volume, including editor Jon Najarian and myself. I delivered remarks on a plenary panel—the basis of which forms my thinking here—on the idea of "graphic modernisms." For that featured session, organizers from the Ohio State University, Tommy Davis and Jesse Schotter, suggested participants conceptualize our working definitions of the graphic. The valences of the graphic in "graphic modernisms" help us to understand the force of comics as an essentially modernist form. I will begin there before touching upon salient connections between modernism and comics, and end by considering a brief example of how comics, a deeply formalist medium defined by its approach to time, helps us to think about the persistence of modernist aesthetic values and practices today.

"The graphic" is a concept I approach often in my work, since the so-called *graphic novel*, or *graphic narrative*—a category of hybrid, word-and-image expression—occupies a lot of my scholarship. Etymologically, "graphic"—both the adjective form (as in "graphic novel") and the noun form (as in "computer graphics")—comes from the Latin and Greek for "drawing or writing." During the 1600s–1800s, a common usage of graphic was *producing by words the effect of a picture*—the term described words that were vividly descriptive and lifelike. The graphic in this understanding is imitative; poetry would be considered graphic because it could be an imitative art in this sense (we see some of this meaning today persist in colloquial sentences that refer to a "graphic description"). Today, "graphic" often, perhaps most commonly, refers to image-driven art, so a widespread sense of the graphic is that it is *of* or related to drawing or painting, and the category "graphic arts"—in which one can get a degree—indicates the arts of drawing or imposing (through etching, digital techniques, or what have you) an image on a flat surface.[2]

Then there is the double valence of "graphic," which relates to earlier definitions but is more recent, in which it has come to mean providing or conveying full detail, synonymous with the *explicit*, and is particularly connected in the public imagination to the representation of sex or violence. This can make the common term "graphic novel" funny sometimes. When a publisher of mine suggested the title *Graphic Encounters* for one of my books, I had to laugh out loud, because it sounds like soft-core pornography. The cartoonist Daniel Clowes has said that the appellation "graphic novel" makes it seem as though he's writing books like *Lady Chatterley's Lover*.

But I think this kind of discomfort or awkwardness with the double valence of "graphic" is productive, because it indicates something about the possibilities of comics. There's an *excess* about comics that makes people uncomfortable, like too much visuality, a plentitude. And this is almost always centered on the expression or representation of the body, whether it's dead bodies—something we see a lot of in the work of comics journalist Joe Sacco—or bodies engaged in sexual behaviors or activities, as in the work of Alison Bechdel, whose graphic memoir *Fun Home: A Family Tragicomic* has provoked objections from students and even librarians.

We can connect this *embodiment* delivered by the graphic form of comics to the earliest attestation of the Greek verb *grapho*, meaning "to write" (from which *graphe* derives, meaning "scratch" or "graze"). The earliest attestation of *grapho*—to write—is in the *Iliad* (17.5999), in the context of a spear wounding a warrior in the shoulder. The example that originally indicates writing as making a mark by incision—as in using a stick on the ground, or a stylus in clay or wax—is actually the Iliadic use of "writing" a wound in a body. So we can understand comics' *graphicity*—with its attention to handwritten form *and* to giving presence to "obscene" bodies, whether dead or sexualized—as revealing the profound connection between the category of the graphic and embodiment.[3] (Writing might be then, in some general fashion, one body wounding another; and also, in comics, embodying wounded bodies by visually articulating them in order to "wound" a reader.) Where does this concept of "the graphic" specifically intersect with visual culture and theories of visuality? Nicholas Mirzoeff suggests "the politics of bringing the subject into presence in space is visual culture"—an idea connected to embodiment and legible in forceful ways in comics.[4]

Literary and visual modernism and comics have clearly informed each other in the early twentieth century and beyond. The curators of the famous (and controversial) 1990 Museum of Modern Art show *High and Low* assert, "When art in the later teens and twenties began to include images from the comics, it was informed by [the] sense of the comic strip as the popular embodiment of avant-garde values."[5] There are rich connections here, but we must further take the comics medium on its own terms: not just as a popular version of modernism, as Adam Gopnik and Kirk Varnedoe suggest above, but also, and perhaps more significantly, as this collection indicates, *as* modernist practice itself, whether avant la lettre or after the traditional period of historical modernism.

For the medium of comics, what we might consider its high modernist period really happened during the late 1960s and 1970s, during the "underground comix" movement in which cartoonists published independent work distributed outside of mainstream structures with no commercial strictures, unleashing new types of stories and new experiments with form. Art Spiegelman explained, "It did feel like this must have been what the cubists were going through. All the magic of being in Paris for the postimpressionist moment did somehow feel like being in San Francisco in the early 1970s."[6] This registered both as an insistent set of references to modernism, often cubism, but also, more importantly, at a level of formal invention linked closely to visual and literary modernist aesthetic practice. Spiegelman described parts of his 1974 story "Ace Hole, Midget Detective," published in the underground title *Short Order Comix*, as "a confluence of Gertrude Stein and pulp fiction" and has explained Stein's push against narrative content and focus on the rhythm of syntactical articulation and its sound as influential (see figure 12.1).[7] One of my dissertation chapters, in a project that aimed to present the contemporary landscape of comics, bears the title "'Rectangular Accusatory Windows': Comics Re-Translate Modernism" (the first part refers to Spiegelman and Françoise Mouly's "comix and graphix" magazine *Raw*). As Spiegelman himself puts it in the afterword to his own republished book *Breakdowns*, narrating his mindset in the early 1970s when he first created the material: "He was on fire, alienated and ignored, but arrogantly certain that his book would be a central artifact in the history of Modernism."[8]

Spiegelman's underground comics focus on how the form represents time—in boxes, or panels, of time—*as* space, as in the framed moments that are juxtaposed on the page in meaningful relation. Could time be slowed down, run backward—or even stopped? Could time proliferate and overlap? Spiegelman brought the rigor of modernist experiment with space, simultaneity, and shifting practices of perspective *and* perception to the comics. His underground comics destroyed a fixed viewpoint, as with cubism, and made readers aware of their own perceptual apprehension. Along with others, Spiegelman created a comics avant-garde of which he was at the forefront. We also see this level of formal experiment registered alongside a tongue-in-cheek acknowledgment of historical modernism in work like Robert Crumb's 1967 "Abstract Expressionist Ultra Super Modernistic Comics," published in the influential underground title *Zap*, which pushes back in different ways on established reading practices for comics (figure 14.1). Here we have entities speaking sounds, speaking a color, and also simply speaking marks.

Here comics demands attention to another valence of the graphic as a methodological imperative—one we see, for instance, in Johanna Drucker's analysis of avant-garde poetry, in which she describes the term *graphic* as including "all aspects of layout and composition by which elements are organized on a surface."[9] Comics is a spatially site-specific form—like avant-garde poetry and many forms of poetry—in which every mark exists in significant relation to others both semantically and extrasemantically. In this way—thinking of a graphic analysis in which "the surface of the page is a problem to solve," as Spiegelman put it, we can understand the consonance between modernist experiment and comics form. And part of this is recognizing both the graphic whole of comics, the abstract composite, and its succession of elements as distinct—and equally necessary—objects of reading.

As I previously observed, comics is a medium that is deeply formalist, consistently revealing the imbrication of the aesthetic and the political in a way that marks its investments, even in the current moment, as aligned with modernist

Figure 14.1. Robert Crumb, "Abstract Expressionist Ultra Super Modernistic Comics," from *Zap* #1, 1968.

belief in the force of form—and also the unresolvability of form. In 2003 W. J. T. Mitchell wrote an essay, "The Commitment to Form, or Still Crazy After All These Years," in which he alleges, "The modernist moment of form, whether modeled on organisms, perceptual gestalten, or structural coherence, may be behind us, but that only means that some new notion of form, and thus a new kind of formalism, lies before us. This will be a formalism we will have already been committed to for some time without knowing it."[10] That energizing new formalism, to me, is evident in the conspicuous, celebrated emergence of the comics field and the surge of incredible comics works that have come out in the last twenty years. However functionally commercial, popular, and even populist these works are, which marks their difference from canonical versions of high modernism, they bear the profound influence—and/or extension—of modernist spatiotemporal experiment and devotion to the imbrication of the aesthetic with the political. And in that way, as Mitchell's comments suggest, and as I suggest in the opening of this afterword, contemporary comics, moving forward from the underground, indicate the enduring value and aesthetics of modernism.

We see this clearly in the in the work of Joe Sacco and Alison Bechdel, cartoonists noted earlier for their conspicuous attention to embodiment. Bechdel, after decades of producing a serial comic strip, *Dykes to Watch Out For*, broke open the contemporary comics field in 2006 with the acclaimed book *Fun Home*, which examines her relationship with her closeted father, who died by suicide when she was nineteen, just a few months after she came out to her family as gay. As with her follow-up memoir *Are You My Mother? A Comic Drama*, which features Virginia Woolf as a character and focal point, *Fun Home* is often analyzed in connection to literary modernism because it is alluringly dense with reference to big ticket modernists, such as Marcel Proust, F. Scott Fitzgerald, Wallace Stevens, and, most conspicuously, James Joyce.

Bechdel considers the biographies and the work of these canonical figures, both of which were admired by her father, in order to research and to reflect on her father's personality and mystery. But references to modernism are not what make this book modernist. Rather, *Fun Home*'s resolutely nonchronological structure, collapsing and layering of temporalities (both thematically and through shaping the space of the page), and its insistence on an unresolvable dynamic of presence and absence mark a characteristically modernist belief in experimental form to address the subjective and the social horizons it interrogates. Its modernism is about the power and attention the story itself, through its unique telling and showing, gives to literary and artistic invention, rather than the names and titles it invokes. And specifically, its graphic modernism not only indicates the visual dimension of its formal experiment but further reveals the significance of the "excessive" bodies it displays to the shape of its story. Those include dead bodies, as in those prepared by Alison's father Bruce Bechdel, a part-time undertaker—particularly those he makes her witness—and living ones, as in Bechdel's controversial scenes of college sex. The contrast between dead and living bodies, between gaps and presence, highlights the artist's own embodied act of artistic creation and contributes to *Fun Home*'s weird and moving temporalities, in which we recognize the loss of Bruce and his absence even when he's present.

Sacco, a Maltese American cartoonist who travels the world to report in comics form on people "crushed by the wheels of history," was the featured speaker at the MSA's Graphic Modernisms conference. He is the creator of five major comics works, including, most recently, *Paying the Land* (2020), about colonialism and resource extraction among the indigenous Dene population of the Northwest Territories in Canada. Sacco's own graphic modernism lies in his intense spatiotemporal innovation and attention to how comics introduces distinct practices of reading that ask readers to be aware of their own perception.

In his essay "The Art of Succession: Reading, Writing, and Watching Comics," Tom Gunning suggests that "comics offer simultaneously two alternative regimes of reading: an overall one that grasps the page as a total design and a successive one that follows the order of individual frames one at a time."[11] His attention to perceiving the "total design" as part of comics reading—the graphic whole of a page—resonates with Drucker's call to heed the graphic—"elements organized on a surface"—to analyze poetry of the avant-garde. The effect of this is that comics, as Gunning argues, is "a medium of new processes of reading." In this fundamental way, comics suggests the *proliferation* of perspectives and temporalities that is characteristic of modernism—its simultaneity, its escape from "exclusive linearity."[12]

We can see this in a page from Sacco's *Footnotes in Gaza* (2009; figure 14.2) that registers, as all of his work does, this perceptual simultaneity—and also returns us to the embodiment of the graphic, in the Iliadic sense of the graphic as a wound. This is a breathtaking page I have analyzed in other writing, including in my book *Disaster Drawn*, but its techniques are consistent across Sacco's oeuvre: it is both dramatic and emblematic. It centers on Misbah, a handyman who survived a firing squad massacre in Gaza in 1956 in the Palestinian city of Khan Younis in which 275 people were killed.

Here the black horizontal background in the upper third, matching seeping pools of black blood, in Sacco's black and white field, creates a T shape with the elongated panel below it. Reading the irregular panels in succession, the temporalities and perspectives are multiplied: the first unbordered panel opens with the discharge of machine gunfire in 1956, followed by a scene of spoken testimony in 2003, in which Misbah, literally surrounded by the past, is pictured before the perspective, exploded across time, then switches back to his own optical view after he was shot, adopting his perspective even during an out-of-body experience before then picturing his body in space again. The words have a material weight on the page as graphic elements in their own right, as Misbah's speech switches from speech balloons to floating text boxes that stamp over the scene of his mutilated body and even jostle outside of the boundary of the left-hand frame. This elliptical breaking up of text across floating boxes, extending speech into space, is a signature of Sacco's comics and

Figure 14.2. Joe Sacco, *Footnotes in Gaza* (New York: Metropolitan, 2009), 90.

is reminiscent of and inspired by a central figure of modernism in interwar France, Louis-Ferdinand Céline.[13] The effect is to slow down the reader between perceptual states of reading and looking, leading the eye over and across the devastating—graphic—pile of bodies, zooming in an upward diagonal—an atypical reading direction—from the ground to the sky and back, asking readers to encounter the wounded bodies. The wounding power of comics' graphic form—its power to inscribe bodies on the page—is part of its great possibility.

Notes

1. For more on McCay see Gunning, "The Art of Succession: Reading, Writing, and Watching Comics," in *Critical Inquiry: Comics & Media*, ed. Hillary Chute and Patrick Jagoda (Chicago: University of Chicago Press, 2014), 36–51; and also the chapter "Time, Space and Picture Writing in Modern Comics," in my *Disaster Drawn: Visual Witness, Comics, and Documentary Form* (Cambridge, MA: Harvard University Press, 2016), 69–110.

2. While definitionally this can include painting, "the graphic arts" these days most frequently refers to drawing and other work that can be printed and circulated.

3. I want to acknowledge my former student Oscar Chavez's dissertation "American Graphicity: Postwar Ethnic Literature and Visual Culture" (University of Chicago, 2019), which develops a concept of graphicity as literary attribute that emphasizes and employs visuality, visibility, and visual culture in an author's probe of race and ethnicity.

4. Mirzoeff, *Watching Bablyon: The War in Iraq and Global Visual Culture* (New York: Routledge, 2005), 16. One of the other most useful definitions of visual culture is W. J. T. Mitchell's, which emphasizes not just the social construction of the visual field but the visual construction of the social. See his essay "Showing Seeing: A Critique of Visual Culture," *Journal of Visual Culture* 1, no. 2 (August 2002): 165–81.

5. Kirk Varnedoe and Adam Gopnik, *High & Low: Modern Art and Popular Culture* (NY: The Museum of Modern Art, 1990), exhibition catalog, 167.

6. Quoted in Patrick Rosenkranz, *Rebel Visions: The Underground Comix Revolution, 1963–1975* (Seattle: Fantagraphics Books, 2008), 4.

7. Gary Groth, "Interview with Art Spiegelman," *Comics Journal* #180, September 1995, 101.

8. Art Spiegelman, afterword to *Breakdowns: Portrait of the Artist as a Young %@&*!* (1977; repr., New York: Pantheon, 2008 and 2022).

9. Johanna Drucker, "Graphic Devices: Narration and Navigation," *Narrative* 16, no. 2 (2008): 121.

10. W. J. T Mitchell, "The Commitment to Form; Or, Still Crazy after All These Years," *PMLA* 118, no. 2 (2003): 324.

11. Gunning, "The Art of Succession," 44.

12. Gunning, 44.

13. Sacco is particularly inspired by Céline's 1932 novel *Journey to the End of the Night*.

SELECTED BIBLIOGRAPHY

The texts below represent a selection of works cited in this collection. This list is intended to provide an introduction and overview, rather than a comprehensive list, of important works in the fields of comics and modernist studies, and to offer a reading list for those eager to learn more. Many of the sources that follow are book-length studies rather than articles, though a handful of especially relevant chapters and essays are included.

Abate, Michelle Ann. *Funny Girls: Guffaws, Guts, and Gender in Classic American Comics.* Jackson: University Press of Mississippi, 2019.

Alaniz, José. "Animals in Graphic Narrative." In *The Oxford Handbook of Comic Studies*, edited by Frederick Luis Aldama, 326–34. New York: Oxford University Press.

Amiran, Eyal. "George Herriman's Black Sentence: The Legibility of Race in *Krazy Kat*." *Mosaic: An Interdisciplinary Critical Journal* 33, no. 3 (September 2000): 57–79.

Auad, Manuel, ed. *Al Parker: Illustrator, Innovator.* San Francisco: Auad Publishing, 2014.

Baetens, Jan. "From Black & White to Color and Back: What Does It Mean (not) to Use Color?" *College Literature* 38, no. 3 (Summer 2011): 111–28.

Baetens, Jan and Hugo Frey. *The Graphic Novel: An Introduction.* Cambridge: Cambridge University Press, 2014.

Ball, David M. "Comics Against Themselves: The Graphic Narratives of Chris Ware as Literature." In *The Rise of the American Comics Artist: Creators and Contexts*, edited by James Lyons and Paul Williams, 45–64. Jackson: University Press of Mississippi, 2010.

Ball, David M. *False Starts: The Rhetoric of Failure and the Making of American Modernism.* Evanston, IL: Northwestern University Press, 2014.

Ball, David M. "Lynd Ward's Modernist 'Novels in Woodcuts': Graphic Narratives Lost Between Art History and Literature." *Journal of Modern Literature* 39, no. 2 (Winter 2016): 126–43.

Barthes, Roland. *The Rustle of Language.* Translated by Richard Howard. Berkeley: University of California Press, 1989.

Beaty, Bart. *Comics versus Art.* Toronto, ON: University of Toronto Press, 2012.

Benedict, Nora C. *Borges and the Literary Marketplace: How Editorial Practices Shaped Cosmopolitan Reading.* New Haven, CT: Yale University Press, 2021.

Benjamin, Walter. *The Work of Art in the Age of Its Technological Reproducibility and Other Writings on Media*, edited by Michael W. Jennings, Brigid Doherty, and Thomas Y. Levin, translated by Edmund Jephcott et al. Cambridge, MA: Belknap Press of Harvard University Press, 2008.

Blackbeard, Bill. "The Kat's Kreation." In Herriman, *Krazy and Ignatz: 1916–1918*, 6–18.

Bogart, Michele. *Artists, Advertising and the Borders of Art*. Chicago: University of Chicago Press, 1995.

Brainard, Joe. *The Collected Writings of Joe Brainard*. Edited by Ron Padgett. New York: Library of America, 2012.

Brainard, Joe. *I Remember*. New York: Granary Books, 2001.

Bramlett, Frank, Roy Cook and Aaron Meskin, eds. *The Routledge Companion to Comics and Graphic Novels*. New York: Routledge, 2016.

Braund, Steve. "The Itinerant Illustration: Creating Storyworlds in the Reader's Space." *Journal of Illustration*, no. 2 (2015): 267–85.

Bukatman, Scott. *Hellboy's World: Comics and Monsters on the Margins*. Berkeley: University of California Press, 2016.

Bukatman, Scott. *Matters of Gravity: Special Effects and Supermen in the 20th Century*. Durham, NC: Duke University Press, 2003.

Bukatman, Scott. *The Poetics of Slumberland: Animated Spirits and the Animating Spirit*. Berkeley: University Press of California, 2012.

Burns, Sarah. "Cubist Comedy and Futurist Follies: The Visual Culture of the Armory Show." In Kushner, Orcutt, and Blake, *The Armory Show at 100*, 345–59.

Busiek, Kurt. Introduction to *Leonard Starr's "Mary Perkins On Stage."* Vol. 2, edited by Charles Pelto. River Forest, IL: Classic Comics, 2006.

Canemaker, John. *Winsor McCay: His Life and Art*. Boca Raton, FL: CRC, 2018.

Carrier, David. *The Aesthetics of Comics*. University Park, PA: Penn State University Press, 2000.

Chaney, Michael A. *Reading Lessons in Seeing: Mirrors, Masks, and Mazes in the Autobiographical Graphic Novel*. Jackson: University Press of Mississippi, 2016.

Chute, Hillary. "Comics as Literature? Reading Graphic Narrative." *PMLA* 123, no. 2 (2008): 452–65.

Chute, Hillary. *Disaster Drawn: Visual Witness, Comics, and Documentary Form*. Cambridge, MA: Harvard University Press, 2016.

Cole, Jean Lee. *How the Other Half Laughs: The Comic Sensibility in American Culture, 1895–1920*. Jackson: University Press of Mississippi, 2020.

Cooley, Kevin. "Picasso, Comics, and Cultural Divides: Why *Krazy Kat* Is a Kubist Kat." *Modernism/modernity* 26, no. 3 (September 2019): 595–616.

Cox, Kenyon, ed. *Documents of the 1913 Armory Show: The Electrifying Moment of Modern Art's American Debut*. Tucson, AZ: Hol Art Books, 2009.

Crafton, Donald and David Nathan. "The Making and Re-making of Winsor McCay's *Gertie* (1914)." *Animation: An Interdisciplinary Journal* 8, no. 1 (2013): 23–46.

cummings, e. e. "A Foreword to Krazy." In *Arguing Comics: Literary Masters on a Popular Medium*, edited by Jeet Heer and Kent Worcester, 30–34. Jackson: University Press of Mississippi, 2004.

Danto, Arthur. *After the End of Art: Contemporary Art and the Pale of History*. Princeton, NJ: Princeton University Press, 1997.

Danto, Arthur. *Philosophizing Art: Selected Essays*. Berkeley: University of California Press, 1999.

Danto, Arthur. *The Transfiguration of the Commonplace: A Philosophy of Art*. Cambridge, MA: Harvard University Press, 1981.

D'Arcy, Geraint. *Mise En Scène, Acting, and Space in Comics*. New York: Palgrave Macmillan, 2020.

Dauber, Jeremey. *American Comics: A History*. New York: W. W. Norton, 2022.

Diepeveen, Leonard. *Mock Modernism: An Anthology of Parodies, Travesties, Frauds, 1910–1935*. Toronto, ON: University of Toronto Press, 2014.

Doane, Mary Ann. *The Emergence of Cinematic Time: Modernity, Contingency, the Archive*. Cambridge, MA: Harvard University Press, 2002.

Dozier, Ayanna. "Wayward Travels: Racial Uplift, Black Women, and the Pursuit of Love and Travel in *Torchy in Heartbeats* by Jackie Ormes." *Feminist Media Histories* 4, no. 3 (July 2018): 12–29.

Earle, David. *Re-Covering Modernism: Pulps, Paperbacks, and the Prejudice of Form*. London: Routledge, 2016.

Eco, Umberto. "The Myth of Superman." *Diacritics* 2, no. 1 (1972): 14–22.

Eisner, Will. *Comics and Sequential Art*. Tamarac, FL: Poorhouse, 1985.

Fahs, Alice. *Out on Assignment: Newspaper Women and the Making of Modern Space*. Chapel Hill: University of North Carolina Press, 2011.

Furia, Philip. *The Poets of Tin Pan Alley*. Oxford: Oxford University Press, 1992.

Gabilliet, Jean-Paul. *Of Comics and Men: A Cultural History of American Comic Books*. Translated by Bart Beaty and Nick Nguyen. Jackson: University Press of Mississippi, 2010.

Gardner, Jared. *Projections: Comics and the History of Twenty-First-Century Storytelling*. Stanford, CA: Stanford University Press, 2012.

Goldstein, Nancy. *Jackie Ormes: The First African American Woman Cartoonist*. Ann Arbor: University of Michigan Press, 2008.

Gopnik, Adam, and Kirk Varnedoe. *High & Low: Modern Art and Popular Culture*. New York: Museum of Modern Art, 1990.

Gopnik, Adam, and Kirk Varnedoe. *Modern Art and Popular Culture: Readings in High & Low*. New York: Museum of Modern Art, 1990.

Gordon, Ian. *Comic Strips and Consumer Culture, 1890–1945*. Washington, DC: Smithsonian Institution, 1998.

Gordon, Ian. *Superman: The Persistence of an American Icon*. New Brunswick, NJ: Rutgers University Press, 2017.

Gray, Harold. *Little Orphan Annie*. Vol. 1, *Will Tomorrow Ever Come? Daily Comics, 1924–1927*. San Diego: IDW, 2008.

Greenberg, Clement. "Avant-Garde and Kitsch." In *Art and Culture: Critical Essays*, 3–21. Boston: Beacon, 1972.

Greenberg, Clement. "Modernist Painting." In *Modernism with a Vengeance, 1957–1969*, edited by John O'Brian, 85–93. Vol. 4 of *The Collected Essays and Criticism*. Chicago: University of Chicago Press, 1993.

Greenhill, Jennifer. "Flip, Linger, Glide: Coles Phillips and the Movements of Magazine Pictures." *Art History* 40, no. 3 (June 2017): 582–611.

Groensteen, Thierry. *The System of Comics*. Translated by Bart Beaty and Nick Nguyen. Jackson: University Press of Mississippi, 2007.

Gunning, Tom. "The Art of Succession: Reading, Writing, and Watching Comics." In *Critical Inquiry: Comics & Media*, edited by Hillary Chute and Patrick Jagoda, 36–51. Chicago: University of Chicago Press, 2014.

Hajdu, David. *The Ten-Cent Plague: The Great Comic-Book Scare and How It Changed America.* New York: Farrar, Straus and Giroux, 1999.

Hansen, Miriam. "The Mass Production of the Senses: Classical Cinema as Vernacular Modernism." *Modernism/modernity* 6, no. 2 (April 1999): 59–77.

Haskell, Barbara. *Lyonel Feininger: At the Edge of the World.* New Haven, CT: Yale University Press, 2011.

Harrington, Oliver W. *Dark Laughter: The Satiric Art of Oliver W. Harrington.* Edited by Thomas M. Inge. Jackson: University Press of Mississippi, 1993.

Hatfield, Charles. *Alternative Comics: An Emerging Literature.* Jackson: University Press of Mississippi, 2005.

Hatfield, Charles and Bart Beaty, eds. *Comics Studies: A Guidebook.* New Brunswick, NJ: Rutgers University Press, 2020.

Heer, Jeet. "Crazy Quilts, Krazy Kats and King's Cartoons." In Maresca, *"Crazy Quilt,"* 6–8.

Heer, Jeet. "Krazy Kat's Colors: The Shadings of George Herriman's Black-and-White World," *Lingua Franca* 11, no. 6 (September 2001): 53–58.

Herriman, George. *"The Family Upstairs": Introducing "Krazy Kat," 1910–1912.* Westport, CT: Hyperion, 1977.

Herriman, George. *Krazy and Ignatz: 1916–1918.* Edited by R. J. Casey. Seattle: Fantagraphics, 2019.

Herriman, George. *Krazy and Ignatz: 1919–1921.* Edited by R. J. Casey. Seattle: Fantagraphics, 2020.

Herriman, George. *Krazy and Ignatz: 1922–1924.* Edited by J. Michael Catron and Bill Blackbeard. Seattle: Fantagraphics, 2022.

Herriman, George. *Krazy and Ignatz in "Tiger Tea."* Santa Ana, CA: IDW, 2010.

Herring, Phillip. *Djuna: The Life and Work of Djuna Barnes.* New York: Viking, 1995.

Hoberman, J. *Vulgar Modernism: Writings on Movies and Other Media.* Philadelphia: Temple University Press, 1991.

Hornby, Louise. *Still Modernism: Photography, Literature, Film.* Oxford: Oxford University Press, 2017.

Howard, Sheena C. "Brief History of the Black Comic Strip: Past and Present." In *Black Comics: Politics of Race and Representation*, edited by Sheena C. Howard and Ronald L. Jackson, 11–22. New York: Bloomsbury Academic, 2013.

Howard, Sheena C., Henry Louis Gates Jr., and Christopher J. Priest. *Encyclopedia of Black Comics.* Wheat Ridge, CO: Fulcrum, 2017.

Huyssen, Andreas. *After the Great Divide: Modernism, Mass Culture, Postmodernism.* Bloomington: Indiana University Press, 1986.

Hutchinson, Ben. *Modernism and Style.* New York: Palgrave, 2011.

Inge, M. Thomas. *Comics as Culture.* Jackson: University Press of Mississippi, 1990.

Jackson, Debra. "'A Cultural Stronghold': The 'Anglo-African' Newspaper and the Black Community of New York." *New York History* 85, no. 4 (Fall 2004): 331–57.

Jackson, Tim. *Pioneering Cartoonists of Color.* Jackson: University Press of Mississippi, 2016.

Jameson, Fredric. "Magical Narratives: Romance as Genre," *New Literary History* 7, no. 1 (1975): 135–63.

Jones, Amelia. *Irrational Modernism: A Neurasthenic History of New York Dada.* Cambridge, MA: MIT Press, 2004.

Kennedy, Martha H. *Drawn to Purpose: American Women Illustrators and Cartoonists.* Jackson: University Press of Mississippi, 2018.

Kern, Stephen. *The Culture of Time and Space, 1880–1918*. Cambridge, MA: Harvard University Press, 2003.

Kidman, Shawna. *Comic Books Incorporated: How the Business of Comics Became the Business of Hollywood*. Oakland: University of California Press, 2019.

Kukkonen, Karin. "Space, Time, and Causality in Graphic Narratives: An Embodied Approach." In *From Comic Strips to Graphic Novels: Contributions to the Theory and History of Graphic Narrative*, edited by Daniel Stein, 49–66. Boston: De Gruyter, 2013.

Kunzle, David. *The Early Comic Strip: Narrative Strips and Picture Stories in the European Broadsheet from 1450 to 1825*. Berkeley: University of California Press, 1973.

Kunzle, David. *The History of the Comic Strip*. Vol. 2, *The Nineteenth Century*. Berkeley: University of California Press, 1990.

Kurtzman, Harvey and Will Elder. *"Playboy"'s Little Annie Fanny*. Vol. 1, *1962–1970*. Milwaukie, OR: Dark Horse Comics, 2000.

Kushner, Marilyn Satin, Kimberly Orcutt, and Casey Nelson Blake. *The Armory Show at 100: Modernism and Revolution*. London: Giles, 2013.

Levay, Matthew. "Repetition, Recapitulation, Routine: Dick Tracy and the Temporality of Daily Newspaper Comics." In "Seriality." Special issue, *Journal of Modern Periodical Studies* 9, no. 1 (2018): 101–22.

Lopes, Paul. *Demanding Respect: The Evolution of the American Comic Book*. Philadelphia: Temple University Press, 2009.

Lutes, Jean Marie. *Front Page Girls: Women Journalists in American Culture and Fiction, 1880–1930*. Ithaca, NY: Cornell University Press, 2006.

Maresca, Peter, ed. *"Crazy Quilt": Scraps and Panels on the Way to "Gasoline Alley."* Palo Alto, CA: Sunday Press, 2017.

McCay, Winsor. *Dreams of the Rarebit Fiend*. 1905. Reprint, New York: Dover, 1973.

McCloud, Scott. *Understanding Comics: The Invisible Art*. 1993. Reprint, New York: Harper Perennial, 1994.

Mendez, Armando. "Something Cool: Alex Raymond, Rip Kirby, and the Rise and Fall of the Photorealistic Comic Strip." *Comic Art* 2 (Winter 2003): 52–63.

Merkl, Ulrich, ed. *The Complete Dream of the Rarebit Fiend (1904–1913)*. By Winsor McCay. Self-published, Ulrich Merkl, 2007.

Meskin, Aaron. "Defining Comics." *Journal of Aesthetics and Art Criticism* 65, no. 4 (2007): 369–79.

Mitchell, W. J. T. "The Commitment to Form; or Still Crazy After All These Years." *PMLA* 116, no. 2 (March 2003): 321–25.

Mitchell, W. J. T. "Showing Seeing: A Critique of Visual Culture." *Journal of Visual Culture* 1, no. 2 (August 2002): 165–81.

Mitchell, W. J. T. *What Do Pictures Want? The Lives and Loves of Images*. Chicago: University of Chicago Press, 2005.

Molotiu, Andrei. "Cartooning." In *Comics Studies: A Guidebook*, edited by Charles Hatfield and Bart Beaty, 153–71. New Brunswick, NJ: Rutgers University Press, 2020.

Munson, Kim. *Comic Art in Museums*. Jackson: University Press of Mississippi, 2020.

Najarian, Jonathan. "*Crazy Quilt*, Advertising, and the *Chicago Tribune*." *American Periodicals* 32, no. 2 (Fall 2022): 109–115.

Nemerov, Alexander. "N. C. Wyeth's Theater of Illustration." *American Art* 6, no. 2 (Spring 1992): 36–57.

Nolan, Michelle. *Love on the Racks: A History of American Romance Comics*. Jefferson, NC: McFarland, 2008.

North, Michael. *Machine-Age Comedy*. Oxford: Oxford University Press, 2008.

Nyberg, Amy Kiste. *Seal of Approval: The History of the Comics Code*. Jackson: University Press of Mississippi, 1998.

Ottley, Roi. *The Lonely Warrior: The Life and Times of Robert S. Abbott*. Washington, DC: Regnery, 1955.

Owen, Ben Novotny. "A Touch of Irony and Pity: *Krazy Kat* in the Breaks." In *Comics Studies Here and Now*, edited by Frederick Luis Aldama, 9–30. New York: Routledge, 2018.

Padgett, Ron. *Joe: A Memoir of Joe Brainard*. Minneapolis: Coffee House, 2004.

Parker, Al. "The Decade: 1940–1950." *The Illustrator in America, 1880–1980: A Century of Illustration*, edited by Walt Reed and Roger Reed, 206–7. New York: Madison Square, 1993.

Peppis, Paul. "Popular Modernism in the Late *Krazy Kat* Comics: Industry and Innovation in the Color Sundays." *Journal of Modern Periodical Studies* 9, no. 2 (2019): 157–76.

Pizzino, Christopher. *Arresting Development: Comics at the Boundaries of Literature*. Austin: University of Texas Press, 2016.

Proctor, Ben. *William Randolph Hearst: The Early Years, 1863–1910*. Oxford: Oxford University Press, 1998.

Quilter, Jenni. *New York School Painters & Poets: Neon in Daylight*. New York: Rizzoli, 2014.

Robbins, Trina. *The Flapper Queens: Women Cartoonists of the Jazz Age*. Seattle: Fantagraphics Books, 2020.

Robbins, Trina. *Nell Brinkley and the New Woman in the Early 20th Century*. Jefferson, NC: McFarland, 2001.

Robbins, Trina. *Pretty in Ink: North American Women Cartoonists 1896–2013*. Seattle: Fantagraphics Books, 2013.

Roeder, Katherine. *Wide Awake in Slumberland: Fantasy, Mass Culture, and the Art of Winsor McCay*. Jackson: University Press of Mississippi, 2014.

Rosenkranz, Patrick. *Rebel Visions: The Underground Comix Revolution, 1963–1975*. Seattle: Fantagraphics Books, 2008.

Sabin, Roger. *Adult Comics*. London: Routledge, 2013.

Saguisag, Lara. *Incorrigibles and Innocents: Constructing Childhood and Citizenship in Progressive Era Comics*. New Brunswick, NJ: Rutgers University Press, 2019.

Sanders, Ed. *Fug You: An Informal History of the Peace Eye Bookstore, the Fuck You Press, the Fugs, and Counterculture in the Lower East Side*. Philadelphia: De Capo, 2011.

Schelly, Bill. *Harvey Kurtzman: The Man Who Created "Mad" and Revolutionized Humor in America*. Seattle: Fantagraphics Books, 2015.

Scholes, Robert and Clifford Wulfman, *Modernism in the Magazines*. New Haven, CT: Yale University Press, 2010.

Seldes, Gilbert. *The Seven Lively Arts*. New York: Harper and Brothers, 1924. Reprinted with an introduction by Michael Kammen. New York: Dover, 2001.

Shamma, Yasmine, ed. *Joe Brainard's Art*. Edinburgh: Edinburgh University Press, 2019.

Smith, Matthew J. and Randy Duncan, eds. *Critical Approaches to Comics: Theories and Methods*. New York: Routledge, 2011.

Smolderen, Thierry. *The Origins of Comics: From William Hogarth to Winsor McCay*. Translated by Bart Beaty and Nick Nguyen. Jackson: University Press of Mississippi, 2014.

Solomon, William. "Slapstick Modernism: Charley Bowers and Industrial Modernity." *Modernist Cultures* 2, no. 2 (2006): 170–88.
Stein, Daniel. "The Comic Modernism of George Herriman." In *Crossing Boundaries in Graphic Narrative: Essays on Forms, Series and Genres*, edited by Jake Jakaitis and James F. Wurtz, 40–70. New York: McFarland, 2012.
Strother, T. Ella, "The Race-Advocacy Function of the Black Press." *Black American Literature-Forum* 12, no. 3 (1978): 92–99.
Tisserand, Michael. *Krazy: George Herriman, a Life in Black and White*. New York: HarperCollins, 2016.
Walker, Brian. *The Comics Before 1945*. New York: Harry N. Abrams, 2004.
Ware, Chris. "A Young Man's Game." In Maresca, *"Crazy Quilt,"* 5.
Weiss, Jeffrey. *The Popular Culture of Modernism: Picasso, Duchamp, and Avant-Gardism*. New Haven, CT: Yale University Press, 1994.
Whaley, Deborah Elizabeth. *Black Women in Sequence: Re-Inking Comics, Graphic Novels, and Anime*. Seattle: University of Washington Press, 2016.
Wilkinson, Alec. "Cubies." *New Yorker*, February 24, 2013.
Willmott, Glenn. "The Animalized Character and Style." In *Animal Comics: Multispecies Storyworlds in Graphic Narratives*, edited by David Herman, 53–77. London: Bloomsbury Academic, 2017.
Willmott, Glenn. "Cat People." *Modernism/modernity* 17, no. 4 (2010): 839–56.
Willmott, Glenn. *Modern Animalism: Habitats of Scarcity and Wealth in Comics and Literature*. Toronto, ON: University of Toronto Press, 2012.
Wolk, Douglas. *All of the Marvels: A Journey to the Ends of the Biggest Story Ever Told*. New York: Penguin, 2021.
Woo, Benjamin. "An Age-Old Problem: Problematics of Comic Book Historiography." *International Journal of Comic Art* 10, no. 1 (2008): 268–79.
Worden, Daniel. "The Politics of Comics: Popular Modernism, Abstraction, and Experimentation." *Literature Compass* 12, no. 2 (2015): 59–71.

ABOUT THE CONTRIBUTORS

David M. Ball is an academy English instructor and program coordinator for the Davis Democracy Initiative at Punahou School in Honolulu, Hawaii. He is the author of *False Starts: The Rhetoric of Failure and the Making of American Modernism* (Northwestern University Press, 2015) and coeditor, with Martha Kuhlman, of *The Comics of Chris Ware: Drawing Is a Way of Thinking* (University Press of Mississippi, 2010). He is at work on two monographs: one on the intersections of comics and artistic and literary modernism, and another on the teaching of visual storytelling.

Scott Bukatman is professor of Film and Media Studies in the Department of Art and Art History at Stanford University. His work has long explored the alternative bodies popular media has produced in droves in comedy, animation, musicals, and superhero media. His books include *Hellboy's World: Comics and Monsters on the Margins* (University of California Press, 2016) and, most recently, *Black Panther*, part of the 21st Century Film Essentials series (University of Texas Press, 2022).

Hillary Chute is distinguished professor of English and Art + Design at Northeastern University. She is the author or editor of seven books, including *Graphic Women: Life Narrative and Contemporary Comics* (Columbia University Press, 2010); *Disaster Drawn: Visual Witness, Comics, and Documentary Form* (Harvard University Press, 2016); *Why Comics? From Underground to Everywhere* (Harper, 2017); and the collection *Maus Now: Selected Writing* (Pantheon, 2022). She has written for venues including *Artforum*, *Bookforum*, the *Village Voice*, the *New York Review of Books*, and the *New York Times Book Review*.

Jean Lee Cole is professor emerita of English at Loyola University Maryland. She is the author of *How the Other Half Laughs: The Comic Sensibility in American Culture, 1895–1920* and formerly the editor of the journal *American Periodicals*. She currently resides in Oaxaca de Juarez, Mexico.

Louise Kane is assistant professor of Global Modernisms at the University of Central Florida. She has a longstanding interest in periodicals and is a general editor of the forthcoming *Oxford Critical and Cultural History of Global Modernist Magazines* series.

Matthew Levay is associate professor of English at Idaho State University and coeditor of the *Journal of Modern Periodical Studies*. He is the author of *Violent Minds: Modernism and the Criminal* (Cambridge University Press, 2019), and his essays have recently appeared in *Modernism/modernity*, the *Journal of Modern Periodical Studies*, and the *Routledge Companion to Crime Fiction*. He is currently completing a book on anachronism in contemporary comics.

Andrei Molotiu is senior lecturer of Art History at Indiana University Bloomington. His publications include *Fragonard's Allegories of Art* (J. Paul Getty Museum, 2007), a book that accompanied the exhibition *Consuming Passion: Fragonard's Allegories of Love* at the Getty and at the Clark Museum of Art, in Williamstown, Massachusetts, which he cocurated. He is also the author of *Abstract Comics: The Anthology* (Fantagraphics Books, 2009). With John McCoy, he curated the exhibition *American Alternative Comics, 1980–2000: "Raw," "Weirdo," and Beyond* at the McMullen Museum of Art, Boston College, and edited, with McMullen, the accompanying exhibition catalog. Molotiu is currently writing a book on the early years of the Spider-Man comic book, under contract with Rutgers University Press.

Jonathan Najarian is visiting assistant professor of Writing and Rhetoric at Colgate University. His work considers the intersection of modernist literature, visual art, and comics. He is currently at work on a book project titled *The Intermedial Era: Collaboration and Contact in Global Modernism*, and his writing has appeared in journals including *Modernism/modernity*, *American Literary History*, *Contemporary Literature*, and *Twentieth-Century Fiction*.

Katherine (Kerry) Roeder is assistant professor in the History of Art, Design, and Visual Culture Department at the Maryland Institute College of Art. Her courses focus on the history of commercial illustration, picture books, and comics art. She has published articles on Cliff Sterrett, Chris Ware, and David Wiesner, in addition to her book *Wide Awake in Slumberland: Fantasy, Mass Culture, and Modernism in the Art of Winsor McCay* (University Press of Mississippi, 2014).

Noa Saunders is a doctoral candidate in English at Boston University, where she is completing a dissertation on the uncertainty of everyday life in twentieth-century poetry, film, and media. Her essays and reviews can be found in *Modernism/modernity* Print Plus and *Against the Current*. She holds an MFA in poetry from the University of Maryland, College Park; her poems appear in *Ninth Letter, Ghost City Review, The B'K, The Shore, Leavings, The Mantle*, and others.

Clémence Sfadj is a writer and comics scholar researching early comic strips with a focus on cartoonists published in African American newspapers. She holds a master's degree from the Sorbonne University and lives in Brooklyn, where she works as an editor.

Nick Sturm is a lecturer in English at Georgia State University. He is a coeditor of *Get the Money!: Collected Prose, 1961–1983* by Ted Berrigan (City Lights, 2022) and editor of *Early Works* by Alice Notley (Fonograf Editions, 2023). More information about his research, scholarship, and teaching can be found at nicksturm.com.

Glenn Willmott works in modernism and in areas of popular culture at Queen's University in Canada. His current interests are in experimental literature, early Hollywood, pulp genres, and comics, informed by economic, social-political, and ecological perspectives. His most recent books are *Modern Animalism* (University of Toronto Press, 2012) and *Reading for Wonder* (Palgrave Macmillan, 2018), and he has chapters on comics in *Animal Comics* (Bloomsbury, 2018), *Modernism and the Anthropocene* (Rowman & Littlefield, 2021), and *The Edinburgh Companion to Vegan Literary Studies* (Edinburgh University Press, 2022).

Daniel Worden is an associate professor of Art at the Rochester Institute of Technology, where he teaches art, comics, and print and visual culture. Most recently, he is the author of *Neoliberal Nonfictions: The Documentary Aesthetic from Joan Didion to Jay-Z* (University of Virginia Press, 2020), the editor of *The Comics of R. Crumb: Underground in the Art Museum* (University Press of Mississippi, 2021), and the coeditor with Jesse W. Schwartz of *New Directions in Print Culture Studies: Archives, Materiality, and Modern American Culture* (Bloomsbury, 2022). He is currently at work on a book about comics and energy.

INDEX

Abate, Michelle Ann, 291
abstract expressionism, 240, 243, 288
"Abstract Expressionist Ultra Super Modernistic Comics" (Crumb), 304–5
"Ace Hole, Midget Detective" (Spiegelman), 11, 260, 266–73, 303
Action Comics, 185–92, 197
Adams, Neal, 178–80
Adler, Jack, 185
Adorno, Theodor, 203, 257
advertisements. *See* advertising
advertising, 58, 67, 89–94, 106, 157–58, 165–73
African Americans: cartoonists, 115–16; newspapers, 113–16; press, 115; readership, 115; women, 113–16, 121–22. *See also* Black
"After the Cubist Food Exhibit" (King), 45
Alaniz, José, 74
Ally Sloper's Half Holiday, 133–35
Anderson, Carl Thomas, 219, 221
animation, 50, 64–68, 285
Apter, Emily, 147
Armory Show (1913), 4–5, 18, 33–48, 71, 90, 184–85, 192–93
Art News, 235–37
Ashcan School, 35–37, 90
avant-garde: aesthetics, 185, 207, 260, 277–79, 301; art, 33, 36, 109, 234–37; comics, 304; groups, 5, 17, 28, 129, 136, 258; literary, 207–21, 304, 307; movements, 48n41, 184, 191–93, 201; music, 15; reactions to, 39–46; techniques, 21, 41–42
Ayres, Jackson, 298

Baetens, Jan, 83n27, 289
Bakhtin, Mikhail, 32n21, 105
Ball, David M., 13, 287, 295
Balla, Giacomo, 187–92
bandes dessinées (BD), 149–50
Bank, The (Chaplin), 59–62
Barnes, Djuna, 6, 10, 87–112
Barthes, Roland, 158, 165, 173
Baudelaire, Charles, 30n4, 106
Beat (writers), 206, 209
Beaty, Bart, 15, 17, 30n1, 147, 149
Bechdel, Alison, 9, 11, 93, 119, 302, 306
Beckman, Bill, 209–10
Bell, Clive, 6
Benjamin, Walter, 30n4, 52, 62, 202
Berkson, Bill, 208, 219–20
Berrigan, Ted, 207, 209–12, 219, 225n37
Black: artists, 113; characters, 122, 146; comics, 126, 127n17; modernism, 118; vernacular, 126; women, 114–16, 121–24, 127n18. *See also* African Americans
Black Rat (Closser), 297
Blackbeard, Bill, 7, 83n28
Boccioni, Umberto, 187–92
Boke Press, 213, 221
Book of Repulsive Women, The (Barnes), 88, 106–9, 112n39
Borges, Jorge Luis, 129, 140
Brainard, Joe, 11, 206–25, 230
Braque, Georges, 38, 44, 264
Breakdowns (Spiegelman), 260, 263, 267, 269, 274, 280n5, 304

Briggs, Clare, 43–44, 46
Brillo Box (Warhol), 238–39, 244
Brinkley, Nell, 10, 88, 90–94, 97, 104–6, 109
Brooks, Gwendolyn, 116
Brunetti, Ivan, 161–62
Bukatman, Scott, 50, 188–89, 293, 301
Burns, Sarah, 41, 44
Burroughs, William, 209
Busch, Wilhelm, 42
Bushmiller, Ernie, 207, 219, 221

C Comics (Brainard), 207, 210–22
Caniff, Milton, 234, 237
Cap Stubbs and Tippie (Dumm), 23, 25–26
capitalism: consequences of, 51, 61–64, 66–67, 127; free-market, 291; infrastructure of, 62; and modernity, 30n4, 58, 65
Caplin, Elliot, 157
Captain America, 159–60, 192
Captain Marvel (Fawcett), 236–37, 239, 251, 254n9
Carew, Kate, 88, 90, 94–97, 100, 104–5, 109
Casanova, Pascale, 141, 150
Caselli, Daniela, 105
Céline, Louis-Ferdinand, 309
celluloid sheets (cels), 50, 59, 65
censorship, 225n7, 261–62, 273, 275–79, 301. *See also* Comics Code Authority (CCA)
Cézanne, Paul, 39
"Cézanne" (Brainard and Padgett), 212–13
Chaney, Michael A., 295
Chaplin, Charlie, 51, 59–64
chronophotography, 42, 51, 68n3, 196
Chute, Hillary, 7, 49, 52–53, 57, 281n27, 282n32
cinema. *See* film
circulation, 57, 64, 141, 144, 149–50, 202, 219, 299n7
Closser, Cole, 285–98
Clowes, Daniel, 302
Cole, Jean Lee, 83n27
collage: aesthetic, 258, 260, 277; in Brainard, 207, 210; cubist, 41, 44
Collins, Jess, 230
Comics Code Authority (CCA), 193, 237, 245, 261, 275–76
Comics Journal, 298n6

comix, 8, 11, 206–10, 219–21, 225nn38–39, 260–62, 303–4
Conrad, Joseph, 29
consumer culture, 16–17, 66–67
Cooley, Kevin, 71
Crazy Quilt (King et al.), 9, 44
Crumb, Robert, 11, 131, 206, 208–9, 221, 223n17, 225n39, 262, 304
Cubies' ABC, The (Lyall), 45
cubism, 37–46, 71, 191, 258, 303–4
cummings, e. e., 5, 7, 71, 258
"Curlee Clothes" (Brainard and Schuyler), 215–18

da Vinci, Leonardo, 246, 249, 263–64
Dada, 136, 184, 188–92, 209, 258
Damrosch, David, 141, 144
Danto, Arthur, 11, 229–30, 236, 238–53
Dark Laughter (Harrington), 126
DC (publisher), 178, 254n9
de Man, Paul, 8, 75
Deitch, Kim, 209–10, 221, 298n7
Deleuze, Gilles, 60
Die Pleite, 136–39
Dirks, Rudolph, 5, 35–36, 71, 80n2
Dismorr, Jessica, 136
distribution. *See* circulation
Doane, Mary Ann, 64
Drake, Stan, 157–63, 172–73, 178
Dream of the Rarebit Fiend (McCay), 42, 49–69, 70
Drucker, Johanna, 304, 307
Duchamp, Marcel: at the Armory Show, 34, 42–43; and *Fountain*, 260; and *Mad*, 231–32, 246; and motion, 4–6, 81n6, 193–97
Duffy, Enda, 193
Dumm, Edwina, 23, 25–27, 29

Earle, David, 141
EC Comics, 230–31, 237, 241–53, 275
Eco, Umberto, 74, 258, 299n19
Eisner, Will, 131, 241
Elder, William (Bill), 231–36, 251, 263–66, 279
Eliot, T. S., 5–8, 108, 113, 135, 149, 184
Elmslie, Kenward, 207, 213, 218–21

"Extended Man and the Kingdom of the Machine" (Marinetti), 197–98

Family Upstairs, The (Herriman), 73–74, 76
Famous Funnies, 132–33
Fantastic Four, 197–201
fashion, 16, 45, 142, 163–71, 175, 188
Fauset, Jessie, 116, 121
fauvism, 46
Fawaz, Ramzi, 222n9
Feininger, Lyonel, 9, 71
film, 50–51, 56, 58–68, 80, 173, 176, 184–85, 196
Fish, Anne Harriet, 142–45, 149–50
Fisher, Bud, 6, 204n16, 259–60
Flash Gordon (Raymond), 23, 27, 184–85, 201
Footnotes in Gaza (Sacco), 307–9
"Foreheads" (Brainard and Guest), 214–15, 218
Foster, Hal, 29, 172
"Foundation and Manifesto of Futurism" (Marinetti), 189–90
Fountain (Duchamp), 204n16, 260
Fox, Fontaine Talbot, 41
Freilicher, Jane, 215–18
Frey, Hugo, 289
Friedman, Susan Stanford, 184
Frontline Combat (Kutzman), 237
Fun Home: A Family Tragicomic (Bechdel), 119, 302, 306
futurism, 8, 41–42, 48n27, 185–93, 197–202

Gabilliet, Jean-Paul, 204n3
Gaines, William, 245
Gardner, Jared, 5, 81n8, 180n1, 192, 280n9, 287
Gasoline Alley, 2–5, 46
Gates, Henry Louis, Jr., 83n29, 113
Gay Comix, 219
genre comics: romance, 127n9, 158–59, 173–76, 178, 180; science fiction, 191, 201; superhero, 159–62, 178, 180, 184–205, 236–37, 268, 289
German expressionism, 46, 71
Gertie the Dinosaur (McCay), 65
Ginsberg, Allen, 209, 221
Girl Before a Mirror (Picasso), 231, 263
Glackens, Louis, 39–40

Glackens, William, 36
Glasgow Looking Glass, 135
Golden Age comics, 140, 185, 208, 236
Gombrich, E. H., 162, 164
Gopnik, Adam, 257–58, 303
Gordon, Ian, 69n33, 204n4
graphic novel, 115, 119, 131, 150–51, 221, 254n10, 302
Gray, Harold, 29, 286, 290–96, 299n13
Green, Justin, 262
Green Lantern/Green Arrow (Adams and O'Neil), 179–80
Greenberg, Clement, 15–16, 18–20, 31n13, 238, 240–41, 243, 255n29
Gris, Juan, 258
Griswold, J. F., 42–43
Groensteen, Thierry, 108, 112n46
Gross, Milt, 258
Guernica (Picasso), 273–79, 282nn33–34, 283n40
Guest, Barbara, 214–15
Gunning, Tom, 50, 57, 68n3, 307

Hajdu, David, 254n11
Hammill, Faye, 142
Hansen, Miriam, 51, 58
"Hard Times" (Brainard and O'Hara), 215–16
Harlem Renaissance, 114, 116, 135
Harper's Bazaar, 142, 166
Harrington, Ollie, 126
Hartman, Saidiya, 114, 116–17
Hatfield, Charles, 96, 132, 147, 149, 192, 207, 225n39
Hayot, Eric, 162
Hearst, William Randolph, 36, 51, 55–56, 66–67, 70, 83n28, 88–90
Heath, Russ, 232–33, 235–36, 253n4
Heer, Jeet, 46, 83n27, 281n20, 299n13
Henri, Robert, 35–36, 39, 90
Herriman, George, 5–6, 8, 15–16, 23–25, 29, 30n4, 70–83, 153n52, 192, 241, 297–98
Hoberman, J., 256n30, 264–65
Hollywood, 19, 159, 174, 178
Hornby, Louise, 52–54, 57
Hughes, Langston, 113–14, 116, 126
Hurston, Zora Neale, 115, 121, 126

"I Do" (Toth), 175–77
illustration: of books, 45; commercial, 26, 34–35, 165, 178; cover, 110n6, 185, 187, 207; in magazines, 26, 133–44, 157, 159, 165–76, 178, 225n38; in newspapers, 37, 88–105
Infantino, Carmine, 193, 195–97
Inge, M. Thomas, 81n8, 280n16

Jacob's Room (Woolf), 184
Jaillant, Lise, 7
Jameson, Frederic, 30n8
Johns, Jasper, 25
Jones, Joëlle, 169
Journal Tigers, The (Swinnerton), 29
journalism, 87–112
Joyce, James, 5–8, 48n34, 142, 184, 306
Juliet Jones (*The Heart of Juliet Jones*), 157, 161, 172, 178, 180n3

Katz, Alex, 215–18
Katzenjammer Kids, The (Dirks), 5, 35, 70–71, 80n2, 270, 273, 279
Kelp-Stebbins, Katherine, 147
Kern, Stephen, 194–96
Kidman, Shawna, 192
King, Frank, 2–4, 6, 44, 45–46
King Features, 144, 147
Kirby, Jack, 174, 198, 230, 241, 298n6
Kiss, The (Lichtenstein), 234–36, 254n8, 266
Kitchen, Denis, 280n10
kitsch, 16, 18–19, 31n13, 202
Kline, Franz, 234
Kramer, Hilton, 215–18
Krazy Kat (Herriman), 5–6, 8, 10, 15–16, 23–25, 29, 70–83, 153n52, 184, 192, 258, 298
Kuhn, Walt, 34–35, 38–39
Kunzle, David, 42, 131
Kurtzman, Harvey, 11, 229–53, 258, 260–62, 265–66, 279, 280n10

La Revista Multicolor de los Sábados, 140, 149–50
Lady Chatterley's Lover (Lawrence), 302
Lady Killer (Jones), 169
Larsen, Nella, 121
Latham, Sean, 130

Lawrence, D. H., 18, 142
Lee, Stan, 198
Leick, Karen, 142
Leja, Michael, 41
Letters of Eve, The (Fish), 142–45
Levay, Matthew, 110n2, 131, 152n6
Lichtenstein, Roy, 16, 229–30, 234–37, 239, 243, 246, 249, 251, 258–59, 266
Little Annie Fanny (Kurtzman and Elder), 230–36, 244, 250–51, 253n4, 266
little magazines, 129–53, 207, 221–22, 246
Little Nemo in Slumberland (McCay), 65, 70, 268, 286, 293
Little Orphan Annie (Gray), 29, 286, 290–96
Little Sammy Sneeze (McCay), 70, 286
Little Tommy Lost (Closser), 284–98
Loos, Adolf, 165
Lord Jim (Conrad), 29
Lorde, Audre, 221
Luks, George, 36
Lutes, Jean Marie, 100
Lyall, Earl Harvey, 45
Lyall, Mary Mills, 45

Mad magazine: and comix, 206; covers, 244–53; and Kurtzman, 230–32, 243–44, 260; and satire, 244–49, 260–66; and Spiegelman, 260–66, 279
manga, 149–50
manhua, 139, 150
Mansfield, Katherine, 136
Marey, Étienne-Jules, 42
Marinetti, F. T., 186, 190–91, 197–98
Marvel (publisher), 178, 198, 201, 203, 230
Mary Perkins: On Stage (Starr), 157, 163–65
mass culture, 16, 87, 142, 144. *See also* consumer culture
Matisse, Henri, 264, 279
Maus (Spiegelman), 7, 260–61, 268
McCay, Winsor, 5, 33, 42, 49–69, 70–71, 241, 268, 277, 286, 292–93, 301
McCloud, Scott: and closure, 79–80, 122, 139, 162; and comics history, 16–17, 141; on icons, 31n16, 32n22, 158, 270; on relation between words and images, 25–26; and sequence, 59, 131; and transitions, 69n20, 282n33

mechanical reproduction, 50, 62, 65–66
melodrama, 159, 161, 173–74, 178
Meskin, Aaron, 131
Miró, Joan, 234, 251, 259–60
Mirzoeff, Nicholas, 303
Mitchell, W. J. T., 297, 305–6
Modern Sketch, 139, 147–48
Molotiu, Andrei, 180n3, 180n9, 222, 266
Mona Lisa (da Vinci), 207, 231, 263
Moretti, Franco, 141, 150
Morice, Dave, 222
Mrs. Dalloway (Woolf), 16
Ms. Marvel (Wilson), 203
Munson, Kim, 47n8
Murry, John Middleton, 136. See also *Rhythm*
Museum of Modern Art (MOMA), 188, 191, 257–60, 303
Mutt and Jeff (Fisher), 260
Muybridge, Eadward, 42, 51–53

Najarian, Jonathan, 48n32, 301
nationalism, 66, 192, 201–2
New Modernist Studies, 6–7, 184, 201, 287
New York School, 206–25
Ngai, Sianne, 49
Nietzsche, Friedrich, 74–76, 185, 190–91
Nightwood (Barnes), 98
Norris, Margot, 75
North, Michael, 6, 75–76, 297
Nude Descending a Staircase (No. 2) (Duchamp), 4, 34, 42, 193–97, 207
Nyberg, Amy Kiste, 254n11

O'Hara, Frank, 213, 215–16, 219, 223n14
O'Keeffe, Georgia, 71
On Stage (Starr). See *Mary Perkins: On Stage*
O'Neil, Denny, 179
O'Neill, Rose, 22, 110n6
1001 Roman, 146–51
Organ, Marjorie, 36, 88–92, 96, 106, 109
Ormes, Jackie, 10, 113–28
Owen, Ben Novotny, 76, 81n6

Padgett, Ron, 207, 212–13, 221, 225nn37–38
Parker, Al, 166–70
Parker, Dorothy, 5, 7

Paying the Land (Sacco), 307
Peppis, Paul, 71, 151n4, 153n52, 297–98
periodical studies, 130–35
photography, 42, 50–57, 104, 165–69, 173, 181n28
Picabia, Francis, 34, 36
Picasso, Pablo: and the avant-garde, 136; and collage, 44; and comics, 5, 7, 71, 266–79; exhibitions of, 34–41, 47n10, 237, 258; paintings by, 234; parodies of, 231, 246, 249, 259–60, 263–64, 266–79; statements by, 270–72, 282n31; and stylization, 19, 46. See also *Guernica*
Pizzino, Christopher, 287
Playboy, 231–33
Plymell, Charles, 208–9, 223n17
Pollock, Jackson, 234, 237, 251
Polly and Her Pals (Sterrett), 16, 31n20
Pop Art, 229–53
popular culture, 5–6, 16, 21, 72, 80, 202–3, 258–60, 287
postimpressionism, 35–36, 303
postmodernism, 191, 213, 238–40, 270
Pound, Ezra, 6, 132, 135
Prince Valiant (Foster), 29, 172
Prisma (Borges), 129, 140, 150
"Prisoner on the Hell Planet" (Spiegelman), 262
prosopopoeia, 271
pulp: fiction, 19, 174, 273–74, 279, 303; magazines, 131, 141, 185, 197; novels, 220

racism, 28–29, 115, 202, 262
Raw (Spiegelman), 252, 258, 304
Ray, Man, 258
Raymond, Alex, 23, 27, 29, 172
"Recent Visitors" (Brainard and Berkson), 219–21, 225n36
Rhythm (Murry), 136–39, 149–50
Robbins, Trina, 110n11, 209
Rodriguez, Spain, 209–10, 224n23
Roeder, Katherine, 18, 50, 80n1, 292–93
romance comics. See genre comics
Rosenkranz, Patrick, 206, 209
Rothko, Mark, 234

Rude Descending a Staircase (Rush Hour at the Subway) (Griswold), 42–43

Sacco, Joe, 11, 281n27, 302, 306–9
Saguisag, Lara, 290–91
Sass, Alek, 36–37
satire, 36–37, 41, 45, 262–63, 279, 280n10
Scholes, Robert, 130
Schor, Naomi, 163–65, 171, 181n28
Schuyler, James, 212–19
science fiction comics. *See* genre comics
Scioli, Tom, 289, 298n6
Short Order Comix, 303–4
Shuster, Joe, 185–88, 191, 202
Seduction of the Innocent, The (Wertham), 245, 275
(Seeing Ourselves) As Others See Us (Jackson), 126
Seldes, Gilbert, 71, 80n4
seriality: in Bechdel, 306; in Brainard, 207, 223n11; of comics form, 70, 180n1, 190–91, 287, 295, 299n18; in Herriman, 72–73, 79–80; in magazines, 146; in McCay, 52–54, 65; in newspapers, 70, 96; in Ormes, 117–18; of photographs, 52; in soap opera, 174; and television, 176
Siegel, Jerry, 187–88, 191, 202
Simon, Joe, 174
Simplicissimus, 136–39
slapstick, 58–64, 82n25, 118
Sloan, John, 36–38
Smith, Jeff, 31n20
Smolderen, Thierry, 65, 162
speech balloons, 54, 100, 135, 212, 235–36, 266, 271, 307
speech bubbles. *See* speech balloons
Spiegelman, Art: and "Ace Hole," 266–79, 303–4; as archivist, 80n2, 279, 281n20, 298n7; as art critic, 257–60; and *Breakdowns*, 260–63, 280n5; and *Mad*, 260–66; and *Maus*, 7, 32; and *Raw*, 252; and underground, 32n20, 206, 210, 262, 266–79, 303–4
"Stamp Out the Family Plan!" (Brainard and Berrigan), 210–13, 218
Stark, Jessica, 222n9, 223n11

Starr, Leonard, 157–58, 163–65, 172
Stein, Daniel, 5, 82n27
Stein, Gertrude, 5, 35, 71, 142, 260, 280n4, 303
Steve Canyon (Caniff), 234, 236
Stewart, Kathleen, 54–56
Street Light (Balla), 187–89
Sueño y mentira de Franco (Picasso), 276–79
superhero comics. *See* genre comics
Superman, 185–92, 197, 202, 204n4, 251, 254n9, 265
surrealism, 9, 32n20, 191–92, 268–73, 276
syndication, 130, 144–51

technology, 52, 58, 62–65, 185, 190, 196–202, 281n20
television (TV), 157, 166, 172, 192
Tisserand, Michael, 5, 81n5, 82n27, 88–89
Tit-Bits, 140, 150
Töpffer, Rudolph, 42, 162, 241, 255n26
Torchy Brown in "Dixie to Harlem" (Ormes), 113–28
Toth, Alex, 175–77
transnationalism, 142, 149
Tung, Charles, 288
Twain, Mark, 94
Two-Fisted Tales (Kurtzman), 237, 241–44, 266
typography, 41, 166

Ulysses (Joyce), 16, 184
Unique Forms of Continuity in Space (Boccioni), 186–87, 191

Varnedoe, Kirk, 257–58, 303
vaudeville, 51, 65–67, 180n9
Vault of Horror, The, 265, 275

"Waffles" (Brainard and Elmslie), 218–19
Walker, Brian, 35
Ward, Lynd, 71, 81n7
Ware, Chris, 44, 298n7
Warhol, Andy, 16, 230, 238, 244, 250–51, 258
Warner, Michael, 262, 280n9
Waste Land, The (Eliot), 6, 48n34, 184
Weimar Republic, 136–37, 139
Weiss, Jeffrey, 5–6

Wertham, Fredric, 245–46, 248, 275. See also *Seduction of the Innocent*
Whaley, Deborah Elizabeth, 116, 123, 126
"What to Do?" (Brainard and Schuyler), 212–13
Whitmore, Coby, 166, 170–71
Willmott, Glenn, 32n23, 81n9, 301
Wimmen's Comix, 219
Wojcik, Pamela Robertson, 295
Woo, Benjamin, 204n3
Woolf, Virginia, 6, 184, 306
Worden, Daniel, 81n8, 151, 153n53, 208, 218, 223n11, 224n29
"Working Girl's Romance" (Toth), 175
world literature, 129–53
World War I, 110n5, 192–93
World War II, 94, 192–93, 201–2
Worringer, Wilhelm, 20–22, 24, 31n16, 31n20
Wyeth, N. C., 166

X-Men, 198

Yeats, William Butler, 94
yellow journalism, 55, 97
Yellow Kid, 70, 97
Young Romance (Simon and Kirby), 174

Zap Comix (Crumb), 206, 208–10, 219, 225n39, 304–5
Zervos, Christian, 270
Zhang, Longxi, 141

www.ingramcontent.com/pod-product-compliance
Lightning Source LLC
Chambersburg PA
CBHW030606230426
43661CB00053B/1868